Guidelines for the Development of a Security Program

Second Edition

James D. Henderson
W. Hardy Rauch
Richard L. Phillips

Reginald A. Wilkinson, President
James A. Gondles, Jr. , Executive Director
Gabriella M. Daley, Director, Communications and Publications
Leslie A. Maxam, Assistant Director, Communications and Publications
Alice Fins, Publications Managing Editor
Michael Kelly, Associate Editor
Mike Selby, Production Editor

Cover Design by Mike Selby. Photo of U.S. Prison, Marion, Illinois by Chris Crawford, courtesy of Federal Bureau of Prisons.

Printed in the United States of America by Graphic Communications, Inc., Upper Marlboro, MD

ISBN 1-56991-069-3

This publication may be ordered from:
American Correctional Association
4380 Forbes Boulevard
Lanham, Maryland 20706-4322
1-800-222-5646

For information on publications and videos available from ACA, contact our worldwide web home page at:
http://www.corrections.com/aca.

Library of Congress Cataloging-in-Publication Data

Henderson, James D.
        Guidelines for the development of a security program / James D.
    Henderson, W. Hardy Rauch, Richard L. Phillips. — 2nd ed.
            p. cm.
        Rev. ed. of: Guidelines for the development of a security program
    / National Institute of Corrections (U.S.)
        ISBN 1-56991-069-3 (pbk.)
        1. Correctional institutions—Administration. 2. Correctional
    institutions—Security matters. I. Rauch, W. Hardy.
    II. Phillips, Richard L. III. National Institute of Corrections
    (U.S.). Guidelines for the development of a security program.
    1987. IV. Title.
    HV8756.H46 1997
    365'.641'068—dc21   97-13898
                                                            CIP

Table of Contents

Section VI: Appendices

Index 283

About the Authors. 305

Foreword

This publication is a revision of a 1987 ACA book of the same name, which for the first time gathered in one place all of the information needed to establish and manage a comprehensive security program in a correctional facility. It was an important work then, and this revision is an even more important one because of the many changes that have taken place in corrections in the intervening years.

Given society's increasing knowledge and concern about corrections, it is more important than ever that we as correctional managers ensure our institutions and their programs are operated in a safe, secure, and humane manner. Our responsibility to the public and inmates is clear. It is equally important that correctional institutions are good places for our staff to work. We owe it to them and their families to be sure that their workplace is as safe as possible. And finally, it is vital that institutions run efficiently and effectively. We must give the public full value for their tax dollars in an era when corrections competes fiercely with schools, roads, and many other public enterprises for scarce tax dollars. This publication can help corrections managers achieve all of those ends: public safety, staff safety, and wise use of public funds.

No correctional institution can run from a "cookbook" of security procedures. Each facility is different, with different staff, inmates, physical plant, and mission. But every institution and every institution employee must adhere to certain fundamentals–key control, tool control, inmate accountability, effective use of personnel resources, and professionalism. These and other basics of institution operations are at the heart of our work, and they are at the heart of this publication.

Actually, the material in these guidelines represents a compendium of generally accepted approaches to accomplishing many of these fundamentals, but it should not be construed as representing the only way. Some of the content will not apply across the board, because of statutory regulations, labor-management agreements, or other good causes. Moreover, the fact these guidelines omit a certain practice should not be taken as an indication that that practice is unacceptable, or that conversely, if a correctional system is not using a practice contained in the guidelines, that it is derelict in any way. Readers should feel free to consider this entire body of material, and adopt what is useful and functional for their system.

The authors of this book are highly experienced corrections professionals who have contributed a great deal individually to the field over the years. But they also have had the benefit of receiving input from a group of other distinguished practitioners–individuals who are putting into practice daily the principles and practices that this book outlines. I am sure that as you read it, you will find many ways to apply it and to improve your institution's security operation.

James A. Gondles, Jr.
Executive Director
American Correctional Association

Preface

Corrections is a fascinating profession. It is far more complicated and challenging to those who work in it than ever could be imagined by someone who has never been involved in the day-to-day operation of a correctional institution.

In one sense, correctional institutions always have been worlds of their own–relatively self-contained entities that often have been characterized as small towns surrounded by walls and fences. Yet, in today's climate of increasing media interest, broader court involvement, and growing public policy interest in them, correctional institutions are more than ever subject to wider scrutiny. The walls, fences, and gates of today's facilities are far less impervious to the public. And that, for the most part, has been good for our profession.

Of course, there are other facets of corrections that are equally important to today's criminal justice scene. Indeed, from a numerical point of view, probation, parole, and a variety of other community-based corrections programs carry the real load in corrections today, in terms of raw numbers. Yet, for those offenders who require some form of custodial confinement, correctional institutions are a necessity, and it is to that segment of corrections that this book is aimed.

Correctional institutions are complex organizations. But at the core, they provide for the security, control, and safety of men and women who by definition have not been able to abide by society's code of conduct. And this is no small matter, particularly in higher security institutions. Inmates try to escape. They try to hurt each other and staff. They try to smuggle in and use drugs and contraband of various types. Even in lower-security facilities, there is a

regular flow of events that require staff involvement to prevent disorder and detect misconduct. And while it is the responsibility of every correctional worker to be aware of and to enforce institution security and safety, the security, or uniformed correctional, workforce has these tasks as its primary mission.

This publication is intended to serve as a guide to the establishment and management of the security program in a correctional institution. However, it is important to note at the outset that there is no one fixed security or management pattern that will apply to every institution. Each facility has a somewhat different mission, staffing pattern, administrative team, physical plant, labor-management environment, and set of historical traditions. These factors ultimately will be just as important in determining the final form of an institution's security program as a body of policy and procedure.

Despite this variety of contributing factors, certain core elements comprise the security program of every well-managed facility. These institutions have a highly visible and actively engaged management staff, a strong workforce management program, a well-defined inmate classification system, an adequate physical plant and equipment, and a fully implemented set of policies and procedures (including such critical elements as emergency procedures, inmate accountability, key and tool control, and inmate discipline). Without these central features, it is difficult to manage any correctional institution.

These topics and others are the heart of this publication. While each institution is not going to use every element of the guidelines, they reflect major activities and procedures in most correctional institution settings. Our hope is that every institution can benefit in some way with a new idea for an improved procedure, with a way to use technology a little differently, or with a new method for managing the security workforce. If that happens, then these guidelines will have accomplished their goal.

As a final note, the principal authors wish to draw readers' attention to the contributors listed in the Acknowledgments section, who took time from their busy schedules to undertake this important project.

Gene Atherton (Colorado) and Jerry O'Brien (Florida) were particularly instrumental in making substantive suggestions for revisions and changes, and in reviewing interim materials.

James D. Henderson

W. H. (Hardy) Rauch

Richard L. Phillips

Acknowledgments

In revising this publication, the principal authors drew heavily on the core material contained in its original version.

In making this revision, a number of outstanding corrections professionals provided significant assistance. Without their help, the final product would not have been as comprehensive or complete.

Judy Anderson
Columbia, South Carolina

Gene Atherton
Colorado Springs, Colorado

Stan W. Czerniak
Tallahassee, Florida

Jerry A. O'Brien
Lake Wales, Florida

Joan Palmateer
Salem, Oregon

Manuel D. Romero
Santa Fe, New Mexico

Introduction

1

Maintaining effective security in a correctional institution is no simple task. It involves coordinating the activities of not only the uniformed security workforce, but also the security-related activities of every other department in the institution. It also involves providing programs and services to inmates in ways that keep them gainfully occupied, and in a fashion that at least meets minimum constitutional standards.

To describe how this can be done, these guidelines are divided into six distinct sections.

(1) This introductory section discusses such things as the philosophy of corrections, the importance of staff, inmate and facility classifications, the place that policy has in institution operations, the role of training, and the value of auditing.

(2) The second section discusses administrative organization, including the central office and institution-level management structures.

(3) The third section relates to the physical plant and equipment issues that are important in managing a modern institution.

(4) Section four concentrates on specific operations and procedures, such as inmate accountability, inmate discipline, programs, gangs, infectious disease concerns, investigative activities, key and tool control, and many others.

(5) The fifth section deals with emergency preparedness and tactical issues.

(6) The final section consists of appendices, containing relevant ACA policies, sample forms, a sample audit format, and roster information.

In looking at the way correctional institutions function today, during this century and particularly in the last few decades, the role of security staff in correctional systems has changed dramatically. During the 1800s and early 1900s, various departments within correctional institutions commonly operated separate from (if not in conflict with) other departments. This separation was especially noticeable between the "security" or "custody" staff and the "treatment" staff. These terms implied separate groups with differing goals. To a large extent, they reflected completely different attitudes toward both inmates and toward the respective groups' feelings about the division of labor within an institution. The uniformed security workforce believed that it did the real work of running the institution and that treatment staff were do-gooders. Likewise, the treatment staff in many cases held the security personnel in low regard because of their (as often was the case in those days) lack of higher education and the perceived routine nature of their jobs.

Fortunately, this situation began to abate during the middle of this century. Conceptually, correctional staff began to see the team nature of their work and began to recognize the valuable contribution both camps were making to institution operations. Some evidence shows, for instance, that the staff member making the most positive impact on an inmate was not the caseworker or social worker, but the job supervisor, closely followed by the correctional officer. The advent of unit management in the 1970s further demonstrated that the custody/treatment dichotomy was artificial, and that employees from all specialties could make not only a contribution to managing the institution, but to helping inmates as they served their sentences.

The true foundation of security is seen not just in physical features of the institution, although they are important. Today we recognize the importance of staff selection, training, and supervision–and we recognize how improved staff effectiveness has become so critical in light of the recent unprecedented growth in the incarcerated population. We recognize the importance of accurate inmate and facility classification systems. And we recognize the importance of programs, policies, and management oversight activities.

Just as critical are the management premises by which a system is run, and the management structure it uses. Policies and procedures must be developed through a rational process, communicated effectively to staff, and their implementation properly supervised. The agency must take advantage of outside resources, when appropriate. Principal among these is the Standards and Accreditation program promulgated by the American Correctional Association (ACA)[1] and ACA's own policies, several of which relating to institution security are contained in Appendix A.

The first function of a correctional institution is to protect the public. This means that security is of primary importance to every correctional agency. An agency that cannot prevent escapes and control violence within its institutions will not be regarded as successful by the community.

To achieve that goal, a healthy security program must be based on a variety of carefully integrated factors and conditions, including:

- A fundamental and clear understanding of the agency's and institution's mission, and sufficient resources to carry out that mission

- A well-structured and well-staffed headquarters organization, responsible for liaison with other agencies, overall budget and workforce management, policy and rule establishment, technical and resource support, and a variety of compliance and oversight activities. In some agencies, these functions extend to regional offices that are tasked with headquarters-type functions for a specific geographic area or group of institutions. These guidelines will not address regional office operations, specifically. However, the reader should understand that in regionalized operations, many headquarters technical assistance, auditing, training, and reporting functions are delegated to regional office specialists, who are able to maintain a close working relationship with institution-level managers in their discipline.

- A comprehensive institution organization, which provides all necessary supporting services to staff and inmates and which includes a well thought-out, agencywide inmate management system

- A high-quality personnel management structure, which includes efficient hiring and training functions

- Careful matching of the institution (layout, design, age, and level of maintenance) with a given type of inmate and a specific staffing level

- The availability of appropriate equipment, including locking devices, door and window hardware, perimeter security devices, and other items used for monitoring and control

- The availability of programs that enhance security by involving inmates in productive use of their time

---

[1] While the publication contains information that is in accord with ACA standards, specific standards will not be referenced.

Staff

2

There is an old saying attributed to one of the early icons of corrections, Austin McCormick that, "Given the right staff, you can run a prison in an old red barn." And while that may be something of an overstatement, its core truth remains. Staff are the key to running a correctional institution.

There are a number of logical points at which to examine the issue of staffing. They are (1) recruitment and selection; (2) initial, refresher, and other specialty training, and continuing professional education; and, (3) supervision. While this guide will discuss elsewhere some of the more concrete workforce management issues such as roster management, this chapter concentrates on these three points.

Recruitment and Selection

Staff recruitment and selection is the starting point for a correctional workforce that is appropriate for the agency's mission. Unfortunately, in the past, corrections was a convenient repository for politically connected individuals who wanted the security of a government job. In many instances, the top agency administrator had no veto over the appointment of subordinate staff. Today, these practices largely have been replaced by civil service appointment systems– a great improvement.

Each agency, naturally, will have a different selection and screening process, which in most cases will be dependent on its governing statutes and regulations. Often, state personnel regulations provide a baseline set of criteria for broad job categories, which the agency has the latitude to expand to define specific institution jobs. In most instances, pay also is set in some broad bands or categories, commensurate with the responsibilities of a position.

Recruitment is no problem in some areas of the country. Particularly in rural areas, where jobs may be scarce, correctional institutions have no trouble in finding willing applicants. In urban regions, and in some other parts of the country where there are competing jobs in the marketplace, correctional institutions have a hard time finding qualified staff. Job fairs, targeted recruitment at schools with criminal justice and sociology courses, and efforts to involve local schools in starting such programs–all can be potential avenues for new staff.

However, a sound recruitment program really starts with the development of a set of hiring criteria (within the boundaries of the applicable civil service regulations). Standards for staff should include:

- *Minimum education level* - ordinarily candidates should be high school graduates or have obtained a General Equivalency Diploma.

- *A minimum level of job experience* - an institution job usually should not be a person's first experience in the work world.

- *Personal and financial responsibility* - prospective job candidates should not be demonstrably vulnerable to personal pressure exerted by inmates.

- *Maturity* - candidates must have the ability to exercise good judgment and understand human nature, and provide a **reasonable** expectation that they are capable **of independent** functioning.

These and other key traits must be ascertained during the initial hiring process, and through the use of interviews, questionnaires, references, and other means. Each agency's requirements in this area differ, but the main concern is to assure the highest possible quality candidates.

Some agencies use integrity interviewing procedures that can help identify in advance staff who may be particularly susceptible to integrity problems. Far better to learn about persistent debt problems, run-ins with the law over spousal abuse, or past patterns of drug or alcohol use before actually hiring an employee. Some agencies require prospective employees, as part of the pre-employment physical examination, to submit a urine sample to be tested for illegal drugs. Sometimes, personnel regulations require that the agency advise the candidate at the time the interview is scheduled that a drug screen is included in the physical. Those testing positive without cause are disqualified, of course, but just the knowledge this test is to be conducted often means that questionable applicants withdraw on their own. Many agencies may not hire a candidate until a law enforcement investigation has been completed.

There is no overstating the importance of ensuring that the workforce is representative, and that the principles of equal employment opportunity are followed. In dealing with an inmate population that is overrepresentative of the minorities in our society, this is a vital concern. Likewise, while state regulations in some cases may impose some limits, agencies increasingly are using female and disabled staff in all correctional settings, including the most secure institutions.

Training

In today's complex correctional environment, the correctional officer is a professional who is required to master a wide variety of skills. A comprehensive, well-organized training program is essential to achieving that end.

Yet, high staff turnover rates, tight budgets, and an atmosphere of crisis management all shape the type of training offered in correctional institutions. In many states, turnover is responsible for up to 90 percent of staff training time being devoted to pre-service orientation and security staff training. In some instances, this has resulted in little or no orientation or training for the clerical, support, or program staff. In smaller jurisdictions, agencies have experienced generalized training shortfalls. This pattern, regrettably common in corrections, is not tolerated in other government agencies or in private industry.

In the past, training was regarded as an unnecessary and troublesome requirement imposed from the outside. Too often, training was the last to be funded and the first to be cut in times of fiscal crisis. However, increasingly today, top administrators know that training is not only the key to starting a new employee down the path to dependable, highly professional performance, but also to keeping skills current for all employees over the years. With this attitudinal shift has come an increased willingness to devote the resources necessary to maintaining a high-quality training program.

To be successful, training programs must be given the total support of the top administrators of the agency. In the end, it is their responsibility to see that the necessary staff and financial resources are found to carry out the agency's training program.

The level of management commitment to the training program is demonstrated by a number of things.

(1) The first indicator of the degree of importance attributed to training is who supervises the program. In the central office, training considerations must be made an integral part of every policy, procedure, and program, and top executives are the ones who can enforce that philosophy. As a practical matter, this means that a deputy director should have specific responsibility for training in his or her portfolio. Every discussion of an operational change must include building in a way to cover training expenses. If that means more positions, more funds, or additional equipment investment, then so be it. Only administrators at the top level can be sure that happens. In the institution, training activities should be supervised at the deputy warden[2] level. This manager can oversee the activities of an advisory training committee, made up of various institution disciplines. Training should be a factor that is integrated into every local decision about a program, policy, and procedure change, and it should be endorsed by staff at the highest level.

(2) The second indicator is the amount and type of operational staff assigned to the training function. Training staff should be assigned full time and should have specialized preparation for their positions. Only well-qualified trainers should be involved. If training is used as a "dumping ground," the program may never accomplish its goals.

---

[2] From this point forward in the guidelines, a named position of responsibility will be understood to include that person's properly designated temporary replacement, or designee.

(3) Third, the space provided for training should be easily accessible and large enough to meet the needs of the agency or institution, and should provide a climate conducive to training. Equipment for various types of presentations should be available and reference materials should be up-to-date and in good repair. Special areas and equipment for such training as firearms, use of chemical agents, and self-defense also should be provided. Training should include the full range of techniques, including: classroom exposure; hands-on activities and exercises; videotape, satellite, and closed circuit television; computers; and on-the-job training. As new methods emerge, agencies should be open to exploring them, as well.

(4) A fourth indicator is the amount of time dedicated to training activities, and training can be very time-intensive. Whenever practical, training should be conducted during staff duty hours. Since operating an institution is a twenty-four-hour per day activity, this is not always possible. Therefore, funds for overtime, or compensatory time off, should be available to staff to compensate them for time spent in training during off-duty hours.

(5) Fifth, the approach taken to management and specialty training also can indicate the commitment management staff has toward training. This category of training is mentioned in detail below, but in brief, without management and specialty training, there is no way an agency can assure the necessary flow of higher-skilled employees. These courses offer some formal means of developing advanced skills.

(6) Finally, management should support an annual evaluation of all training programs, to determine that they meet the agency's needs, and to help in program revision and activity planning. Vigorous follow-up means top management really wants the program to improve.

Training is not a static process. As new departmental policies come into force, they should be incorporated into the training program at all levels. As legal and societal forces operate on the agency, new procedures may have to be implemented. As new types of offenders or new inmate problems (such as the threat of HIV) become realities, new strategies must be implemented. In every one of these instances, the agency's training program is the vehicle for the necessary management response.

Training staff themselves must receive specialized in-service preparation for their positions. Full-time personnel should complete forty hours of training-for-trainers each year.

An advisory training committee, composed of departmental representatives, should direct the actual training program. Features of the program should include: training program evaluation, the provision of adequate library and reference services, and the use of resources available from other public and private agencies.

Initial Training

Training programs for new staff are vital in setting the tone for their entire career. Many, if not most, employees enter correctional work with little or no relevant correctional training or education. For this reason, new staff should be exposed to training at the very beginning of their tenure, ideally after only a brief familiarization with their home institution. The training academy or other initial training experience is a time to provide fundamental correctional information to set standards and expectations, to show approved methods, and to teach the policies and precepts that should guide new staff members throughout their entire career.

Initial training should concentrate on both practical topics and policy familiarization. Actually, these two areas should be fused to the greatest degree possible, for truly functional policy blends easily into the operational area. As departmental policies change, they, too, should be incorporated into the training program. Also, it is an unfortunate, but true, adage that once new staff complete their training, experienced employees almost seem compelled to neutralize that training by showing them how things work in the "real world." Training must anticipate that as well, and give trainees good reasons for adhering to what they have been taught, despite social pressures to the contrary.

All new correctional officers should receive at least forty hours of orientation and training prior to independent assignment. These sessions should include the following: orientation to the purpose, goals, and policies and procedures of the institution and parent agency; working conditions and regulations; inmate responsibilities and rights; and an overview of corrections, in general. The agency should have a specific suicide intervention program, which may include direct, constant supervision, as well as active participation by mental health staff in managing suicide cases. For line staff, recognizing the signs of potential suicidal ideation is a critical training element, particularly for employees working with new inmates and those assigned to special housing units.

New correctional officers also should receive an additional 120 hours of training during the first year

Training Areas

- Communication skills
- Crime scene preservation
- Cultural diversity
- Fire and emergency procedures, including disturbance indicators
- Firearms training
- First aid and Cardiopulmonary Resuscitation (CPR)
- Inmate rules and regulations
- Key control

- Interpersonal relations and crisis intervention
- Report writing
- Rights and responsibilities of inmates
- Safety procedures
- Self-defense
- Signs of suicide risk and suicide precautions.
- Use-of-force regulations and tactics

of employment and an additional 40 hours of training each subsequent year of employment. That training should include the items listed in the box above.

Trainees should be evaluated closely in their performance and response to the training. The capability should exist to terminate trainees for unacceptable performance or other conduct which clearly demonstrates their unsuitability for correctional work.

Refresher Training

Regular refresher training for all staff is equally important. Aimed at both general correctional skills and specialty training, this program is an acknowledgment that all employees lose the skills and knowledge that they have been taught, unless they constantly use them or are retrained.

The goals of refresher training should include the following:

- An improvement in the skills of supervising and interacting with inmates

- An increase in personal effectiveness, with a resulting increase in organizational efficiency and economy

- An increase in the ability to recognize, understand, and solve problems common to correctional institutions

- An opportunity for greater job satisfaction and broader career service

Refresher training can allow correctional staff to gain other benefits, as well:

- Advancement in rank and salary

- Personal development

- Greater ease in handling work assignments

- Development of sound judgment

- Greater knowledge of occupational hazards

- Improvement in working conditions

- Increased dignity and pride in employment resulting in the development of a professional attitude

- Greater understanding and practice of institutional philosophy and policies

- Greater job satisfaction

A particularly important example of the need for refresher training is in the area of firearms and the use of force. Every tower officer or other armed staff member is entrusted with life-and-death responsibilities. Once an employee is through with initial firearms training, there must be a refresher training program or requalifying procedure to insure that competence is retained and that all staff issued lethal weapons are thoroughly familiar with the circumstances under which they may be used. To not have such a program in place is an invitation to serious injury, perhaps death, and certainly costly litigation.

There are other areas, such as fire control, disturbance control, and self-defense, in which staff regularly should be requalified, as well, so that they are as well prepared as possible to deal with the eventualities of institutional duty. To that end, the agency must identify high-priority specialty retraining programs, and provide them to all staff.

Of course, training is not a unilateral activity, and there is no reason why staff cannot maintain and upgrade their skills through other avenues, as well. In addition to the agency-provided training program, correctional officers and other staff also should consider taking outside training from other sources, such as community colleges, and local, state and national professional associations, to improve their skills.

Management and Specialty Training

The agency also must have a separate program for developing and training managers, supervisors, and staff in specialty areas. Most people are not naturally born with the necessary skills to be good managers or supervisors. Assessment programs and close supervisory attention can identify good candidates for these positions. However, few of these candidates, if any, will develop to their full potential without training specifically directed at amplifying and expanding their inherent talents. For that reason, every agency needs programs that move supervisory and management candidates into developmental assignments that plumb their abilities, and provide the training and high-quality supervision necessary to fully realize their potential. This is particularly true as agencies expand and new managerial teams must be assigned to additional facilities. Staff need to be mentored and trained not only in correctional basics, but also in budgeting, personnel management, and other related administrative skills.

To accomplish this end, many agencies now offer in-house specialty and management training; others contract out the development and provision of such programs. Leadership academies or seminar programs, special management track assignments, or other methods also can be used to serve this purpose. Whatever strategy is used, the goal of this process should be to develop a cadre of continually maturing midlevel and administrative personnel who have been carefully screened and trained over the years, and who readily are available to handle additional responsibilities as the needs of the agency so require.

Moreover, there is every reason to believe that litigation by inmates, individual employees, unions, and the federal government will continue to shape corrections. And while every employee should have a basic working knowledge of correctional law issues, managers, in particular, should be well-versed in the legal principles and rulings that govern their work. The old adage "ignorance of the law is no excuse" has particular relevance in corrections. Inmates still are entitled to numerous rights based on the Constitution, the Civil Rights of Institutionalized Persons Act, the Americans with Disabilities Act, and the Religious Freedom Restoration Act. Failure to recognize these and other rights may subject correctional personnel to civil liability. Consequently, it is imperative that agency training personnel be thoroughly informed of correctional law developments and their significance for both administrative rules and regulations, and for the instruction they provide in staff-training programs.

In some cases, training deficiencies of an agency are painfully highlighted by litigation. In others, training becomes part of the eventual solution. In either instance, it is clear that correctional agencies have a direct responsibility to provide training in specific job functions, as well as on the rights and responsibilities of staff and inmates. Supervisors have been held liable for failure to train (or to supervise the training of) subordinate employees, where such failure resulted in the denial of constitutionally protected rights. For example, if a correctional officer misuses a weapon against an inmate without receiving proper training, supervisors may be held responsible for any injury. However, proper training and supervision of training should reduce the legal risk, even in cases where a properly trained officer does not act in accordance with his or her training. The importance of training also is stressed in American Bar Association, Department of Justice, and American Correctional Association guidelines.

The quality of staff training itself, its curriculum content, hours of delivery, mode of delivery (centralized, local, institutional, or on-the-job), and the credentials and skills of the training supervisor and staff also may be critical factors in reducing potential liability. Moreover, wardens and other managers regularly are called upon to testify in court, and their decisions and practices are being subjected to careful court scrutiny. Training can be critical in actually preparing those staff to give effective testimony and more effectively represent the program or activity in question.

Supervision

Once employees are hired and trained, it would be nice to be able to send them on their way, and not to worry about them the rest of their career. Yet, once the employee comes out of the academy, the real work begins, and continues until the day that the employee leaves the service of the agency. Supervision is the key to getting the long-term value out of the agency's selection and training investment.

The nuts and bolts of supervision include timekeeping, tracking patterns of leave abuse, and other important, but seemingly mundane things. A later section of these guidelines discusses the need for an effective workforce management system, that includes managing rosters, timekeeping, and keeping and tracking performance records. These certainly are core elements in a supervisor's role. However, this section will focus on other, less obvious, aspects of supervision. Each agency and institution will have its own system for doing such things, but they are important for several reasons.

First, agencies must fulfill their legal and public policy requirements to ensure that public funds are spent wisely, and that means that positions are allocated, filled, staffed, and monitored properly. Second, if staff are not properly supervised and assigned, important security coverage is compromised. Third, serious morale, equity, and security problems are created when employees are not on duty as required, without proper justification.

In the real world, some staff members are late, take their "Friday" or "Monday" off sick a bit too predictably, or show up out of uniform. Only a very few employees know every policy and procedure; an even smaller number keep up with all of the changes that inevitably occur in those regulations. And, it is virtually impossible for any one staff member to know all of the day-to-day changes in facility operations that are typical of a correctional institution–things like intelligence information about drug trafficking or a possible escape plot. Supervisors are the key to successfully managing these issues and every other aspect of a security program.

Keeping staff familiar with policy and procedure, and ensuring that they are implementing those policies and procedures fairly and consistently, is a constant and central part of supervision. This is particularly true of key policies and plans regarding accountability, hostages, bomb response, escape, and tool and key control. Staff not only have to know policy, but also how it is to be applied. Supervisors have to be sure that procedures are being carried out as consistently as possible in every part of the institution. They also must be sure that if situations require immediate deviation from policy, that the proper authorization is issued. And finally, every employee –supervisor or not–knows that some policies are just not practical, or that events or other changes have rendered them unworkable. Thus, when line employees and supervisors see that policies are not working, the supervisor is responsible for conveying that information to higher management officials who are in a position to change them.

Keeping staff up-to-date on the latest information that may affect their job performance is vital, as well.

If intelligence information indicates a possible escape attempt, officers must be alerted. A recent news event (a change in sentencing laws, for instance) may put the inmate population on edge, and incoming staff must be told. If there is a major operational change, such as in commissary operating hours, officers need to know what to tell inmates. Supervisors are the key to all of this type of information-related activity.

Supervisors also are the upward channel in the organization for information. Line employees need to be able to tell their supervisor if they receive or observe important information about some inmate activity. Supervisors are the route staff use to relate suggested policy changes. Of course, sometimes an employee simply needs to be able to ventilate with a supervisor. This act can indicate to the supervisor how that employee or the entire institution is doing.

These components of supervision and the others mentioned later in this publication are important. But to do them properly requires one other element: supervisory visibility. While the workload of top supervisors may be high for any number of reasons, it

Source: Oregon Department of Corrections

Supervisor visibility: a superintendent visits a classroom.

is imperative that the warden, his or her executive staff, department heads, and shift supervisors regularly tour the institution and make themselves available to staff and inmates. The degree of communication and credibility that this engenders is invaluable in the administration of any facility.

Without this kind of attention on a constant basis, it is only a matter of time until administrators lose contact with the realities of day-to-day operations, and are unable to see firsthand how their subordinate supervisors are performing. This visibility strategy allows administrators to be on-site throughout the facility, and to personally communicate their standards of conduct and performance. More importantly, when they tour the institution, they must seek out performance information and insist that standards be maintained. If they do not, then the standard of acceptable performance automatically becomes whatever level is in force at the time, as opposed to the expressed ideal. Only by personally conveying and communicating the expectations of the administration, and regularly following up with those who carry them out, will slippage in critical areas be avoided.

This approach extends especially to special housing units (administrative segregation, disciplinary detention, protective custody, death row, and so forth), where critical problems quickly can develop from relatively small issues. In high-security settings particularly, the presence of top staff communicates one more important factor to other personnel. The fact that administrators move confidently throughout the facility, clearly conveys that working conditions for line staff are safe.

Staffing Patterns and Levels

Many administrators believe they never have enough employees to cover institutional needs. To resolve this issue, various formulas have been designed to determine the number of positions needed for adequate institutional operation. However, no fixed formula will meet the needs of every agency. Historical factors in a facility, physical plant variations, the labor-management environment, programs and services provided, and the actual custody classification of the inmates, all have an impact on staffing. Any specific staffing guidelines must be reviewed with these realities in mind.

Some agencies use fixed staffing guidelines to determine the number of positions that are assigned to a specific institution. This approach has the benefit of using an equitable model for each institution, thereby reducing the potential for local administrators to believe they have been allocated too few staff;

every institution in the system with certain categories of posts or activities receives the same number of positions. This approach has several serious drawbacks. It does not account for physical plant differences. It does not account for different types of programs. It does not account for the different features of an inmate population that on the surface may appear homogeneous, but, in fact, can differ significantly across institutions of apparently similar security levels.

For that reason, this publication does not advocate any single set of staffing guidelines. They exist, and in fact, many are quite good for the agency involved. But invariably, when one looks at the detail of their application, they inevitably become modified with exceptions, waivers, and other variances. For that reason, this publication recommends a more individualized approach to determining staff complements and describes it later.

Whatever system is used to determine staffing allocations, as programs and inmate populations change, the institution's managers should make appropriate adjustments in the staffing pattern. In many agencies, the failure to respond to constantly rising inmate populations with corresponding increases in staffing has led to serious security problems. Because the increase in inmate numbers may be gradual and the mechanisms for securing additional staff members can be cumbersome, some institutions cannot balance their interim needs without incurring large overtime expenses.

Possible methods for avoiding unnecessary overtime expense and achieving necessary security within existing staffing levels include the implementation of three strategies:

(1) Unit management which can assist in maintaining positive staff/inmate relations by assigning a multidisciplinary staff to each housing unit, scheduling their work hours optimally, and placing their offices in the housing units

(2) Direct supervision by security staff, in lieu of indirect supervision. Officers involved in direct supervision circulate among the inmates in the housing areas instead of remaining behind locked doors in unit control centers. Proponents of this style of supervision assert that security problems can be avoided and better observation can be maintained by increasing contact between inmates and officers. In high-security settings, a combination of direct and indirect supervision is a viable option, with

proper procedures in place to ensure staff safety

(3) Increased reliance on the correctional worker concept, which properly apportions (where permissible) some security functions to nonuniformed staff

The improved staff/inmate relations that result when officers and inmates get to know each other as individuals–through any or all of these approaches–can promote more effective security.

Unit Management

Until the last few decades, the management structures of virtually all correctional systems were departmentalized or centralized. Individual managers were given the responsibility for programs or functional areas such as security, education, food services, medical services, religion, and facility maintenance. This type of organization tended to separate employees into groups who were more interested in internal department goals than in the broader concerns of the institution.

In recent years, many correctional systems have begun to change to a different type of management structure, one that is more decentralized. This approach commonly is called unit management, stressing a total team approach to many aspects of an institution's mission. Unit staff members are delegated major decision-making responsibilities that formerly would have fallen to central department heads such as the chief of security or chief of classification, the deputy warden, or even the warden. For instance, in a typical unit management system, the unit staff is delegated authority to make decisions about some forms of inmate discipline, work programs, educational and vocational training assignments, leisure time activities, orientation programs, and release plans.

Unit staff have their offices in the housing unit and are available to inmates through most of the day, and on evenings and weekends. They may be responsible for providing security shakedowns, conducting counts and safety/sanitation inspections, enforcing contraband control, making daily notations in unit logs, and conducting security inspections of the unit. While unit staff members have many responsibilities, maintaining high security standards always will be a prime consideration and as a result, continuous cooperation between the unit staff and the security department is a must.

In general, unit management has the following major objectives:

- To divide large groups of inmates into smaller, well-defined clusters whose members are encouraged to develop a common identity and close association with each other, and with unit staff members

- To increase the frequency of contact and the quality of relationships between staff and inmates by placing decision-making personnel in close proximity to the inmates being controlled

- To provide better observation of inmate activities, improve inmate accountability and control, and detect problems before they become critical

- To provide different programs, strategies, and interventions for each inmate, depending on his or her needs, abilities, and interests

Most staffing patterns call for a minimum of one unit manager for every 200-300 inmates. The unit case manager is responsible for case management matters within the unit and assists in other unit operations as directed by the unit manager. Typically, there is about one case manager for every 100 inmates. Under the unit management system, correctional counselors selected from the security service are responsible for inmate counseling, with about one counselor for every 100 inmates. There should be a unit secretary for not more than every 200 inmates. Unit correctional officers should be assigned to a unit for an extended period (nine months to a year, including rotation through all three main shifts). They are an integral part of the team, interacting with other unit staff and contributing to the decisions made in the unit. Other team members may include an education advise and a mental health representative.

The unit team (described above) meet at least once a week to conduct case reviews, interview inmates, and make program decisions. Because unit staff (as a group) know the inmates perhaps better than anyone else, their input into the process creates a strong atmosphere for making decisions.

Some benefits of unit management can be obtained only by staff being around and being available to inmates during nonworking hours. While counselors and others should be visiting work sites on a regular basis, a great deal of activity and interpersonal contact occurs in the unit in the evening and on weekends. Thus, to meet the needs of inmates and the institution, the nonsecurity members of the unit staff should be scheduled to work on evenings and weekends. Unit managers should develop a schedule that includes each member of the staff working at least one evening each week. Weekend coverage should be rotated on an equitable basis, and include the unit manager.

Direct Supervision

The last two decades have seen the emergence of "direct supervision," as opposed to "indirect supervision," models for facility operations. Indirect supervision results from a combination of staff assignment and design features that tend to keep staff and inmates separate. Often, indirect supervision institutions have control centers in the housing units, from which staff operate door controls remotely and communicate with inmates over speakers or through other electronic means. This lack of regular, direct staff contact with inmates tends to reinforce the social distance between staff and inmates, prevents staff from learning more about inmates and what is going on in the institution, and inhibits the development of a constructive relationship between staff and inmates.

Direct supervision, which is highly compatible with unit management, relies on a more open design, in which staff circulate through the units in physical contact with inmates. Staff interact personally with inmates, and also actively are involved in patrolling the unit, searching cells, conducting security inspections, and performing other fundamental tasks. Staff and inmates know each other better, and from that dynamic, there is a much stronger interpersonal foundation for managing individual inmates and the institution, in general. Direct supervision is the general population supervision model chosen by many correctional agencies today.

Correctional Worker Concept

Supervision in the correctional setting has a unique aspect in that every employee in the institution has a vested interest in maintaining the security and safety of the facility. From this concept comes the idea

Source: Dworsky Associates

Modern, direct-contact designs can be safe and effective for supervising most offenders.

Source: CRSS

Indirect contact operations rely on secure control centers to safeguard staff and control many unit operations.

that all correctional staff–no matter what their job specialty–are correctional workers first, and specialists in a particular occupational area second.

The correctional worker concept is not new. Many correctional systems for years have established the expectation that all staff share a certain amount of responsibility for traditional security tasks. Training and evaluations reflect this expectation. And while in some correctional systems, stringent union contracts prevent full implementation of this concept, it slowly is gaining acceptance throughout the country.

Under this concept, all staff are provided a common base of training in fundamental correctional skills, such as inmate accountability, key control, searches, and other tasks. Having received that training, an individual employee may be called upon to use it in any number of ways that are reasonably related to that person's day-to-day work in the institution or to the overall mission of the facility, that includes maintaining safety and security.

Several examples may be useful. Under this approach, a laundry employee with inmate workers would be called upon to account for those inmates throughout the day, rather than having a separate correctional officer post for that purpose. A maintenance shop employee would be expected to conduct security inspections of the physical features (bars, locks, windows, and so forth) of his or her shop area. An industrial shop employee would be required to be accountable for all tools in that area or in use by any inmate workers in the shop. These core tasks, which are reasonably related to the person's normal duties and are easily integrated into the daily routine, reduce the need for a uniformed security staff presence in various areas of the institution.

In an emergency, the value of a large body of staff who are trained in core security skills is immediately evident. First of all, when an emergency alarm sounds under this system, every available staff member responds whether on the security force or not. This provides a far larger response force–one that in most cases stops an incident before any more harm can be done or before it spreads. But this approach works effectively in other crises, as well. Case managers can be assigned to provide secondary coverage in a housing unit, backing up correctional staff. Maintenance staff can be issued weapons and assigned to security posts during an escape hunt. Business office personnel may be assigned to assist in processing inmates in the aftermath of a disturbance. In short, staff from any department can be used to supplement the "formal" security workforce when there is a pressing need to do so.

This concept does raise the issue of potential supervisory problems at least conceptually, as employees from various disciplines perform security-related tasks. However, since it has been in day-to-day practice in many large correctional systems for years, there appear to be few real reasons why the correctional worker concept cannot be applied in all correctional institutions.

The benefits of such an approach accrue to management, the individual, and the total institution. Because employees in such a system are trained more broadly in the full range of institution operations, they are more flexible and more knowledgeable, and ultimately, more effective and more promotable. Moreover, because every employee has a heightened awareness of the importance of security and inmate accountability, the overall security status of the institution is greater. That, in turn, creates a safer working environment for all employees, security and nonsecurity.

Classification and Facility Security Levels

3

Today's correctional institutions seem to have a greater proportion of more dangerous inmates, inmates with significant histories of substance abuse, violence, and other problems. Because population levels still are rising in most systems, the problems of safe, effective security are on the rise. Classification is a sorting-out process that places inmates in the most appropriate security level institution, under the proper degree of staff supervision. Classification also aids decisions on which programs and services are most likely to be beneficial for individual inmates. Properly done, a good classification system can make the job of the security staff much easier and safer.

To achieve the proper match between inmates and the joint attributes of staff and physical plant, most correctional systems use a two-part nomenclature to reflect the two different elements of this process. Inmate custody level systems identify the degree of control and supervision that inmates need, through the use of an objective inmate classification system. Facility security levels are identified as a result of an objective assessment of the physical and staffing features of institutions. These parallel structures lead to a system for assigning inmates to institutions that provide the degree of control and supervision they require (ideally, no more, and no less).

The Classification Process

In modern corrections, each agency should have a systematic method for identifying the proper custody level for each offender in custody. The primary feature of this system should include a means of assuring that inmates are not held in a more restrictive custodial setting than necessary to insure their continued safe (that is, safe for the public, staff, and the inmates themselves) confinement.

Housing high-security inmates in too low a security setting presents obvious problems–escapes, assaults, intimidation, and other internal management problems. What is not quite so obvious is that confining an inmate in too high a security setting for his or her actual needs is also fraught with problems. The confinement of low-security inmates in a high-security setting, first of all, is dangerous for those individuals. It unnecessarily subjects them to the threats and physical attacks of more aggressive, hostile inmates. It also is more costly than necessary to house lower-custody inmates in a maximum-security institution. It costs a great deal more, in terms of staff and other security-related operational costs, to house a given inmate in a high-security setting than it does in a lower-security setting of the appropriate classification.

The fact that newly constructed high-security beds are more costly places them at a premium, and if for no other reason, makes it necessary for administrators to carefully review and analyze the patterns of confinement in their agency to better use available bedspace. This is particularly relevant as inmate populations continue to climb and new construction costs for high-security beds still are growing rapidly.

To meet these management needs, objective classification instruments may be used to determine an inmate's custody needs. Staff within a particular system can develop these classification methods on their own or rely on systems developed by the National Institute of Corrections or other parties. Custody categories developed by any of these methods reflect the degree of physical control and staff supervision that an inmate requires, and will determine (to a large

15

degree) the inmate's institutional designation and types of programs to which the inmate will have access.

The most important aspect of classification, as it relates to these guidelines, is the determination of which inmates are most likely to be dangerous to others or which present severe escape risks. This process is referred to by various names: security screening, custody determination, escape potential assessment, or violence prediction. Some systems perform this task at a central intake facility; others do it at the institution level. By any name and at whatever location, this process serves the same vital function –assisting staff members in determining which inmates are most likely to disrupt the orderly operation of the institution. Security staff do not necessarily need to know the details of classification, but they should be aware of the general scheme in use in their system. This publication describes only the basics of classification, since agencies use different methods.

Other major features of the classification process should include:

- A method for initially assessing and periodically revising inmates' security categories that are established in parallel with the security features of the system's institutions

- A means of assuring that custody assignments are imposed consistently, and never as a form of punishment

- Inmate understanding of, and participation in, the classification system

- A method for providing sufficient latitude to staff to override system-generated classifications, based on their professional judgment

- A process that provides for ongoing review and validation of the system, and that ensures its reliability and objectivity

Initial Classification

Initial custody decisions should be based to the extent possible on actual relevant behavior. The frequency, recentness, and severity of past behavior is the best indicator of future similar behavior. At intake, the following criteria most frequently are reviewed:

- Severity of current offense

- Length of sentence

- Type of prior commitments

- History of escapes and attempts

- History of violence

- Type of detainer

The use of these criteria in a risk-screening instrument permits a general prediction of the security needed for each inmate. However, no classification device can predict correctly and unfailingly all risks. Thus, an override capability must be built into the system (to allow staff to exercise professional judgment) and must be monitored continuously by staff to prevent abuses.

In addition to typical intake assessment factors, there must be a provision for identifying inmates who are management problems or who have special needs. They fall into several categories:

(1) Potentially dangerous inmates, such as those with a history of assault or predatory behavior

(2) Those who require protection and separation because they may be in danger from other inmates

(3) Those who, by reason of their offense, criminal record, or institutional behavior, require particularly close supervision

(4) Those who received unusual publicity because of the nature of their crime, arrest, or trial, or who are involved in criminal activity of a sophisticated nature, such as organized crime

(5) Gang members; these offenders should be identified at the earliest possible stage, so that basic management decisions can be made. Staff training in tattoo and other gang-related symbolism is important in this regard.

(6) Those with special needs, including those defined by age, infirmity, mental illness, retardation, and other medical problems

(7) Where appropriate, the classification system also must take into account validated management and security needs of female inmates that are different from those of male inmates.

Table 3-1, and the accompanying narrative that follows, represent one custody classification model among the many available. Reduced to narrative form, Table 3-1 has the following practical implications.

Community custody inmates pose the lowest level of risk and direct supervision is not required, although intermittent observation may be appropriate

Table 3-1 – Inmate Classification Chart

Typical Supervision Levels in Relation to Inmate Custody Categories

ACTIVITY	COMMUNITY	MINIMUM	MEDIUM	CLOSE	MAXIMUM
OBSERVATION	Occasional; appropriate to situation	Checked at least every hour when outside the perimeter of the institution	Frequent and direct	Always observed and supervised outside cell	Direct, always supervised
DAY MOVEMENT	Unrestricted	Unrestricted	Unescorted but observed by staff	Restricted, on a check-out/ check-in basis	Always restrained when out of cell, handcuffed and in leg irons
NIGHT MOVEMENT	Unrestricted	Under staff observation	Restricted, on a check-out/ check-in basis	Escorted and only on order of watch commander	Out of cell only in emergencies and in restraints, with approval of watch commander
MEAL MOVEMENT	Unrestricted	Under staff observation	Supervised	Supervised and may be escorted or fed in cell or on cellblock	In cell or in unit
ACCESS TO JOBS	All, both inside and outside the perimeter	All inside perimeter and supervised outside jobs	All inside perimeter, none outside perimeter	Only selected day jobs inside perimeter	In cell or directly supervised
ACCESS TO PROGRAMS	Unrestricted, including community-based activities	All inside perimeter and selected outside perimeter	All inside perimeter, none outside perimeter	Selected programs/activities; none outside perimeter	Limited to programs within unit
VISITS	Contact; periodic supervision; indoor and outdoor	Contact; supervised	Contact; supervised	Contact	Noncontact for selected cases
LEAVE THE INSTITUTION	Unescorted	Unescorted	One-on-one escort; inmate at least in handcuffs; strip search	Armed escort, inmate in restraints; strip search	Armed escort, full restraints; strip search
FURLOUGH	Eligible for day pass* and furloughs	Not eligible for day pass* or furlough	Not eligible for day pass* or furlough	Not eligible	Not eligible

DEFINITIONS: * Day Pass: Permits inmate to be away from institution only during daylight hours; whereas a furlough means overnight for at least one (or more) nights.

under certain conditions. Community custody inmates may be permitted to participate in jobs and programs outside the facility's perimeter.

The minimum-custody category is reserved for inmates who pose a relatively low risk of escape or few management problems. They may move around the institution during the day under general supervision, but at night, they should be under general supervision. Minimum-custody inmates may be eligible for escorted trips and supervised assignments outside the facility perimeter.

Inmates assigned a medium-custody designation may be permitted to move around the facility during the day. Supervision of medium-custody inmates should be frequent, with direct observation of their programs and activity areas. During the night, the movement of medium-custody inmates should be on a controlled basis. These inmates should be placed in handcuffs and accompanied by an escort when they travel outside the institution. Inmates in this group are eligible for all programs and activities inside the perimeter.

Like maximum-custody inmates, close-custody inmates should be under constant supervision, but they may be managed in small groups. All movement for close-custody inmates should be restricted. During the day, these inmates should move on a controlled basis, and at night, they should be under escort, with the approval of the shift supervisor. When leaving institutional grounds, close-custody inmates should be placed in full restraints. Inmates in this group should not be eligible for furloughs and should be assigned only to selected daytime jobs and programs, inside the institution's perimeter.

Maximum-custody inmates require constant supervision; they present serious escape risks or pose serious threats to themselves, to other inmates, or to the staff. Maximum-custody inmates should be confined one to a cell and managed individually. They should remain in their cells at all times, except when they are removed for authorized activities. When outside of their cells, maximum-custody inmates should be escorted in restraints by at least one staff member. When these inmates must go outside the institution, they should be placed in full physical restraints, including handcuffs and waist chains, and should be accompanied by at least two armed escorts, supported by other armed officers, as the situation dictates.

Reclassification

In addition to initial classification, a reclassification, or periodic case review system also must be in place. This is necessary to allow for reevaluation of

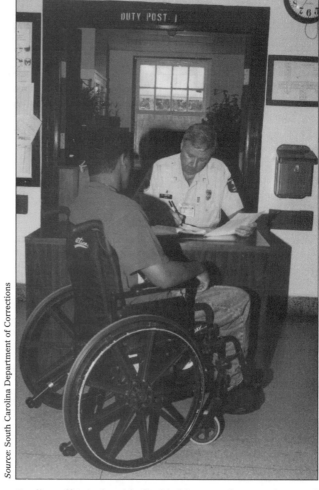

Source: South Carolina Department of Corrections

Dealing effectively with disabled inmates is not only sound corrections, but a legal necessity under the Americans with Disabilities Act.

each inmate's security needs as time passes, sentences progress, detainers are dropped, conduct records are established, and other factors intervene. Typically, this involves consideration of such factors as the following:

- Percentage of time served

- Type and frequency of disciplinary reports incurred

- Involvement with drugs or alcohol in the institution

- Mental and psychological stability

- Staff assessment of level of personal responsibility

- Family or community ties

- Program participation

- Job and quarters conduct

The reclassification system should reliably suggest the need for a custody reduction (when these factors so indicate), and, in some cases, may result in transfer to a lower-security institution as a sentence progresses. It also should be just as reliable in helping staff identify inmates whose conduct suggests the need for higher security measures, and consequent transfer to an institution where custody and supervision levels are greater.

Women and Special Needs Cases

Classification also has to consider the special cases. Yet, in years past, very little attention was paid to women inmates or those with special needs: the mentally ill, the retarded, the aging, the disabled, and substance abusers.

Women

First, women inmates are, indeed, special needs inmates. But they are different from other categories of special needs inmates in an important way. The other special needs discussed in this section have a disability or dysfunction of some type. Women are not disabled or dysfunctional by virtue of their sex. This is an important distinction, when we as a society are working hard to overcome a history of gender-based discrimination. Nothing in this discussion implies that women inmates are less capable in any way than men inmates, or that they require special treatment, only treatment that is proper and required to meet the special medical and social needs they bring to confinement.

From a historical standpoint, women inmates traditionally were placed in institutions that were intended to provide a suitably safe, secure environment, but which in many instances, did not have the same range of programs and services that were made available to male offenders. Specialized health care and family services were not a priority, although some systems provided excellent programs in these areas. Training programs were limited to those associated with stereotypical female roles.

Mentally Ill and Retarded

Similarly, in the past, mentally ill and retarded offenders were handled as best as the staff could do. No treatment programs were available. Such inmates were generally "hid out" somewhere in the system unless they presented serious management problems, in which case they were treated just like any other inmate and placed in special housing, often for long periods of time. They were vulnerable to predatory inmates. Many were unable to participate in or understand the nature of typical institution activities.

Elderly

Aging inmates are a reality in corrections. The length of sentences is increasing in most systems, and older offenders bring with them a wide range of health problems. They also are, as a group, more vulnerable to younger, more aggressive inmates. Many systems have set up special geriatric units to help these inmates cope with daily institution living.

Disabled

Institutions always have had disabled inmates, and in one way or another, they have met their needs. Yet, more often than not, that meant that the disabled inmate had to forego participating in many programs, and did not receive the full range of services available. In some cases, it also meant that they were preyed upon by others. Today, with the advent of the Americans with Disabilities Act, institutions are required to take affirmative steps to assure that disabled inmates' needs are met through reasonable accommodation to those needs, not by ignoring them.

Substance Abusers

Finally, substance-abusing inmates have been a regular fixture in institutions for generations. Today, with the popularity of lengthy drug-related sentences, mandatory minimum terms, and abolition of parole in many jurisdictions, the number of incarcerated substance abusers has increased dramatically. While relatively low numbers in the past meant that on-the-side programs were sufficient, today most institutions have, or need to have, specific, much larger-scale programs to help these inmates.

Current Practice

Each of these categories of special needs inmates requires special attention in today's correctional world. But those types of treatment should not impact on the need for infusing those programs with sound security practices. Such practices may involve providing proper supervision for a family visiting program, being aware of the need to properly and safely handcuff a pregnant inmate, training security staff in special techniques for working in a mental health or geriatric unit, or any other similar situations. Whatever the situation, security operations can and should be custom-tailored to serve the overall needs of the institution and these special needs offenders, without jeopardizing public safety.

Automation

Many correctional systems are integrating the classification process with computerized systems for maintaining basic inmate identification and program information. If properly designed, reliance on a real-time, online computer system dramatically can improve communications, enhance overall management decision-making, and quite likely eliminate many duplicate records in the agency. Prime among the records that possibly could be eliminated would be central office files that many agencies maintain, since ultimately all relevant records can be maintained in the computerized system, which all authorized staff could access.

Facility Security Levels

When inmates with high-security needs are placed in a low-security facility, escapes and security-related incidents are inevitable. Conversely, when inmates requiring minimal security are assigned to high-security institutions, expensive resources are wasted and inmates are exposed to potential harm. Thus, a crucial factor in maintenance of control and security is attaining a good match between facility security level and inmate-custody category. That implies a need for a method to categorize institutions by their security capabilities, such as internal design, perimeter security features, staffing patterns, equipment, and other factors.

In many of its publications, the American Correctional Association refers to five different facility security levels: (I) Community, (II) Minimum, (III) Medium, (IV) Close, and (V) Maximum. But this is, by no means, the only facility security scheme that can be used. Some systems, for instance, have fewer facility security levels and use inmate "grade" classifications to differentiate the supervision levels needed for offenders. Names can be used for facility security levels and letter grades (such as AA, A, B, C, D) to indicate degree of inmate custody or supervision.

While each agency has its own descriptions and criteria for categorizing facility security levels, ordinarily, they rely on a review of factors such as the following:

- Type of perimeter security

- Existence and operation of towers

- Use of external mobile patrols

- Use of detection devices

- Type of housing arrangements

- Nature of internal architectural features, such as reinforced concrete construction, security glazing, corridor grilles, control centers, electronically controlled steel cell doors, and so forth

Table 3-2, and the accompanying narrative, show one set of definitions and criteria for consistently assigning facilities a security level.

Community security, or Level I facilities, employ open housing within a defined perimeter. They do not employ detection devices, do not have external patrols, and make only limited use of institution staff members for supervision. Level I facilities include the following types of institutions: institutions employing no perimeter security systems, prerelease units with access to the community, and other nonsecure community correctional program settings appropriate to the needs of the inmate.

Minimum-security housing (Level II) may consist of either single cells or rooms, multiple-occupant rooms, or dormitories, according to the facility's physical design. Open housing units should be within an appropriately secure institution perimeter. The perimeter may consist of a single fence, or clearly designated unarmed "posts." While Level II facilities employ no perimeter detection devices, they may use intermittent external mobile patrols. Most Level II facilities place a strong emphasis on programs and activities.

Housing in medium-security institutions (Level III), ideally, should consist of living units with single cells or rooms. However, the reality of today's crowded institutions is that most are double-bunked and that some even use dormitories. Level III facilities should have a secure perimeter with a double fence, outside mobile patrols, and detection devices. Typically, Level III facilities provide a wide variety of programs and activities.

Close Security–Level IV–requires a facility with secure housing and a secure external perimeter similar to that of a Level V institution. Although there may be little apparent difference between the physical design of the two highest security classifications, Level IV facilities may house larger inmate populations. The security hardware equipment needs of a Level IV institution are essentially identical to those of a Level V.

In addition, the custody categories of the inmates in Level IV facilities require single cells secured by heavy-duty hardware, including security doors and windows. Cells may be outside cells, and the equipment employed need not be as secure as that used for Level V.

Direct supervision should be provided at all times when the inmates are outside their cells. While correctional officer/inmate ratios remain high, Level IV

Table 3-2 – Facility Security Features

Typical Design Features Relating to Facility Security

SECURITY LEVELS	I	II	III	IV	V
PERIMETER	None	Single fence	Double fence and/or unarmed "posts"	Double fence Secure entrance/exits	Same as IV and/or wall and secure entry/exits
TOWERS*	None	None*	Combination	Combination of intermittent tower and/or patrol surveillance	Same as IV with tower and/or patrol surveillance
EXTERNAL PATROL	None	Intermittent	Yes	Yes	Yes
DETECTION DEVICES	None	Optional	Yes, at least one type	Yes, more than one type	Yes, extensive
HOUSING	Single rooms and/or multiple rooms or dorms	Single rooms and/or multiple rooms or dorms	Single cells or rooms	Single outside or inside cells	Single inside cells
LIGHTING	Minimal	Some lights on perimeter and interior	Entire perimeter and interior compound illuminated	High-intensity illumination of all perimeter and interior areas	High-intensity illumination of all perimeter and interior areas

*Towers may be used for control of traffic and/or pedestrian movement.

DEFINITIONS: Inside Cell: A cell which is contained on four sides within a cellblock: in other words, if inmates escape from the cells, they are still confined within the building envelope.

Outside Cell: A cell within a wall or window on the outside of the building. If inmates escape from the cell, they have escaped from the building.

facilities should place greater emphasis on program staff than do Level V institutions. Inmates only should be placed in full restraints under armed escort when they are outside the facility itself.

Maximum security, or Level V facilities, represent the highest security in a correctional system, providing highly secure housing within the most secure perimeter. This level of security also may involve providing separate management procedures for various activities, including food services and exercise. Level V facilities should be small, with a maximum population of about 500 inmates.

A wall, or double fences with razor wire and/or a wall with detection devices, should separate the facility from the community. The entire perimeter should be supervised by armed officers in towers, as well as an external mobile patrol system. Inmates should be housed in single cells. Housing units should be supervised by at least one officer at all times, including the periods when inmates are locked in their cells. When officers are in close proximity to cells or working with inmates, two officers should be present. Cells should be secured by heavy-duty hardware, including security doors and windows, locks, and other equipment.

Frequent searches for contraband and weapons should be conducted. All out-of-cell movement should be restricted to movement inside the facility and carefully should be controlled and supervised by the staff. Restraints such as handcuffs, leg irons, and waist chains may be used, as required by department policy.

Where inmate work assignments are appropriate, they should be closely supervised, with inmates being required to pass through metal detectors and to undergo body search procedures before leaving the work area.

Crowding

Dealing with crowding is likely to be an issue that correctional administrators are going to have to cope with for the foreseeable future. Sound classification can help moderate somewhat the adverse impact of crowding. At the macrolevel, the central office has to work to obtain necessary bedspace and other resources, as well as to properly assign inmates throughout the system. But at the institution level, there are no simple solutions to this problem. Exceeding a facility's population design limits has a serious impact on the safety of the staff and inmates alike. Many agencies use the following general principles to manage crowding.

At the central office, long-range planning should be undertaken, including studying inmate population projections, and making provisions for new institutions or modification of existing facilities, to meet the system's future needs. This should include ensuring that new bedspace is accompanied by a commensurate amount of program space, and the funding and positions to operate those programs. The agency's objective classification system should be used to its fullest to properly disperse the population, with the central office closely monitoring the population and

Source: U.S. Bureau of Prisons

Double bunking is a reality in all but the most secure institutions in the country today.

easing crowding by making appropriate adjustments through transfers between institutions. Also, systemwide, the dangers of crowding must be weighed against institution-security levels; crowding may present less risk in medium-security facilities than in maximum- or minimum-security facilities. Alternatives to incarceration, including early release programs, parole, work release, halfway houses, and probation, should be used fully.

At the local level, as population density increases, staff must be deployed optimally to maintain sound security and supervision, as well as programming. Local administrators must be alert to prevent deterioration in basic services, including medical, food, commissary, laundry, recreation, sanitation, and visiting programs. Staff should be alert to unusual demographic changes in the population, and must prevent racial or ethnic imbalances in job, program, and housing assignments. To the extent possible, adequate numbers of inmate jobs and other programs should be provided.

Auditing

4

The primary purpose of conducting security audits is to identify weaknesses or deficiencies in a security operation so that corrective actions can be taken to strengthen it. Secondary reasons include determining if institutional procedures and actual practices comply with agency policy and procedure, and assessing whether security resources are being used in an effective and efficient manner.

Auditing Philosophy and Structure

The agency should consistently implement an audit philosophy and practices that emphasize the following purposes:

- Promoting the audit process as a valuable management tool, rather than a negative experience by institutional staff

- Seeing improved institution safety and control as the ultimate goal of audit processes

- Viewing security auditing as a proactive approach that detects weaknesses in security before they lead to significant failure

- Seeing the audit process as an opportunity for the institution's security program to be seen by professional peers

- Using institution staff as audit teams to provide credibility and support to the audit process

Those establishing and carrying out the audit system must establish an expectation that the process will be a cooperative venture, in which institutions are provided expert assistance to strengthen their security programs. Unfortunately, auditing tends to be confrontational. Auditors believe that for an audit to be credible, they must find something wrong. Institution administrators, on the other hand, prefer (not surprisingly) to avoid any adverse audit findings. Although the fear of receiving a negative audit report can act as a powerful motivator, it also can cause facility staff to pay undue attention to paper and pencil issues, while neglecting important operational concerns. In addition, undue pressure often is brought upon subordinate supervisors and staff to ensure that there are no issues of noncompliance. The major concern becomes one of covering yourself rather than trying to uncover real weaknesses in a security operation. In this situation, there is little likelihood that issues will be explored mutually for the benefit of the facility involved. As a result, security suffers as less obvious, but more critical, deficiencies may not be disclosed until revealed by the inmate population.

For maximum benefit and credibility, security audits should be conducted by individuals who have experience managing security programs. Sometimes tensions between auditors and institution staff are attributable to selection of auditors who lack "real life, hands-on" experience in the area that they are auditing. They tend to focus on paper/procedural deficiencies rather than on operational issues involving security hardware, gate procedures, perimeter configurations, lighting, workforce, and emergency preparedness, and so forth. There are many benefits that result from using experienced former or current chiefs of security to conduct audits. In addition to providing credible audits, an environment is created

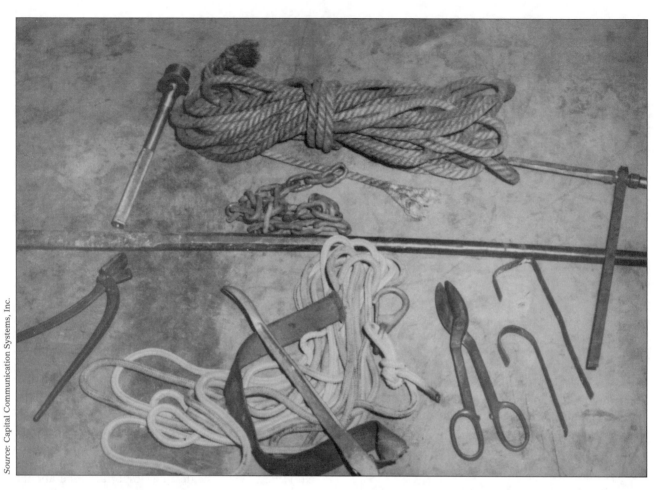

Source: Capital Communication Systems, Inc.

Above and below: Contraband control procedures are one of the many areas that should be subject to auditing.

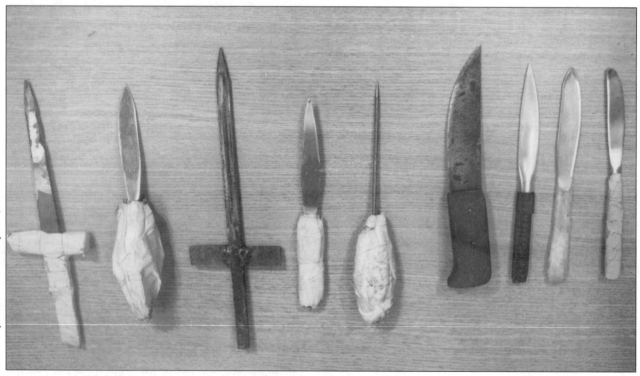

Source: Capital Communication Systems, Inc.

where chiefs can measure their own operations against those of their peers. Also, experienced security managers are usually in a much better position to recognize serious deficiencies that might otherwise be overlooked by inexperienced auditors, and to prescribe workable corrective actions. In this way, auditors are not viewed as judges or scorekeepers, but, instead, as experts who are there to provide technical assistance. Also, auditing using institution staff provides a good source of training for employees who are being developed as managers and supervisors, allowing them to see the different ways others deal with issues and problems.

Institutional staff should be encouraged to identify deficiencies. If an audit is approached with a "score card" mentality, staff will not want to help uncover weaknesses because in doing so they invite a possible unfavorable comparison to other institutions. The same can be said for the effect on institution administrators; if a warden is preoccupied with the audit's final score, the emphasis will be on minimizing the number of deficiencies. If, however, the "score" is not an issue, wardens will be more inclined to encourage their staff to help uncover deficiencies so that they can be corrected.

Types of Audits

There are several different types of audits, and each of these is important. Taken together, a combination of these methods will go a long way toward assuring sound security operations.

External Audits

External audits (that is, audits conducted by personnel outside the level of the organization being audited) should be conducted by agency staff who are well versed in the agency policy and procedures governing the department being audited. Identification of resource use, policy compliance, and management effectiveness are specific functions of the audit process. These audits should be conducted at least annually, and more frequently, if indicated. A fully documented report of the findings of the audit should be provided to the warden of the institution within a reasonable period of time, preferably thirty days. Particular attention should be given to repeat deviations or shortcomings. The agency headquarters should require a follow-up report from the institution, describing the actions taken as a result of the audit, within sixty days of the receipt of this report.

Internal Audits

Internal audits should be conducted at the institution level at least annually, by institution staff. These internal audits should be scheduled at intervals midway between external audits so that the institution is audited at least once every six months. The criteria for both external (agency) and internal (institution) audits should be the same. A copy of each internal audit should be forwarded to agency headquarters for review and comparison with prior external audits. Again, particular attention should be directed to correction of past deviations.

Conducting a Security Audit

The audit should begin with a complete tour of the entire facility, and include all housing units, medical services, academic, vocational, and educational buildings, kitchen, dining room, maintenance, warehouse, armory, control center, sally ports, gates, perimeter posts, towers, and any prison industries. This tour not only will provide a complete overview of a particular operation, but also can show facility staff the importance of the audit. The audit team should be encouraged to not only use audit questionnaires, but continually to be alert for any other security-related issue(s) that they might encounter.

Auditing should determine whether:

- Institution procedures comply with agency policy

- Procedures are sufficient to prevent security problems; if there are any actual security deficiencies, the audit process should identify the specific actions needed to correct them

- Procedures are specific enough to account for each relevant task

- Actual practices are in accord with written procedures

- Staff are capable of appropriately responding to hypothetical situations posed by the auditors

Institutional security audits should include, but not be restricted to, the areas in the chart on page 26.

Appendix B contains a basic audit outline, which contains an array of audit topics and areas. However, the distinctly different policy requirements of each agency also should be incorporated into the audit structure, to assure staff are following every important aspect of relevant policy. Consequently, audit guidelines should be established at the agency level and updated as policies change. The guidelines should

---

Security Audits

–Accountability of inmates

–Admission and orientation

–Armory

–Cell equipment

–Clothing services

–Contraband control

–Control center

–Emergency preparedness and response procedures

–Entrances

–Equipment

–Evidence handling

–Food service operations

–Housing unit operations

–Inmate personal property

–Inmate programs and activities, and their relationship to security

–Internal auditing

–Investigative supervisor operation, to include intelligence-gathering and analysis, storage of contraband and evidence, and other related topics

–Key control

–Mail room

–Medical services

–Perimeter security

–Post orders

–Rear entrance

–Receiving and discharge

–Roster management

–Searches of all types

–Security inspections

–Security staffing

–Special housing unit operations

–Tactical issues

–Tool, equipment, and hazardous material control

–Transportation of inmates

–Urine surveillance programs

–Use of force (lethal and nonlethal)

–Weapon and chemical agent use

–Visiting

–Warehouse operations

---

ensure that institutions are in compliance with applicable laws, regulations, and policies, and that they conform to the standards of regulatory bodies and professional organizations, such as the American Correctional Association.

In the course of the audit, the team should:

(1) Question security staff about their knowledge of all procedures and how they would respond to hypothetical situations

(2) Review post orders, post charts, daily and master rosters, and so forth

(3) Review logs on all posts and observe actual post performance

(4) Stage simulated emergency situations, to observe and make an assessment of staff's reaction (including a debriefing)

(5) Check tool and armory signout sheets, tool inventories, and other records

(6) Observe actual searches of inmates and inmate property

(7) Observe actual security inspections

(8) Review and observe the entry and exit procedures for delivery vehicles and outside work details

(9) Review randomly selected security equipment such as chemical agent dispensers, radios, and body alarms, and walk-through metal detectors

During formal counts, the team may split up to observe actual count practices as they occur concurrently in the control room and in several housing areas. For the most part, however, the audit should be conducted as a team. In this manner, differing viewpoints and perspectives can be discussed, which will contribute to the thoroughness of the audit.

It is important to visit all perimeter posts during daylight and darkness hours. Ask questions concerning use of force and helicopter-assisted escapes. Also, examine lighting, sight lines, and the perimeter's configuration for strengths and weaknesses.

Accreditation

While not an audit process in the same category as those mentioned, American Correctional Association accreditation is a powerful tool for ensuring high-quality institution operations in general, and security, in particular. It provides a well-validated, structured way for institution staff to evaluate their own operations and to improve or upgrade them, as necessary. It also is the means to receive an objective outside evaluation based on professionally recognized standards.

This publication is not the place to discuss the accreditation process in detail. However, this book's authors are thoroughly convinced that accreditation is the most practical avenue a correctional agency has to ensuring safe, humane, and constitutional operations. The reader is urged to consider the important and long-lasting value of the accreditation process and to further explore it through the American Correctional Association.

Managerial Structure

5

The Central Office

The establishment and management of agency-wide standards for security practices, and the necessary procedures and resources to implement them, are the responsibility of the agency's central office. Usually, the agency's security administrator is responsible for the overall management of security operations.

The Security Administrator

An agency's security administrator usually has the following duties:

- Reports to a deputy director and serves as a technical resource on institutional security

- Develops, reviews, and updates a comprehensive body of central office policy in security-related areas and ensures that all such policy is in accord with American Correctional Association standards

- Reviews the security-related policies of other disciplines for aspects of those policies with security implications

- Serves as an advisor for the development of local institutional policies, building on central office security policies

- Reviews all locally issued policy statements for compliance with central office security policies, and for innovative features which can be incorporated into central office policy or disseminated to other institutions

- Maintains a clearinghouse of technical information on security practices, hardware, and devices; supplies field locations with specifications, product data, and other information to support local acquisition of security technology, equipment, and supplies

- Coordinates aggregate purchases of security equipment and supplies when large purchase orders are cost-efficient or beneficial for administrative reasons

- Develops standards of agency wide uniformity for security equipment including firearms, chemical agents, and protective gear

- Maintains a collection of contemporary journals, publications, and professional materials for the use of field security personnel, and serves as reference resource for field security personnel

- Serves as a resource person for agency public information staff, on media inquiries about agency operations; with proper authorization, may directly respond to media inquiries regarding security issues

- Conducts special investigations for the agency head, in cases of serious disturbances, escapes, or conditions of emergency requiring high-level administrative inquiry

- Provides on-site technical assistance to institutional staff on new procedures, new equipment, and redesign of existing facilities

- Serves as resource for architectural and design staff in the conceptualization and execution of new agency facilities

- Represents the agency at state and national conferences of security managers

- Advises the head of the agency on security-related personnel matters

- Conducts special security training and management activities for field staff, and provides input on security issues in overall agency training.

- Coordinates all special investigative functions at the central office level, including tracking general investigative activities in field locations

- Oversees the agency's security audit program, including setting the schedule for audits, training staff in auditing, and conducting security audits, to include authority to conduct follow-up reviews to assess compliance with previous audit findings. Auditing is a key duty of the central office security administrator because it involves applying the sum of all of the other duties to an institution's day-to-day operations. Indeed, in addition to policy development and technical assistance, auditing probably is in the top three most important duties for the central office security administrator.

Where agencies have regional offices, the responsibilities of the security administrators in those offices are a subset of the security administrator, as determined by the central office security administrator.

Policy

Given the variety of activities, people, and contingencies that institution operations involve, there is no way to ensure secure, consistent, constitutionally sound operations without a body of policy and procedure that tells staff what to do, how to do it, and why. In some systems, policies are well-developed based on a rational policy development process and cover each necessary topic. In others, there is more reliance on traditions and past practices, sometimes without having had a formal review for completeness and legality.

In every agency, though, things change–new policies have to be developed and old policies updated to meet new needs. For instance, with the emergence of HIV, many agencies were without formal policies on the control and management of infectious diseases. Even for agencies with a complete policy system in place, situations such as this point out the need to take every opportunity to analyze the changing needs of the system and its various elements, and to develop functional policies and procedures that meet those needs. There are a number of publications that can assist in the development of new policy, and the revision of existing policies. ACA and other publishers and organizations offer books and guides on this issue.

Even so, writing policy is not enough. Even the best policies must be communicated to staff in ways that will help them apply them fully and effectively. Training materials should be developed to demonstrate the functional relationship between policy and institutional operations, with particular emphasis on those based on any newly developed concepts and procedures. Both initial training (whether locally or in an academy setting) and periodic refresher training must contain core information about policies. In training line staff, the rationale for specific policies should be explained carefully, and staff should be impressed with the importance of compliance. Then, to achieve compliance at the operational level, line supervisors and mid-level staff must be sufficiently familiar with and convinced of the value of the policies, so that they can, in turn, effectively supervise line staff.

Also, standing orders, or post orders, developed from policies are important to sustain and reinforce the training effort. In one sense, they are every bit as important as the policies themselves, because in a properly structured post order system, these are the actual documents staff will see regularly–not the formal policies themselves. For that reason, compilation of post orders should be done in a careful and highly practical fashion, one that distills the essence of relevant policies that apply to that post.

Although it would be nice to think that once policy was developed and staff were trained in it, that the job was done, this is not true. Staff supervision and oversight are absolutely critical to making sure that policies are carried out. The day-to-day efforts of first-line and higher management personnel are the key to this process. As they tour the institution, review information that passes over their desks, and talk to staff and inmates, they constantly must be alert to the status of policy compliance. Immediate corrective action is important, so that staff do not get the message that supervisors tolerate noncompliance.

The second facet of oversight is through a formal audit or program review process. This often has two elements: an internal audit function at the institution or department level, and an external audit function by the agency or by some other entity, such as the

American Correctional Association. By scheduling formal audits of each area of institution operations (and the policies that govern them) and then enforcing compliance with any deviations, the agency can be sure that policies are being followed in an effective manner.

Yet, development of a policy does not mark the end of the process; it is only the beginning of a continuing cycle. A complete policy system involves not only policy formulation and training, but regular policy review, audits of policy compliance, feedback from staff, reformulation of policy in accord with that feedback, and retraining, as necessary. In a well-managed correctional system, this is a constant process and necessarily will proceed in different stages for the various segments of an agency's operations.

The Security Manual

The security manager is responsible for developing, maintaining, and publishing the central office security manual. This publication (often in looseleaf form) should contain all agency security policies, as well as detailed instructions for their implementation. It should include, but not be limited to information on the subjects listed in the "Security Manual Topics" box, on the next page. The agency's manual (copies of which should be provided to all institutions' chiefs of security) should be reviewed and revised annually.

Reporting

Reports on all critical incidents and other security activities should be submitted to the central office security administrator on a regular basis. The agency should specify the format for these reports, and which of them should be reviewed by higher officials. Subjects of these reports should include, but not be limited to those listed in the Security Manual Topics box.

Relationships Between Security and Other Specialties

Security and security staff are the focus of these guidelines, and security is an overarching concern in an institution–a concern that should permeate every department, program, and policy. At the central office level, it is very important that the security administrator coordinate every security policy, procedure, and program with other administrators. Likewise, there will be few institution programs that do not involve some security concerns, and so other central office program managers must be equally diligent in coordinating their activities with the security administrator.

In this way, it will be less likely that a policy or program developed in headquarters will have inherent security conflicts or flaws in it.

This is perhaps no more true than in agencies that use unit management. Headquarters' security staff must be diligent in working with their unit management counterparts to assure that each mutually agrees on each procedure or program enacted in these respective departments. Because unit managers in institutions have direct interaction with, and input into the duties of, correctional staff, it is imperative that these two disciplines are talking to each other and that the central office administrators communicate closely and regularly.

Institution-level Structure

The institution security organization ordinarily parallels that of the central office. A chief of security oversees the entire security program, with shift supervisors, senior correctional officers, and correctional officers comprising the entire workforce. While titles may differ from system to system, generally, the functions are the same. From this point forward and for the sake of brevity, these guidelines assume (unless otherwise stated) that the chief of security is responsible for the security-related tasks that are discussed.

The security workforce usually is the largest and most complex department in an institution–responsible for security in all institutional areas, twenty-four hours per day, seven days per week. The chief of security is the local official who is responsible for managing the security workforce. This individual assures that the functions itemized in the security manual are carried out efficiently and professionally through the uniformed security workforce, as well as through the efforts of all departments. But it is vital that the security department maintain proper working relationships with other institutional departments as well, because security is not just carried out on the perimeter, at the entrances, or in the housing unit; security is a concern in every area and department of the institution.

The development and maintenance of an individual institution's security manual is the responsibility of each facility's chief of security. Institutional security manuals should contain local policy and procedures pertinent to the unique characteristics of each facility. Local policy and procedures should be consistent with those described in the central office security manual. For reasons of institutional security, the contents of institutional security manuals and emergency plans must be kept confidential, although

Security Manual Topics

- Accountability
- Admission and orientation
- Armory
- Cell equipment
- Clothing services
- Contraband control
- Control center
- Emergency preparedness and response procedures
- Entrances
- Equipment
- Evidence handling
- Food service operations
- Housing unit operations
- Inmate personal property
- Inmate programs and activities
- Internal auditing
- Investigative supervisor operation, to include intelligence-gathering and analysis, storage of contraband and evidence, and other related topics
- Key control

- Mail room
- Medical services
- Perimeter security
- Post orders
- Rear entrance
- Receiving and discharge
- Roster management
- Searches of all kinds
- Security inspections
- Special housing unit operations
- Staffing levels
- Significant staff meetings
- Staffing levels
- Tool, equipment, and hazardous material control
- Transportation of inmates
- Urine surveillance programs
- Use of force (lethal and nonlethal)
- Weapon and chemical agent use
- Visiting
- Warehouse operations

they should be maintained in locations convenient to key staff.

Before discussing the details of the organization of the security service, we first must discuss one of the true fundamentals of institution management–supervisory visibility.

Supervisory Visibility

This subject was discussed to a certain extent in an earlier chapter, but it is important enough to bear repeating. Policies and procedures in many systems stress the importance of supervisory and administrative staff making regular rounds, walking tours, and performing inspections of the institution. There are good reasons for doing so, and particularly in the

security department. The chief of security and shift supervisors have a special responsibility in this regard.

Security supervisors at all levels (and other administrative staff, as well) should tour the facility regularly to let inmates and line staff know they are aware of what is going on outside their offices in all areas of the institution. These activities reinforce security procedures through constant observation, and ensure that the administrative staff comes into contact with as many of the facility's operational employees as possible. The regular appearance of supervisory staff in and around the institution assures staff and inmates of the administration's continuing interest in them. It reinforces a teamwork approach to the entire facility operation.

However, managers should do more than just conduct inspections. They should pay special attention to operational details and converse with line staff, soliciting suggestions and concerns. Shift supervisors should visit work and housing areas, recreation and other program areas, the dining room and kitchen, and, particularly, special housing units. In addition, they should be aware of any unusual activities or procedures that may require further action.

This visibility strategy is extremely valuable in keeping inmate problems to a minimum, as well. Inmates often will be less likely to protest issues if they believe that supervisory personnel are listening to them and dealing personally and fairly with lesser concerns. Inmates can make an objectively small incident very big in their minds, if they think that no one is listening and that no one will answer them honestly and in a timely way. Personal inmate contacts by supervisors can set the tone for every employee to deal openly and honestly with inmates.

Supervisory visibility and active involvement in operations are important for yet another reason. Security work can be repetitive; staff must anticipate serious events that may not happen for long periods of time, if ever. Under those circumstances, it is easy to become complacent. Supervisors must be alert to this complacency, and be ready to counter it. As a further measure, some jurisdictions use security performance testing or exercises to heighten staff alertness. Some of the tests involved include: attempting to pass someone through a perimeter access point with fraudulent identification; creating a situation where staff are counting a dummy in an inmate's cell; removing a high-security key from a key distribution point, and so forth. If administered with sensitivity to staff's concerns and safety, a system of this type can make a significant difference in the level of job performance throughout the facility.

Post Organization and Post Orders

Posts are established to assign distinct duties to correctional officers in various locations in the institution. Ordinarily, posts are broken down into two categories, by the number of days they are active and by the number of hours they are active in a day. For instance, posts first are identified as seven-day, five-day, or two-day, and then eight-hour, sixteen-hour, or twenty-four-hour, in nature. All rosters and post orders clearly should state the hours of duty for the employee assigned to a specific post. For most posts, the basic hours of duty ordinarily should not exceed eight hours, excluding lunch.

Rotating staff among posts is desirable for several reasons. Employees gain a broader perspective on the total function of the institution, enabling them to better understand how each post interrelates with others. Rotation also provides a fresh view of the post's function and is an important part of an ongoing internal review of institution operations. Finally, rotation allows officers to share the responsibilities of the more stressful jobs and alleviates the boredom of certain posts.

In facilities where post rotation is in effect, officers should be assigned to all three major shifts during a specified time period. For instance, under one such system, staff typically are assigned to the midnight (12-8 AM) shift for one interval, the evening (4 PM-12 AM) shift for an interval, and the day (8 AM-4 PM) shift for two intervals. With three-month intervals, this means that in the course of one year, officers will have been equitably assigned to all three shifts.

Rotational assignments are determined by institution need and staff abilities. The chief of security decides which posts require the most experienced officers, and assignments are made accordingly. Because an employee only can gain experience and expertise by training and exposure to these critical posts, less experienced officers should be assigned to these areas under the supervision of experienced officers. This should be an essential part of any rotation program.

Post orders are based on the institution's policies and procedures, and emphasize the officer's responsibility for custody and security. In addition to stating the hours of duty for each post, they describe routine procedures, and the special duties and responsibilities of the post. Each set of post orders should contain a specific chronological section listing the regular activities to be performed on the post. A general section also should be included, containing excerpts from important policies, such as those regarding inmate accountability and hostages. A list of all program statements relative to the post should be included in the description of duties for that post. Under unit management, the chief of security may involve the unit manager in developing post orders for the unit. Staff should be required to review post orders before assuming a post. A signature sheet that documents the review should be attached to the post orders. See a sample signature sheet in Appendix D.

Each housing unit's post orders must specify that the assigned officer maintains detailed records of pertinent information regarding inmate activity. This housing unit information then is submitted to the shift supervisor for review and inclusion in the official report for that shift.

On armed posts, the post orders must contain instructions for the proper care and safe handling of firearms and specific instructions stating under what circumstances their use is authorized. All officers assigned to armed posts must be thoroughly familiar with the firearms assigned to that post. Post orders for armed posts and those controlling access to the institution perimeter must contain the agency's hostage statement, indicating that any employee taken hostage is without authority, regardless of rank.

Post orders for outside work details should contain information about the type of supervision appropriate for the custody of the inmates. They also should list the schedule of watch calls [3] or other periodic accountability checks that are required of the post.

All post orders must be prepared in looseleaf form and kept current. Each page must be numbered, dated, and initialed by the chief of security. When any page becomes difficult to read, it should be retyped or reprinted on the computer and then reinitialed by all concerned. Unless the nature of the post is such that inmate access cannot be prevented, a copy of the post orders must be kept on all posts.

A master file of post orders should be kept in a convenient central location (staff lounge, shift supervisor's office, control center, front entrance post, and so forth) designated by the chief of security. Copies of post orders should be continuously available for inspection or reference by any interested employee. This enables an employee assigned to an unfamiliar post on very short notice an opportunity to study the orders before assuming the duties of the post. Other department heads should be given copies of post orders when their departments are involved.

An annual post order review should be structured so that about one-twelfth of the post orders are reviewed each month. That way, there is no once-a-year rush to review and reissue the complete body of post orders. Computerization of the post orders and the review schedule can be a significant aid to staff as they complete this process.

The Security Workforce

The security workforce carries out the policies and procedures of the institution. Under the chief of security, correctional officers of various ranks work assigned posts.

The Correctional Officer

The role of today's correctional officers is more involved than simply opening and closing doors, or standing watch in a tower; it is both interpersonally and technically far more complex than in the past. In addition to many technical skills, officers must understand the agency's philosophy, the mission of their institution, and the limits of their authority. In terms of daily contact, the correctional officer is the most important employee in an inmate's life.

A correctional officer also must be able to communicate to supervisors about inmates' conduct–the actions, reactions, and interactions that signal not only how that inmate is acting, but also the tone and atmosphere of the institution. Simple behavior changes can signal progress resulting from positive treatment or indicate tension that might lead to a disturbance.

Senior Correctional Officers

By virtue of promotion on the basis of experience and demonstrated capability, senior correctional officers should be assigned to the most responsible line assignments in the institution, including, but not limited to the control center, entrance posts, and high-security or special housing units. They may serve as officer-in-charge of living quarters or a specific group of quarters; they may orient and supervise new inmates, supervise the disposition of personal property and funds of newly committed inmates, or serve in short-term assignments on any post as a troubleshooter or to improve operations.

Under some circumstances, a senior correctional officer can be assigned as an acting shift supervisor. While this is a less-than-desirable situation, it ordinarily would occur on the morning shift, or on the day shift, Monday through Friday. A senior correctional officer also can be assigned as the acting supervisor responsible for a particular area in the institution (the factory or yard, for instance), under the direction of the shift supervisor.

Supervisory Correctional Officers

The next level in the supervisory chain of command is the correctional supervisor. Correctional supervisors oversee each of the main work shifts for security staff, but they also may be responsible for an area of the institution, such as a special housing unit,

---

[3] A watch call is a regular phone call made during the evening and morning hours by a staff member, to the control center or some other central point, so as to ensure that the employee is safe on his or her post throughout the tour of duty.

the industrial complex, or a large recreation area. Often, there are two ranks of supervisors. The higher rank requires independent functioning as the shift supervisor or special investigations supervisor, and the lower rank is designated for supervising specific areas or functions, such as the factory or yard. A supervisor of the lower rank may be assigned to the position of day watch shift supervisor, if required for training or relief. When this occurs, he or she must be under the direct supervision of the chief of security.

A shift supervisor is most effective out of his or her office among line employees and the inmate population. Although paperwork is a vital part of a supervisor's responsibility, it never should be so overwhelming as to preclude his or her spending the majority of the time in direct contact with staff and inmates. Through accessibility, the supervisor can recognize the strengths and weaknesses of subordinate employees and provide the direction and support required by personal observations.

Special Investigations Supervisor

The special investigations supervisor is an officer of shift supervisor rank who coordinates the investigation of criminal acts committed by inmates, staff, or other persons on institution property. The responsibilities of this position include, but are not limited to:

- Gathering intelligence about ongoing, illegal staff and inmate activities
- Taking appropriate action to curtail illicit activities
- Investigating criminal activity, acts of violence, and escapes or attempted escapes
- Providing accurate and detailed accounts of incidents to appropriate agencies
- Maintaining information on gang activity of all types
- Training staff in the protection of crime scenes, preservation of evidence, and proper documentation

Correctional Counselors

Many systems have established the position of correctional counselor (as distinct from case manager) for officers who are assigned from the correctional complement to counseling activities. In most systems, counselors are specially trained for this role, either through college or in-house training programs. A counselor may be responsible for the following:

- Conducting individual and group counseling
- Providing information regarding inmate adjustment in all areas of the institution
- Informing supervisory personnel of problems requiring attention
- Improving communications between inmates and staff. This is a key counselor function. When inmates are able to obtain authoritative information through the counselors, this process can counteract rumors, eliminate a primary source of misinformation and unrest, and serve as a major contact between the inmates and the administration.

The counselor's working hours should be scheduled to minimize interruptions of inmate programs. Most contacts should coincide with the inmates' nonworking hours.

Details of Managing the Security Workforce

Effective use of the workforce consists ideally of having the right staff, in the right place, at the right time, and doing the right job. Obtaining the right staff was discussed earlier in this publication. This chapter is about the remaining three elements.

In an era of scarce financial resources, optimal use of available institutional staff is a necessity. The principles of efficient use of the workforce must be custom-tailored to each correctional facility within the total system. While there may be a variety of common funding and entitlement factors within a system, the actual use of allocated staff must be done on an institution-by-institution basis. Nevertheless, a number of common, basic management tools can be applied in virtually every correctional setting to deploy available staff effectively. We will examine each of the following items:

- Complement determination
- Relief factor analysis
- Centralized roster management
- Position tracking system
- Recapitulation of workforce utilization

Complement Determination

These guidelines do not recommend the across-the-board use of fixed staffing guidelines. Every institution, its population, and its programs is unique, and requires a customized determination of its staffing needs. Using an individualized approach to determining the correctional complement is a relatively straightforward, but important, task. However, a great deal of effort is needed to accurately determine how many security staff an institution needs.

The first step is a detailed analysis of every post in the institution. This is an appropriate point to highlight the often-misunderstood, but critical difference between posts and positions. A post is an official duty station that is occupied by an employee for a certain period of time (twenty-four hours a day, seven days a week, for instance). A position represents a single employee who has days off, vacation time, sick leave, and other benefits that reduce that person's availability to be assigned to a post. As an example, five-to-six positions are required to staff a twenty-four-hour, seven-day post.

A complement assessment should determine the optimum and necessary hours and days of operation, of course, but also should look objectively at the duties performed. Can they be done more efficiently? Can they be combined with duties of another post? Can they support another post? Is the post actually needed? This time-consuming, but fundamental, analysis will yield a breakdown of posts by days of activation (seven-day, five-day, and so forth) each week, and a parallel breakdown of the number of hours per day each post should be staffed (eight hours, twenty-four hours, for instance) each day.

This initial tabulation of all posts does not take into account days off, sick leave, or other factors. It simply is the raw number of posts for which coverage must be provided, broken down again by days the posts are to be staffed (two-day, seven-day, and so forth). The shift relief factor (calculated as outlined in the next paragraph) should be multiplied against the number of posts in each category to arrive at the total number of positions for each category. By adding the number of positions for each category, you can derive the total number of positions needed for the institution.

Relief Factor Analysis and Computation

Developing sufficient information to compile an accurate shift relief factor is central to assuring an adequate workforce. The shift relief factor is a multiplier applied to the number of posts in a given facility, to determine the actual number of staff who must be on board to cover all posts. It is essential that those reviewing and approving the budget for facility

staffing know and understand how the shift relief factor compensates for around-the-clock operation, days off, vacation days, holidays, sick days, training, and other leave days such as funerals, injury, and perhaps discipline time.

The figures provided as a result of shift relief factor computations ordinarily are supported by data provided by the personnel staff of the agency, and often will apply throughout a whole system. They must reflect actual usage patterns, as well as the statutory entitlements for holidays and other factors that impact on post coverage.

The chart on page 37, with sample numbers, provides a relatively simple method for calculating the relief factor.

To calculate the total workforce needs of the institution, the total number of specific posts must be multiplied by the specific relief factor associated with that category of post. This calculation yields the total number of positions required to staff the institution for a year. A sample tabulation of such a workforce analysis is included in Appendix D.

Centralized Roster Management

Once this data is available, a coordinated central roster can be established. Without a coordinated assignment system, one or more shifts in an institution could be operating with excess staff and the others with a shortage, with no method of compensating for the shortage other than by resorting to overtime. To avoid this situation, a master roster can be compiled as a basis for the coordinated assignment of all security personnel. From the master roster, daily rosters may be derived that show the actual array of staff available to each shift supervisor. These daily rosters provide the basis for an accurate assignment system, but also are important for timekeeping purposes as documentation of workforce used. A sample of a master roster and one shift's derivative daily roster is included as Appendix D. While this sample roster is based on the "block of seven" [5] system, there are other workable systems for aligning staff posts.

Rosters should encompass the following features:

(1) Staff assigned for the efficiency of the service, not the convenience of employees

(2) Centralized rosters (coordinated with pay periods) to enable staff to structure ideal days off for each post. For instance, a rear gate post, if used at all on weekends, would be a relatively undemanding assignment,

(continued on page 38)

Shift Relief Factor

Post coverage:

7-day post, coverage provided for 365 days per year [4]	(52 weeks x 7 days)
6-day post, coverage provided for 312 days per year	(52 x 6)
5-day post, coverage provided for 260 days per year	(52 x 5)
4-day post, coverage provided for 208 days per year	(52 x 4)
3-day post, coverage provided for 156 days per year	(52 x 3)
2-day post, coverage provided for 104 days per year	(52 x 2)
1-day post, coverage provided for 52 days per year	(52 x 1)

Using this information, the relief factor for an agency or an individual institution can be calculated using the following process:

STEP

1. Number of days per year that the agency is closed, and no services offered — 0(a)

2. Number of days per year post is active — 365(b)

3. Number of regular days off per employee per week (usually 52 weeks/year x 2 days off per week) — 104(c)

4. Number of vacation days off/employee/year — 14.6(d)

5. Number of holidays off per employee per year — 12(e)

6. Number of sick days off per employee per year (should be actual average for facility staff) — 8(f)

7. Number of other days off per employee per year (including time off for injuries on the job, filling vacancies, military leave, funeral leave, unexcused absences, disciplinary time off, special assignments, and so forth) — 0.6(g)

8. Number of training days per employee per year — 8.3(h)

9. Total number of days off per employee per year [(c) + (d) + (e) + (f) + (g) + (h)] = (i) — 147.5(i)

10. Number actual work days/employee/year[365-(i)] — 217.5(j)

11. Lunches and breaks (j) x 0.0625 downtime factor — 0(k)

12. Actual work days per employee = (j) - (k) — 217.5(l)

13. Shift relief factor = (b) divided by (l) — 1.68 - 7 day posts

[4] Base year: The base year is 365 days.

and thus ideal for a relief officer. The regular day off for such a post should be Saturday and Sunday. Similarly, it would make little sense to have the regular visiting room officer off on the heaviest visiting days, so the days off on that post should be selected accordingly

(3) The use of some type of "relief brackets" that allow staff to organize permanent assignments in concert with their relief posts, to efficiently deploy all available staff

(4) Coordination of annual leave and training, so the institution has a consistent number of staff on leave throughout the year, except for periods set aside for any institutional training for the entire staff

(5) The use of a regular relief and sick/annual relief structure, so that staff know the post requirements when working on relief, rather than moving around from post to post on a frequent basis

(6) The use of regularly scheduled eight-hour shifts that begin and end in the same calendar day, although in instances where twelve-hour shifts are employed that may not be possible

(7) The regular post rotation of correctional staff, ordinarily at intervals of three to twelve months each, depending on local conditions and labor-management agreements

(8) The restriction of assignments to fifty-two weeks; tower duty ordinarily should not exceed twelve weeks. This latter time is arbitrary, but it reflects a typical roster length. The limitation itself is intended to ensure that no one officer is assigned to this relatively boring post for too long

(9) The rotation of shift supervisors two weeks prior to the effective date of the regular assignment roster, so they can become familiar with the duties of all posts before line staff change

(10) The rotation of probationary officers every four weeks during their probationary year, to provide broad correctional experience on all posts and shifts; probationary posts should be so designated on the quarterly roster. An asterisk, or other method can be used for this purpose

(11) Elimination of the use of terms such as "utility" and "escort" as assignment designations; post titles should reflect clearly the duties actually performed by the officers. If the duties of an assignment are widely varied, the post should be named to identify the major responsibilities identified in the post orders

(12) Methods that ensure officers are not required to assume a post without at least seven and a half hours off-duty order to assure maximum alertness and efficiency on duty

Centralized roster management ordinarily requires an assignment officer to manage the system, but the benefits of coordinated scheduling quickly should recover any additional staff time involved. This post is ideal for keeping all time and attendance records, and compiling a total recapitulation of all workforce used within the department and loans to other services, to ensure optimum use.

Position and Employee Tracking Systems

One general problem in the analysis of many existing correctional rosters stems from the difficulty in following positions from their original allocation through to their present one. In many correctional systems, no method exists to prevent a position from being requested under justification for a critical security need, and then being reprogrammed into a less important area at a later date, without administrative review at a high level.

To remedy this problem, the agency should establish a position tracking system in concert with the approved master roster, to ensure that proper accountability and use are enforced regarding all allocated positions. Every allocated position should be assigned a distinctive number and its use and incumbent should be associated in a formal structure. Whenever the position becomes vacant, proper approval should be obtained from the central office before filling it. Similarly, whenever it becomes necessary to convert a position from one use to another, a written rationale should be prepared by the institution and reviewed by a designated official (ordinarily

---

[5] This is the method of assigning staff that is reflected in the sample rosters; five posts and two relief officers are aligned together in the "block of seven."

in the headquarters' office). These items should be filed with other documentation regarding that position so as to provide a permanent record of why the original position was converted.

At the department level in the institution, a separate, individual employee-level assignment record system should be maintained on each officer, beginning with the first day of employment. This record often is maintained on a 5 x 8 card, but increasingly such records are being maintained on computers. In either case, the record should include the employee's full name, date of birth, date of entry on duty, dates of promotion, and chronological listing of posts assigned. Deviation from normal rotation should be noted after the assignment entry (in other words, job-related self-improvement, training to assume more responsible posts, limited assignments for health reasons, specific need of the institution, and so forth). Having such a record also will allow supervisors to equitably assign staff to posts as future rosters are developed.

Recapitulation of Workforce Use

Each roster system must include a method for recapitulation of all personnel services provided to the institution by the security department. The system should account for every hour of paid staff time, and reconcile those numbers with the positions and salary dollars allocated to the agency.

The typical system used involves a relatively simple tabulation of the totals of all use categories daily, usually on the daily roster itself. The recapitulation should include a complete summary of all leave in every category, as well as all assignments, both within the department and as loans to other services. Staff then periodically total all categories for reporting purposes; the total on the recapitulation must equal the total authorized complement. A sample of such a tabular report is contained in Appendix C.

Other Workforce Management Issues

Professionalism

In past generations, corrections had the reputation as being the refuge of corrupt political hacks and patronage workers who could not find better jobs. Today, we know better. Many people in corrections have worked hard to see that the nature of agencies and their staffing has changed. But the media still portray many correctional staff in a negative light,

and that means that the public's opinion of the profession is still low.

Professionalism must be a touchstone for everything staff do. Having authority that extends to life-and-death issues is a serious responsibility. A consistent, high-level ethic should pervade everything security staff, and all other employees, do. Correctional officials cannot tolerate illegal, immoral, or unethical conduct in their organizations. They cannot afford to allow staff to project an unprofessional appearance. They cannot afford to be involved in conflicts of interest or even have the appearance of a conflict of interest. Public confidence is too hard to gain and too easy to lose.

Each agency should have a clearly stated code of conduct for its staff, a code that sets expectations in areas such as:

- Providing humane, fair treatment of inmates

- Respecting all laws, and the legal rights of staff and inmates

- Setting boundaries for relationships with inmates, their families, friends, and associates

- Defining permissible use of agency property and resources

- Outlining regulations for outside employment, particularly those jobs which may require the use of firearms

- Avoiding a conflict of interest, or the appearance of a conflict of interest

Various jurisdictions may require other areas of ethical consideration for its employees, so this is not an all-encompassing list. But it is suggestive of the main areas in which correctional employees should be sensitive regarding their personal conduct.

The area of conflict of interest warrants particular concern. They may involve the security administrator who accepts favors from the munitions company supplying the agency, the procurement official who is far too willing to award contracts to firms that have ties with organized crime, or the correctional officer who goes into business with the brother of an inmate. These and many other situations can arise if employees are not trained in clear and firm ethical standards of conduct.

Staff also need to be aware of the need to respect inmates' legitimate disabilities, religious beliefs, and other established rights. The possibility of litigation seems to grow daily for violating legal rights under the Americans with Disabilities Act, the Religious Freedom Restoration Act, and the Civil Rights of

Incarcerated Persons Act. Training and supervisory expectations should make clear the requirements of these laws, and the way the agency expects staff to comply with them. It is important to display professionalism on a daily basis.

Sexual harassment in the workplace is another significant area where staff professionalism is implicated. It is never permissible for staff to make unwanted sexual advances or contact of any kind with an inmate; in many jurisdictions, it is a criminal act under specific statutes enacted to protect inmates. But it also is impermissible under the law for staff to sexually harass other employees. Each agency will have a different way of articulating this policy and its approach to sexual harassment under current law. So, again, training is vital in providing employees at all levels with concrete information on how the agency views this problem.

Outside agencies, such as the state police, ordinarily investigate allegations of illegal activity in correctional institutions. But most agencies have an internal affairs office or some other staff investigative function, which may be paired with an ethics office in investigating questionable, but apparently not criminal, employee practices of those types.

Clothing

In recent years, uniforms for correctional officers have been modernized, in both material and style. In line with more casual dress trends in today's society, some officers may try to substitute personal clothing for various items of the uniform, detracting from the professional appearance of the officer. Agencies should require that the complete and correct correctional service uniform be worn by all uniformed staff at all times while on duty.

Most agencies provide uniforms or a uniform allowance to all staff required to wear uniform dress, sometimes to include safety shoes for posts such as a rear gate. Search crews and other staff whose jobs may involve unusual working conditions may be issued special clothing items. Each agency also should make provisions to issue foul weather clothing to correctional officers assigned to outside posts during inclement weather. As a related matter, each institution should have a reasonably sized locker room for staff to use to change clothes, if they desire. In many facilities, showers also are available for employees.

Procedures for issuing, storing, and accounting for all official clothing should be established. These items, which potentially lend themselves to use in an escape, should be located in a secure area, preferably outside the facility.

Professional appearance is an essential, personal, aspect of staff being able to enforce order and discipline in the institution. In line with this interest, correctional officers should not wear jewelry or ornaments that detract from the overall appearance of the uniform or which may present a safety hazard. Examples of items that could be used to cause injury to the officer (because they could be grabbed by an inmate during an altercation) include: necklaces worn outside the shirt or blouse; large, dangling earrings; and other such items.

Language

A related issue in portraying a professional image is that of the language staff sometimes use. Employees often try to portray a toughened image by using vulgar or profane language. Doing so is highly unprofessional and suggests that staff are functioning at the level of inmates, many of whom use that type of language. Supervisory staff should set the tone in this regard and insist that staff use proper, professional language in all of their duties.

A second aspect of professional language has to do with nicknames and the loose talk that sometime becomes part of an institution's permanent jargon. Calling special housing unit recreation yards "pens" or "dog runs" conveys the image that inmates in the yards are somehow less than human. "Feeding" inmates, rather than serving them meals, conjures up the negative image of feeding animals. Calling a tactical group by a whimsical, even popular name that suggest staff aggressiveness may seem to build staff morale, but it also portrays a less-than-professional image. It also may cast into doubt the propriety of their actions if they later are accused of using too much force in managing an inmate.

These topics suggest the need for training that covers key aspects of ethical and professional conduct. Certainly, the best time to give that training is when an employee is starting his or her career. But it also should be reinforced through annual refresher training sessions and in the day-to-day supervision activities that go on throughout an institution.

Supervisory Meetings

Supervisors in the security department should meet periodically, ideally at least once a month. This is a prime opportunity to discuss programs and problem areas of general concern. A definite time and date should be established for these meetings (For example, 8:30 AM on the first Wednesday of each month). The warden and deputy warden(s) of the institution should be invited to attend, as should department supervisors and other interested persons. The chief of security ordinarily should be responsible for the compiling and distributing the agenda in advance, and should chair the meeting. Minutes should be kept and distributed to the warden, deputy warden, and the central office security administrator, but minutes need not be routed to all those who were in attendance.

At these meetings, supervisors should discuss current and potential operational issues, and staffing concerns. In many systems, this is the time when supervisors evaluate the progress and performance of probationary employees. If this is done, then a written evaluation should be prepared for each employee, which includes performance and training needs. Specific comments regarding performance and progress, and the advisability of retention or termination, should be drawn to the attention of the chief of security and the personnel officer.

Automation of Security Management

Managing the security workforce is an increasingly complicated job. To the extent that modern technology can reliably help with that task, correctional managers should be eager to embrace it. While technology issues are mentioned in many other relevant sections of these guidelines, several points bear special mention.

(1) To the extent possible, control centers and other entry-related operations should be automated. This includes elements such as computerization of basic records, automation of gate and grille controls, and use of closed circuit television, motion-detection, biometrics, [6] and other technologies to enhance entrance security.

(2) Automation of rosters can be an immense time-saver for the management of the security workforce. Commercial packages are available for this purpose, but agency staff may develop an in-house system. It not would only generate daily rosters and optimize workforce deployment, but also could be used to track leave usage, loans to other services, overtime funds, and even tardy staff. These systems can be invaluable in developing information to justify agency budget requests to legislative bodies.

(3) Inventory systems in the private sector increasingly rely on bar-coding and computerization to accurately and efficiently track all items. Such systems can be developed and used to track armory equipment and expendables, inmate property, commissary stock, or other items.

(4) While electronic monitoring of inmate activity primarily has been a community programs option, recently, electronic tracking of inmates in an institution has become a possibility. Such a system could provide the opportunity for: conducting dependable, real-time counts without inmates returning to their cells; enforcing off-limit zone enforcement; enhancing perimeter detection; providing evidence of an inmate's presence at a crime scene; accumulating accurate management information, in terms of inmate movement and program activity; and reporting of staff tours.

Theoretically, such a system also could be used to track staff, supplementing the personal safety that a body alarm provides. In a time of emergency, for instance, the location of all personnel in the institution could be ascertained, and if hostages are taken in an institution-wide takeover, tactical personnel would have positive information on their location throughout the crisis. While retrofitting such equipment may not be practical in existing institutions, the time may come when it would be deemed practical and desirable for new construction.

Computers can assist in gathering and organizing information on security program performance, staff effectiveness, and the workload. Systemwide data collection on grievances, incidents, urine testing results, transportation activity, numbers of inmate visitors, and so forth can help agencies respond to not only internal operational needs, but also legislative requests for information, to hold correctional systems accountable for resources.

Elsewhere in these guidelines are references to other applications of technology, in areas such as digitized data recording, high-technology scanning capabilities, and others. Agencies should be alert to developments in the field and to their applicability to specific institution needs.

Controlling inmate access to computers is important. As correctional systems become increasingly reliant on automation, and as local and wide area networks are used to link stand-alone systems, the risk increases for computer tampering, or "hacking." Computers can be an excellent teaching tool, and there is no reason why inmates cannot use properly supervised instructional computers. But many inmates are computer literate and could penetrate staff computer systems if given the opportunity. Consequently,

---

[6] This involves using specific body measurements (retinal patterns, shape of a hand) to identify a person entering or leaving an institution.

inmates must not be permitted to access any computer that contains agency data of any type, nor any computer that is linked to a network or a modem. Moreover, inmates should not be permitted to write computer programs other than as part of an instructional program, and then only with positive assurance that the program will not run on a noninstructional computer.

Also, while this is a highly technical area that goes beyond typical security issues, management personnel should be concerned that agency computers are not vulnerable to outside penetration. The use of suitable safeguards such as passwords, physical access control and software/hardware "firewalls" can provide a relatively high degree of assurance that only the most dedicated computer expert could access the system. But agencies also should examine the level of background investigations, password management, and post-employment dependency that its computer operations have on contractors who do computer work for the organization. There are significant vulnerabilities in this area that every agency should address in its computer security plan.

Leave Policies

Annual leave should be scheduled at an employee's request, with first consideration given to the needs of the institution and any applicable labor-management agreements, or other regulations or statutes. In the case of the security workforce, the security and safety needs of the institution clearly involve assuring a certain minimum number of staff are available to operate all essential posts, allowing for some variation in total complement. An equal number of employees should be on leave each period throughout the year. Centralized roster management is a key to achieving this balanced leave scheduling.

Sick leave should be granted only when the employee is unable for physical or mental health reasons to report for duty. All employees must notify the institution as early as possible before the start of their shift, of their inability to report for duty due to illness. Local custom and requirements may vary, but ordinarily employees reporting "sick" should call in to the shift supervisor on duty.

Supervisory personnel should monitor potential sick leave abuse cases, and intervene, when necessary. In some instances, medical certificates may be required to substantiate sick leave above certain levels. Highly questionably circumstances, such as repetitive use of sick leave before or after days off or holidays, may require the employee to justify any sick leave taken. Many systems–frequently because of state regulations–require this step to be taken if

more than three days of sick leave are involved and a pattern of questionable leave use already has been established. Prior written notification to the employee may be required in some instances, before such justification is demanded.

Personnel Evaluations

Where permitted by the labor-management agreement, records documenting each officer's quarterly performance should be maintained in the shift supervisor's office, when they can be appropriately secured from unauthorized access. In most cases, these working records will not be classified at the same level as the employee's official personnel file, and thus keeping them in this location is permissible. In some systems, however, state personnel regulations may impose specific storage requirements that only may be achieved by storing such records outside the secure perimeter.

Evaluations should include elements such as: ability to manage inmates, communication skills, writing ability, knowledge of policies and procedures, personal characteristics and appearance as they relate to job performance, job interest, dependability weaknesses, and strengths. All performance ratings should be completed by the shift supervisor and reviewed by the chief of security. If the institution is operating under unit management principles, correctional officers assigned to units for the majority of the rating period should be rated with input from the unit manager. Evening and midnight shift correctional officers assigned to units, and not under direct supervision of the unit manager, should be rated by the shift supervisor with a review by the unit manager.

Formal quarterly performance reports are typical in many agencies, but additional comments should be entered on the performance card as necessary (but not less than monthly) throughout the rating period. A monthly evaluation form should be completed on each employee on probationary status. A supervisor should review the evaluation monthly with the probationary employee.

When performance-based entries are made, they should be called to the officer's attention at the time of notation, and the officer should be required to initial the card. If an officer refuses to initial an entry, a notation to that effect should be made by the supervisor. An officer should be permitted to see his or her card at any time, but must not be permitted to see another employee's performance evaluation, except when authorized in writing by the employee concerned.

Properly documented evaluations serve as a guide when completing annual performance ratings, which ordinarily are completed on the employee's anniversary date (in other words, date of entry on duty or date of promotion to the present grade). A new card should be started to coincide with the beginning of the new rating period, and the old card retained for one year, after which it should be removed and destroyed.

Security's Relationship with Other Departments

As a practical matter, the chief of security is the central figure in an institution. This sentence does not say that the chief of security is the most important figure, or the most powerful, or even the most authoritative. What it says is that the chief of security is the person around whom virtually all of the institution's activities revolve. And, if that person is not constructively and actively involved in the security-related aspects of every department, then it is likely that operations will suffer.

How does this positive interaction happen? It starts with communication among all department heads. Personal meetings between department heads and the chief of security, attendance by the chief at departmental meetings, attendance by unit managers at meetings the chief has with shift supervisors, and many other such forms of interaction are essential in maintaining a smooth day-to-day operation. It certainly extends to the security staff providing key security-related training to all staff from all departments about core security skills. Whether or not an institution is operating under the correctional worker concept, training in certain security skills and knowledge builds a common professional bond among staff of all disciplines.

All of this requires a certain willingness by all involved to share authority. It requires every department head to acknowledge that security is the common theme throughout the institution, and that his or her department is not exempt. It requires that the chief of security also acknowledge that the security department is in existence, to a certain extent, to achieve the smooth and secure functioning of the other departments. Those mindsets reflect a professional approach to running an institution, and they produce an effective management atmosphere.

Buildings

6

Design Elements

Institution design is a critical factor in determining how the security of an institution is organized. This includes not only the layout of buildings and perimeter security features, but the nature and number of internal design barriers, lines of sight, the types of security systems, and the types of security technology and equipment used. It also includes things like installing handcuff ports and locating showers in cells in special housing units, or situating showers and phones in general population units so that officers can see them easily. These are things that make an institution far more workable on a day-to-day basis. Including proper layout and operational elements at the time of original design is far less expensive than adding them later.

Starting with the specific mission of the institution, designers must be aware of the general impact of a building's configuration on its security. The central office security administrator and other key staff should be integrally involved in every stage of this process.

Architectural Issues

Basic layout is critical, and architectural personnel should strive for the best possible sight lines for supervisory staff. Campus plans and open-layout housing units, versus corridor-system plans with traditional cellblocks, are particularly appropriate for providing good surveillance and a more relaxed atmosphere. In an institution with a campus-style layout, inmates in the compound can be observed easily by staff members whose main responsibility does not include direct supervision. In fact, some institutions have been designed so that the warden and other top staff members can survey virtually the entire inner compound from their offices. Conversely, architects also should be aware of design details that can make supervising the compound more difficult. These include items such as awnings and porches that provide access to rooftops, indentations and blind spots in walls, and construction materials that lend themselves to contraband concealment or fabrication. Design materials should be prudent, low-cost, and attractive.

Architectural staff should design the physical plant so it will support programs in proportion to the number of beds in the institution. No new facility ever should be designed and built without sufficient work and program areas to support the entire population.

The general design of the physical plant also must include adequate space for staff offices, work and factory space, and inmate programs and services. Design also has an impact on housing unit supervision and unit management. New institutions and those being renovated should include sufficient office space in, or in the immediate vicinity of, housing areas, to allow all assigned unit staff to be readily available to inmates. This ordinarily includes space for a secure file storage area and a small conference or meeting room. Work areas must be provided, so that each inmate has a worthwhile job.

Size is an important factor, as well. Ideally, a total institution should be no larger than 500 inmates, but today's reality is that many are much larger. When the population exceeds 500, it becomes increasingly difficult to maintain a healthy atmosphere, promote open communications, provide programs tailored to individual needs, control tension, and ensure the safety of both staff and inmates. In recognition of that reality, when possible, larger facilities should be subdivided into sections that house no more than 500 inmates. This makes them more manageable.

Correctional systems requiring increased capacity sometimes have resorted to "clustering" two or more facilities on a common site, into a correctional complex. Reasons for this strategy include the economies of scale inherent in larger operations, capital savings incurred in the sharing of certain service functions, and the difficulty of obtaining sites, particularly close to major urban centers. In the past, decision makers were urged to avoid this clustering approach, the thinking being that while there were some direct savings, there also were substantial and less apparent indirect costs. However, many agencies have challenged this notion with apparent success. These shared-service facilities sometimes have a "super administrator" or "super warden" while others allow individual facility administrators to operate with relative autonomy. In activating correctional complexes, it is important to avoid building into the organizational structure the inherent management problems of larger, older institutions that modern designs have helped neutralize. If complexes are planned, organizational structures and security policy should be designed to ensure the independent operation of programs in each facility, to the greatest extent possible.

In many respects, some of the most important security features in an institution are built into individual areas, such as control centers, housing units, armories, commissaries, mail rooms, pharmacies, locksmith shops, and cashier's offices. Secure walls, doors and hardware, fixtures, and other design elements are important. These factors can ensure that individual functions within the institution can be isolated when necessary, and also are capable of deterring and preventing inmate penetration or escape.

Housing unit design and construction features, in particular, drive the functional security level of an institution. Cost and actual functional need must be consistent with the security mission of the institution. These elements are carefully played out in the realities of wall construction materials, types of cell toilets, selection of security hardware, and other design features. For example, while unified stainless steel toilet/sink fixtures are available, the actual security needs of the inmate population justify the high cost of those fixtures in only the highest security applications.

Building roofs should be reasonably free of potential hiding places. This general requirement is imperative for structures that are part of the perimeter itself for example, an entrance structure that is aligned with the perimeter fence system and is an integral element of the perimeter security system.

Secure perimeters surrounding both the institution and inmate housing areas allow for more relaxed internal operations and a reduced need for constant inmate observation. In the event of a general disturbance, strong perimeters give the staff time to address the emergency and bring it under control before unrest extends to other housing units or to the nearby community.

Landscaping is an integral part of overall security design, in that it contributes to a wholesome working atmosphere for staff. However, any shrubs and trees that are placed should not jeopardize institutional security, nor obscure sight lines.

In general, designers should strive to provide sensory stimuli and avoid an atmosphere of watchful intrusion, which can add to tension and stress among staff and inmates alike.

Staffing Impact

Facility design has an immense impact on staffing. Most agencies recognize that the initial construction cost of an institution is only about 10 percent of its overall lifetime operating expense. The other 90 percent includes operating costs, mainly personnel expenses. Consequently, a staff-efficient institution will save an agency immense amounts of money over its lifetime. On the other hand, a staff-heavy design will be an expensive albatross for the life of the facility. There are several schools of thought on how to address this at the practical level.

In recent years, many institutions have been designed without perimeter towers. By substituting mobile perimeter patrol posts, agencies initially can avoid creating the need for a large number of positions. The cost implications of this strategy are significant. Consider that one tower, staffed twenty-four-hours a day, typically requires five to six positions to cover (depending on the agency's relief factor). At a cost of $40,000 a year (not unusual for a correctional officer's salary and benefits), a single tower can cost $200,000 or more a year. Multiplied by eight towers (and offset by the expense of two twenty-four-hour perimeter patrol posts) as much as $1.2 million a year can be saved.

The use of unit control centers, or "bubbles" can be a very costly design element. While such posts can and should be used in maximum-security units, placing them in typical close-security housing areas (much less lower-security levels) is a waste of personnel resources. This also runs completely counter to

Source: CRSS

The construction of an institution determines, to a large degree, its mission.

the use of unit management and direct supervision models that promote open interaction and communication with inmates.

The design of the units themselves can increase or decrease staffing requirements. For instance, in special housing units, if cells are designed with properly controlled showers in them, then fewer escort staff are needed to supervise inmates going to and from common showers. Similarly, in general population housing units, proper placement of key design elements can improve supervision and reduce the need for extra coverage on certain shifts.

Finally, proper incorporation of technology into the design can make the institution more staff-efficient. Cameras, remotely actuated gates, and other methods can reduce the number of staff required in some areas. While these technologies cannot totally substitute for staff (officers still have to conduct security inspections and search inmates at key traffic points to intercept contraband, for instance), in many ways technology can reduce staffing requirements.

Equipment

Despite the initial thought that equipping an institution should be straightforward, it actually is a challenge of some magnitude. The world of corrections has expanded in the last decade, to include a wide array of manufacturers and vendors, whose products seem to offer a bewildering number of choices. Those choices often can be limited by the realities of budget limitations, or the practicalities of actual program usefulness.

In this section, the basic equipment needs of an institution's security program are addressed. No particular brands are endorsed, nor should the generic product characteristics mentioned here preclude shopping for other technology products. Technology is changing so quickly that it would be impossible to list all of the features that are current on every device today. And even if it were possible to do so, a year from now, some would be obsolete and additional options would be available on others.

All security equipment should be approved by the central office security administrator. This requirement actually points out an important personnel need in most systems. While the ACA and other criminal justice organizations can provide some guidance on technology issues, it is desirable to have a staff member specifically assigned to review, assess, and recommend procurement of security technology devices. This can assure consistency in procurement, appropriate selection of devices in new construction and for retrofitting of existing facilities. It also can lead to a more cost-effective use of agency funds. Because each system's needs are different, an in-house specialist can be of great value in deciding what newly developed systems should adopt.

While technology is an excellent aid to security, no security system should be built solely around it. Closed-circuit television can assist with some tasks, but on-site human supervision enables an institution to really control inmate interactions. Speakers or intercoms can be helpful communication aids, but personal interaction with staff allows both staff and inmates to build personal relationships and confidence that pay off in a tense situation. A motion sensor or other detection system can provide information, but it still takes an officer crawling through a tunnel, looking under a truck body, or inspecting a plumbing chase, to find out whether security systems have been compromised.

Facility-related Equipment

With that human factor in mind, the following are basic security-related equipment items that an institution should have.

Emergency Generator: An emergency generator should provide backup capability in the event of a power outage. The generator and all critical switching gear should be located outside the secure perimeter. The control center, armory, towers, phone system, detection systems, radio systems, command center, and other key areas should be on this emergency power system. The system should be tested at least monthly and emergency battery-powered lighting should be available at the site of the generator in the event that it does not work properly.

X-ray or other Scanning Equipment: X-ray or other suitable technology should be used to screen

49

packages, briefcases, purses, inmate property, facility mail, and warehouse products for contraband as they pass through the perimeter. In some high-security locations, in addition to scanning all incoming items, inmate commissary packages being delivered to locked housing units are scanned. In all such cases, a procedure needs to be in place to periodically test the equipment for proper functioning, and for assuring the safety of those around it. In addition to x-ray technology, ion spectrometry scanning devices are a possibility. They are far more sensitive and provide dependable results in the detection of drugs and explosive materials. Magnetic resonance imaging technology offers extremely good possibilities of providing expedient, reliable body cavity searches without the medical/legal implications associated with high-intensity x-ray examinations. With proper safeguards for all constitutional rights, passive millimeter wave length imaging can be used in low-intensity forms to provide thorough searches of the human body through clothing.

Walk-through Metal Detectors: Walk-through metal detectors at all entrances and key internal traffic points (pinch points going into factory and shop areas, for instance) enhance the surveillance of all inmates and nonstaff moving through those points. *Pinch points* refer to traffic points through which most (if not all) of the inmates going to and from an area must pass. They are the logical places to locate metal detectors and to conduct other searches, as well. These devices should be calibrated carefully and regularly checked (and recalibrated, as necessary) to ensure that they are working properly and detecting all metallic objects above a certain mass threshold.

Perimeter Detection System: A perimeter detection system should be installed on the inner fence of all fenced facilities, and in an appropriate location on walled perimeters. This is an important method for giving staff enhanced surveillance capability. These systems are of varying types, and in many institutions, a full perimeter system involves the use of more than one technology. For instance, a "shaker-wire" system, a type of alarm that detects shaking motions, may be called for on fences, while a series of microwave fields may be used at a rear gate area. Although a principle dating back many generations, a taut-wire system may be effective for some applications. In some cases, climate conditions may call for a geophone-based system, rather than a fence-based system. The geophone-based alarm detects vibrations through the ground, such as would be caused by an inmate moving in proximity to a detector-equipped fence. Alarm zones in such systems should be identified visibly in such a way that they can be seen from both sides of the fence. This can enable staff to respond quickly to the area of an alarm announced over the radio. Most detection systems are monitored in the control center. Many offer fixed or mobile annunciator panels (a type of monitor that visually presents the site plan of the institution, including the perimeter fence and alarm zones) that can be installed in towers or patrol vehicles. Whatever system is chosen, each institution should have procedures in place to deal with false alarms, and to test the system on each shift. The integrity of the fence itself should be checked under the institution's security inspection system.

Fence Wire: Razor ribbon and rolled razor wire should be installed on the fences, and between them, to deter inmates and intruders from trying to breach fenced perimeters. Such wire also can and should be used on interior fences, building roofs and walls, and in other locations, where appropriate. Fence wire configurations will vary in accord with the institution's security mission, the terrain, and the fence configuration. However caution should be exercised to ensure that the wire rolls do not actually provide some support for a timber or heavy fabric "bridge" over the fences. A 4-3-2-1 stack is a preferred configuration for higher-security institutions. With a four-layer thickness of razor wire at the ground level thinning out to a single layer at the top, the stack configuration makes climbing a fence much more difficult. However, a single roll on the top of a fence may be sufficient for low-security locations.

Lighting: The department should develop standards for minimum and average lighting levels on perimeters. The standards may call for a higher level of illumination on the perimeter than elsewhere in the compound. High-mast lighting fixtures can enhance security considerably in the compound, as well as on the perimeter, increasing staff safety and reducing the opportunity for escape attempts. Many firms design the installation of such lights using a computer program that analyzes a plot plan of the site and identifies optimal light placements, minimizing shadows between buildings and in other normally dark locations. In some installations, it may be desirable to design a lighting system that operates at one level during normal activities and is augmented by higher-intensity lights if an alarm is activated.

Tower Intercoms: All towers should be equipped with open intercoms, connected both to the other towers and to the control center. This system allows tower staff to instantly report any unusual happening they observe, while at the same time reaching for equipment or repositioning themselves in the tower for better vision or readying weapons fire.

Standardized Key Storage Cabinets: A standardized storage cabinet should be used for all institutional pattern and spare keys. The acquisition or construction of this piece of equipment can significantly enhance the key control program. The cabinet should be capable of storing multiple keys on hooks, along with identifying information for the keys; rapid access, through a multipanel design of some type, is desirable.

Key Machine: A key machine pays for itself relatively quickly in the time and service charges saved when staff no longer have to obtain duplicate keys commercially. This capability also can free up the locksmith's time for repairs and maintenance in the institution.

Audiodialer: Automatic, sequential, dialing equipment is available. It allows the control center officer to dial (without any further action) every staff member whose phone number is logged into the dialer, and to convey a prerecorded message to report to the institution. Ordinarily, supervisory staff, emergency response teams, and medical personnel are called first. Then, additional line staff are contacted.

Two-way Radio Systems: Multichannel radio capability is critical in today's correctional environment, allowing staff to communicate confidentially by switching to an alternate frequency. In an emergency, radio communications used for command personnel can be on one channel, while other staff in inmate areas can use the other. In the case of facilities which are located near other radio sources on the same frequency, the second channel prevents a great deal of confusion in day-to-day radio communications. Radios used in the secure areas of the facility, in contact with inmates, ideally should be capable of receiving only one channel. Then, in the event inmates gain control of one of these units, all response and command communications can be on an alternate frequency. Some systems also are available with scrambled signal capability, but these are of primary use in circumstances where more sophisticated monitoring of radio traffic by the public is likely to be a problem. Such units should be evaluated carefully to determine if the additional capability is worth the cost and complexity they entail.

Procurement and operational staff should remember that authorization must be obtained from the Federal Communications Commission before staff can operate on any radio frequency. The power output of the base station and the portable radios should be sufficient to establish a clear communications link between radios anywhere near the institution, including the maximum distance that staff are expected to travel during an escape search. When installing a new radio system or a new variety of radio, it also is important to test representative portable units throughout the institution to be sure there are no "blind" spots where transmissions are unreliable. It also is important, in a day and age when printed circuit boards are incorporated in so many other security devices, to ensure that the radio frequencies in use do not induce currents in any other critical circuitry, which could result in a security grille being inadvertently activated, for instance.

Closed Circuit Television: The use of closed circuit television (CCTV) as a security tool is very cost-effective for many applications. CCTV is an excellent device for monitoring fence lines, rooftops, tunnels, and corridors, and can aid in the identification of people passing through sally ports. Some closed circuit television cameras can be set up to detect motion in their field of view and alert the control center if someone is in an unauthorized area. However, closed circuit television should not be used alone to monitor inmates in their regular duties and functions. There is no electronic substitute for personal interaction between inmates and staff. Also, closed circuit television in areas like the yard, corridors, and special housing units, may be installed in conjunction with taping equipment, so that staff will have concrete evidence of misconduct or criminal acts. This is particularly valuable in the visiting room, which is a prime avenue for contraband introduction.

Public Address Systems: These systems allow the control center officer or other designated staff members to make general announcements throughout the institution, to summon individuals, and to alert staff to emergencies. Because institutionwide paging causes unnecessary disruption in areas unaffected by specific announcements, zone paging is recommended. A listen-in/talk-back function adds the capability to monitor a specific location or to conduct conversation.

Automated/Remotely Actuated Gates, Grilles, Doors: These devices are regular features of correctional institutions today. Any number of entry control technologies are available, and the choice of a specific application depends on many factors. Rather than discuss the relative merits of chain-driven, pneumatic, or other methods of operation, or the benefits of buttons, computer touch-screens, or trackballs for actuating them, the following principles are important:

- Controls should be simple; it does very little good to have a state-of-the-art system if staff find it cumbersome to use or hard to learn.

- The operating system always should have a manual override or fallback mode; in the event of power failure or other crisis, staff always should be able to physically open the doors.

- Doors that might be used as emergency entrances or exits always should have keyways and handles on both sides; staff should always be able to gain entry to any area.

- To the greatest extent possible, the system should be maintainable with in-house resources; cost considerations are critical in an institutionwide system such as this, which is in constant use, and, therefore, is subject to constant wear and tear.

Control Center Equipment

Control center operations are discussed in detail on pages 75-81 in this publication, which should be read in connection with this information. Modern institutions rely on a combination of basic technology and high technology. Starting with a modern console with strategically located controls, operations in this critical location should be designed for ease of use. Adequate storage must be available for a wide range of equipment items, to include the following:

- A well-organized key board, with alphanumeric coding, should have separate sections for regular, emergency, and restricted keys. Many agencies use a rolling storage cabinet that moves easily into place for key issue at shift change, but can be moved out of the way at other times.

- Adequate card files or other storage media for inventories of all post equipment; gate passes; inmate, staff, and volunteer identifying information; and other similar information items. Local policy should be clear on the means of identifying nonemployees (such as volunteers and contract employees) and the areas of the institution they may access. Color-coded pass or ID card systems can be used to improve travel in and around the institution, although they never should be substituted for proper identification procedures authorizing anyone to leave the institution.

- Computers, in whatever configuration are required to support the facility's operation. This may include use as word processors or to maintain count records, but also could include a comprehensive system that controls all doors, alarms systems, and staff/inmate data.

- Television monitors and controls; the monitors should be positioned, if possible, so that any inmates in the vicinity cannot see what is on the screens.

- Monitors, controls, and storage/battery recharge racks for radios, personal body alarm systems, fire alarms, and perimeter detection systems are necessary. Monitors are needed to pick up radio frequencies assigned to other law enforcement agencies with whom the institution may have contact in an emergency.

- An intercom system connected to all key posts is necessary.

- Override controls for high-security remotely actuated doors, grilles, and gates elsewhere in the institution are important.

- Gas masks (ideally with vocal capability), should allow control center staff to issue instructions if chemical agents are employed in the vicinity and infiltrate the area, or in the extreme event that chemical agents had to be dispersed in the control center as a deterrent to inmate takeover. These masks typically include a microphone built into the inside of the face compartment, and have a small battery-powered speaker beside the mask, which can be heard easily by others when smoke or gas has been deployed.

  Gas masks and self-contained air packs mounted on wall racks should be in all control centers and towers where there is a possibility of smoke or gas being blown into an area and disabling staff who have particularly vital security responsibilities.

- Selected ordnance, including chemical agents; depending on agency policy, firearms and ammunition may be stored here, as well.

- Storage boards or racks for restraint equipment, chemical agents, and protective gear are vital.

- Bolt cutters for removing jammed restraints, and other basic tools are necessary, perhaps including a cutting-torch set.

- Storage areas for staff's personal items and clothing are necessary.

- A toilet and sink in a private area may be necessary.

Unit control centers should be equipped with a subset of this equipment, as determined by the agency. Obviously, keys and ordnance items should not be in these areas. If a toilet is not included in the control center's design, then other staff on the unit can provide relief for the officer in the unit for that purpose.

Telephone Equipment

In the past, telephone systems in correctional facilities usually consisted of two separate systems–one operating inside the institution, and the other extending outside the institution. This latter system also was used for what formerly were relatively rare inmate outside phone calls. The inside system typically was installed and operated by the institution. The outside system normally was provided by the local telephone company and was comparable to most regular business systems. Telephones with access to outside communications were located in secure areas, and inmates were restricted from using them unless under direct staff supervision.

Today, things are a bit more sophisticated. The inside telephone equipment usually provides access to outside lines, and a separate inmate telephone system also is in place in most locations. Each of these telephone systems specifically should be designed for the institution, and capable of functioning as an integral part of the institution's security system. All new phone installations now are solid-state, combining the security features of the inside telephone system with the flexibility of the outside system. This resolves many of the installation, interface, operational, and maintenance problems associated with the traditional dual system. Printed circuit boards can be replaced easily when problems develop, and additional capabilities can be added in modular fashion. A necessary feature of all systems is battery-operated backup capability, in order to maintain communications in case of an interruption in the institution's electrical supply.

Cellular phones are a reality of modern life that have significant benefits in the correctional environment. They can be carried by command staff at all times, to allow almost instantaneous communication in an emergency. Escort staff can carry a phone, allowing them to call the institution or local police from any location if there is a problem. Bus and van crews can carry them on the open road, in the event of a breakdown, sick inmate, or other unusual situation. In the event the main phone system is inoperable, cell phones provide a backup. All in all, this is a relatively inexpensive, yet valuable technology that every institution should be using in some form. However, inmates never should be permitted access to a cellular phone.

Staff should be required to regularly test the emergency elements of the phone system. Once a week on the morning watch, test calls should be made on the emergency alarm number from a variety of locations, as a test of the system's functioning.

The staff phone system should include the following special features:

- A watch call feature that enables each officer making an inmate count to call a special number. These calls "stack" onto an open line in the control center for continuous and simultaneous communication until the count clears.

- An emergency alert feature that is initiated by dialing a special number, and which activates an emergency network that simultaneously rings predesignated phones including those in the control center, and other command locations such as the office of the warden and chief of security.

- A no-dial alarm that is activated when a handset is removed from its base instrument for at least fifteen seconds prior to dialing. This alarm also indicates the location of the instrument being dialed.

- An executive right-of-way feature that allows staff at certain phones, such as those in the warden's office or the control center, to interrupt calls if lines are busy, thus enabling an emergency call to be completed immediately.

Inmate phone systems should have the following minimum capabilities, unless otherwise prohibited by law or regulation:

- Phones should be armored and firmly anchored to a fixed object in a location that allows for good staff supervision.

- Inmate phones should not be capable of making outgoing calls without going through an operator or automated process to ensure calls are placed properly.

- Ideally, staff should be able to exert positive control over who inmates call, and to control the length of the call. Some systems allow automatic debiting of the inmate's commissary account to pay for calls, rather than requiring the calls to be collect. The use of some automated systems may require obtaining permission from prospective call recipients before adding that person to the inmate's approved call list.

- Staff should be able to monitor all inmate phone calls as they take place, and to identify both the phone from which the call is being made and the number to which the call is being placed. Monitoring can be done in "real time" by tower officers, through later review of monitoring tapes during the morning watch, or by special staff assignments in furtherance of an investigation. In facilities where phone call monitoring and intercept capability are available (for inmate and staff calls), employees must have clear instructions on the proper use of the system. In jurisdictions where taping of random calls is permitted, the regulations clearly should define the parameters for legal interception.

- Recording capability for all calls should be in place, and if possible, extended-play, multi-track recorders should be used, with the tapes retained for a reasonable period, in the event that later investigative efforts require their review. Some phone systems now available permit linking recorded conversations with computerized records of the inmate, phone called from and the number called, so as to be able to accurately reconstruct telephone activity as part of an investigation.

- In special housing units, staff should install phone jacks on the range near the cells, so that phone calls can be made from within the cell. Some institutions are experimenting with radio-based portable phone systems, which have sufficient range to allow their use in an open cellblock, and do not require the wiring that individual phone jacks entail. These options free up staff time and reduce the amount of out-of-cell traffic that a more typical central phone system generates in special housing.

Ordnance

Requirements for firearms, gas, and specialty items (stun guns, custody control belts, and so forth) are best established by each agency, and particularized for each institution. A facility located in an urban area will have perimeter security and weaponry needs very different than those of an institution in a rural location. The types of weapons needed for crowd control inside a corridor or yard are much different than those encountered if a tower officer were to come under fire from a sniper outside the institution. Consequently, the balance of this section will provide only the most general description of the types of firearms and potential uses they may see.

Rifles. There are at least two broad categories of rifles in correctional use: those in daily use in towers

and patrol vehicles, and those issued to snipers. Typically, tower weapons are short, small-caliber, autoloading, clip-fed weapons that are easy to handle and bring to bear on a moving target. Many agencies now use .223 caliber weaponry for this purpose. These weapons generally are intended to be used against a distinct target (such as to stop an escape) or to fire warning shots to stop inmate disturbances. Sniper rifles tend to be larger bolt action weapons, with telescopic sights, and of a heavier caliber, such as .30-06 or .308 Nato. These weapons should be used only under the most carefully controlled situations, with close controls over when staff are authorized to discharge them against a human target.

Shotguns. Twelve-gauge shotguns have multiprojectile capability; they can fire different types of armaments, including solid lead slugs, pellets of varying sizes, or specialty rounds with wood, rubber, or plastic components. Their principal use is for crowd control (with wood, rubber, or birdshot, not the larger "buckshot" rounds). Shotguns have an immense intimidation impact, and often the sight alone of these weapons (without even firing them) can bring disruptive inmates under control.

Handguns. Handguns in .38 caliber formerly dominated the correctional scene. But agencies increasingly are moving to high-capacity, semiautomatic 9 mm pistols that give staff as many as eighteen rounds of defensive or responsive firepower. Tower weapons should be equipped with a lanyard loop, to prevent them from being dropped to the ground.

Gas Projectiles. Typically, single-shot 37 mm weaponry is used to project gas shells, although some multiround 37 mm weapons are available. Projectiles range from blast dispersion rounds that are short-range in nature to long-range rounds that are intended to reach distant or barricaded areas.

High-volume Gas Dispensers. These devices, which can be large aerosol containers or gasoline-powered units that use the exhaust stream to propel the chemical agent, can be very effective in dispersing extremely large volumes of gas in housing units, gyms, or other large enclosed spaces. They may be somewhat less effective in open spaces, but still may have some utility there, as well.

Other Specialty Ordnance. "Stingballs," "flash-bangs," "beanbag" rounds, and other special munitions are of importance in retaking housing units, but their use also has proven successful in more open areas, as well. Each institution should have a preselected array of these rounds in its armory to support tactical operations. Stingball munitions are like small grenades that, when exploded, expel a large number of hard rubber balls that sting and confuse inmates, but do not ordinarily penetrate or do serious or permanent injury to those in the area. Likewise, beanbags are munitions that consist of a dense dust or small pellet-like material, contained in a durable but flexible container (a bag, if you will), such that when it hits inmates it knocks them down, but ordinarily does not penetrate the body.

Specialty Control Devices. In this category are Tasers, other handheld electric stun devices, and electric custody control belts. These units are capable of stunning or shocking an inmate who, otherwise, is uncontrollable. Special training and supervision requirements should attach to the issue and use of these devices.

Standardization of armory equipment is encouraged in all institutions. This especially is advisable for reasons of training, scale of purchasing, and exchanging of equipment between institutions. The following chart is a basic list of standard-purchase items.

Patrol vehicles, as opposed to escort or inmate transportation vehicles, are intended to serve as a mobile response post in the event of escape or intrusion. This latter point is not insignificant; the possibility of inmates having outside assistance in an escape attempt is a reality, including the use by outsiders of gunfire to suppress towers and perimeter patrol staff as inmates try to breach the perimeter. Patrol vehicles should be equipped with items from the chart below.

Personal Equipment

Individual employees may be issued the following items:

Personal Body Alarms and Receivers. For years, institutions depended on personal contact and watch calls (scheduled phone calls to the control center by staff in remote areas) to ensure the personal safety of

Standard-purchase Armory Equipment

- Chemical agents appropriate for indoor and outdoor use, including CS, CN, and OC in various dispensers (grenades, projectiles, aerosols)

- Other ordnance, including smoke grenades, stun rounds, stingballs, flash-rounds, and parachute flares

- Appropriate ammunition for all weapons

- Gas masks with and without speakers

- Replacement gas mask canisters

- Protective helmets and face guards

- Disturbance control batons

- Electronic stun equipment and handheld restraint devices

- Beanbag and other close-range rounds

- Jumpsuits, coverall type

- Protective shields

- Bulletproof, or attack-resistant, vests

- Portable cutting torch, backpack type (for use in cutting locks and bars in an emergency)

- Handcuff covers, plastic ("black boxes")

- Handcuffs, standard, nickel-plated steel, 10 ounce

- Handcuffs, hinged, nickel-plated steel

- Leg irons: standard, nickel-plated steel with approximately fourteen and a half inch chain

- Waist chains: chains, case-hardened steel

- Handheld metal detectors

- Plastic cuffs (for temporary use only) When tactical staff or other employees use temporary plastic restraints to control large groups of inmates, it is important that those restraints be applied properly. Many systems have found the double-loop type plastic cuff to be particularly effective. However, because they are less secure than typical handcuffs, and can be abraded or cut, they should be replaced as soon as possible with regular handcuffs.

Tower Equipment

Towers should be equipped with the following items:

- Weapons as determined by the agency, but typically a 12-gauge shotgun; .223 clip-fed, autoloading rifle; 9 mm autoloading pistol; 37 mm gas gun; and, appropriate munitions to support those weapons

- Appropriate gun rack/ammunition storage area

- Binoculars

- High-powered flashlight and spotlight capabilities

- Intercom linked to other towers and the control center

- Body armor and Kevlar helmet for officers to wear

- Toilet and sink

- Storage area for officer's personal items outer garments, lunch, and so forth

- Megaphone or other loudspeaker capability for hailing inmates on the yard, or civilians trespassing or approaching the vicinity of the tower

- Annunciator panel for fence alarm system (optional); this electronic device receives signals from an alarm system and visibly displays where those alarms have been triggered

- Radio with multifrequency capability, and charger (optional)

staff. While these still are sound practices, personal body alarms provide a much higher level of assurance that staff can alert supervisory personnel in the event of an emergency. Devices on the market range in sophistication from a simple tone-alert model, or one that emits a loud sound to alert nearby staff, to those with a limited voice capability to the control center. Whatever model is chosen, these devices give a greater opportunity to respond effectively and quickly to crises. Not only is staff safety greatly improved, but quick intervention facilitated by body alarms can prevent a small disturbance or assault from building to unmanageable proportions before responding staff can arrive. Some of these alarms are activated positively, using a shielded button; others may be of the "man-down" type, where a certain period of time in a nonvertical position may trigger the alarm.

Pagers, Tone and/or Voice. Pagers are relatively inexpensive and reliable tools for contacting key

Patrol Vehicle Equipment

- Weapons as determined by the agency, but typically a 12-gauge shotgun; .223 clip-fed, autoloading rifle (perhaps a carbine model); 9 mm autoloading pistol in appropriate holster comfortable for wearing while driving or sitting for long periods; and, appropriate munitions to support those weapons

- Appropriate automatic locking gun rack and a secure ammunition storage area

- Binoculars

- High-powered flashlight or spotlight

- Megaphone or other loudspeaker capability

- Radio with multifrequency capability

- Radio-controlled, annunciator panel for fence alarm system

- Body armor and Kevlar helmet for officer

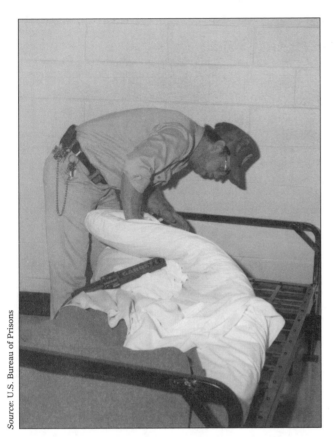

Source: U.S. Bureau of Prisons

Cell searches should include the use of a handheld metal detector.

personnel, such as administrators, department heads, members of tactical groups, and medical personnel. Their usefulness is unquestioned, and is challenged only by the increasingly low cost of cellular phones. However, nonofficial pagers and cell phones (including those belonging to inmate visitors, repair personnel, and other visitors) should not be allowed in the institution, so that they do not fall into the hands of inmates, who could use them for illicit purposes.

Handheld Metal Detectors. Handheld trans-friskers or portable metal detection devices will improve the capability for individualized searches throughout the institution. This emphasis should be particularly strong in the special housing unit; all inmates moving in this unit should be scanned whenever they are out of their cells. The rear gate and front entrance should be equipped similarly.

Key-related Items. Every staff member carrying keys should be required to use a method of reliably affixing the keys to their person when they are not in use. This may involve a belt keeper, chain, or retractable cable. Key pouches often are used to conceal key profiles and prevent keys from catching on things as the officer moves. Key shields should be considered for all large security keys, preventing inmates from observing key profiles and cuts.

Infectious Disease Prevention Equipment. Staff should have the option of carrying latex gloves on their person, in the event they must come in contact with bodily fluids, such as when handling urine samples or performing searches of various types. Safety shields for performing CPR also are a common preventive device for officers today. Belt-mounted pouches often are used to carry these items.

Flashlights. Some systems issue staff flashlights, while others require officers to procure their own. Ordinarily, agency-owned lights are issued on a durable receipt system from the control center, as other equipment items. This system relies on small metal or plastic tags with an employee name or number on them. A tag is given to the issuing person when keys or tools are issued to the owner of the tag. This durable receipt, or "chit," is placed on a hook or other location from which the keys or tools are removed when they are issued.

Perimeter Security

8

Fences, buildings, and walls form the perimeter of correctional institutions, and are the last major line of defense against escape and intrusion.

The Perimeter Barrier

Walls and towers form the perimeter of many older correctional facilities providing solid security with relatively little maintenance. But the cost of free-standing masonry or concrete walls has essentially precluded their use in new construction for many years. While certainly not a part of most original designs, alarm systems can be installed in conjunction with walls, ranging from simple taut-wire setups on the top or inner surface of the wall, to microwave fields and vibration-sensitive geophone-based systems near the inner base. Alarms of all varieties are typical at fenced institutions, however.

Buildings form the perimeter in some of the oldest and newest correctional institutions in use today. Many older penitentiaries used the cellhouse walls as part of a larger walled perimeter. Newer urban detention centers and a few other high-security designs employ the same strategy, but without a separate wall around other portions of the property. In some cases, these installations do employ supplementary fencing or alarm systems; others rely solely on towers or perimeter patrols to ensure no inmates leave the property. But for the most part, institutions of this type rely primarily on the building envelope for security.

Today, though, fences are the most common type of perimeter security used in correctional construction. As is the case with technology in doors, there are many types of fences and alarm systems, and this publication does not cover all of the options available to an agency. However, a number of basic principles should be considered when designing or redesigning a fenced perimeter.

- The institution's terrain should be as level and clear as possible, so as to allow clear lines of sight and weapon fire; a significant cleared boundary should exist around the perimeter, free from trees, high weeds, or gullies. Where towers are in use, fences should be aligned with the towers, in consideration of the terrain. (Rolling terrain or other geographic features may have an impact on the placement of towers.)

- Heavy-gauge galvanized fencing remains the type of hardware used in most installations. However, several new designs and combinations of chain-link, fine-mesh, and overhead curvature also appear to have promise.

- Typically, two twelve-foot fences with rolled razor wire, and with a minimum twenty to thirty foot separation, comprise a medium-high security application, with the amount and configuration of wire varying according to the security level involved. The separation prevents potential escapees from easily jumping to the second fence if they have reached the top of the first one, or from easily straddling the fences with devices such as ladders. It also provides adequate space to place rolls of security wire between the fences while leaving a pathway to apprehend potential escapees trapped between the fences. Rolled stainless steel razor wire is a typical element in most perimeter fence configurations today, on both the inner and outer fences. The outer fence should have more such wire at the bottom of the fence than at the top, to prevent potential escapees from easily reaching the top.

- The ground between the fences should be sterilized, spread with an impermeable plastic, and then covered with gravel or crushed rock; weeds and vegetation that grow between the fences should be suppressed. A clearly marked no-access zone should be maintained inside and outside the fence; this will prevent inmates from approaching too close to the inner fence, and will stop pedestrians and vehicles from nearing the perimeter to assist in an escape attempt or an attempt to introduce contraband.

- In the last few years, some correctional systems have adopted electrified fences as an inner escape barrier. Strictly speaking, these fences are not for intrusion or escape detection, but rather for pure deterrence. In facilities where such fences are installed, due regard should be given to providing inmates with several forms of notice about the lethal

nature of the fence. Any such fence system should include the installation of a low, non-lethal warning fence with appropriate warning signs posted in all major languages used by the inmate population. Of course, institutions should provide appropriate signage in all necessary languages in other areas, as well.

- Secure entry gates should be constructed in the fence near towers or at regular intervals, so that staff can enter for routine maintenance, to kill vegetation, or remove inmates who have attempted to escape and have become entangled in the wire. The fence should be anchored into a poured-concrete curbing. This curb can prevent easy penetration of the perimeter, and somewhat deter escape attempts. Also, without being stabilized at the base and properly tightened, many vibration-based electronic detection systems may not function optimally. The curbing serves to dampen the vibration in the fence material.

- Perimeter detection systems should be installed to enhance security on the inner fence, assisting staff in detecting tampering

Source: Capitol Communication Systems, Inc.

The appropriate use of rolled razor wire can significantly strengthen a perimeter.

with the fence, or outright attempts to escape over it. This is especially true during inclement weather which reduces tower or patrol officer visibility. Because conditions vary from site to site, no single system is best for all situations.

During the 1970s, numerous problems occurred with these systems, largely because of the eagerness of both clients and vendors, many of whom were on the "bleeding edge" of what was then a relatively new technology that had not then been broadly tested in the field. In addition, a frequent problem then was the lack of in-house specialists to maintain the systems on a daily basis or at least on very short notice.

The importance of this point should not be overlooked; it may be better to forego a state-of-the-art detection system unless there is a resource commitment to adequate upkeep and timely response to system malfunctions. Proper technology selection depends on multiple factors, including topography, vegetation, wildlife, weather, soil conditions, background noise, and staff response time.

- Blind spots (such as in rear gate areas) may be monitored by closed circuit camera, with monitors located in the control center, or perhaps in a tower. Finally, strategically placed mirrors can be installed at selected locations in the vicinity of towers and external armory entrances, to compensate for blind spots. With some tower designs, for instance, it is possible to visualize an inmate or unauthorized civilian moving to the base of the tower undetected, and from there attempting to escape or take over the tower. Mirrors are a cost-effective means of safeguarding these key areas. Razor wire also may be installed around the towers to prevent a takeover of any type.

Tower and Mobile Perimeter Patrols

Twenty-four-hour surveillance of the outside perimeter fence generally is provided through either towers or mobile vehicular patrols patrolling the fencelines.

Towers

Towers provide a good view of the perimeter but are very expensive to construct, and even more costly to operate. Each twenty-four-hour tower post requires the assignment of five or more officers, when vacations, sick leave, and relief time are considered. This cost calculation alone has caused many agencies to adopt perimeter patrols for institutions without walls. Towers must be constructed securely and designed for maximum visibility in all directions, and windows must be designed to open quickly to accommodate the firing of weapons.

Generally, towers are located outside truncated fence corners to provide clear sight lines between the fences in both directions. Additional towers may be needed at intermediate points on the fence line because of the facility's configuration or to maintain a maximum distance of 600 feet between towers. Any greater distance between towers renders them questionable for accurate gunfire and serviceable only for observation. While modern high-powered rifles produce a relatively flat trajectory, tower officers also should be provided with sighting charts that indicate the measured distance to various points within sight of the tower, so that they can gauge more accurately elevation for any long-distance firing.

To ensure good sight lines, tower floors should be a minimum of thirty feet above the ground level at the adjacent fence line. If a typical (nonhigh-mast) perimeter lighting system is used, the design should provide that the eye level of tower officers is above the level of the lights.

In some high-security institutions where it is believed there may be a threat of weapons fire from civilian accomplices of inmates, ballistics-resistant glazing has been installed in tower windows. Storage space for weapons and ammunition must be included in the tower. Other equipment-related issues are discussed in an earlier general chapter on security equipment. Searchlights should be available in towers; usually, they are mounted on the tower's cab.

If meals are not brought to the officer, a small refrigerator usually is provided for food storage. Toilet facilities must be included and designed so that a tower officer using the facilities still can see outside and along the fence lines.

Perimeter Patrols

The primary alternative perimeter surveillance system, now in growing use, is the mobile patrol. Typically, two mobile patrol vehicles (often pickup trucks), each staffed by one officer, patrol the perimeter during active program hours. Some systems use only one patrol vehicle when inmates are locked in their housing units and the probability of escape attempts is reduced substantially. At night, the patrol vehicles

Source: Capitol Communication Systems, Inc.

Mobile perimeter patrols are an effective way to reduce costly reliance on towers in all but the most secure operations.

should operate with their lights off, so that the drivers' night vision is not compromised.

Each mobile patrol vehicle should be equipped with a two-way radio, to allow patrol officers to stay in constant contact with the control center, other mobile vehicles, and any foot patrols. The vehicle should be equipped with an annunciator panel, and the perimeter detection zone should be divided into zones that are indicated on the panel. If a detection zone is violated, electronic sensors simultaneously should alert the patrol and control center officer by an audible tone and a visual signal. The visual alarm, displayed on the car and control center monitors, indicates in which zone activity is occurring. The mobile patrol officer then can respond to the alarm, investigate the activated zone, and take appropriate action. Other perimeter patrol equipment is covered in an earlier general chapter on security equipment.

Perimeter Lighting

Effective perimeter security also requires a good exterior lighting system. The traditional method is to place lights at 100-foot intervals along the entire perimeter, with additional lights placed at building locations both inside and outside the fence and at other locations around the compound. In recent years, "high-mast" lighting systems have become popular. Each fixture in these systems illuminates a very large area and provides suitable visibility at ground level. By using only a few high-mast light poles–usually five to eight, each 100 to 120 feet tall–the entire compound and perimeter can be illuminated adequately with considerable savings in both capital and operating costs.

An economical method of providing satisfactory light quality is to combine equal numbers of sodium vapor and metal-halide lamps in each high-mast light fixture. The lamps on each high-mast pole can be wired in two groups, individually operated from the control room. Under this system, operating costs can be reduced by using only one set of light elements (at a lower light and power level) while inmates are locked in their housing units. The system can be designed to activate the second set of elements if an alarm of any pre-identified category is triggered, increasing light levels, as needed.

Helicopter Deterrence

Just as inmates look to entrances when other portions of the perimeter are made more secure, alert security also must anticipate that escape (by way of outside assistance) may come from above. Since most institution yards are not large enough for a fixed-wing aircraft to land, the most viable option for this type of escape is a helicopter, or possibly a gyrocopter. Agency policies vary greatly on this topic. Some prohibit firing on the helicopter, in the belief that hitting a rotor or fuel tank could cause a disastrous crash inside the institution, injuring or killing staff and inmates alike. Others permit firing on the craft if it is clear of buildings.

Most agencies do take the position that in the interest of protecting innocent parties (except in the case of self-defense) lethal force must not be directed at the aircraft. Typically, lethal force may be directed at inmates who are attempting to gain access to the aircraft, however. Whatever the policy, the institution's escape plan should address this issue. At a minimum, the plan should direct staff who see an aircraft entering the institutional airspace to make all possible efforts to wave or signal the aircraft off, perhaps using lights.

It is appropriate for prison architects to consider the manner in which buildings are clustered, and the arrangement of lighting masts and other "ground clutter," that can interfere with helicopter escapes. Additionally, wire may be strung across open yard spaces to prevent or discourage helicopter landings. Institutions should consult both engineers and pilots in the process of developing their aircraft deterrence system. Design staff should consider the possibility of an aircraft-assisted escape in laying out the compounds of new institutions. Provision for ground clutter, availability of supports for deterrence wires, and appropriate lines of sight by the perimeter patrol posts should be factors in any new project, or major renovation work, as well.

Accountability

9

Inmate accountability, the staff's ability to locate and identify inmates at any point in time, is the very heart of institution security, from minimum-security camps to maximum-security penitentiaries. In the public's eye, the primary function of a correctional facility is to confine inmates, to keep them off the streets, and out of society until they are ready to return. As a result, every correctional system needs a clear and practical set of procedures to ensure accurate accountability for the entire inmate population.

Accountability procedures fall into two general categories:

(1) Counts and other regularly scheduled procedures for physically tracking the number of inmates in custody, including all routine and emergency counts, and

(2) Supporting procedures that provide interim accountability throughout the institution, such as pass systems, gate passes, and ID cards

Counts

Timing

While ACA standards require a minimum of one count per shift, and agency policies vary, a commonly used and highly recommended system relies on a total of five counts each day, with the following sequencing:

(1) Midnight, or as close to midnight, as possible. This count should be the official institution count for the day.

(2) Middle of the morning watch. A count in the middle of this shift reduces the possibility of an escape remaining undetected during the long morning period when there is a relatively low level of supervision.

(3) Before opening the institution for the day. This early count, usually held between 5:30 and 6:00 AM, ensures that all inmates are accounted for before heavy activity periods commence.

(4) End of workday. This count, taken late in the afternoon, ensures that all inmates are present and that no inmates are hiding and waiting for nightfall to breach the perimeter.

(5) Lockup count. Taken when all inmates are secured for the night, the lockup count ensures that the entire population is accounted for before the morning watch, when staff levels again will be low.

Specific times to conduct counts should be established by each institution, with security as a top priority. In most cases, count times should not interfere with regularly scheduled programs or meals. At the end of the day, a standup count should be required. In standup counts, inmates are required to stand at the doors of their cells or at the ends of their beds to demonstrate that they are physically present and are not deceiving observers through the use of dummies or other simulations.

Count Records

Staff should control the count at every stage, from making up and maintaining the master count sheet to accurately taking and recording the count.

The master count record should be maintained by the control center officer, and throughout the day the control center should be advised of moves of any kind, including housing changes, work assignment changes, hospital admissions, and all other movement. In addition to tracking internal housing unit transfers, officers on perimeter gate posts must keep track of all inmate movement through the perimeter. This system allows the officer who ultimately takes the count to know in advance how many inmates should be counted in each area, and not to rely on count numbers as they come in to shape the count process.

The master count sheet should be subdivided by unit, range, and floor, and also should provide space to list any departments with outcounts (inmates away from the unit). A base reference number for the correct count in each unit is arrived at by subtracting the number of outcounts and empty beds from actual unit capacity figures. Unit capacity is the number of habitable spaces. At the time of the count, these baseline figures should agree with the total head count of each unit.

Outcounts should be listed in a separate column of the master count sheet. They should not be aggregated with the counts of the units from which the inmates originated. Unit count totals, when added to outcounts, should equal the total count of the institution.

No count can be considered cleared until all signed count slips are in and verified against the master count sheet. The control center officer should retain all count slips, outcount slips, and official count sheets for at least thirty days. A sample official count form is included in Appendix D.

Any errors in the official count records should be crossed out in red, with the correct number entered above. Any errors, corrections, or other unusual circumstances should be documented in a specified addition to the count sheet.

The officer receiving the count should advise staff when the official count is in agreement with the master count; many systems require two recounts after a miscount, to be certain that the final count is correct. After a correct count is formally called in, it should be followed by a count slip, with no alterations or corrections, signed in ink by the staff member(s) conducting the count.

If a unit's physical headcount does not agree with the recorded number on the master count sheet, the officer receiving the count should order a recount without informing the staff member performing the count of the expected number. Agency policy should state whether a picture count is needed and how many recounts are necessary after an incorrect number is reported.

No inmates should be involved in maintaining count records or otherwise involved in any part of the count process; doing so would place them in a position to modify or otherwise affect count records and perhaps facilitate or conceal an escape.

Outcounts

An outcount is an enumeration of inmates who are outside their assigned housing at the time of a formal count. Supervisory staff should minimize outcounts, limiting the number of inmates outside housing units to those who are truly necessary to institutional operations at the time of the count.

Outcounts should be submitted for supervisory approval, on a specific outcount form, no less than one hour before the time of the count. This lead time is necessary to ensure accurate compilation of the master count and to avoid last minute changes that create bookkeeping problems and delay clearing the count.

The shift supervisor should be provided the name, register number, and unit of each inmate who will be outcounted. Once the outcount information is approved by the shift supervisor, the form should be taken to the control center, and its figures should be included in the master count sheet being compiled. Inmates being outcounted should not be permitted to return to their assigned unit or leave the outcount area until the official count has been cleared. Outcount slips are not acceptable as count slips. Staff counting inmates in approved outcount areas should still turn in a proper, signed count slip.

Count Procedures

Counts should be announced on the institution's public address system, other available audible devices, and the institution's radio system. The shift supervisor should personally take at least one count on each shift.

No inmate movement should be permitted during counts. During a count, all televisions and other equipment should be turned off, and all activity should cease. Nothing should distract staff during a count except major emergencies such as escape attempts, fires, or life-threatening medical crises.

In single cell units, staff should lock all inmates in their rooms for the official counts. In units where inmates cannot be locked in rooms for the count, at least one covering officer should be assigned to aid the regularly assigned staff member. Both officers should count the inmates and compare their findings, and both should sign the count slip.

The unit count should be called in by phone and the unit count slip prepared in ink. The counting staff should remain in the area until the institution count is officially cleared.

Staff must be sure that they are counting living, breathing flesh, as dummies have been used successfully in many escapes. Flashlights should be used at night to ascertain that each inmate is still in place, but consideration should be taken to not unnecessarily wake the inmate. Institutional disciplinary procedures should clearly specify the consequences for inmate actions that disrupt or delay a count.

Emergency Counts

Emergency counts are official counts taken at unscheduled times, after unforeseen events, such as disturbances, when inmates are believed to be missing, after lengthy power failures, or following or during periods of heavy fog or other inclement weather that might facilitate an escape. Indeed, in locations where typical weather conditions make this an important issue, staff should identify restrictions on inmate movement, posts which should be staffed, and internal and external security changes necessary to ensure inmates do not escape during periods of inclement weather, including fog.

The shift supervisor should be authorized to call for a count at any time for these reasons, or when in his or her professional judgment there is cause to do so. Control center records should be organized so that an emergency count can be completed quickly and accurately. Recall should be sounded and inmates should be required to return to their housing areas. The master count sheet should be prepared immediately, with verbal or telephone outcounts approved by the designated supervisor. Emergency counts taken at night should disrupt inmates as little as possible; lights should not be turned on unless a picture count is necessary.

Picture Counts

A picture count involves direct comparison of every inmate with his or her photograph, to determine which inmates are not in their assigned locations. A picture count should be taken whenever an inmate is believed missing or when repeated recounts create a problem in verifying the count. The number of recounts (on a regular or emergency count) necessary to trigger the picture count should be established by agency policy.

For a picture count, inmates should be required to stand at the doors of their cells or, in dormitory-type quarters, at the ends of their beds. Each inmate's picture should be carefully compared with the occupant of the cell or bed to ascertain that every inmate is present in his or her assigned living space.

A prerequisite for picture counts is an accurate, up-to-date picture card system. All housing units should maintain a picture card for each assigned inmate. The minimum information on the card should be the inmate's name, register number, job, cell or bed assignment, and photograph. In addition, sentencing data or other details that aid in the management of the unit may be added.

Supporting Systems

In addition to counts, there are a number of other procedures that institutions should use to further enhance inmate accountability.

Census Checks

A census check is an informal area count that verifies that inmates are in the proper location during the periods between formal counts. It should be conducted both in housing units and on the site of all work details. At a minimum, census checks should be conducted at the beginning and end of each work period, but they can be done at any time of the day. For instance, in the evening, when large, predetermined numbers of inmates leave the unit for programs and the unit otherwise is locked, staff in both the unit and

Source: Maryland Department of Corrections

Counting inmates is one of the central activities of prison life.

the program area should conduct census checks, if possible. Layins, idles, sick-call cases, and all other inmates without assignments should be accounted for in their housing units. Inmates in the unit who do not belong there should be ordered to go to their job or program assignment. Census checks on the job should involve an informal count of all inmates present and a reconciliation of that number with the number of inmates assigned. Census checks are particularly important in crowded institutions, where many inmates may congregate in areas such as housing units. Copies of forms that can be used for this purpose are included in Appendix D.

Ordinarily, a report of an informal census check should be made only if an inmate is missing, although in housing units the officer should note the census in the unit log. Censuses can be conducted during nighttime hours as well, taking on the features of a count, since all inmates should be in their housing units except for the few who may be on night job assignments such as the powerhouse.

Every facility should conduct a general census once a month, on a random basis, for the entire institution. This procedure involves stopping inmate movement and counting the inmates where they are located at that time. Each unit and department should have a running accountability record for all inmates in that location at all times, so the actual number of inmates counted should agree with the predetermined figure. All of the separate census count totals called in to the control center should be combined into a total facility count. Even in facilities where running totals are not kept, taking this census periodically but without notice keeps staff and inmates more aware of the institution's accountability requirements. The census can help staff learn if inmates are hiding during the day, perfecting escape routes, engaging in sexual activity, or fabricating contraband. Supervisors and administrative staff can learn which departments or staff are deficient in their procedures and weak in accountability.

No matter what census system is used, staff should be impressed with the importance of immediately reporting inmates who are missing or out of bounds. These are often signals of improper activity, and they should be investigated at once.

Pass Systems

Whether an institution's inmate movement program is based on controlled movement, individual movement, mass movement, or a combination of methods, pass systems can improve accountability between counts. Passes can be required at specified times, for movement between specific parts of the institution, or for selected categories of inmates.

Under a pass system, staff are issued pass books, from which they issue signed, individual movement passes to inmates. Movement on a pass should be preceded by a phone call, although in some situations, phone calls for routine movements (such as callouts) may not be practical. Phone calls should be used for nonroutine passes, however.

All passes should include:

- The inmate's name
- Register number
- Department originating the pass
- Name and signature of staff member originating the pass
- Time and date of issue
- Destination
- Time of arrival
- Signature of receiving employee

The pass system should include provisions for regulating the number of inmates in any one area at a time. This can be done in conjunction with controlled movement and callout systems. The effect of such a policy is to reduce the buildup of large numbers of inmates, which inadvertently can happen in areas such as medical and casework. Passes should be issued only by staff and pass books must be controlled strictly. They should be issued from and returned to a central location, usually the control center.

Local policy should indicate which employee should take follow-up actions if the inmate does not arrive on time and should clearly state the travel time considered excessive. The inmate should surrender each pass upon return to the originating area. Staff members receiving inmates moving on passes should examine all passes used, determining if the travel time taken was excessive and investigating all significant delays. Institutional policy should establish that inmates moving without passes during periods of controlled movement are subject to disciplinary action.

At the end of each day, passes must be reconciled against all stubs to ascertain if any inmates are missing and to ensure that no passes have been lost or stolen. Passes also may be reconciled against the unit log, if the local accountability system permits a second check of this type.

Picture Card Systems

Staff must not rely on personal knowledge to pass inmates through the perimeter. Indeed, accountability systems for traffic points, such as perimeter gates (and, in some cases, critical internal access points) should include a picture card system that positively identifies every inmate entering or leaving the facility. This picture card or gate pass must be approved by the chief of security or deputy warden, and should bear the inmate's name, register number, custody classification, job, and a current photograph. Passes should be laminated or embossed with a seal over the authorizing signature, to prevent forgery. Some systems have adopted computer-coded pass systems that automatically track inmates in and out. However, the use of these systems does not eliminate the need for personal identification of all inmates moving through gate areas.

To maintain these passes in an orderly manner, a gate pass board should be used. The typical board has two sections, one (organized either alphabetically or by work detail) for inmates who are in the facility, and the other one for inmates who are outside. When an inmate passes through the gate, the gate pass should be moved to the corresponding section, providing a ready check on the status of all inmates with approved passes.

Inmates who are moving through gates or other control points without gate passes, such as those who are being released or are going out to court, should be subject to a different identification process. The gate staff should be provided in advance with a release list with pictures of all prospective releases. Exceptions to this requirement may be made in emergencies.

When a staff member escorts a nongate pass inmate to the gate for release, several steps should be taken.

- First, the gate officer should confirm the release by phone with the control center or the receiving and discharge staff. Second, the releasing officer should carefully compare the inmate with the photograph provided to ensure that the proper individual is being released.

- In emergencies, special procedures should dictate the steps to properly identify an inmate being removed from the institution. This may include having someone from the records office, or a supervisor, come to the gate personally to deliver a photo and take a fingerprint of one finger for official records.

Running counts should be maintained at gates where inmates enter and leave the facility on a regular basis. This system can be kept in conjunction with the use of the gate passes.

Crew Kit Cards

In addition to gate passes for inmates who are approved to move through the perimeter for outside work details, every work crew should have a separate crew kit packet. It should consist of an easily carried leather or vinyl pouch containing an identifying card on each assigned inmate. Like gate cards, crew kit cards should be laminated or embossed, and include the picture, custody classification, sentence data, and other important information about each inmate on the crew. This system can enable supervising employees to have a better method of identifying their inmates, as well as an improved means of telling them what kind of inmates they have on their crews, since it is important that official information about their inmate workers is conveyed to the detail supervisors.

The crew kit folders or packets should be stored in the control center when not in use. The kits should be updated during morning watch to ensure that they accurately reflect all inmates in every job category. When an inmate is added to or removed from the crew, the appropriate card should be removed from the packet, in order that accountability checks easily can reconcile the inmates on hand with the cards in the packet.

As a related issue, many systems operate on the principle that it is best to assign to outside details only those inmates who do not require armed escort. This can be accomplished by careful classification screening. In any case, armed staff never should be in direct contact with inmates on outside work details. Doing so would make them highly vulnerable to being overpowered by the members of the work party.

In another individual inmate identification process, inmates are issued photo ID cards, which they must carry on their person. One method of use includes requiring inmates to surrender their card to the housing unit officer when entering the unit and to pick it up when leaving. In this way, it functions like a gate pass for the purpose of unit accountability, and can be required to be produced at other points in the institution, as well.

Callouts

Every facility should have a callout or master pass system to record and authorize certain inmate movement for prearranged activities, such as school, medical or dental appointments, interviews, or other necessary programs. Callouts are compiled from inmate names submitted by staff who have set up appointments at specific times with those inmates. The lists should be distributed to the various areas of the institution each morning. Staff members supervising inmates throughout the day still are responsible for issuing passes to the inmates on the callout sheet.

In facilities where standing passes are issued for regular programs (such as school), a standing pass list should be issued. This provides staff with an easy means of verifying the authorization of all inmate movement on passes.

Controlled Movement Systems

In addition to other accountability systems, many institutions use some form of controlled movement as an alternative to total individual movement or unregulated mass movement systems. This involves permitting inmates to move during the day only at certain specified intervals, with doors and grilles locked at other times.

For instance, under such a system, the institution is secured (with all inmates at work, in programs, or in the housing units) until the top of the hour. When a controlled movement announcement is made, for the next ten minutes, inmates can move from area to area. Then an announcement is made that the movement period is over, and all doors and grilles are locked again. Ordinarily, controlled movement programs are somewhat more relaxed on evenings and weekends, although that need not be the case.

Lockdown

A lockdown is the most extreme form of inmate accountability and control. During lockdowns, inmates are fed in their cells or in the central dining area on a very limited basis. Under the most strict conditions, all inmates moving out of their cells are escorted or placed in restraints.

Lockdowns ordinarily are triggered by an unusual incident or emergency in the institution or a staffing crisis. Historically, they have been used in the aftermath of killings, disturbances, strikes, or other major disturbances, to preempt future problems while the staff regains control. As inmate tensions or other emergency conditions abate, the level of control gradually is reduced.

Long-term lockdowns are recognized by most correctional administrators as being undesirable. Most institutions are neither staffed nor designed to operate for more than a short period of time without allowing inmates typical access to the dining area, showers, and recreation. If long-term confinement of this type is required, then special management procedures (costly and controversial in some quarters) are the inevitable route that should be pursued, in all likelihood for only those inmates considered the most dangerous or disruptive.

Armory Operations

10

Correctional institutions require an armory to provide for the secure storage of firearms, ammunition, and other security equipment. This area must be inaccessible to inmates and other intruders, but not so remote from the main staff traffic patterns that equipment issue is inconvenient or excessively time-consuming.

Design and Access

The entrance to the armory must be outside the institution's secure perimeter, but it may be in any "outside" structure. It usually is best to situate the armory as part of, or near, the front entrance, since this location is accessible easily to staff in emergencies. Because they have similar security requirements, the armory and locksmith shop sometimes are located in the same area. The armory should be equipped with a telephone, emergency lighting, a radio, and perhaps an intercom to the control center, and the area outside the entry.

The materials used to construct the armory must provide maximum security and safety; it must be absolutely impregnable. Ideally, the armory entrance should be under constant supervision by either a correctional post or a camera. In addition, the entrance to the armory should be protected by a security vestibule.

The room should be equipped with a reinforced pass-through in the solid metal door, or a Dutch or split door with screening to prevent movement over the bottom half of the door into the armory. This arrangement provides a safe, secure method for issuing weapons and equipment. Two issue and storage points may be useful, to keep the lethal weapon-related functions apart from those involving the storage and issue of disturbance control equipment only.

The armory should be of sufficient size to provide adequate space for the storing, cleaning, and maintaining of weapons and related emergency response equipment. Adequate space and proper storage cabinets, shelving, and racks not only will make issue easier, but also will make it much easier to inventory all items. With the proper layout and organization of contents, a complete inventory of even the largest armory should take no longer than one hour. Some procedural steps can save time, as well; for example, full ammunition boxes can be counted intact, and only loose rounds counted individually. A workbench area for cleaning and maintaining weapons is essential.

Ammunition should be stored in metal cabinets or cases. The entire area should be climate-controlled to minimize deterioration of supplies by variations in temperature or humidity.

If the armory and lockshop are in the same location, additional square footage is required to conveniently accommodate both functions. However, to avoid contaminating weapons with metal filings, key-cutting should be sufficiently separated from the weapons' storage area. While armories as small as 150 square feet may be functional, it is possible that as much as 400-500 square feet could be needed for storage of significant quantities of disturbance control equipment, weapons, and expendables, particularly in a large or extremely high-security institution.

Traffic into the armory should be limited strictly to those with an official need to be there; only the armory officer (and locksmith if this is a joint area) may enter alone. All staff entering the armory should sign an official log that provides a permanent record of everyone who is in the area, including the armory officer and locksmith.

The key to the armory should be highly restricted and a signed ledger must be established to record entry. Preventing unauthorized access can reduce the likelihood of theft, tampering, or other unauthorized activity in this critical area.

A backup armory key (as well as a control center key) should be maintained in a secure location, to provide prompt emergency access. Ordinarily, this location is a tower or a secure locker elsewhere outside the perimeter. These keys should be issued only in a bona fide emergency; every instance when this key is issued must be logged and a copy of the entry sent to the chief of security within twenty-four hours. These keys also must be rotated and checked regularly, to ensure their proper functioning.

The warden also may authorize the establishment of subarmories for small numbers of weapons held for quick access in an emergency. These areas must be outside the secure perimeter, and access should be tightly controlled, but streamlined.

Armory Procedures

During regular business hours, Monday through Friday, an armory officer should be responsible for the armory's operation. Outside of regular business hours, the shift supervisor should assume this responsibility. The armory officer should be specially trained in handling and maintaining weapons. Additional officers may be assigned to assist in the armory during emergencies.

Types of ordnance are discussed in more detail elsewhere in this publication, but in brief, specifications for this equipment (and ammunition) should be developed by the agency for each facility. All equipment stored in the armory must be approved by the chief of security and be in accord with agency standards approved by the central office security administrator.

An individualized approach is necessary because a facility with difficult terrain or a very limited buffer zone in an urban area would not need the same weapons as one in a rural area, where long-range shooting outside the perimeter would not jeopardize public safety. However, even in urban settings, a limited quantity of long-range weapons may be appropriate in the hands of trained staff for use inside the compound to protect lives. Thus, firearms selection and deployment decisions are best made by the agency.

However, firearms in use throughout the system should be standardized to the greatest extent possible. While every type of firearm may not be used in every institution, all pistols, shotguns, and rifles should be the same caliber and type. This uniformity simplifies training and facilitates cross-assignment of staff between institutions and during emergencies.

Gas equipment can be standardized more easily, in view of the range of items available on the market. The 37 mm projectile is a standard for shoulder-held weapons, and although specialized adapters are available for 12-gauge shotguns, their adapted use reduces the weapon's flexibility for its prime purpose.

Agency policy should specify the types of gas to be used: CS, CN, or OC (pepper) and the circumstances under which it is to be employed. Except in the most life-threatening emergency, CS gas should not be used indoors. Larger facilities should have a high-volume chemical agent dispenser, to generate extremely large quantities of gas without using pyrotechnics or projectiles.

All chemical agents should be stored in the armory, except for authorized amounts in the control center, towers, or a designated subarmory. Inventories and the continually issued 5 x 8 inch "bin cards" used to maintain the inventory should reflect the actual amounts on hand at all times. Receipts should be given for all chemical agents issued. Local policy should specify all out-of-armory storage and use conditions for any small aerosol gas dispensers employed for forced cell moves or other specialized purposes. In no case should aerosol dispensers be stored in housing units or carried on a regular basis by staff in contact with inmates.

Categories of chemical agents should be separated in storage, and clearly marked as to type to avoid incorrect issue and use in an emergency. Outdated gas being saved for training purposes should be stored separately from current supplies to prevent inadvertent issue. These items can become unreliable or even dangerous as they deteriorate with age. Chemical agents usually have a shelf life of no more than thirty-six months from date of receipt; the expiration date should be etched on the container at the time it is received. Other expendables, such as batteries in flashlights and voice-amplified gas masks, must be tested for serviceability and sufficient stocks of fresh spare batteries must be available.

Sufficient quantities of the items listed in Chapter 7 on equipment should be procured and stored for easy issue, to equip a major portion of the staff. Some agencies have adopted the position that basic protective and defensive equipment (helmet with face shield, jumpsuit, and baton) for 25 to 30 percent of the workforce should be readily available.

All weapons, ammunition, chemical agents, and defensive, detection, and communication equipment should be inspected and inventoried by the armory officer at least once each month. This inventory should include the amount on hand, the amount issued, purpose of issue, and to whom issued. Inventories on firearms should include serial numbers, brand names, and assigned location of the equipment.

All defensive equipment (such as gas masks, handcuffs, helmets, leg irons, disturbance control batons, and so forth) should be inventoried, as well. Although these items do not have serial numbers, their exact location and quantity must be known.

An official inventory must be conducted at least once each year. A report of these inspections and inventories, with any discrepancies noted, should be directed to the chief of security. The armory officer and shift supervisor should conduct quarterly inventories of all ammunition, chemical agents, firearms, and emergency equipment. All inventories should be typed and signed by the inventorying staff member; these inventories should be jointly signed by the armory officer and the supervisor conducting the inventory, and should be performed on a regular basis.

All weapons stored in the armory must be unloaded; a weapons unloading barrel or other similar device should be available at every location where weapons might be unloaded.

Many agencies take the position that personal weapons may not be stored in an institution armory. However, if the agency permits this practice (as presumably would be the case for staff who are required to live on institution property and who have no other safe place to store personal weapons), those weapons and any personal ammunition should be checked into the armory by the armory officer. They should be kept in a locked cabinet that is separate from all institution weapons and ammunition. A receipt should be issued for each, and a copy of that receipt should be provided to the owner. A copy of a form that could be used in such a situation is included in Appendix D, but additional record keeping may be required to comply with agency policy. Staff members should be required to sign for personal weapons when checked out, and safeguards should be in place to ensure that personal weapons are not inadvertently issued to staff in an emergency.

Agency firearms that are assigned to a specific staff member should be prominently tagged so that they are not issued to someone else. This situation would be most commonly encountered when sniper rifles are sighted for the exclusive use of a specific tactical team member.

The armory officer and at least one other experienced employee should be assigned to issue equipment during emergencies. A copy of a sample issue form is included in Appendix D.

Immediately following an emergency, the armory officer should conduct an inventory to ascertain that all equipment is accounted for and properly cleaned. Written records must be maintained for routine and emergency issue of all security equipment. All ammunition and weapons should be signed for on issue slips that list the serial number of the weapon, the number of rounds of ammunition, and any other equipment, such as a holster. Escape kits containing firearms, ammunition, and other equipment, should have pre-prepared issue slips attached.

Anytime a firearm is discharged, the shift supervisor should be notified immediately. A complete written report should be submitted to the chief of security. No staff member should be permitted to use a personal weapon or ammunition on duty. This includes no use of personal weapons in towers, escort activities, or escape hunts. Only official weapons and approved ammunition may be used.

Firearms should not be permitted inside the institution unless authorized by the warden. Law enforcement officers should be questioned about possession of firearms or ammunition prior to entering the institution, and they should be required to place any weapons or ammunition in a secure weapons depository located outside the institution.

Tower and patrol vehicle weapons and ammunition should be shown on the armory inventory as to location, date of issue, and specifics on the actual items at that remote location. On-site inventories of tower and patrol equipment should be conducted at each shift change, with a copy of that inventory submitted to the shift supervisor.

The institution must have an inspection system that ensures all firearms and defensive equipment are serviced, cleaned, and are functioning properly. All weapons should be inspected at least semiannually. Normally, these functions are delegated to the armory officer, with periodic inspections conducted by the chief of security or the shift supervisor.

Unserviceable weapons either must be repaired or replaced. In the former case, only qualified service personnel should make repairs. In the latter instance, the weapon must be decommissioned according to agency policy. Serviceable parts may be stripped to repair other weapons. Then, the serial number must be destroyed and the item rendered completely unusable by cutting it apart with a torch or saw. In all such instances, the inventory should be amended to reflect shipment to a repair shop or decommissioning. Serviceable weapons that are no longer necessary for the institution's use must be disposed of in accordance with agency regulations.

Control Center

11

The control center is the "nerve center" for the entire facility and is staffed twenty-four hours a day. In most institutions, the control center officer observes and controls the institution's entrance and exit traffic, records all inmate movement and tracks the count, monitors fire and security alarm systems, operates communication systems, issues keys, maintains key inventories, and operates telephone equipment. Each of these activities has a critical impact on the institution's orderly and secure operation.

Construction and Design

The control center is often a part of the administration building and preferably is located a suitable distance from the front pedestrian sally port, so that staff assigned to the control center can observe the entrance area. Where the institution's design lends itself to this approach, the control center should allow clear observation of entrances to the visiting, admissions/discharge, and administration facilities, and as much of the main compound as possible.

The entire envelope surrounding the control center, the staff working area, toilet, janitor's closet, sally port, and electronic equipment room should be of secure construction to prevent unauthorized admittance. The inner walls, such as those between the janitor's closet and the control center, do not require security construction.

Walls should be constructed of reinforced block or poured concrete. There should be no partial walls with nonsecure extensions to the ceiling. Dropped, unreinforced ceilings should be strengthened to prevent unauthorized entry from adjacent rooms. Any ventilation grilles or other openings within the control center should be secured with appropriate security bars.

The control center entrance must have a sally port, a vestibule entrance with two doors that are interlocked so only one can be opened at a time. The sally port must be constructed so the control center officer can see inside to ensure that no unauthorized persons have entered. In certain circumstances, it may not be possible or practical to construct a new sally port in the control center. However, it may be feasible to install grilles in the adjacent corridor on either side of the entrance door to the control center to provide an improved level of isolation.

If the control center has windows, they should be constructed carefully with reinforced frames and ballistic-resistant glazing. The glass in the control center should be tested extensively to ensure durability and impenetrability during a major assault by inmates. Many institutions now install tubular steel barriers or tool-resistant steel bars over the security glazing, to ensure total security.

An adjacent room of sufficient space often is needed for supporting equipment, including telephone equipment, battery backups, and computers. If entry to this room is not through the control center, then it should have a sally ported entrance. If the equipment room is adjacent to the control center, the sally port to the control center can serve as a secure entrance for both spaces; if the room is below or above the control center, a second sally port is recommended, as is closed circuit television monitoring of this entrance.

In facilities where the armory entrance is reached through the control center, special attention should be given to security during weapon or other emergency gear issue. A split or Dutch door precludes casual access to the armory during these periods.

The control center key board should be located close to a window with a secure pass-through. The board should have separate, color-coded sections for regular, emergency, and restricted keys. This is a separate color-coding system from that often used on the emergency keys themselves, however, and regular issue keys for color-coded emergency locks should not be color-coded. The board may be designed with folding doors to conceal its contents or placed on a rolling base so that it can be moved out of the way during nonpeak issue periods.

The control center key pass-through should have a drive-in-bank-type drawer or some other form of baffled construction to prevent the introduction of a bomb or incendiary device into the control center. It should, however, be large enough to accommodate radios and other typical issue items that may be issued from this post. Due to their size, gas equipment, bolt cutters, and other items should be issued through the sally port or an adjacent secure location that is supervised and remotely controlled from the control center. In general, issue of such items from another secure location is preferred, again to avoid distracting the control center officer in an emergency, as well as to minimize the number of occasions when the control center door is opened.

The control center should have a means for the emergency disposal of keys if a takeover is imminent. In most cases, this need is met by a trap or chute in the floor to a secure vault below, or an appropriately constructed vault with a tamper-proof drop chute securely affixed to the control center floor.

This area should have a separate heating and air conditioning system, and temperature and air exchange conditions must be regulated to prevent deterioration of chemical agents and to minimize danger in the event of leakage. Dehumidification equipment may be necessary for gas supplies to be maintained under optimum conditions.

The control center should be organized so that one person can monitor all equipment and devices, and operate them easily. The design of the consoles in the control center should minimize inmate visibility of the operation of the electronic equipment, while ensuring that the control center officer faces toward the main traffic areas being monitored. The control center should have raised-access flooring such as that used in a computer room, to facilitate wiring and maintenance of the equipment.

Because the officer must remain inside the control center at all times, a toilet and janitor's closet should be provided inside the secure envelope of the control center.

Storage space should be provided in the control center for certain emergency equipment, including crowd control batons, helmets, shields, first aid kits, and perhaps tear gas. However, space considerations often cannot be ignored, and other secure storage in the immediate vicinity of the control center (with the lock to the area controlled remotely from the control center) can serve equally well, as long as it is not in an inmate-access portion of the facility. While the use of such an area means that a staff member must be there to issue the equipment, it also means that the control center officer is not distracted by equipment issue from other important duties.

The control center should be online to the emergency power generation system. In addition to the power for various emergency, communications, and security systems, a separate, standalone lighting system should be included, in the event the main backup generation system fails. There should be at least one battery-operated radio in the control center at all times, as well as a direct phone line to the outside. This is particularly important with the advent of more complex electronic phone switching and PBX systems. Although most of these systems have separate battery backup, their main boards may fail due to power surges or other problems associated with a major power blackout. Therefore, at least one direct outside line, which does not go through the main board, is needed. A cellular phone also can perform that function.

Staffing and Access

Control center staffing requires flexibility in response to changing workloads throughout the day. It is difficult to generalize on this topic because facilities vary widely in design and security requirements. However, a few principles are common to most institutions.

Generally, the control center needs a minimum of two staff members during significant parts of the day and evening. The morning watch rarely requires more than one officer between midnight and the time when inmates are unlocked for the day or when the first main shift comes on duty. Control centers typically require additional staff at shift change time, and during periods of heavy inmate or staff program activity and traffic. The assignment of an activities officer or some other staff member to handle key issues frees the regular officer to monitor communications and traffic flow in and out of the facility.

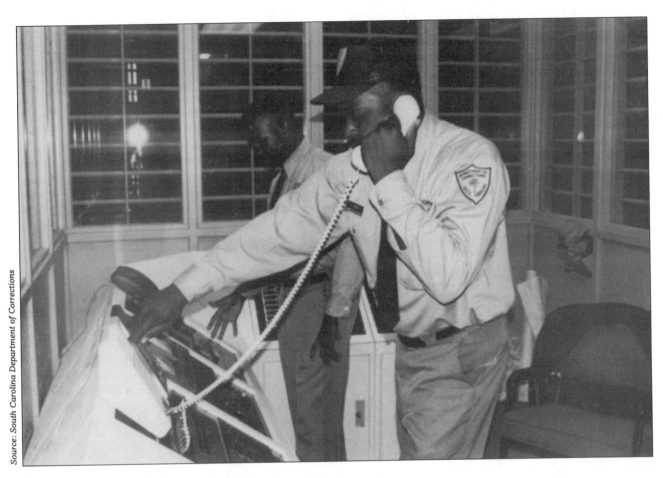

Source: South Carolina Department of Corrections

Above and below: The control center is the operational hub of the institution.

Source: Corrections Today

If closed circuit television is used to monitor the visiting area, an additional staff member may be needed during visiting hours. Similarly, if there are other high traffic or high activity areas that are monitored by closed circuit television, more staff are necessary during peak usage times. In institutions where armory operations are consolidated with those of the control center, additional staff are required when firearms or other equipment are issued. The armory officer, in many cases, could provide this assistance, but when that person is not available, additional help must be assigned.

During periods of peak activity, incoming telephone calls to the institution may be answered by a receptionist or switchboard operator in another area. At night, when the receptionist is not needed, incoming calls may be switched to the control center.

Employees should not be permitted to actually come into the control center to pick up their keys or for any other casual purpose. This area is critical to the operation of the institution, and nonessential traffic should be eliminated, as it increases the risk of a security breach.

Inmate crews never should be assigned to work in the control center. Any maintenance work in the areas immediately adjacent to the gate and grille controls, communications devices, emergency equipment, and the key board is clearly a sensitive task. Even minimum-security inmates constitute a great risk, and using them in this area should not be permitted. The maintenance staff of the institution should be the only ones to perform work in such a sensitive area.

Inmates never should be permitted in the immediate vicinity of the control center sally port when the outer door is open. To do so would constitute an extremely serious breach of security. The risks in terms of staff safety–for takeover in this area as well as takeover of the entire institution–are extremely serious.

An emergency key to the control center should be kept in a secure location outside the institution's secure perimeter so that the control center can be opened if the officer suddenly is incapacitated. Other critical emergency keys must be kept in an area that is totally secure from inmate takeover. It does no good to have the emergency keys to the special housing unit in the control center if the control center itself is physically vulnerable, or is in a location where inmates conceivably could block staff from accessing the keys.

Control Center Procedures

General

In most institutions, the control center is a key traffic point. To ensure that no unauthorized persons enter or leave the institution, control center procedures clearly must state the types of identification and conditions required for passage through the control center area. Identifying staff and inmates entering and leaving the institution is only part of the problem. Inmate visitors, contract employees, volunteers, and repair personnel also must pass through this point.

A well-defined system must be established to ensure that only those with proper authorization enter the secure portion of the institution or leave the premises. The control center officer must be able to rely on personal knowledge of the individual, picture identification, electronic means of verifying physical attributes, or other similarly reliable means to identify those seeking to exit or enter. In the event that an individual cannot be satisfactorily identified by these means, control center officers must have another staff member confirm the entrant's identity. If no one can identify the individual, then he or she should not be allowed to pass through.

In most institutions, counts are taken in the control center or an adjacent, equally secure area. See additional information on this topic in Chapter 9 on inmate accountability.

A systematic log of events occurring on the control center post is vitally important. These events include, but are not limited to, all commitments and discharges, alarms, miscounts, and the issue of restricted and emergency keys. These entries should be made in addition to any other record system required, such as the separate logging of emergency or restricted key issuance. A copy of such a form is included in Appendix D.

Key issue is a typical activity in most control centers. Procedures should specify the various categories of keys, the issue procedures for each category, and the persons to whom the keys may be issued. The procedures for issuing restricted and emergency keys should be a prominent part of the key control policy. A log or other permanent record must be kept of keys issued.

The policy also must clearly specify the persons to whom keys may not be issued. Ordinarily, volunteers, contract staff, and other part-time employees may not be issued keys. Inmates should not be issued keys, except where limited access to vehicle keys is permitted for official purposes, or if inmate room keys are in use.

Source: Oregon Department of Corrections

Key issue must be from a suitably secure location, and keys should be organized in a way that ensures quick, easy storage and issue.

Backup keys for certain critical locations–the armory, lockshop, and the control center itself–must be located elsewhere. Often, they are kept in a tower or in a secure repository elsewhere outside the perimeter, with the keys to that repository themselves under strict control.

The control center officer should have clear instructions as to what equipment should be issued, to whom, and under what circumstances. Equipment such as batons, chemical agents, gas masks, and bolt cutters only should be issued under specified circumstances. Flashlights, restraints, pagers, radios, keys, and other regular use items can be issued on a durable chit system using small metal or plastic tags, to ensure proper accountability.

Emergency equipment stored in the control center must be controlled strictly. Each agency should establish guidelines for the types and quantities of chemical agents stored in this location. For simplification of inventory and control, these quantities should be kept to a minimum, and staff members should have firm guidelines on the circumstances that

warrant the use of each kind of gas, as well as a clear understanding of which officials may authorize such use.

Chemical agents, in particular, must be stored under controlled conditions that preclude casual handling or accidental discharge. They should be stored in a separate area of the control center, with a posted inventory that reflects at all times a running total of the amounts on hand.

Other items of emergency equipment may include batons, additional restraints, bolt cutters, tool kits, fire extinguishers, or in rare cases, gas guns. A shadowboard is desirable for storage of items like bolt cutters, restraints, and batons. Bulky equipment, like portable cutting saws or hydraulic rams, cannot be stored on the shadowboard. All of these items must be controlled strictly and issued only under necessary circumstances.

Inventories should be required every shift on some items, and daily on others. Every shift change should involve signing over all chemical agents permanently stored in the control center. For items in continual circulation, like keys, a daily inventory (ordinarily on the morning watch) provides the necessary safeguards.

Communications

The control center post orders clearly should outline staff responsibility in maintaining communications within the institution. Since most, if not all, of the communications equipment is centralized here, it is important that the control center staff knows how to use it effectively. Ordinarily, this equipment includes radios, teletypes, computers, pagers, personal body alarm receivers, intercoms, telephones, emergency alarm systems, and closed circuit television equipment. There should be instructional information for each of these systems in the post orders and, if necessary, in separate manuals.

When and if incidents or other specialized activity must be logged, the post orders clearly should describe both the circumstances and the recording procedures.

Staff using radio equipment should be aware of the Federal Communications Commission (FCC) regulations on the official use of assigned radio frequencies. The FCC requires that all assigned frequencies be used for the purpose intended and that base station operators identify the station by using assigned call letters and numbers. Brevity in radio communications should be encouraged. If call codes and signals are used, personnel must be trained in their proper use. The FCC prohibits the use of foul or obscene language in radio transmissions.

All communications equipment should be clustered conveniently for efficient staff use. In many cases when the officer is not able to answer a hand-held instrument immediately, a speaker phone speeds responsiveness.

Racks of battery chargers and other items related to issue equipment should be located near the issue window. Phone equipment, personal body alarm receivers, and radios should be placed in logical locations.

An inspection system should be in place, to ensure proper functioning of all communications equipment. Any equipment failures should be reported to the designated supervisor or maintenance staff member. He or she should establish an inspection system to ensure that all equipment is functioning properly at all times. Maintenance contracts should be considered for highly technical or specialized equipment items that require elaborate testing or repair. Phone numbers for repair services or on-call repair staff should be available readily for use by the chief of security or maintenance chief.

Personal body alarm systems may have a receiver/decoder installed in the control center, with individual transmitters issued to employees assigned in living quarters, and other areas deemed appropriate by the administration. These alarm systems should be tested at the beginning of each shift, and the control center officer should log the results of those tests.

In facilities with towers, intercom capability among the towers, and between the towers and the control center, is strongly recommended. Intercom capability permits staff on perimeter posts and in the control center to be aware of the activities at all other posts. When an emergency occurs on the perimeter, staff in the control center do not have to wait for a phone call or radio transmission; they can hear what is happening and respond accordingly.

Typically, the institution's closed circuit television monitors are located in the control center. A second set of monitors can be installed in another location, and monitoring activity switched to that location during peak activity periods in the control center. Post orders clearly should state the parameters for this activity.

Despite the prevalence of personal body alarms in many systems, during nonbusiness hours, some institutions have staff on all posts call the control center by phone every half-hour. This is done as a basic, low-tech, safeguard against an employee being injured, held hostage, or otherwise disabled for a lengthy period of time without other staff knowing it. The use of body-mounted, headset phones can allow control center staff (or those on other telephone-intensive posts) to perform other operations while talking on the phone, streamlining operations considerably.

Emergencies

Control center post orders clearly must state the necessary steps in case of fire, disturbance, hostage situation, work or food strike, escape, power failure, or other institutional emergency. Copies of the emergency plans for each of these situations should be in the control center. Staff assigned there must be trained in them and prepared to carry them out at once. Staff readiness is particularly important, because, in an emergency, supervisory personnel may be preoccupied with containing or responding to the problem and must rely on control center staff to initiate key aspects of the emergency plans.

A comprehensive hostage statement should be included in the control center post orders because of the possibility of a hostage-type escape attempt at that location. Control center staff should thoroughly understand that no person under duress has any authority, and that no inmates will be released with hostages in their custody.

A staff call-up procedure is an important feature of emergency-response procedures. Many institutions have automatic sequential dialing equipment; when the control center officer activates the dialer, every staff member whose phone number is logged into the dialer automatically is called with a prerecorded message to report to the institution. Usually, the call sequence is in command order, so that supervisory staff, emergency response teams, and medical personnel can be called first. An alternate method, which has been effectively used for years, is the pyramid system. In this method, staff are assigned a specific group of employees to call, and they, in turn, call another group, who call yet another. In this way, a relatively small number of calls by any one person still results in a large number of staff being contacted.

Traffic Control

Records of inmate traffic fall into two categories. The first is commitment or discharge activity, which should be subsumed into the count records. The second, a picture card system, is necessary when the control center monitors inmate traffic from one area of the facility to another. This system should include the name, number, housing assignment, job, and picture of every inmate in the facility.

In facilities where the control center manages the inmate visitor flow, an accurate count of all visitor traffic is imperative. This requires close coordination among staff who process visitors and visiting room officers. The control center officer should have minimal involvement with visitor processing and should be concerned only with visitor identification.

The control center should maintain a complete picture file of all staff. This file enables new employees and officers recently assigned to different shifts to identify legitimate staff members with whom they have not become familiar.

Picture ID systems are discussed in Chapter 12 on entrance operations. In brief, they should include a picture for each staff member, authorized volunteers, contract employees, and any student interns, as well as photo-based gate passes for inmates who are authorized to pass through. Ideally, the control center should have a picture ID card for every inmate, in addition to the photo on the gate passes.

Identification procedures for inmate visitors ordinarily do not include taking photographs. Blacklight (and sometimes fingerprint comparison) systems are used and are effective in preventing inmates from leaving the facility disguised as visitors.

Inmate work crews rarely should be processed out through the control center area. However, if crews do use this route, then crew kit pouches for each such crew should be maintained in the control center. They should be returned at the end of the workday by the crew supervisor. If a crew continues its work past the change of shifts, the new supervisor should return the crew kit. Crew kit folders should be stored in a rolling rack that easily can be moved into the control center for updating and rolled out again the following day for access by staff members who are drawing crew assignments.

Entrances

12

Institutional entrances are vulnerable to serious security breaches–primarily escapes and the introduction of contraband. It also is axiomatic that as you tighten security in other portions of the perimeter, then the entrances become more attractive to inmates as a means of escape. For those reasons, it is important that procedures exist to ensure complete security at all entrances.

Entrances sometimes are categorized into four groups: front, rear, pedestrian, and vehicular. A few facilities combine pedestrian and vehicular functions at the front entrance–a practice that is not recommended. Most combine those functions at the rear gate. For the purpose of this publication, front entrances will be defined as encompassing only pedestrian traffic involving staff, visitors, or inmates. Rear gate operations will be considered to include other pedestrian activity, as well as vehicular traffic.

Operating Procedures

General

Applicable laws and rules regarding contraband and searches, as well as potential penalties for violation of those regulations, should be posted clearly at all entrances. Every entrance post must have a clearly written set of post orders containing, at a minimum:

- A description of general duties

- A chronological list of duties to be performed during the shift

- The agency's standard agency hostage statement, specifying that no hostage has any authority while under control of inmates

- Instructions for handling and storing firearms

- Other specialized information particular to that institution or post, including a collection of other relevant institutional and agency policies, such as those defining contraband and describing how visitors are to be processed

Procedures for each gate post should be written in sufficient detail to enable any staff member assuming that post to perform the required duties with minimal supervisory assistance, but should include clearly described procedures for requesting supervisory assistance. This is especially important for entrance posts, because errors made there can have serious repercussions.

All visitors should be required to sign into the facility in a bound logbook maintained for official record-keeping purposes. To ensure that those entering the institution are informed of the applicable rules and regulations, a standard sign-in form should be used, stating restrictions on contraband, cameras, recorders, drugs, medications, and other items that apply at that particular facility. The record of incoming individuals should be subdivided into categories including official visitors, volunteers, contract employees, inmate visitors, repair persons, salespersons, and others.

The logbook for visitors should contain at least the following information:

- Name

- Date

- Time in and out

- Purpose of visit

- Means of identification (driver's license, birth certificate, agency identification, or other means)

- Department or person visited

- Remarks

Visiting logs should be turned in daily to the chief of security and retained for a minimum of thirty days, to enable staff to reconstruct visiting patterns of a particular inmate or investigate a particular visiting day.

Also, a current inmate roster should be available to staff at the entrance processing inmate visitors. A card or file folder system may be used for tracking visits, although some facilities have automated this process.

Inmates who are to be officially released from custody must be properly identified. An official release order should be prepared in advance and properly authenticated by a supervising official. The control center officer and the officer staffing the entrance post should have identical copies of the order, including a picture for direct identification purposes. Local procedures should be very specific about the sequence and content of the identification process.

Armed law enforcement personnel are an everyday part of the traffic pattern of a typical institution. However, there must be safeguards to insure that weapons, ammunition, and other hazardous items do not enter the facility. Ammunition constitutes a risk only slightly less than a weapon, and safeguards must be implemented to insure that no loose ammunition, magazines, speed-loaders, or chemical agents come into the institution. A weapons-unloading barrel or other safe method of unloading firearms should be at each entrance.

Source: CRSS

Effective vehicle sally port operations are vital to perimeter security.

Design and Equipment

A mechanical, electronic, or procedural interlock system must be in place at all sally port gates, which prevents more than one of the two sally port gates, grilles, or doors to be opened at a time. This system can be used to detain people or vehicles until properly identified and searched, and to prevent unauthorized access or exit. An emergency override may be built into the system if it is thought necessary, but if an override is incorporated, sufficient safeguards should be in place to prevent its casual use.

If a tower officer controls the gates, then that person needs to be able to see if the officer on the ground is under duress. This is a particular concern if inmates are assigned to the gate area. The officer on the ground should stand clear of all other persons, in full view of the tower officer who can see a clear signal that it is okay to open the gate. The gate should not be opened by the tower officer unless he or she receives a distinct signal from the officer on the ground.

All gate controls must be in a secure location, typically in the control center or tower. When an open sally port is in use, the gate controls should be interlocked so that both gates cannot be opened at the same time. Visibility from the control center or individual approaching the tower is important for proper identification and, if distances are great, installation of closed circuit television may be considered. It is particularly important to have procedures that ensure tower or control center officers controlling sally port entrances positively can determine that the officer at the gate is not under duress.

Because these posts must be staffed at all times, they should have rest room facilities, running water, and other personal comfort fixtures. The entire gate area should be well lit, with clear lines of sight from any tower controlling the gates to the ground post area. Entrance staff should have metal detection equipment, a phone and radio, and an ultraviolet light for inspection of blacklight imprints on visitors.

Gates where inmates are processed out on a regular basis need a crew kit card or gate pass board. This board holds the cards and helps in accounting for inmates. Constructing this board on rollers allows easy movement from the inner to the outer gate, facilitating movement of the cards as inmates move in and out.

Storage lockers must be provided for items that visitors cannot take into the visiting room. These lockers should have individual locks, with a removable key that visitors take with them into the visiting room and return to the locker after the visit. A secure coat rack must be available, with a checkout system to prevent theft by other visitors.

A safe weapon-unloading receptacle and a high-security weapons locker should be provided for law enforcement personnel and staff authorized to carry weapons outside the facility. Ideally, tower or control center staff should control the outer door of the weapons repository. Inner compartments with individual locks and keys keep weapons safe from tampering by others accessing the main gun locker.

Metal-detection equipment should be provided and tested on a regular basis, with recalibration, as necessary. Many metal detectors are affected by the proximity of large moving metal objects. Care should be taken in installation to shield against such interference. Staff members also should be aware of the possible effects of perimeter detection devices on the operation of metal-detection equipment.

As in many other areas of institution operations today, agencies increasingly are turning to automation and other computer-related devices to help manage these processes. Physical attribute identifiers (identifying hands, fingerprints, retinas, and so forth) and picture card systems provide a technological advantage in assuring positive identification of inmates, staff, inmate visitors, and facility guests. In the face of growing inmate populations and institutional systems, the challenge of managing movement of authorized persons through security barriers must be supplemented as much as possible, albeit by reliable, tested methods. In general, maintaining basic visitor information (and even advanced digitized information) in a computer is an excellent time-saver. However, these technologies should in no way eliminate the need also to use personal identification methods in processing visitors.

Gate Staffing

The number of staff required at each entrance post depends on the design of the facility. Clearly, staff either must be close enough to the gates to properly identify traffic through the area, or must use closed circuit television to enable proper identification.

Schedules or rosters should fit the prime activity periods for each entrance post. In the case of a rear gate, weekends off is logical, since most delivery and work detail traffic is during the week. If the post were staffed at all on a weekend, it would be ideal for a relief officer. Conversely, the front entrance officer should be on duty on weekends, when visiting traffic is heaviest.

Tact, diplomacy, and familiarity with regulations are necessary for individuals staffing entrance posts. At armed posts, employees not only must be properly trained in the type of weapon involved, but also must have the maturity and good judgment to handle the additional responsibility that weapon use may entail. Alertness, good powers of observation, and a knowledge of overall institution policies are also necessary.

Rear Gate Operations

Concerns for both vehicles and pedestrians should be included in developing procedures for rear gate operations.

Vehicles

Vehicular traffic into secure perimeters should be kept to an absolute minimum. Vehicular gate operations should be properly staffed to provide for 100 percent search and identification of all traffic going through that point.

Signs should be posted at all traffic locations approaching the institution entrances. The signs should include information about prohibited acts and contraband, as well as directions for inmate visitors, deliveries, and authorized official guests.

Where possible, large vehicles should time their departure to coincide with the clearing of institutional counts.

No inmates should be in the sally port when a vehicle is passing through or being searched. Employees escorting inmates through the gate area must stand clear of the gate before signaling the officer controlling the gate to open it. Inmates never should be permitted to loiter in the gate area or to obtain possession of the keys to gates.

If a vehicle must come into the institution and it is too long to close both sally port gates, the shift supervisor should provide additional security in the vicinity of the gate to ensure no inmates escape as the vehicle moves through the gate area.

Staff vehicles parked in close proximity to any vehicular gate must be restricted to a designated parking area; personal staff vehicles should not be permitted to enter the institution. When vehicles are unattended, they should be locked securely and should contain no contraband, weapons, ammunition, or other hazardous items. Staff should be advised that vehicles are subject to search within the laws of the jurisdiction involved.

Records and logs should enable reconstruction of all traffic for a thirty-day period, and ID photos of inmates should be a part of the inmate identification process. It is not sufficient to send the name and number of all inmates approved for daily work outside the institution, or for transfer, and to use that information as the sole means of identification. Picture photos must be used to identify the inmates being released.

At a minimum, those entering the institution with a delivery of any type should present picture identification, and staff should log the following information:

- Name of driver

- Company represented

- License number

- Time in and out

- Purpose of entry

- Name of escorting employee

- Signature of person clearing vehicle in and out

Many systems require drivers or other visitors coming inside the institution to surrender their picture ID, which is held at the gate (or control center for inmate visitors, for that matter) until they leave. A clip-on pass of some sort often is issued to provisionally identify the person while in the institution.

Drivers of commercial delivery vehicles should declare the contents of their entire cargo, to avoid placing firearms and other hazardous materials intended for other locations in proximity to inmates. The gate officer should search the vehicle for contraband. This inspection must include all compartments, under the hood, and other areas where contraband is likely to be hidden. Use of a pit or inspection well is recommended, but mirrors and automotive "creepers" also can be used. Drivers should be required to sign a statement that they are aware of the items considered contraband and that none are in their possession, or in the vehicle in question. Once the inspection is complete, the driver and officer conducting the search should stand clear, and the officer should indicate that the vehicle may pass through the gate.

Inside the facility, all commercial vehicles must remain under constant staff escort, including while they are being unloaded and loaded. Officers escorting vehicular traffic should not ride in the cab; they should be in the back to properly supervise the load, or follow on the ground where the entire vehicle can be observed.

When vehicles are leaving the institution, they should drive to a preidentified stopping point, or "deadline," well short of the inner sally port gate. The driver should dismount, move well away from the vehicle, perhaps to the front or rear of the vehicle to show that they are not under duress, and give an all clear signal.

The gate officer must properly identify and search the vehicle and driver as required before clearing them through. Inspection before release involves a thorough security check of all compartments, including the engine, the underbody, the inside of the cab, and the rear cargo box. The officer must inspect the trailer of a semitrailer or the body of a straight truck from the inside to ensure that no false compartments or other hiding places have been concealed. He or she should use an inspection well or creeper, in conjunction with a mirror, to perform the underbody inspection. Only then should the inner gate be opened.

If it is not possible to thoroughly search a vehicle before it leaves the compound, either it should be unloaded or held in the sally port through a count. Large loads should be held inside the institution, after being searched and sealed, for a minimum of two counts, to prevent inmates from successfully escaping by concealing themselves inside cartons or false compartments in the vehicle itself.

Trash dumpsters inside the institution must be taken out regularly, but only after a thorough search. Probing rubbish and other materials for hidden inmates should be a regular procedure for dumpsters, garbage trucks, and other bulk cargo loads that are loose enough to penetrate with a long pole. In addition, they should remain inside the institution for at least one clear count before removal, or compacted inside the perimeter.

Any vehicles left unattended inside the secure perimeter must be disabled by removal of the rotor, distributor cap, or by other means. These vehicles must be locked and parked within view of a tower.

There should be a barrier at the rear gate to deter and prevent vehicle-assisted escapes. Such a barrier should be fabricated and installed, either as an in-ground post, suspended reinforced V-shaped barricade, or some other method to prevent a successful escape attempt by inmates commandeering a vehicle inside the compound and crashing the gate.

Rail traffic is rare, but when it occurs, it should be handled by similar procedures. Considering the power of a typical locomotive, a small tractor-style vehicle of limited power is preferable for use inside a compound. These smaller vehicles either can be rail or rubber tire-based units of sufficient capacity to slowly pull a loaded rail car out of the facility with regular sally porting, but not so powerful as to create an unusual risk of ramming a gate if inmates are able to commandeer it in an escape attempt.

Emergency vehicle entry also is an important consideration, and access procedures for emergency vehicles should be clear and streamlined. Staff should anticipate how to process an emergency vehicle into the institution when a van, bus, or truck is in the sally port. Identification, search, and inventory procedures may be minimal, but they must be well known to all staff working the post, and provide a sensible balance between thoroughness and speed. Ambulances (carrying medications and needles) and fire trucks (carrying many potential weapons) require particularly close supervision.

Staff members should question drivers about weapons, but should not delay the entry process unless a weapon is declared and must be secured. Although procedures should not unduly delay entry and exit, staff should not open both sally port gates at the same time. Supervisors should notify the gate that the vehicle is on the way and provide an escort to stay with it the entire time it is in the facility.

All institution vehicles moving in or out of the secure perimeter should be governed by the same rules and regulations prescribed for commercial and other traffic. Searches, sally porting, and driver activities must conform to these patterns of security procedures. Constant staff escort may be a local option, depending on the security level of the facility.

Pedestrians

It is desirable to have a positive method for tracking staff who are inside the institution. This can be done using a variety of methods. In some systems, nonemployees entering the institution are required to surrender their picture ID until they leave the institution, providing a positive check on persons as they depart.

Inmate traffic through gates should be kept to a minimum; the greater the amount of traffic, the greater the risk for contraband movement or escape.

A walk-through metal detector should be used to search all inmates, drivers, and nonofficial visitors entering the institution. This provides a way for staff to ensure that metallic contraband, such as a gun, is not introduced into the facility. Anyone who sets off the metal detector then should be searched by a hand-held transfrisker or small portable metal detection device. But these searches should go beyond the use or metal detectors, and should include regular inmate pat searches and irregular but frequent strip searches in a private area adjacent to the entrance.

Inmates entering and leaving the facility should be limited in the items they are permitted to carry. Local regulations specifying a minimum amount of personal effects reduces the likelihood of contraband movement through the entrance. The inmates should surrender their property at the gate, and be personally searched one at a time, and moved through the perimeter. Then, the property can be searched at staff's convenience.

Inmates should not be assigned to work continuously in the gate area itself, and should be permitted in the sally port only for janitorial duties. Other inmates should be restricted from the sally port unless they are being processed through the gate for an outside work detail.

Cross-circulation of inmate traffic in the gate area must be avoided by having an organized method for routing traffic or identifying individuals moving through the gate, and preventing searched and unsearched inmates from mixing. Traffic patterns must ensure that searched and unsearched inmates do not come into contact with each other.

The identification procedures associated with inmate releases must be positive and easily used. A standard picture identification system (as referenced in Chapter 9 on accountability) can ensure that all inmates released through vehicular entrances are authorized for such release.

Front Gate Operations

Proper identification procedures should be posted prominently in the pedestrian entry area. Individuals who do not have a photographic ID or other approved identification should be denied visiting privileges, or, in questionable cases, referred to a supervisor for a final determination.

Front entrances, in particular, should use ultraviolet ink stamping procedures, with randomly varying stamps. Staff members clearing visitors out of the facility should check for the presence of the stamp using an ultraviolet lamp.

Inmate traffic through the front gate should be minimal. In those rare cases (a front lobby orderly, for instance) where an inmate moves regularly through the front sally port entrance, a gate pass should be used, of the same type and maintained in the same manner as those at the rear gate. These cards, with basic identifying information and a picture, should be moved from one area of a slotted status board to another to reflect the inmate's location in or out of the institution.

Some institutions have procedures that call for all staff members to be searched as they enter the institution. However, in most agencies, this procedure has been found to be generally ineffective in detecting unauthorized materials. It is true that there is some deterrent, but the larger effect of this procedure is to demoralize those searched. Staff are given the inescapable message that they are not trusted. Employees presumably are screened, interviewed, and investigated in the preemployment process. Routine searches betray the confidence that otherwise is attributed to them in handling firearms, government funds, costly equipment, and even human lives. In cases where the agency has a reasonable belief that a particular employee is introducing contraband, regulations always will be available to search that person, pursuant to the same probable cause test that applies in the community.

The officer on the front entrance post never should open an entry gate unless he or she verifies the identity of the individual approaching the gate, using the required identification procedures. When the officer is in doubt, the person seeking admittance should not be allowed to pass unless the officer knows the identity of the person. When there is any doubt at all, other staff should be called to investigate.

Ideally, package deliveries should take place at the rear gate, but if delivery at the front gate is necessary, delivery personnel should not enter the facility. To expedite this process, a weather-protected storage and inspection area should be constructed as a part of the entrance complex.

Food Service Operations

13

Food service is a critical department. The regular provision of nutritious, appetizing, visually appealing meals is a major element in maintaining the morale of the inmate population. Even if food is prepared elsewhere and delivered to the facility, many basic security-related activities have to be carried out in connection with food service operations. Sometimes, correctional officers are assigned to the food service department, where they play an important role in overseeing security of the food preparation process. As a result, security staff need to have a solid understanding about how food service staff accomplish their mission.

Several basic operational areas are involved in a successful food service operation. They are divided roughly into three segments: kitchen (or preparation-related) operations, dining room operations, and satellite meal service. Satellite meal service is covered in Chapter 20 on special housing units. This chapter focuses only on the first two areas.

Kitchen and Food Preparation Areas

Food service personnel should work in close cooperation with security personnel to develop policies and procedures that assure proper custody, control, and security in the kitchen and related areas. These policies should ensure:

- Counts and census checks are accurate. One commonly used method calls for inmates to sit in one section of the dining area and move to another area when their names are called. No matter what method is used, inmates should remain in one place during all such counts, unless their presence is essential to the preparation of the meal.

- Provisions are in place for any necessary backup for food service personnel when counts are made

- Control is maintained of all hazardous tools, "hot" food items, and contraband

- There are provisions for controlling inmate traffic in and out of the food service department

- Conduct regulations for inmate workers are posted and enforced

- Inmate work areas in the food service department are the subject of daily searches and shakedowns, and inmates are searched on both entering and leaving the food service department on every work shift

- Inmates are not allowed outside the food service department with unauthorized food items

Hazardous Items

Procedures must be in place for the control of hazardous equipment and materials representing potential risks, including cutlery, saws, and cleaning solutions. Knives and other kitchen tools are among the most hazardous forms of contraband an inmate can possess, and control of them is so important as to require special attention to the following elements.

Knives and tools should be etched with a department identifier and a tool number, and then stored securely in locked containers. Locked shadowboards with an expanded metal front should be used to store knives and other kitchen tools, and to allow staff easily to ascertain the presence or absence of tools. The expanded metal front prevents inmates from tampering with or stealing the items on the board, while allowing staff to see what is on the board and what is not. The inventory for items on the shadowboard should be in the cabinet itself.

Knives and other implements should be issued to authorized inmates only, with a durable chit or log system used to record the name and number of the inmates to whom such items were issued, along with the time of issue and return.

Knives should be used only under proper staff supervision. When in use, knives should be cabled and locked to work station tables. By attaching the tool to the work table or other fixed item with a high-strength steel cable, the inmate cannot use it away from the authorized area. This cabling system is not, however, a substitute for proper storage and inventory procedures when these implements are not in use.

One staff person per shift should be designated as responsible for the control, safekeeping, and tracking of all knives and hazardous tools, and that person should possess the only key to the storage cabinet.

In addition to the inventory in the immediate vicinity of the storage area, the responsible employee should maintain a separate, complete inventory of all tools in the department, keeping a copy in the food service department, and furnishing another copy to the control center and the chief of security. Local institutional policy may require additional record-keeping procedures.

Meat cutting saw blades should be stored in the control center.

Yeast, dough, sugar, fruit juices, raisins, mace, nutmeg, hot pepper compounds, and any other similarly abuse-prone food items must be inventoried and secured at all times. Quantities of these items stored inside the institution should be kept to a minimum. Because of its potential for misuse in the fermentation of unauthorized beverages, kitchen yeast and dough should be used under tight controls, and ideally should be handled and accounted for by only one food service employee. Yeast should be stored in a secure box in a refrigerator or other suitable designated area, and the storage box should be anchored to the floor or wall. Inventory records should be kept in the yeast storage box, including the date and quantity of issue, balance on hand, receipt for withdrawal, and the initials of the employee making the withdrawal. Once removed from storage, yeast should be kept under close supervision until such time as it is thoroughly incorporated into the food being prepared.

Broken or worn items should be disposed of by turning them over (with the appropriate receipt) to the tool control or armory officer. Replacement tools should be marked and inventoried prior to being used.

In the event of loss or misplacement of a knife or hazardous tool, the food service manager and the chief of security must be advised immediately. A thorough search should be made, including the questioning and searching of all inmates who may have had access to the item. These inmates should be detained in the food service department until the item is found or they are cleared. A written report to the warden should be prepared following any loss.

Security staff are not responsible for actual food preparation in most facilities. But because they may be called upon to supervise kitchen crews on occasion, it is important to review some other related areas of kitchen operations.

Among the safety practices that should be highlighted are the following tasks:

- Reporting defective equipment

- Avoiding hazardous shortcuts

- Keeping aisles, stairs, and paths of travel free from obstructions

- Storing supplies and materials neatly, avoiding the danger of overhanging and falling objects

- Maintaining orderly work areas, with no objects protruding over the edges of counters, ranges, or shelves

- Labeling all cleaning supplies clearly and storing them separately from food supplies

- Disposing of bottles, trash, and scraps in the appropriate manner

- Avoiding slips and falls by mopping floors in sections to leave dry areas of passage, and cleaning all spillage immediately

- Using the proper tool for each job

- Maintaining proper lighting levels in hallways, stairs, and storage areas

Fires present acute problems in correctional facilities, and staff working in food service must be sensitized to the extreme importance of fire prevention. Compliance with fire regulations is mandated by federal, state, and local legislation. Among the procedures necessary for fire prevention are development of procedures to minimize dangers of fire and explosion, rules banning smoking in warehouse areas, specification of storage area contents, and arrangement to keep aisles and potential evacuation routes clear in the case of emergency.

Sanitation is an issue in food service, and regular inspections should be carried out to ensure that the highest possible levels are maintained. A sample sanitation inspection form is in Appendix D.

The following practices are recommended to maintain high environmental and sanitation standards:

- Routinely clean walls, floors, and ceilings in all areas

- All work and storage areas must be clean, well lit, and orderly

- Although this can present search problems, overhead pipes should be eliminated or covered by a false ceiling, as they are a hazard in food preparation areas because they collect dust and might leak, thus leading to possible contamination of food.

- Ventilation hoods should be designed to prevent grease buildup or condensation that collects on walls and ceilings or drips into food or on food-contact surfaces. Filters or other grease-extracting equipment should be readily removable for cleaning and replacement if they have not been designed for easy cleaning in place.

- To prevent cross-contamination, kitchenware and food-contact surfaces of equipment should be washed, rinsed, and sanitized after each use and after any interruption of operations during which contamination could occur.

- Food-contact surfaces of grills, griddles, and similar cooking equipment plus the cavities and door seals of microwave ovens should be cleaned at least once a day. This does not apply to deep-fat cooking equipment or filtering systems, which are cleaned periodically at the discretion of the food service staff.

- Surfaces that do not come into contact with food should be cleaned as often as necessary

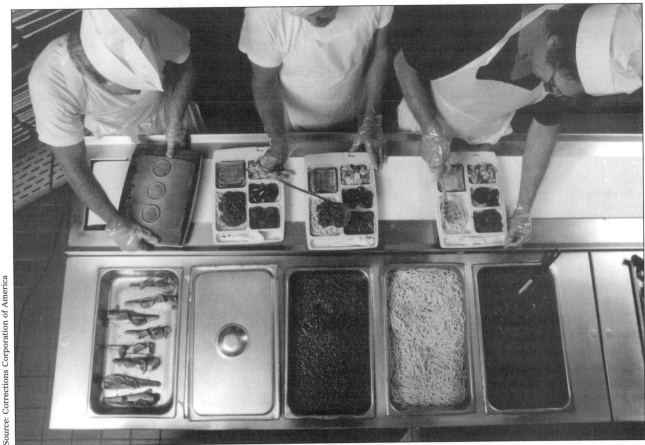

Source: Corrections Corporation of America

Food service is a critical function and must be carried out in an orderly, well-supervised manner.

to keep the equipment free from the accumulation of dust, dirt, food particles, and other debris.

- Manufacturers' instructions should be followed for the cleaning of all equipment.

- An adequate number of insect/rodent proof containers should be available for garbage and refuse disposal; they should be kept covered and cleaned frequently.

- Protective shields should be provided for all lighting fixtures, to prevent broken glass from falling onto food or other preparation-related areas.

Flies, ants, roaches, and silverfish can be kept to a minimum when food service personnel:

- Keep floors and walls clean

- Keep shelves, cupboards, and floors dry

- Keep all food covered

- See that screens and windows fit tightly and are in good repair

- Keep doors closed

- Screen supplies upon delivery

- Store all food supplies on pallets, skids, or in covered containers

- Spray, when allowed by the institution, at night when all food, dishes, and utensils, are stored and covered

Dining Room Operations

While the food service manager should be responsible for the overall supervision of the dining room operation, security staff coverage is an important element of dining room operations. The following considerations apply to this aspect of food service security concerns:

- Inmate conduct in the dining room is the joint responsibility of the food service and security staff.

- A sufficient number of correctional officers must be posted in or near the dining room.

- Meals should be served under conditions that minimize regimentation, but prevent "double-backs" and other portion-control problems.

- In high-security institutions, polycarbonate or heavy plastic serving utensils should be used, rather than metal items. All utensils should be accounted for after each meal.

- Tables should be arranged in a manner that permits free seating and ease of movement, while permitting ready supervision.

- Security personnel should conduct pat searches of inmates going in and out of the dining room.

- The food service supervisor–not security staff–is responsible for instructing the dining room workers in their duties, keeping floors and tables clean. Major cleaning should occur after all inmates have been served, have eaten, and have left the dining room.

Housing Unit Operations

14

In some respects, housing unit operations are the heart of an institution. Inmates live here, spend a major portion of their spare time here, and interact closely and regularly with each other and with staff. Ironically, though, this is the shortest chapter in the publication. That is because virtually every aspect of housing operations–accountability, searches, security inspections, and many others–is covered in a separate chapter. What this chapter is intended to do is highlight a few key areas.

The post orders for housing units (as for every other post) should be clear about what officers are expected to accomplish. They should contain the daily routine described in the sections on waking inmates, searching those going in and out of the unit, supervising inmate workers in the unit, searching cells, performing security inspections, ordering supplies, and performing many other duties.

Unit officers constantly should be aware of unusual incidents, inmate contacts, or other noteworthy activities in the unit, and report them to the proper supervisory personnel.

The demands of congregate living require that staff set and maintain high standards of cleanliness and high standards of housekeeping. Personal property limitations need to be a requirement in every unit.

The assignment and supervision of unit orderlies, or porters, is an important aspect of unit operations. Officers should insist that orderlies maintain the common areas of the unit in a high state of sanitation and orderliness.

Likewise, individual inmates must know that officers will be inspecting their cells and holding them to high standards as well.

Personnel assigned to housing units need to intervene immediately to prevent the deterioration that will soon set in if they tolerate lower standards. The appearance of an institution communicates to staff and inmates something about the way staff feel about them. If priorities of a neat, clean, orderly institution are strong, morale will be higher.

Coverings over cell fronts or windows not only look unsightly but they prevent staff from properly supervising activity inside the cells. Staff should be aggressive in requiring inmates to remove them when they are first seen.

Television viewing in common areas of the unit is a regular feature of institution life. Staff should make sure that programming is equitably distributed. Measures to reduce television sound levels include use of dedicated television rooms, hard-wiring speaker plugs in common areas and issuing headphones, or in a more modern adaptation of that strategy, using a small radio transmitter that sends the television voice track over a specific FM radio frequency, which the inmates then tune with a personal radio.

Officers must account for inmates moving in and out of the housing unit. If inmates are not tracked inside the institution on a regular basis, then no matter how secure the array of outside barriers, there is no way of assuring that the institution is running safely and securely. This refers to escape prevention, of course, but also concerns control of inmate activity inside the institution. Knowing where inmates are in the institution at all times will prevent them from easily perfecting escapes, but also will cut down on other impermissible activities such as sexual activity, assaults, and fabrication of contraband. Unit officers

A clean, uncluttered housing unit is not only safer, but easier to supervise.

must make deterring and detecting these activities a high priority.

The use of handheld transfriskers or small portable metal-detection devices should be a regular routine in housing units. In addition to searching inmates as they come and go, these devices are also an aid in searching mattresses and other similar areas for metallic weapons. Machines that detect solid plastics exist but are not in typical use today.

Housing unit staff should conduct security, fire, and sanitation inspections on a daily basis. Copies of forms used to document such inspections are included in Appendix D.

When unit management is in use in an institution, unit officers should maintain a close relationship with the unit manager and other members of the unit team. One of the key benefits of unit management is the communication channel that it opens up between line and management personnel, and officers should take advantage of this opportunity to educate top management about what really is going on at the line level.

Supervisory staff actively must oversee housing unit operations to ensure staff are following policy closely; the onsite visit is the best method for doing so. There is no other effective means of determining whether searches are thorough, inmates are tracked carefully, or other activities are properly carried out throughout the day. Shift supervisors also should visit these posts during heavy traffic times to provide advice and assistance and to observe activity when problems are most likely to occur. Supervisors visiting housing posts also must review the post orders and discuss them with the officers working the post. This enables post orders to be changed through natural evolution of duties, or as a result of routines and procedures in other departments that may have an effect on unit operations.

Key Control

15

Absolute control of all keys is a must for a correctional institution. To maintain effective security, the staff must control the doors, grilles, and other locking devices that comprise physical security, both inside and outside the perimeter. Good key control is not only a program or system, it is a skill that every staff member must learn and practice. Its fundamentals must be incorporated into every institution's operations and be ingrained into every staff member's work habits.

All institutional policies and procedures regarding key control must be written clearly and available for staff for reference, but inmates must not have access to these policies or to the record-keeping systems that support them. Inmates should not be permitted to establish any base of information about the institution's locking system. Staff never should underestimate the capability of inmates to acquire knowledge of locking system technology and to pass that knowledge on to other inmates.

Within larger correctional systems, where common locking systems are used, an information exchange policy should be established for chiefs of security. With such a policy, if keys are compromised in one facility and the same keys are used elsewhere, the other facilities can make appropriate changes before inmates become aware of the situation.

In addition to initial policy formulation, each institution must establish a documented method for annual review and revision of the key control policy and program. As portions of the institution are used for different purposes, or as inmate programs or custody classifications change, the array of locks and the procedures that support the locking system also must change.

Descriptions and Categories of Keys

Policy clearly must define the various categories of keys used in the institution so that staff is aware of the different accountability requirements for each category. These categories ordinarily include:

Backup keys: Keys to a limited number of critical areas (control center, armory, lockshop) maintained in a separate, secure key repository located outside the secure perimeter.

Emergency keys: Keys maintained on key rings and kept separate from all regular-issue keys. They provide prompt access to all parts of the institution during fires, disturbances, or other urgent situations.

Inactive keys: Keys no longer used, but which are retained as spares and backups for unused locking devices. These are also keys maintained separately for other purposes, including storage for other institutions within the system.

Master keys: Keys that are cut so that one key may actuate more than one locking device in a series of locks from a single manufacturer.

Pattern keys: Keys from which all other keys for a particular lock or series of locks are cut. They are maintained separately from all other spare or blank keys.

Restricted keys: Keys that allow access to sensitive areas of the institution. Special authorization must be obtained before they are issued to anyone other than the employee designated to draw them on a regular basis.

Security keys: A broad reference to keys that, if lost or duplicated by inmates, would facilitate an escape, or jeopardize the security of the institution, institutional property, or persons. Urgent remedial action is necessary if a security key is lost, compromised, or missing.

Vehicle keys: Keys to motor vehicles operated by institution staff (or in some instances inmates) for official purposes, including tractors and other specialized machines located inside or outside the secure perimeter of the facility.

The Issue System

Keys must be issued from a central, secure location, usually the control center or a similar reinforced area not accessible to inmates. All keys must be returned to this location, either at the end of the workday or when employees leave the facility. The major features of this issue system should include a fixed, multiple-panel key board in the key issue area. Hooks on the board, arranged in alphanumeric rows and columns (A-4, for instance, indicating a key on the first row and fourth column of the board), are used to store the key rings themselves. Hooks should have no more than one ring on them; multiple rings on one hook make it impossible to have accurate, prompt key accountability.

Some agencies also use a rolling, portable key board which can be moved into place for key issue at shift change, and then moved to a more convenient location within the control center for the balance of the shift. Portable key boards (small locking cabinets with handles) sometimes are used in small departments or issue zones, for vehicles in an institution garage, for instance. They are considered less desirable, and their use should be approved in advance by the warden. Portable boards should be returned to the key issue area daily, and full accountability for the keys on them must be maintained.

Vehicle keys also may be maintained separately in a secure area; a parallel accountability system for vehicle keys must be employed, using durable chits, inventories, and documented daily counts. A chit is a plastic or metal tag with an employee's name (or a unique identifying number for that staff member), which is used as a receipt for issue items such as keys and equipment.

When a key ring has been removed for authorized use, a chit should replace it. Special "not in use" chits should occupy all empty hooks that are not needed for active key storage. Only a limited number of chits should be issued. If the chit system uses identifying numbers on the tags, a log book containing employee names and number assignments should be maintained. No temporary chits or paper receipts for keys should be used without the approval of the head of the security department. Loss of a chit should be reported immediately, followed by a written report. All chits are to be turned in when an employee is terminated, resigns, retires, or otherwise leaves the facility.

Under this issue system, each key ring has two metal tags attached. One tag is engraved or stamped with the key ring designation–the alphanumeric hook assignment on the key board. The other tag indicates the number of keys on the ring. Both tags should be permanently affixed to the key ring. Keys must be properly inventoried and identified through a distinctive number stamped on the key itself.

Only the locksmith should be able to remove keys from the rings, and for that reason, key rings themselves should be bonded closed–either by welding, epoxying, or soldering. This measure will insure that accurate counts are possible, and will eliminate the temptation for staff to remove a key from a ring to loan to another individual for a short period of time.

Restricted and emergency keys must be stored on sections of the key board that are separate and distinct from regular issue keys. Color-coding the different sections of the board reduces the possibility of inadvertent issue of keys under the wrong circumstances or to the wrong individuals. Many systems store restricted and/or emergency keys in small glass boxes or compartments, with a key opening or constructed in such a way that the glass must be broken to obtain the keys.

The pass-through used to issue keys and other small items of security equipment should be a sliding drawer similar to a bank deposit bin. This will prevent the introduction of a bomb or incendiary device into the area through the pass-through.

With the warden's approval, a highly limited number of nonsecurity keys may be issued permanently. Typically, these include keys to top administrators' offices, staff housing, the cashier's office, and so forth. Chits should be submitted for these keys, as well. However, special identification should be provided on the key board hooks for permanently issued keys. The locksmith should inventory these keys, on the rings of those to whom they are issued, not less than quarterly.

The institution should develop procedures for reporting and taking corrective action regarding lost and broken keys. These procedures should include an immediate verbal report, a written follow-up report, search procedures, immediate inventory of any affected areas, and identification and change of other

Emergency keys must be identified properly and secured from unauthorized use.

locks using the keys in question. In large correctional systems where the same lock may be used in other facilities, information regarding the compromised key should be conveyed to those institutions, as well. Any parts of a broken key should be recovered, if possible, and turned in to supervisory staff.

All staff post orders should outline the specific key control responsibilities of that post, including checking the number of keys on a ring at the time of exchange and calling in a key count at an established time. Staff also must record the key count in the post log. For assignments where keys do not leave the post, procedures should explain how to exchange chits. This should start at the key issue point, where the oncoming officer exchanges a chit of his or hers for the chit of the officer on post with the keys; when he or she reaches the post, the staff member going off duty receives their chit in exchange for the keys.

At a minimum, record-keeping in the control center or key issue room should include a continuously maintained index system for tracking the keys on the issue board. An alphabetical card file or other equally effective system should be established and cross-referenced on the following information:

- Key ring number (number of assigned keys)

- Key ring hook number (title of the key ring)

- Key number (lock and location)

- Location of lock (key number)

Record-keeping for restricted and emergency keys must be kept separate from the log for permanently issued keys. The log procedures for these special keys should include:

- Name of employee to whom the key was issued

- Date and time issued and returned

- Number of the ring issued

- Name of supervisor authorizing the issue

- Signature of employee drawing the ring (selected categories)

- Signature of authorizing official (selected categories, such as restricted keys)

The control center staff should check the key board for completeness and accuracy at the beginning of each shift. Once a day, ordinarily on the morning shift, it is important to account for all of the institution's keys. To do this, the locksmith should provide the control center with the current institutional key count. All staff members having keys on their post should call their counts into the key issue point. There, the totals should be added to the number of keys remaining on the key board. The final tally should agree with the key count provided by the locksmith. Documentation of this process should be forwarded daily to the chief of security.

Key Handling

Written procedures should describe key handling requirements for all staff. When keys are carried, they should be concealed either in a pocket or in a pouch secured to the employee's belt by a metal clip or chain. A chain should be used to attach rings with large security keys to the clip, so that the keys remain connected to the clip at all times. A key chain is recommended for all keys to reduce the possibility of theft or loss. Key shields should be installed on large security keys, to keep inmates from easily observing key profiles and cuts.

Procedures must be established to ensure that perimeter keys are not carried into the secure compound, and that security keys do not leave the facility. Security keys must never leave the institution grounds. Policy must specify steps to be taken if keys inadvertently are taken out of the institution. Inmates must never handle security keys. Duplication, alteration, marking, manufacturing, or making impressions of locks or keys should be prohibited. Similarly, any key

Areas of Restricted Key Issue

- Commissary sales and storage areas
- Property and valuable-storage rooms
- Evidence storage areas
- Personnel records storage rooms
- Warehouse (general and food service)
- Armory and/or weapons vault

- Lockshop and any other key or lock storage areas
- Cashier's office
- Inmate records office
- Pharmacy
- Other areas the warden designates as having special security requirements

impression material, lock picks, key blanks, or other lock or key making paraphernalia should be declared contraband. Disciplinary procedures should provide penalties for inmates possessing, fabricating, or otherwise attempting to duplicate locks, keys, or other items.

Management staff and the locksmith should be cautious about the keys they carry. The status associated with carrying certain keys can create a security risk when inmates unnecessarily come in contact with the keys or people carrying them.

Keys never should be thrown from one staff member to another or slid from one point to another across a desk or floor. Keys never should be left in locks or used to lift or pull open a lockable door or hatch.

No force should be used to operate any locks. If locking mechanisms bind or malfunction, supervisory staff must be notified at once.

Staff should not mention key or lock identifying information in the presence of inmates. With the exception of proprietary information on locks, no manufacturers' code numbers should be stamped on keys. A local institution code number should be used instead, but the key cut combination code must not be stamped on keys.

Restricted Key System

Restricted key issue procedures should be established for the areas of the institution noted in the above box.

Restricted keys should be on a separate, distinctly marked area of the key board and should be issued only to authorized staff with supervisory approval. A record should be maintained to document the issuance of restricted keys. No restricted keys (or emergency keys for that matter) ever should leave the institution. Different levels of restriction may be

established, according to the sensitivity of the area to which the keys allow access. In some cases, sealed envelopes or glass-door compartments should be used to secure critical keys such as those for the lockshop, armory, and pharmacy vault.

For critical keys, the issue log also should contain the signature of the person authorizing the key issue. In many cases it may be desirable to have a separate form documenting such issuances; this form should be forwarded to the chief of security by the next working day. Appropriate procedures must be established to restrict access to all key depositories, especially the storage cabinets used for pattern or restricted keys. Keys to these areas should be maintained separately, on separate rings, in glass lockboxes in the control center or key issue room. Only the locksmith should have a twenty-four-hour issue key to the box. Such access should be restricted for everyone else.

If the armory is in a separate location, its keys should be maintained in similar fashion on the armory officer's and shift supervisor's twenty-four-hour checkout rings, with access to other personnel limited. Under no circumstances should inmates come in contact with keys to the armory, lockshop, and entrances.

Certain keys may be restricted during fog or limited visibility conditions. This will ensure that critical departments or sensitive sections of the facility are not activated until all necessary inmate supervision procedures are in place, or until the bad weather abates.

Emergency Key System

Emergency key procedures are critical in a correctional facility and must be detailed clearly in institution policy. Staff must be able to access every part of the facility without delay during a fire, disturbance, or other crisis. Keys on each emergency key ring should provide responding staff access from the point of key issue–in some cases from the front entrance completely through the area or zone the key ring is intended to serve. There is reasonable disagreement on whether, in such a situation, an emergency key ring with a key to a perimeter gate should go into the secure portion of the institution. However, many practitioners believe that in an emergency it is likely that perimeter alertness will be higher and staff will be alerted, and so the possibility of a problem resulting is very low.

The emergency key system must anticipate the worst–no power, no lights, no computers, and no hydraulic or pneumatic actuation of locks. The system also must account for a need to access a given area through more than one entrance. Just one set of emergency keys to the special housing unit, for instance, would not allow for simultaneously using multiple points of entry or evacuation in a crisis. There should be a separate set of keys leading to, and through, each possible entrance/exit in the target building. This may be somewhat costly, but it is immensely important to ensure effective emergency response.

In an emergency, employees who are unfamiliar with the area and its key system may be the only ones responding, so the system must be virtually foolproof. The coding or identifying system employed is not as important as staff familiarity with the method. There are a number of means to quickly and easily identify which key fits which lock. These include the following:

- A color-coded system, with each key handle dipped in colored plastic or epoxy paint to match a colored dot or painted area located at the lock site where that key is used

- Attachment of a simple floor plan drawing on a durable tag attached to the key ring, reflecting the location of all locks opened by the keys on that emergency ring

- Use of metal tags displaying lock/key information, kept in tabular form so as to be easily retrieved and cross-referenced

- Notched keys to assist staff in matching lock and key in smoke, the dark, or other low-visibility situations

Whatever system is adopted, all staff must be trained in it, so that in a time of crisis, anyone issued any set of keys can use them for their intended effect.

Emergency keys must be maintained on a separate key board or on a separate section of the main key board, clearly distinguishable from all other keys.

In either case, the storage area allotted should be made distinct from other key storage areas by being painted red. An alphabetical listing posted adjacent to the board should indicate the locations served by each ring and the corresponding key ring number.

Emergency keys should be rotated into use regularly, so as to prevent uneven wear from rendering them unusable when placed in service. Emergency keys must be tested periodically, not only by the locksmith but by others, to assure that personnel unfamiliar with the peculiarities of the locks involved can operate them effectively. If only the locksmith tests the keys, it is difficult to ascertain if they will function for all of the staff. This can be done by tactical staff as part of their training, and supervisory staff should be involved in this process for training purposes, as well. These tests must be documented in a bound ledger and cosigned by the chief of security. Any deficiencies or needed repairs should be noted in the ledger and appropriate follow-up actions should be taken.

Emergency keys to the perimeter locks and gates, control center, and armory must not be stored inside the facility on the emergency board. Instead, they should be kept in a tower or other secure repository located outside the perimeter, accessible only to appropriately identified and authorized personnel. This prevents inmates from escaping directly through the entrance if they were to gain control of the emergency key board.

Inmate Key Issue

Inmate use of keys should be very limited, and covered by written policy that clearly describes the limits of this program. Inmates only should be issued nonsecurity keys, such as to the door of their room in a lower-security institution, or to a vehicle they are authorized to drive. Only staff should issue inmates keys.

A receipt, such as a durable chit, should be used, and staff should recover all keys when inmates are moved for any reason. Other than personal room keys, all keys must be turned in at the end of each day, but depending upon the staffing pattern and institution configuration, that also may be required.

Locks secured by keys issued to inmates must be unique. No other similarly keyed lock should be in use anywhere else in the institution, and they should have a different keyway than other facility locks. Procedures for issuing keys to inmates who drive institution vehicles should include appropriate check-in and checkout, as well as interim accountability or key counts by supervising staff members. Additional procedures should be developed for inmates who are permitted to drive personal vehicles when involved in approved community activities. The facility should retain a duplicate key set, enabling staff members to move such vehicles for reasons including reparking, or recovery in the event of rearrest or other return to custody.

The Lockshop

If a separate lockshop is maintained, its physical security should be equivalent to that of the control center. It should be located outside the secure perimeter of the facility, if possible. Otherwise, it should be in an area where there is no inmate traffic and other traffic can be easily monitored and controlled. Ideally, a remotely controlled lock (monitored by closed circuit TV from the control center) and sally ported entrance should be part of the design.

The lockshop should have adequate space not only for the basic tools necessary for lock repair, but also for neat, orderly storage of all spare parts and other minor equipment incidental to the maintenance of the institution's locking systems. All spare and pattern keys, locks, parts, and key-making equipment should be maintained in this secure area. Key-making must be a completely secure operation. Ideally, it should not be conducted immediately adjacent to the key issue point, but if it is, complete and secure physical separation must be provided.

Equipment

The typical lockshop should contain the following equipment, the minimum needed for a comprehensive key storage and maintenance program:

- Key duplication machine
- Proprietary or locally fabricated key storage cabinet
- Drill press
- Vice
- Hand drills and bits
- Assorted files, saws, and hand tools
- File cabinet
- Card files
- Assorted shelving and cabinet storage area; all tools should be shadowed and stored in accord with the tool control policy, and an inventory should be maintained on all tools

- Portable tool box, with inventory
- Computer for maintaining lock and key inventory records (optional but recommended)

Storage

A specialized key cabinet should be used to organize all pattern and blank keys. Appropriate staff should be trained in how the key storage system operates, but the key to the cabinet should be restricted. Only authorized staff should have access to these keys, which never should be issued as regular issue keys.

Spare parts for locks and supplies of padlocks for the institution should be maintained in a neat and orderly manner.

Worn or discarded locks and keys should be cut up and disposed of by the locksmith. Inactive keys should be stored in a separate secure area, with appropriate restrictions on access. A written inventory of inactive and discarded locks and keys should be maintained.

Adequate safeguards should be established for the delivery of lock and key supplies and equipment. All lock-related purchase orders must specify delivery procedures to the outside warehouse and include a specification for hazardous material labeling. Clear delivery information will help avoid the inadvertent routing of sensitive materials to the inside warehouse.

Types of Locking Devices

Procurement of locking devices and keys should be centralized. Keys or locks should not be purchased or put into use except by the locksmith. Only dead bolt or dead lock mechanisms should be used in areas accessible to inmates; snap or dead latch mechanisms should not be permitted in those areas. Padlocks should not be used on doors in lieu of, or in addition to, a security-type lock.

The sally ports at all front and rear entrance doors and gates, control centers, and other high-security locations should be interlocked electrically, or have appropriate procedural safeguards to ensure that both doors are not opened at the same time. Entrance and exit doors to inmate living quarters must conform to the specifications listed in the applicable fire code. Removable core lock cylinders should be phased out and replaced by standard lock cylinders.

Master keying should be permitted only when absolutely necessary, and for a minimum number of doors; ordinarily, these keys are used only on emergency key rings. However, a suitable setting for master keying could be an education department (on doors with no security implications) or a dormitory in which inmates are permitted to carry their own keys. However, institutionwide grand master keying or other systems where a single key can open many doors should not be permitted because of the considerable security risk the presence of master keys represents. The prohibitive cost of re-keying the many doors involved when master keys are compromised or lost offsets any advantage of staff convenience.

Padlocks used by inmates to secure their own belongings should be of a single type sold in the inmate commissary or store. These locks should belong to a master key series so that they can be opened by staff members during routine searches or in other appropriate circumstances. The use of nonstandard locks by inmates should be prohibited. Nonstandard locks and locks that have been plugged or rendered inoperative by a master key should be cut from their hasps and confiscated.

Lockshop Records

Records in the lockshop must be more complete than those at the point of key issue, and must be sufficient to reconstruct not only the facility's entire lock system, but also the history of its lock use, and provide a basis for projected procurement needs.

The lockshop should contain a blueprint of the entire facility, indicating the location and type of all locks in use. This is an invaluable aid in planning facility use. The blueprint is also critical in an emergency, when emergency keys or other contingency plans may need to be modified.

The locksmith should maintain a copy of all purchase orders to aid in preparing future budgets. A keying history should be maintained in a permanent log so that the rationale for the original keying scheme, or previous schemes, is available for review.

Changes in key rings, locations, or locks should be made by the locksmith only, with the authorization of the chief of security, who also should be the only staff member who may authorize nonroutine key duplication. Any changes in inventory, lock deployment, or key use immediately should be accompanied by a notation in the appropriate records.

All key blanks and other critical items should be on perpetual inventory. This means that as items are added or subtracted from stock in the storage area, the inventory record is updated. These systems must be maintained in a way that it is possible for any authorized staff member (not just the locksmith) to check the inventories.

Key records (which lend themselves very well to computerization) should cross-index all keys alphabetically, numerically, and also against key ring numbers. This provides a structured method of controlling and inventorying all key blanks and pattern keys in the institution. These records must show what keys are on each ring, what each key fits, and where each lock in the institution is in use. Keys opening multiple locks must be identifiable so that if one is lost, it immediately will be evident which lock(s) must be changed. This system also provides a safeguard against a key to an entry lock being used anywhere inside the institution. The control center should have a duplicate copy of the alphabetical location listing but which does not indicate the storage cabinet hook numbers.

Record-keeping for each key should be cross-referenced by the following:

- Location, filed alphabetically, indicating which lock the key fits, with perimeter locks and keys identified separately

- Lock make and model, including brand name and manufacturer's number

- Key code number

- Key rings on which the key is included

- Key ring hook number of each ring containing the key

- Emergency key rings containing the key (if any)

- Hook number in the storage cabinet, should be filed numerically and indexed to location; which lock the key fits; lock make and model, including brand name and manufacturer's number; and manufacturer's number for blank key stock.

The control center should have a duplicate copy of the alphabetical location listing which does not indicate the storage cabinet hook numbers.

Cut keys and key blanks should be kept in the storage cabinet with a copy of the current inventory. In addition, the locksmith should maintain inventories for all other storage areas, including those for inactive or space keys. These inventories can be kept by hook or bin number, as appropriate. All key inventories must be perpetual. The actual number of copies and blanks for any given key in the storage area always must agree with the information on its record card. Computerization of these records can be a significant time- and effort-saving step.

A perpetual inventory should be maintained of all locks, keys, and equipment in the lockshop. An internal inventory of the lockshop should be conducted quarterly by a supervisory staff member other than the locksmith, with an inventory report forwarded to the chief of security. In addition, the locksmith should make an inventory of all permanently issued keys. This inventory should be logged quarterly and maintained with all other lockshop records.

Staffing

In most institutions, the "locksmith" is a separate position. Occasionally, he or she also has the responsibilities of the armory officer. However, reliance on the locksmith to perform maintenance or custodial duties is inappropriate in all but very small institutions, and should be permitted only in cases of emergency. Some facilities also employ an assistant or part-time locksmith. In many large, older institutions, maintenance of aging locking systems requires additional staff on a regular basis and justifies more than one position.

In some institutions, the locksmith reports to the maintenance chief. However, while there may be some apparent overlap of skills and duties between this employee and some maintenance personnel, the principal duties of the locksmith relate to institution security, and are closely intertwined with security operations. The locksmith should report to the chief of security.

It also may be advisable to have one or more alternate locksmiths, who either can be detailed for assistance on special projects or major lock renovation jobs, or who are being trained by the regular locksmith. These persons can be evaluated for future career development in this area as they work with the locksmith, and can fill in when sick leave, annual leave, or training takes the regular locksmith away from the institution.

The locksmith is expected to operate with a great deal of independence. However, some lock-related areas require the approval of the chief of security, including approving all significant changes in key and lock use, reviewing key control procedures in other departments, attending department staff meetings to discuss the key control program, and organizing regular training sessions to enhance institutional key control effectiveness.

Other department heads are responsible for implementing key control procedures in cooperation with the chief of security. Each department head should adhere to the principles of sound key control and promote these principles within the department. Each employee, in turn, is responsible for learning and implementing the local procedures for carrying out key control policy.

Prison Gangs*

16

Prison gangs first began attracting national attention during the 1970s and 1980s because of the increasing incidence of gang-related violence in correctional institutions. The influence gangs wield is surprisingly strong, despite the small proportion of gang members in most institution populations.

In the past, research into gang structure suggested they were generally somewhat disorganized. Unfortunately, today, there is ample evidence that gangs are employing higher levels of organization, both in and out of prison. Indeed, a number of street gangs with major prison components are sophisticated and highly organized, with branches in institutions and local communities across the country.

In the correctional setting, gangs have been responsible for problems such as:

- The introduction and distribution of drugs

- Intimidation of weaker inmates, extortion, and strong-arming

- Violence between gangs and among individual members

- Threats and intimidation against staff

- An increase in racial and ethnic tensions, leading to wider disturbances

These problems are most often the result of activities directed by gang members against other inmates in the course of their business transactions, rather than actions taken against the institution or staff.

Several basic facts provide a starting point for the balance of this section:

- The number of inmates involved in a typical prison gang varies widely.

- Typically, gangs use violent tactics to carry out their activities.

- The essential elements of gang member behavior include loyalty to the group, adherence to a code of secrecy, and obedience through fear, intimidation, and threats of violence.

- Membership in gangs most often is based on race or ethnicity; prior association with a group of "homies" also plays a significant role in influencing membership decisions.

- Other factors of strong importance may be shared political or religious beliefs or shared lifestyles.

- Most gangs display a high degree of macho camaraderie.

- Many gang members have little regard for human life, and the legal consequences of violence do not deter them.

- Rule-making within gangs varies, with a significant number of groups dependent on the whims of their leaders.

---

* While the nomenclature "prison" has been employed only rarely throughout these guidelines, this is an area where popular usage requires it. A portion of the original information in this section was abstracted from "Prison Gangs: Their Extent, Nature and Impact on Prisons," a 1985 report prepared for the U.S. Department of Justice by the Criminal Justice Institute, South Salem, New York.

- An individual inmate's membership in a gang often is influenced by past association with current gang members or through general acceptance of current gang values.

Membership in a gang often is perceived as a lifetime commitment. Leaving the gang is an act of betrayal and, in many cases, evokes harsh punishment or death. For some members, gang membership ends when the participating inmate leaves the institution; for others, membership transfers seamlessly from the community to the institution, and back to the community.

Gang leaders often are distinguishable from their followers by their mental abilities, physical prowess, seniority, willingness to commit violent acts, and through the display of charismatic qualities. However, the leader may share authority with, or derive power from, a council or committee, or other senior gang members. In some gangs, leadership tenure is relatively brief. In others, usually those with strong community components, leaders may hold their position for many years. Leadership changes occur either by the assertion of a stronger personality or by central committee choice. Only a few gangs appear to function without permanent leadership.

Gang members derive their status from their ability to control other inmates and activities in the institution. Money, drugs, and personal property are tools to gain power and status, and are used to demonstrate the gang's ability to control and dominate others while providing protection, goods, and services to its members. The nature of financial and service transactions varies widely among gangs. Many gangs seek to assert status in relation to other gangs, some of which may have been their rivals in the community.

The degree to which gangs cause administrative problems varies widely from gang to gang and from institution to institution. Estimates of the portion of serious gang-related management problems have ranged as high as 85 percent.

Although the incidence of gang-related assaults on officers has increased over the years, gang members generally avoid contact with staff, as much as possible. Staff are viewed by participants as hindrances to, but not constraints on, gang-related activities.

Gang membership and behavior dominates the lives of gang participants. While some members participate in institutional activities, the demands of the gang leave them little time for many normal institution programs.

With the exception of necessary contact in the conduct of business transactions, gang members ordinarily avoid association with nonmembers, who nonetheless are viewed as weak and controllable; this reinforces the members' self-image of superiority. However, areas that have seemed the most influenced by gangs in the past include legitimate clubs and selected programs, since they are excellent vehicles for concealing gang activities.

Gang members tend to confront nonmembers more frequently than members of their own or other gangs. Confrontations between members of different gangs can bring severe retribution, but the presence of intergang alliances within institutions seems to prevent some retaliatory incidents.

On the surface, visiting is the institutional activity least affected by gang operations. Actually, gangs work to preserve visiting privileges, because they are a major means of communicating, and conveying money and drugs between the gangs and the street. Communication between gangs and gang members in different institutions, with visitors as intermediaries, is a growing concern. Many, if not most, prison gangs now have counterpart gangs on the street, and some gangs use the institution as a base for criminal activity in the community. One special concern has been the occurrence of murders of retribution outside the institution.

Identifying Gang Members

Until recently, there were few effective methods for identifying ongoing gang activity inside institutions. Many accepted means of systematic intelligence-gathering do not work well when applied to gangs, particularly infiltration by informants. When gangs have their origins in neighborhoods, where members would have known each other for years and are strongly bonded together, it is very hard to penetrate the gang structure. However, in recent years, more attention has been paid to this issue, and the related areas of tracking and controlling gang activities, and considerable progress has occurred.

Methods for developing composite information that can help identify gang members are listed in the box on page 105.

Controlling Gang Activity

Because the nature of individual gangs, institutions, and jurisdictions varies so widely, many different approaches have been taken to controlling gang activity. The most effectivities strategies start with early identification of gang members, using methods noted above. The divergence in approaches comes with regard to the deterrent and control measure

Techniques to Identify Gang Members

- Self-admission

- Visual evidence (including tattoos, clothing, and colors

- Use of hands signals and other signs

- Case histories reflecting past gang membership

- Debriefing of former gang members

- Reports of other agencies

- Possession of gang literature or hit lists

- Association with other gang members

- Correspondence

- Home address

- Photographs

- Visitors

- Informants

that are used. At the macro level, these various strategies include:

- Mainstreaming gang members, with higher levels of supervision and control throughout the system

- Separation of gang members and the isolation of gang leaders, either in separate institutions or separate units within the system

- Movement of gang members to facilities outside the state

- Aggressive prosecution of gang-related crimes

- Institution-wide lockdowns

At the microlevel, there also are things that institution staff can do to control gangs. These include:

- Monitoring the incoming inmate flow for obvious gang signs (such as tattoos, gang pictures in personal property, and gang colors) to identify gang members as soon as possible

- Monitoring housing, visiting, and job assignments to ensure, to the extent possible, that there are no unusual aggregation of gang members in any one area

- Forbidding gang colors and visible gang-affiliation signs

- Monitoring correspondence, phone calls, and visits for general and specific intelligence-gathering

- Quickly segregating gang-affiliated individuals who display disruptive or potentially dangerous conduct

Receiving and discharge staff should be particularly alert to the signs of gang membership as they process and interview incoming inmates. The investigative supervisors should network with other investigative resources to keep abreast of the latest developments in the gang scenario not only in their own state, but nationwide.

To improve overall controls, correctional facilities organized with centralized management systems, or with large, crowded inmate populations, should consider adopting unit management and direct supervision practices that place staff members in closer contact with inmates. Increased staff-inmate interaction and communication can reduce inmate perception of the facility as their own "turf" and can increase the likelihood that gang activity will be observed and curtailed.

Information on both success and failure in controlling gangs should be shared among agencies, to minimize the use of less effective approaches and to spread information on those that are more effective. In recent years, a number of organizations have been developed to aid in the documentation of information about successful screening and tracking systems. Members of these official groups share information on gang participation and operations with other component facilities, other law enforcement organizations, and similar intelligence-gathering groups in other jurisdictions.

Receiving and Discharge (R&D) Operations

17

In most institutions, security personnel are integrally involved in the process of receiving and releasing inmates. Typical receiving and discharge operations include the following functions:

- Identifying committing personnel, and authenticating their authority to commit an inmate

- Identifying and obtaining proper documentation of the legality of the commitment itself

- Searching the inmate and his or her personal property

- Inventorying all property and properly disposing of all items

- Separating inmates into any appropriate categories, through screening or initial interviews to avoid potential problems

Because policy cannot cover every possible situation, receiving and discharging staff must exercise good judgment in their decisions. It is imperative that supervisory staff be kept informed of activities in receiving and discharging.

General

To provide a safe and secure area for intake and release processing, the physical layout of the receiving and discharge area is of utmost importance. The area must be arranged so as to prevent searched and unsearched inmates from coming in contact with each other. New commitments and inmates being released also must be kept separated at all times. There should be an adequate number of holding cells

or areas to provide for this separation. Procedures should provide for the search of all holding cells or areas prior to and after each use.

- Hardware in the cells should be hardened. There should be adequate windows in the door and walls to allow staff to properly supervise inmates in the area.

- A private area for conducting intake (including social and medical) screening must be available.

- An appropriate number of lavatories and toilet facilities must be available in the receiving and discharge area to accommodate the maximum number of inmates that may be processed in the area at any given time. Wash facilities must include an adequate number of sinks supplied with hot and cold water. Hand soap and towels or air blowers must be provided. It is recommended that shower stalls be available for inmate use, when necessary.

- The receiving and discharge area must have sufficient secure space to process, secure, and hold property belonging to inmates on writ, property of incoming inmates, and property deemed discarded or abandoned. There also must be adequate space to store release clothing and clothing for writ/court dress purposes.

- It is strongly recommended that receiving and discharge officers wear a radio and body alarm. It is also suggested that a set of handcuffs and a cuff key be part of the regular issue. (Many staff now carry restraints as a part of their daily equipment, making control of handcuff keys quite difficult. Account-ability is critical for all such items, whether they be in receiving and discharge, a locked housing unit, or other areas of the institution. The locksmith should be responsible for accounting for all handcuff keys–an admit-tedly difficult task.) The keys for the receiving and discharge area should be clas-sified as restricted keys.

- The chief of security should provide addition-al staff coverage, and develop additional security safeguards for operations, in receiv-ing and discharge when large numbers of prisoners are being processed, such as bus or multiple van movements, or when inmates with particularly dangerous records are being processed.

Receiving

Receiving operations are varied, and require the application of considerable skill and experience. Only the most qualified officers should be assigned to this post.

- Many law enforcement officials enter receiv-ing and discharge. It is critical that they are properly identified prior to entering and exit-ing the institution. Credentials, badges and

Intake operations include proper identification of all inmates being committed or released.

any advance authorizing paperwork should be inspected closely. Special attention shall be given to ensuring that all weapons and ammunition are properly secured prior to entry into the facility.

- The name of the delivering officer should appear on the commitment documentation and must coincide with the officer's personal identification. All commitment documenta-tion must be reviewed carefully to prevent early or late releases, delivery of inmates to the wrong facility, or identity mix-ups among prisoners.

- Positive identification of each inmate is criti-cal. In addition to the verification of an inmate's identity upon entry into the institu-tion, it again should be verified when the inmate is removed from the holding area for intake processing. The identification process should include verbal questioning of the inmate as to name, date of birth, offense, and register number (if one has been assigned), and a comparison made against existing pho-tograph, fingerprints, and physical descrip-tion data, when available.

Receiving and discharge staff must be familiar with the criteria for receiving inmates at their facility. Voluntary surrender inmates or inmates delivered for commitment without a designation, or who do not meet the medical or security criteria of the facility, must be reviewed closely. The final decision to accept or refuse a commitment shall be made by the warden.

It is the committing officer's responsibility to complete a receipt prior to receiving and discharge staff accepting the prisoner. By signing that receipt, the receiving official accepts full custody of the inmate. The committing officer should retain the orig-inal receipt with the original signature of the receiving authority. The receiving and discharge staff retains a legible copy. All receipts should document a mini-mum of:

- Name of the inmate

- Register number of the inmate

- Date of transfer

- Time of transfer

- Name and authority of the officer relinquish-ing custody of the inmate

- Name, agency and signature of person accepting custody of the inmate

Inmates and all their accompanying personal property are to be thoroughly searched before movement inside the secure area of the institution. Inmates shall be pat searched before entry into the institution and a handheld metal detector shall be used as soon as restraints are removed.

Inmates shall be escorted to receiving and discharge by institution staff, if possible, using a route that does not allow visual or verbal contact with general population inmates. Ordinarily, all entrances to receiving and discharge should be secured during the intake process, and inmate orderlies or workers should not be present in receiving and discharge during the intake process.

After a thorough strip search has been performed, if possible, new arrivals should be allowed to take a shower before intake clothing is issued. Staff should have an adequate supply of clothing and shoes appropriate for the season and climate for new commitments. A variety of sizes must be maintained in receiving and discharging to ensure proper fit, and odd-sized clothing should be available for unusually sized inmates, if not in receiving and discharge, then elsewhere in the institution. Inmates who have been searched should not be allowed to come in contact with those who have yet to be searched. Cross-circulation patterns in the receiving area must be avoided.

Receiving and discharge staff are responsible for the timely processing of inmate property, both in giving allowable items to the inmate and for the mailing of unauthorized items. Special care must be given to detect any contraband that may be hidden in personal property. Clothing that is not considered usable, jewelry, lighters, watches, and other items of small monetary value that are contraband should be destroyed in accordance with local procedures.

Inmates may retain legal material if it relates to ongoing litigation or is research material not available at the institution.

Married inmates may be permitted to retain a wedding ring, provided it is a plain ring and contains no stones. Local regulations may permit religious medals, medallions, pendants, and so forth, to be worn in an appropriate manner as long as the item cannot be used as a weapon or in a manner that would disrupt the security or orderly operation of the institution.

Articles identified as valuables must be sealed in an envelope with the inmate's name and register number clearly marked on the outside, and stored in a locked, fire-retardant vault, safe, or cabinet. Other property such as Social Security cards, driver's license, legal documents, and so forth, may be stored within the same package to eliminate storing property in two areas. Clothing should be stored in a secure room inaccessible to inmates and unauthorized personnel.

A file should be maintained in a separate location to hold the original copy of the personal property record. Inmates should be present during the inventory and search of their property. This function may be conducted in the absence of the inmate when the inmate's presence would jeopardize safety and security of the facility, or if the inmate is absent from the institution. The following procedures apply when searching inmate property.

(1) Staff shall ensure that the inmate does not have access to the property until it has been thoroughly searched and inventoried on the personal property form. The inmate should not assist in the inventorying, packing, or unpacking of property. The receiving and discharging area shall be arranged so a desk, table, or counter separates the inmate from the property to be searched.

(2) Searched items must be kept separated from unsearched items. Staff shall separate items according to appropriate disposition (in other words, kept, stored or mailed). Inmates must elect whether unauthorized items are to be mailed home or destroyed.

(3) All clothing must be thoroughly inspected. Special attention must be given to pockets, seams, hat bills, hat bands, collars, waistbands, linings, cuffs, belts, and places where there is more than one layer of material.

(4) All commissary items must be thoroughly searched. Coffee, sugar, laundry soap, or other granular substances that have been opened may be poured into another container for inspection prior to returning them to the inmate in the original container or the container used for the inspection. Shampoo, body oil, and similar items must be searched with a probe, pencil, or metal detector, or scanned if such equipment is available.

(5) Special care shall be used when inspecting any religious items, such as medicine bags, bibles, religious headgear, and so forth. The chaplain may be consulted to determine if articles are of religious significance. Local regulations should specify allowable religious articles.

(6) Shoes shall be searched thoroughly, looking particularly for hollowed-out heels or cavities. The soles of shoes must also be inspected, as flat items such as hacksaw blades often are hidden in this area. Scanning equipment is recommended strongly for inspecting shoes and other hard-to-inspect items.

Normally, tennis shoes from the community and shoes with air pockets or pumps should not be authorized, as they provide a particularly convenient hiding place for contraband.

(7) Staff must inspect books thoroughly. Books should be opened and the pages searched. Special care must be given to inspecting the binding and covers as they are excellent hiding places for drugs and other contraband.

(8) All electronic devices authorized for possession should be searched very carefully; the use of epoxy or distinctive paint on screws and other fasteners, after the search, will allow staff searching the item in the future to determine if tampering has occurred.

(9) Pictures, picture frames, photographs, and photograph albums require special attention as they frequently are used to conceal contraband.

(10) Questionable items that cannot be thoroughly searched should be x-rayed, if possible. Items that cannot be searched without destruction or alteration shall not be permitted in the institution.

(11) Staff are to ensure that all shipping containers/boxes, wrapping materials, and so forth, are treated as "hot trash" (high risk) and not given to the inmate.

Inmates should not be assigned clerical duties in receiving and discharge. Packaging and inventorying personal property, taking fingerprints, filing forms, taking photographs, and so forth must be done by staff only. Inmates may be used in receiving and discharge for janitorial duties or tailoring, if no other resources are available, but only under direct staff supervision at all times. They may not be in the area while other inmate(s) and property are being processed.

Other Processing Issues

Receiving and discharge staff serve a critical role as they are often the first point of staff contact for new inmates. Offenders often are committed while under the influence of, or may be withdrawing from, the effects of drugs or alcohol. They may be psychologically unstable or angry and upset over their current situation. Therefore, it is important that staff be attentive and alert at all times. Receiving and discharge staff must exhibit a professional and caring approach while performing their duties. It is extremely important for receiving and discharge staff to detect any unusual or volatile behavior and report it immediately to appropriate institution staff.

In addition to the physical processing of the inmate and personal property, receiving and discharge staff also often are involved with intake screening interviews, observing behavior of inmates, and advising them of rules and regulations. To avoid processing delays, any other staff involved in intake processing should be notified promptly when new admissions are received. The staff member responsible for processing the new admissions should ensure the medical department clears each inmate, and that he or she receives a social interview. If an inmate exhibits unusual or aggressive behavior, receiving and discharge staff shall contact medical or mental health personnel, or the shift supervisor.

All new inmates are to receive a copy of the institution's rules and regulations and sign a receipt indicating that they received this information. Staff who witness the inmate's completion of the form also must sign the form. If the inmate refuses to sign, the witnessing staff shall so indicate in the space provided.

Staff should prepare an admission folder consisting of all relevant documentation. This folder should

Source: Corrections Corporation of America

Staff interviews are an important source of information during the admission and orientation process.

Source: Corrections Today

Modern technology–in this case, computerized fingerprint mapping–can be a real asset in modern institutions.

include fingerprint cards, social and medical intake screening forms, inmate commissary account card, Admission and Orientation (A&O) handbook materials, and forms documenting the fact that the inmate has been advised of the rules of the institution.

Photographs of inmates must be of a quality that provides an easily recognized likeness, and must include the inmate's register number and date of commitment. The number of photographs to be taken will vary depending upon the institution's needs. Digital photography systems are available that greatly can streamline the use of photographs for other purposes.

It is imperative that legible fingerprints on all inmates are promptly submitted to the Federal Bureau of Investigation (FBI). Consequently, fingerprints shall be taken at the time of commitment, with appropriate identification data entered on the fingerprint cards.

Staff may encounter situations due to permanent or temporary physical characteristics which call for different fingerprinting techniques. The use of special inking devices similar to those used to fingerprint deceased inmates may be necessary to obtain clear, legible fingerprints from bent or crippled fingers.

Releases

The following procedures should be in place for processing all releases from the institution:

- Receiving and discharge staff must review release paperwork to ensure all forms necessary for release are present. Any forms requiring the inmate's signature should be executed and the appropriate distribution made.

- Institutional departments may request notification of an inmate's release; this ordinarily is done the business day prior to release. Local procedures specifying departments and method of notification should be established. Coordination is critical between receiving and discharge staff and the records office staff.

- Inmates may bring their personal property to receiving and discharge for inventory and pack-out the day before the scheduled release.

- On the date of release, ample time should be allowed to complete the required release steps, including: search, form completion, provision of dress-out clothing, arrangement for necessary medication, receipt of release funds, receipt of property, and final clearance. Staff must ensure that all processing is completed prior to the inmate's scheduled departure time.

- Staff must ensure that all inmates are properly identified prior to release, using fingerprint and photo comparison, and by verbal questioning of the inmate as to name, date of birth, offense, and register number. It is critical that at the time of release, a thumbprint be taken of the releasee, and that print must be compared by the releasing staff member with the thumbprint on file, to verify the identity of the inmate.

- Before actual release, receiving and discharge staff should conduct a visual search of the inmate. Clothing worn to receiving and discharging should be taken from the inmate, who should be dressed in appropriate clothing

111

for the type of release. Once processed and searched, the inmate must be placed in a secure area separated from unsearched inmates while awaiting departure. Most systems allow inmates to have court or release clothing mailed to the institution.

- When escort and medical trips are processed through receiving and discharge, the inmate should be dressed in institution clothing and shoes. Local procedures should be developed to handle furlough releases.

- Inmates may require medication to be taken with them on either temporary or permanent release. This is a decision made by medical staff. However, receiving and discharge staff must ensure that the releasing individual has been provided any authorized medications prior to leaving the institution.

- Before actually releasing the inmate, an identification verification should be conducted by a second employee, who also will sign the release authorization form.

- In the case of institution transfers, receiving and discharge staff should provide information regarding the inmate's criminal and medical history, as well as institutional behavior to transporting officials. This information is critical in maintaining custody and control of the inmate en route to the new destination.

- Law enforcement officials may arrive at an institution to pick up an inmate, and already have other prisoners in their custody. If permitted by local procedures, law enforcement officials may bring these prisoners into the institution to provide for their comfort and security while conducting transactions within the institution. Staff should provide an area for the prisoners' comfort and allow for supervision of the prisoners, as necessary. Inmates allowed temporarily into the facility under these circumstances must undergo the same search as regular commitments, prior to entry into the facility.

Staff must exercise extreme caution when processing inmates for transfer to other law enforcement agencies. A thorough visual search shall be conducted by receiving and discharge staff on the inmate and all clothing and property prior to relinquishing custody of the inmate. Receiving and discharge staff shall run a handheld metal detector over the inmate's body prior to departure. Special procedures may be implemented for maximum security and other inmates having special security needs. The chief of security should be consulted in these cases, as additional staff may be necessary.

It is recommended that the receiving law enforcement officials also conduct their own search prior to accepting the inmate(s) for departure. An area should be provided for the receiving officials to personally search the inmate. If the inmate is to be ready for departure immediately upon the transporting official's arrival, receiving and discharge staff shall conduct the search, dress out the inmate and place him or her in a holding cell or room which previously has been searched. These procedures do not relieve the transporting officers of any search and security responsibilities their own agency may prescribe. Staff shall escort the transporting officials and the departing inmate(s) to the institution entrance to ensure that contact is not made with other inmates prior to departure.

Searches

18

One of the basic requirements for maintaining control in an institution is imposing close controls on the introduction, fabrication, storage, transportation, and use of contraband. Consequently, searches of inmates, their personal property, the physical plant of the institution, vehicles, visitors, and occasionally staff, for contraband are an integral part of institutional security. Effective searches cannot be done only by remote surveillance or simple cursory inspections, but rather must be done by the personal action of trained, professional staff.

Searches should emphasize the following:

- Detection and prevention of the manufacture of weapons, escape paraphernalia, and other impermissible items

- Discovery and suppression of contraband traffic among staff and inmates

- Recovery of stolen or lost items

- Discovery of waste or destruction of government property

- Discovery of hazardous areas or circumstances that otherwise might remain undetected in other inspection programs

Institution policies should describe the types of items considered contraband and should contain general instructions on how to search particular areas. These policies should indicate specific locations, traffic points, and categories of individuals to be searched.

Contraband

In most jurisdictions, contraband is defined as any item in the following categories:

- Any weapon, gun, firearm, unauthorized tool, drug, intoxicant, explosive, corrosive, flammable, or other item not issued by, or under the direct supervision of, a staff member using prescribed procedures

- Cash, currency, or items of value not permitted within the institution

- Items not issued through approved channels or not approved by the appropriate staff member

- Items not approved for purchase in the institution commissary or approved only for special purchase, such as a sweat suit or other such items which cannot be stocked by the institution due to inventory considerations.

- Items not approved for mail delivery to the inmate or not approved for a visitor to introduce

- Items otherwise approved but altered from their original approved condition

- Unauthorized items passed from one inmate to another

- Items reasonably believed to be usable to assist in or effect an escape

- Personal items or valuables whose ownership cannot be determined

- Excessive amounts of any authorized item

- Any other article specifically prohibited by statute, policy, or regulation. This final category can take unusual directions. For instance, inmates in one institution were found to have taken hot peppers grown in a horticultural vocational training program and were planning to use them as a disabling substance, since the base material in the peppers is the same as that used in OC chemical agents. The disposition of contraband is a companion concern.

Institution policy should cover the following areas:

- Disposition of inmate personal property; typically, the inmate is given the options of sending it home, destroying it, or donating it to the agency

- Accounting for and storing in a secure area all items—particularly weapons, drugs, money, or anything of inherent value—and the preservation of the chain of evidence for any items likely to be used in prosecution or litigation

- Handling of contraband received in the mail, including returning the item to the sender, if it is not otherwise illegal

- Issuance of a receipt to the inmate or other person from whom the contraband was confiscated

- Disposition of any agency property located among the contraband items

- Assurance that all appeals have been properly exhausted before any property is disposed of or destroyed

- Provision of proper legal opinion regarding any items that are the property of noninmates

- Disposal schedule to prevent accumulation of contraband for which there is no retention value

- Adequate records about witnesses to property disposition

- Method of reconciling items disposed of with inventory records

- Assurance that disposition methods are of no personal benefit to any staff member

Inmate Searches

Search practices must be founded on a well-written, current body of policy that gives sufficient guidance for day-to-day operations, while leaving staff enough flexibility to make necessary adjustments for individual situations. Separate policies should be written for searches of inmates, visitors, and areas, in recognition of the differing procedures and limitations for each.

As a general caution for all searches, staff need to be highly aware of the possibility of being cut or harmed by deliberate inmate action or accident during searches. Whether a needle and syringe in a pocket, a razor blade concealed under a locker shelf, or by some other method, proper precautions should be taken to avoid such incidents in conducting all searches.

Inmate searches should be frequent, unannounced, and conducted in a professional, dignified manner, and if possible, in a private location. Staff of the same sex as the inmate should conduct searches whenever practical, but in cases where assault, escape, or loss of contraband is imminent, any staff member may search an inmate.

Inmate searches fall into four categories and each will be discussed:

- Frisk or pat searches

- Strip or visual searches

- Cavity searches

- Remote instrument searches

Pat Search

A frisk, or pat, search involves a manual search by staff of a fully clothed inmate. A metal detector also may be used to conduct this search, in addition to the staff member running his or her hands over the inmate's clothing. This search can be conducted on either a routine or random basis in any part of the institution. While privacy is advantageous and under certain circumstances even desirable for pat searches, they may be conducted in any location of the institution.

The general guidelines for conducting a frisk or pat search are as follows:

(1) Inform the inmate that he or she is to be searched.

(2) Have the inmate empty all pockets and remove any coats, hats, or other outer clothing items.

(3) Be careful at this early stage to ensure that the inmate does not throw away any item that may contain contraband.

(4) No item should be returned to the inmate until it has been thoroughly searched and the search of the inmate is complete.

(5) To begin the actual search, have the inmate face away from the searching officer and spread the arms horizontally to the side and the legs approximately shoulder width. This stance reduces the inmate's ability to assault the officer conducting the search. In cases necessitating somewhat improved controls in the interest of staff safety, the inmate may be required to place hands against a wall or other surface and move feet back from the surface.

(6) From the back, with the inmate's arms and feet spread, start at the inmate's head and neck and move hands across the shoulders and down the arms, thoroughly passing over every part of the arms, including into the armpits.

(7) Moving back to the torso, pass the hands over the back, the entire chest, and the abdominal region, with attention to the waist, waistband, and belt, as well as to collars, cuffs, seams, and linings of all clothes.

(8) Next, move down the outside and inside of each leg, including the crotch.

(9) Inspect shoes, soles, linings, insoles, and heels, as time and circumstances allow.

Source: Corrections Corporation of America

Thorough searches of offenders is one of the keys to suppressing contraband in an institution.

(10) Follow essentially the same procedures for female inmates, with particular attention to items that may be concealed in the brassiere.

Strip or Visual Search

A strip or visual search requires moving the inmate to a suitably private area where he or she is to remove all clothing and submit to a visual inspection of the body, including the outer portions of all orifices and cavities. Many institutions have installed privacy booths in areas where strip searches are regularly performed. These also can help eliminate cross-circulation of searched and unsearched inmates. Most jurisdictions permit these more thorough searches if there is any reasonable belief that an inmate may be conveying contraband. Because of inmates' increased sensitivity to these more personal types of body searches, the utmost in professionalism should be displayed during this and successively more intrusive searches.

Categories of inmates that may be strip, or visually, searched to ensure adequate security are the following:

- Newly committed inmates

- All inmate transfers from other facilities

- All inmates after visits

- All inmates returning from court or other appearances outside the institution

- Inmates suspected of attempting to introduce or transport contraband

- Inmates admitted to or discharged from detention or segregation units

- Inmates who participated in a disturbance or escape attempt

- Inmates returning from outside work assignments

The general guidelines for conducting a strip or visual search are as follows:

(1) Inform the inmate that he or she is to be searched.

(2) Instruct the inmate to remove all clothing, including hat, scarf, headband, false teeth, and wig.

(3) Conduct a thorough search of the clothing, including shoes, for contraband.

(4) Examine all bandages and casts, using a handheld metal detector, if available.

(5) Instruct the inmate, once unclothed, to face the officer and spread arms and legs for visual search.

(6) Have the inmate run his or her hands through the hair vigorously to dislodge hidden items. Alternatively, the staff member may do this using disposable plastic gloves.

(7) Have the inmate open his or her mouth and remove any dentures or bridgework. Use a flashlight to inspect the inside of the mouth, including under the tongue.

(8) Check the inmate's nose and ears, again using a flashlight if necessary.

(9) Have male inmates raise the scrotal sac and peel back the foreskin, if present. Have female inmates lift breasts to ensure nothing is hidden underneath.

(10) Have the inmate bend over and spread the buttocks for a visual inspection of the anal area for any protruding objects or signs of contraband. Have females also spread the vaginal opening for the same purpose.

(11) Have the inmate spread all fingers and display both open hands at the same time, turning them over for inspection of top and bottom.

(12) Finally, have the inmate raise each foot and wiggle the toes, turning the foot up for an inspection of the sole of the foot.

(13) Have the inmate dress after all clothing is inspected.

Cavity Search

A cavity search includes the manual or instrument inspection of oral, anal, or vaginal cavities by medical staff to detect the presence of contraband. Because of the sensitive and potentially embarrassing nature of this search technique, it must be done in privacy, with dignity and professionalism on the employee's part. A visual search should be conducted prior to the cavity search. However, because of the intrusive and potentially harmful effects of a cavity search, the following additional conditions need to be in place:

(1) The agency should have a clear written policy explaining the legal grounds and specific procedures for conducting a cavity search.

(2) This search should be authorized in advance, in writing, by the warden.

(3) Whenever possible, the written consent of the inmate should be secured before attempting a cavity search.

(4) Cavity searches only should be conducted by the medical staff or outside medical consultant; employees may not conduct a cavity search if it is likely to cause injury to the inmate.

(5) Cavity searches should be restricted to digital intrusions and the use of instruments such as anoscope, otoscope, vaginal speculum, nasal speculum, tongue blade, and simple forceps.

(6) If an item is located, it may be removed if the removal is easily effected by means of one of the simple instruments noted above, or digitally.

(7) Strict documentation should be maintained of the probable cause for the search, inmate consent (if given), authorizing official, witnesses, and findings of the inspection.

As a related measure, the institution also should have procedures in place for the use of "dry cells" to confine inmates who may have ingested contraband with the intent of passing it out of their system at a later time. Supervision and search requirements for the use of such cells should be known to all supervisory personnel and line staff who are involved in placing and supervising inmates in this status.

Instrument Search

An instrument search involves the use by medical personnel of x-ray, sonogram, fluoroscopic equipment, or surgical examination to detect contraband. A qualified medical person is required to conduct a remote instrument search, which ordinarily should not be performed without approval of the warden. This type of examination ordinarily should be used only for medical reasons and only with the consent of the inmate. The agency should develop carefully researched guidelines for institutional staff to use in implementing policy in this area. Justifications for this examination include the presence of a foreign object that may perforate an internal organ or ingestion of contraband substances in balloons that, if not removed, may rupture and cause the death of the inmate.

Documentation must be compiled on the probable cause justifying the search, the inmate's consent (if given), the authorizing official, any witnesses, and the findings of the inspection or surgical procedure.

Searches of Other Persons

Inmate Visitors

An official notice concerning contraband and searches should be posted in English and Spanish at all entrances. Inmate visitors should be subjected to a careful search of their persons, packages, purses, and other items before entering the secure portion of the facility.

If necessary, to ensure that no contraband is being introduced, and if provided for by department policy, a pat search may be required to gain entry. The traffic flow in the entry area should ensure that a visitor awaiting search procedures cannot pass contraband to a visitor already processed, and cannot hide contraband for later removal by an inmate.

A walk-through metal detector supplemented by a handheld transfrisker are two pieces of virtually indispensable equipment for processing visitors. Anyone who activates the walk-through unit must be thoroughly searched by the transfrisker.

A blacklight procedure should be used for all nonstaff (inmates as well as official visitors) entering the facility. For this procedure, the institution should maintain a supply of several different hand stamps with varying patterns. These stamps are used in conjunction with an ultraviolet reflecting ink and pad to stamp the back of each entering visitor's hand. When a visitor exits the visiting area, and before he or she leaves the secure portion of the facility, an ultraviolet or blacklight is used to examine his or her hand to authenticate the person's status as a visitor. By varying the stamp daily, the possibility of a duplicate being obtained and used in an escape attempt is reduced.

If a staff member suspects that a prospective visitor is under the influence of any substance, that employee has the authority to deny the visit. Appropriate supervisory review and procedural safeguards may be included in local policy as well as in the entrance and visiting room post orders.

Official Visitors

Each agency should establish a uniform policy for the search of official visitors, including other law enforcement and correctional personnel, probation officers, judges, lawyers, and members of the legislature. These procedures should specify which individuals will be searched, as well as any other limitations or requirements for processing them into the facility.

Vendors, Repairpersons, Volunteers, and Contract Employees

While agency policy varies regarding searches of individuals in these categories, in general, all of these individuals should be required to pass inspection by metal-detection equipment, and to leave any unnecessary packages or other items outside the secure portion of the institution. For the most part, vendors and repair personnel should be under direct staff escort at all times. All tools and repair equipment should be inventoried and searched before being allowed into the institution.

In the case of volunteers and contract employees, purses and similar personal items may be allowable, depending on the degree of background investigation and staff supervision provided. In higher-security facilities, a greater measure of restriction will apply to these individuals.

Staff Searches

In most correctional facilities, staff are not searched on a regular basis before entering the institution, because that approach to contraband suppression generally is ineffective, and serves only to demoralize employees by conveying the impression that they and their fellow employees cannot be trusted. While the deterrent value of these procedures is arguable, the adverse morale factor is clear. Since most jurisdictions permit searches of anyone (including staff members) with probable cause–and in view of the fact that most cases against staff are developed from either inmate or outside informants–regular staff searches are not recommended except when evidence exists that the employee probably is involved in the traffic of contraband or other illegal activity.

Search Location

Inmate searches can and should take place at any time and in any location in the institution. While most searches should be unpredictable, certain locations in a correctional facility offer prime opportunities for fixed-search programs. Standard fixed-search locations are receiving and discharge areas, all gates to the institution, entrances to housing and segregation units, entries to industrial and maintenance shop areas, the visiting room entrance, and other key traffic points.

Cells

Searching cells is a time-consuming operation, so it is important to proceed systematically. The following is a procedure for searching a cell for contraband and indications of an escape attempt:

(1) Staff should search cells the same way each time until it becomes automatic; this will promote efficiency and thoroughness.

(2) Remove the inmate from the cell, strip search and escort him or her to another secure area. When the search is complete, strip search the inmate again before he or she returns to the cell.

(3) Before entering the cell, secure the cell door in the open position to avoid being accidentally locked in the cell.

(4) Before searching the cell, look at the items that are about to searched. See if anything is out of the ordinary. If so, examine that item carefully.

(5) Start the search with the bed and use it as a workbench when finished searching it. Remove the mattress and other bedding and examine above and below the bunk and in any crevices between the bunk frame and the wall. Look under the bed and check for items suspended from springs or fastened to the bedframe. With the mattress removed, examine the upper side of the bedframe and springs. Examine the bedframe supports to ensure that they have not been partially sawed through for easy removal.

(6) Examine the mattress and pillows by rolling them lengthwise and widthwise. Check the sides and ends for cuts or tears in their covering. Any indication of re-sewed seams calls for a more careful examination, including opening the seams for extensive probing. A transfrisker is very effective in finding metallic contraband in these items.

(7) Examine the remaining bedding. Pay special attention to any seams or double thickness of the cloth.

(8) Search the locker next, one shelf at a time, and return all items to their original positions. Examine all surfaces of the locker. Contraband may be taped to the underside of shelves or concealed in shelf ledges, supports, legs, or false sides or backs of the shelves. Also, examine any paper used to line shelves.

(9) Check all clothing (including dirty laundry) piece by piece. Pay special attention to seams, double thickness of material, and pockets.

(10) Open and check individually every item (letters, books, magazines, toilet articles, and so forth).

(11) Examine coat hangers; certain types of plastic hangers are excellent places to conceal contraband.

(12) Check all footgear, including linings, soles, and heels; feel inside shoes all the way to the toe and remove the inner soles and any removable arch supports.

(13) Shake talcum powder containers and squeeze toothpaste tubes. Remove a small portion of the contents of commonplace items to check for illegal substitutions. Check to see that cakes of soap have not been hollowed out.

(14) Look in, under, and behind the wash basin and in the drain, overflow, and gooseneck water seal (if accessible). Contraband may be suspended in the pipes or hollows on wires or threads, or stuck on with glue or tape.

(15) Examine the toilet carefully, inside and out. Because inmates are aware of the officer's reluctance to examine these fixtures, they are favorite hiding places. Check under the base of the toilet, behind the toilet where it connects to wall, and the toilet drain. Contraband also may be passed through the gooseneck of the toilet into the sewer pipe and be suspended by wire or string, the other end of which is tied to a small block wedged in the water seal.

(16) Examine the toilet paper holder and all rolls of toilet paper to make certain that currency or other contraband is not rolled up within the roll.

(17) If there are electrical outlets or other similar access panels in the room, remove them and inspect the cavities.

(18) Examine any brooms or mops for items concealed in broom straws or mop heads.

(19) If there is a radio, examine it carefully. Remove the back, check the battery well, and examine the electric cord.

(20) Carefully remove any pictures from frames and examine the frame and the backing material. Remove all wall coverings; remember, even steel walls may be cut, with the cuts concealed behind calendars and pictures.

(21) Carefully scrutinize the walls, ceiling, and floor for indications of sawing, digging, cutting, defacing, or other possible signs of an escape attempt.

(22) Look for indications that mortar has been removed and replaced with a substitute. If the concrete is of poor quality, it is easy for the inmate to gouge out holes as hiding places for contraband.

(23) Check heat or ventilation duct openings for indications of tampering or concealed contraband. Look for strings, thread, or wire holding something suspended in the duct.

(24) Look around interior and exterior window frames and the outside window ledge. If ledges have a covering of any sort, be sure that nothing is concealed beneath them.

(25) Examine window bars for evidence of tampering. Be alert for any wires, strings, or thread fastened to the bars and suspended outside the window.

(26) Carefully examine the cell door or grille, and the wall in which it is set. Pay particular attention to the areas above eye level. Examine the bars and cell door locking device for signs of tampering, and check the area with the door in both the open and closed positions.

Once an inmate's belongings have been searched, they should be put back where they were found. Not only is it good security (let the inmate wonder about what exactly was searched), but it should foster some goodwill and avoid unnecessary hostility on the part of inmates. Inmates usually accept searches as a necessary part of facility operations and accept a properly conducted search without resentment. What an inmate will resent is unnecessary damage to a cell and its contents during the search. Officers must remember that inmates appreciate courtesy and consideration, but resent inconsiderate treatment of their belongings. Clothing, letters, photographs, and commissary purchases are important to inmates, even though the items often have little monetary value.

Preservation of evidence and chain of custody is of paramount importance. All contraband removed from the cell should be documented carefully in the following manner: day, date, and approximate time of discovery; exact location in the cell where each item was found; name and register number of the inmate(s) or occupant(s) of the cell; and a precise description of each item found. If money is recovered, list it by denomination and serial number. Handle all evidence as little as possible to preserve fingerprints.

Nonhousing Areas

The following information should serve as a guide for developing a general search plan for other portions of a correctional institution:

- Common-access areas of the institution (including housing units, shops, and program areas) should be inspected at least weekly on a schedule established by the chief of security.

- When performed by security staff, inspections in other areas of the institution ideally should be conducted in the company of the department head or manager of that section. This facilitates access to otherwise secured areas and assists in advising the staff conducting the search on questionable items.

- Staff immediately must isolate and report any security hazards discovered such as weapons, tools, home brew, or escape paraphernalia.

- Visiting areas (including trash, furniture, shakedown areas, and toilets) should be thoroughly searched before and after visits.

- The perimeter should be searched for items hidden next to or under fences.

- Yard areas should be inspected carefully. Use a metal detector to locate buried weapons and other contraband. Yards adjacent to roadways should be inspected for items thrown over the fences.

- All institutional buildings and crawl spaces should be checked for evidence of tunnels. Also check desks, file cabinets, and shelving particularly in areas that are not under frequent staff supervision.

- The vicinity of all visitor traffic points should be searched regularly to discover items hidden or thrown by visitors that are intended for inmates. Visitor holding areas and gates should be scrutinized carefully.

- The ductwork and plenums (air chambers) that carry air to and from the building and into individual rooms, should be searched on

119

a regular basis, not only for breaches in security, but for signs that they are being used as places of concealment for contraband.

- Tunnels, utility corridors, and plumbing chases should be searched, since they are poorly supervised areas where inmates, if they can gain unauthorized access, can fabricate and conceal unauthorized items, or use the area in an escape attempt.

- Areas outside the secure perimeter should be searched for contraband to help stem the flow of contraband into the institution.

- Inside and outside receiving areas (docks, ramps, and so forth) should be searched regularly, as they are likely places to conceal contraband or escape paraphernalia.

- Shops, vocational training, and industrial areas have a wide range of possible contraband hiding places and should be searched regularly; vents, block and brick walls, workbenches, machinery, bins, toolboxes, covered openings, elevator shafts, outbuildings, lockers, and staff-only areas also should be searched.

Mail Room Operations

Fluoroscopic examinations should be conducted on all packages (for both staff and inmates) coming into the mail room, to locate contraband that otherwise might go undetected, or that might require dismantling or destruction to otherwise search thoroughly. All incoming correspondence and packages also should be manually inspected for contraband before being given to inmates.

There should be no inmate workers in the mail room. An inmate's presence in this area constitutes a security risk, not only because of staff inattentiveness, but also because of the likelihood that sooner or later employees will become overly familiar with the inmate and begin to rely on him or her to do other tasks.

Incoming inmate packages should not be opened in the inmate's presence unless there is a barrier or screen between the inmate and the staff member opening the package. Under the wrong conditions, an inmate could seize contraband in a package and run out of the area before staff could intervene. Corrugated boxes and other packing material from all packages for both staff and inmates should be secured in the mail room until they can be disposed of outside the institution.

If the institution permits inmates to receive electronic equipment or other major items from the outside (televisions, radios, musical instruments), an internal inspection should be carried out by someone familiar with the nature of that item, to ensure no damage inadvertently is done to the item as it is inspected. For electronic devices, staff should then epoxy or paint all screws, to allow easier detection of tampering or use of the device to hide contraband.

A shadowboard and inventory should be provided here, as in any other area of the institution, to assist in accounting for handheld metal detectors and other tools used by staff.

Vehicle Searches

Incoming

Supply traffic is necessary to the life of an institution, but it also provides a prime avenue for introducing contraband. Vehicle searches, including searches of official vehicles, must be thorough and consistent if they are to deter and detect dangerous items. This section should be read in connection with Chapter 12 on entrance procedures.

Mobile equipment such as trailers, towmotors, mowers, and other vehicles provide unlikely locations for contraband at first glance. However, staff must be conscious of the possibility that they can be used as mobile contraband depositories, and any vehicle regularly entering the institution should be searched for hidden compartments and contraband.

Of particular concern would be any commercial semi-trailer truck traffic. Long-haul truckers commonly carry weapons of various types, and they may not be anxious to declare and surrender them. Also, the elaborate nature of many modern over-the-road tractor-trailers makes them very hard to thoroughly search in a reasonable amount of time. In most instances, if a commercial trailer must go inside, it is better to use an institution tractor or other method of conveying the load inside, rather than permit the commercial tractor inside.

Normal search procedures at the gate should include removal and storage of all hazardous items while the vehicle is outside the perimeter. These would include firearms and ammunition, of course, but other items, such as flammables, also should remain outside. Searches should include all compartments, visible frame members and components, the undercarriage itself (using a mirror, inspection pit, or other method) as well as the cargo area and cargo. No

Source: Corrections Corporation of America

Careful vehicle searches are an important part of entrance operations.

vehicle should be passed in or out of the institution without a thorough search of all of these areas. Finally, escort of all vehicles coming into the compound will reduce the likelihood that any remaining contraband concealed on board is conveyed to inmates.

Outgoing

Vehicles leaving the institution should be searched as well. The search procedure should start with the driver dismounting from the vehicle after it reaches the vicinity of the gate, and standing away from it so that staff can see that he or she is not under duress. Then, a complete search, using the same techniques as employed on the incoming search, should be conducted. Particular attention should be directed toward the possibility of false compartments and other areas where an inmate could be hidden.

Equipment and Supplies

Shakedown crews and other staff members conducting searches should be equipped with the following items:

- Suitable walk-through metal detection units for fixed search points

- Metal detectors (transfrisker and portable ground type)

- Flashlights

- Mirrors and extensions

- Jumpsuits or overalls

- Plastic or rubber gloves

- A secure storage area for all contraband items

- A supply of ziplock and other plastic bags for securing contraband pending disposition or for use in preserving items as evidence

Recordkeeping

Documentation of searches enables staff to reconstruct patterns of contraband fabrication, storage, and movement, and provides a ready means of ensuring that no particular area is either ignored or oversearched. Local procedures should clearly outline the reporting systems that are necessary to support the search program, and include the following features:

- Description of reporting requirements for each search category

- Description of all searches in housing units, including documentation of date, time, cell

121

number, person inspecting, remarks, inmate's name and number, and contraband found

- Distribution method for all required standard forms

- Requirements for supervisory review of all recordkeeping systems

- Description of a follow-up recordkeeping system for disposition of confiscated items

Supervision and Monitoring

The chief of security has overall responsibility for assigning search duties to staff on the roster, assigning any centralized shakedown or search crews to specific areas or tasks, and coordinating searches by individual staff. He or she also is responsible for all recordkeeping systems related to searches and the accounting, storage, and disposition of contraband. The chief of security may delegate operational responsibility for portions of the program to other supervisory staff in the security department, including: the investigative supervisor, for evidence-type contraband; the locksmith or armorer, for broken files, blades, and other tool or weapon-type items; and the shift supervisor, for day-to-day recordkeeping functions.

Other department heads with specific search-related responsibilities, such as unit managers, industries superintendents, or shop supervisors, may be called upon to provide staff for regular searches in their own area or in other areas in time of institutional emergency.

First-line supervisors, in particular, continually must be active in reviewing line staff search activity to be sure that the proper techniques are used, that searches are properly distributed throughout the area in question, and that accountability and corrective action for items discovered are complete and in accord with policy. By showing an active interest in this vital program, they will convey to their subordinates the importance of search duties on the overall security and safety in the institution.

Drug/Alcohol Testing

The use of contraband drugs is an unfortunate fact in modern institutional life, and test-based surveillance programs are an effective means of detecting this usage. While efforts to suppress the flow of contraband into an institution are the first line against substance abuse use while in custody, almost certainly in most institutions some drugs will find their way in, and some institution-made alcoholic beverages will be made. Except for the most tightly controlled institutions where noncontact visits are the norm and staff are very diligent about searches for home brew, drug and alcohol testing are necessary tools. And even in those locations, testing can be useful to deter inmates and to prove the effectiveness of the preventive measures staff take.

Consequently, each institution should have programs of urine and alcohol testing that monitor specific groups or individual inmates who are considered high risk for substance abuse. These should include testing of:

- All inmates involved in community activities or who have any community contact

- Randomly selected members of the entire population, each month

- Known drug users, suspected drug users, and inmates who have tested positive in prior tests

- Saturation tests, where an entire work detail or housing unit, for instance, is tested as a deterrent and detection tool

Since the cost of a full-fledged test program may be high at first, staff may wish to consider testing at first only high-risk groups, such as known users and those in contact with the community, and as more resources become available, add other categories.

If funds are available, emerging technology makes other drug detection methods available. Units now on the market allow staff to obtain a sample of dust from a ventilator, for instance, and detect whether drugs have been stored there. The same method can be used to determine if drugs have been on any surface in a cell, or even on an inmate's clothing. These can be useful adjuncts to other available testing means.

The following procedural elements should be a part of every urine test program:

- Only institution staff may supervise urine collection, and record, mail, and process samples and results.

- The sample should be collected in private.

- Staff of the same sex as the inmate tested shall supervise directly and continuously the giving of the urine sample.

- Procedures should be in place to ensure the chain of custody on all samples throughout the test process.

- Staff should be issued latex gloves to wear while handling all samples.

- Appropriate procedures should be in place to ensure the inmate's name is not associated with the sample itself; a coded number should be the only identifier that is on the sample that goes to the test laboratory.

- If an inmate is unwilling to provide a urine sample within a specified period of time, staff shall prepare an incident report.

- The agency should develop specifications regarding the laboratory to be used for the analysis, the types of drugs to be tested for, and the procedures to be used for retesting inmates.

Alcohol testing can be done at the local level, using portable test equipment maintained in the shift supervisor's office. An inmate may be required to provide a breath sample for this purpose whenever a staff member has a reason to believe the inmate may have been consuming alcoholic beverages, or whenever the inmate has been in contact with members of the community. Refusal to submit a breath sample should be grounds for an incident report and the basis for a presumption that the inmate actually has consumed alcohol.

A summary of the results of all substance tests should be reported to the central office. In this way, administrators can identify early indicators of security system failure and "hot spots" in certain portions of the inmate population.

Canine Operations

The use of canine units in institutions for a variety of purposes is accepted practice, when appropriate controls are in place. This portion of the guidelines will provide information on the general organization of canine units, and specifics on their use in searches. Later sections will cover their use in escapes and tactical operations.

A specific staff member should be identified as being responsible for the operation of the canine unit, including:

- Developing and implementing training for assigned staff and canines

- Developing programs for the care and maintenance of canines and kennels

- Preparing all required reports

- Developing and managing the unit's budget

- Selecting, or having input into the selection of, unit personnel

- Being familiar with facility designs, with emphasis on knowledge of entrances and exits

In addition to any other assigned duties, officers assigned to the canine unit will be trained to handle dogs, including, but not limited to the following situations:

- Tracking

- Controlling the crowd

- Detecting narcotics

- Searching cadavers

- Detecting weapons

- Detecting explosives

- Searching for articles

Canine dogs may be trained in tracking, detecting, and controlling of crowds. Training will be on an ongoing process, to include, but not be limited to obstacle courses, daily exercise and daily routines/drills. Canine unit staff will familiarize all other institutional staff with canine operations in initial and refresher training.

All incidents involving the use of force by a canine unit shall be reported and investigated in the same manner as other use-of-force incidents. All injuries suffered by staff or inmates during an encounter with a canine dog, will receive prompt medical attention, or attention as soon as practical. A medical report shall be submitted to the warden.

Canine units may be used to seek out and locate contraband, under strict supervision by qualified handlers. The detection dogs may be used in all areas where contraband is suspected, as well as periodically in any area, as a preventative measure. This may include:

- Search of vehicles entering agency property

- Search of visitors, staff and inmates entering or on agency property

- Search of articles entering institutional property

- Detection canines also may be used for any special institution events, either at entrances or at the completion of the events, when detection canines may search the area

Controlled substances to be used in detection training must be acquired from local, state, or federal law enforcement agencies by completing "U.S. Official Order Forms" supplied by the Drug Enforcement

Agency (DEA). In the event that controlled substances are unavailable from a law enforcement agency, they may be secured from any licensed pharmaceutical firm. No contraband substances obtained from inmate searches may be used.

The canine unit supervisor should be responsible for the controlled substances used for canine training purposes. These items are to be maintained on an inventory, in a separate locked container, in the institution armory. The key to this container will be a restricted key. The inventory and a scale shall be maintained within the container. The substance shall be weighed anytime it is removed and weighed each time it is returned. The weight, time, date, and signature shall be recorded in the inventory.

The canine supervisor and a shift supervisor jointly will verify the inventory, at least monthly. After the odor/aroma of the controlled substances has decreased to the point that its value for training purposes is lost, it shall be disposed of in the manner prescribed by the DEA and its disposal logged in the inventory.

Training

As with many other aspects of institutional operations, every newly hired employee does not have the correctional skills necessary to conduct thorough searches. These skills are best instilled through hands-on training using model cells, actual searches of other persons, and demonstrations of actual contraband concealment techniques. Also, new staff are not initially attuned to the sophisticated concealment techniques used by inmates, nor do they have a clear picture of the ways that seemingly innocuous items can be used for unauthorized purposes. That knowledge also must be instilled through initial and ongoing training.

Training sessions should have a major section that includes an opportunity for staff to perform actual searches in both controlled and real situations. In concert with the live aspect of this training, other sessions should inform staff of the latest techniques used by inmates to conceal and fabricate contraband. As inmates develop new methods for this purpose, the staff needs to be updated on them.

Security Inspections

19

Security inspections are an integral and absolutely essential part of the custodial operation in a correctional facility. Without actual hands-on inspection, there is no way to ensure the complete integrity of the devices and physical features that comprise the physical security of an institution. Security inspections are separate from all other search systems, and should be documented separately.

Scope of the Program

The institution must have a specific policy that describes the security inspection system in detail. Local policy can be patterned on an agencywide policy, but it must be custom-tailored to meet the needs of the facility in which it is applied. The policy should identify the responsible staff members at each level of the program. It should break the institution into manageable inspection zones and specify the staff responsible for coverage in those zones. It also must describe accurately the reporting system that supports the actual inspections. Copies of forms used in such a system (both monthly and daily) are included in Appendix D.

Each zone identified for the system should have the following characteristics:

- The zones generally should be in one area or in adjoining areas reasonably related to each other. Exceptions can be made for roving posts that logically cover scattered areas of the institution, but to the degree possible, each zone should be relatively self-contained.

- The zones should be of a reasonable size not so large as to overburden a staff member nor encourage shortcutting.

- The zones should be reasonably related to the duties of the post to which they are assigned. Whenever possible, employees should be assigned to inspect their own workplace and its immediate environs as opposed to other departments. Convenience and familiarity with the area result in better inspections.

Policy should establish clearly the timing of the inspections for each zone, because different zones, and components of some zones, may require different inspection intervals. For instance, the fence line and certain features of special housing units may require inspections on every shift. In less secure portions of the facility, a daily inspection may be sufficient. For lower security institutions or areas of lower concern, a weekly inspection is sufficient. Supporting forms should specify these intervals.

Local policy should state the method for inspecting various parts of the institution, and should state which areas and security features will be inspected visually, which will be tapped, and which will be probed or checked by other means. These inspection methods include the following:

- **Visual inspection:** Look for bent bars, irregular surfaces, broken or cracked fittings or parts, loose mortar fillers such as putty or papier-mache, uneven wear or use patterns, fresh paint, and other signs of tampering or damage. Any irregularities in color, texture, shape, or appearance warrants closer inspection. Wall coverings should be suspect as potential hiding places.

- **Tapping**: Vigorous hammer strokes set up sound waves that assist in distinguishing between solid and otherwise damaged or tampered bars, sashes, and other solid metallic security fixtures. Leather, plastic, or wooden mallets should be used for this purpose. Any inconsistency in sound produced from bar to bar in a set of adjacent bars warrants closer inspection.

- **Probing with instruments**: Putty knives and other metallic probes are used to inspect the edges and corners of surfaces that otherwise might escape notice. Particular attention should be paid to locating loose mortar, cracks or cuts in metal surfaces, and other irregularities that indicate a security breach.

Written procedures should prescribe the techniques for inspecting each type of security feature. For example, policy should specify that all bars will be tapped with a certain type of mallet and struck with a force sufficient to generate a solid sound indicating that the bar has not been cut, sawed, or otherwise tampered. Similar and more elaborate descriptions of the inspection techniques should be included in the written procedures available to staff for reference.

The items to be inspected should, at a minimum, include:

- Locks and lockboxes

- All security fittings such as screws, bolts, hinges, bars, window mullions, and sashes

- Doors, screens, grilles, braces, brackets, windows and frames, fences, walls, ceilings, and floors

- Drains, manhole covers, air chambers, tunnels, and key mortar joints

- All exits, gates, and internal cutoff fences

- All perimeter wire and detection and surveillance systems

Source: Corrections Corporation of America

Security inspection systems should include regular, close-up inspection of all fence systems.

- All electrical junction and transformer equipment servicing perimeter lighting and detection systems, as well as the perimeter fence or wall itself

- Staff also should be alert to other security, safety, or procedural problems, such as fire hazards, accumulation of excess property, or hidden contraband

As portions of the institution are assigned different purposes or as actual physical plant changes take place, the procedures that support the security inspection system must be reviewed and revised. Post orders and other supporting documents must be written to include the inspection system, and they must be revised when changes are made in the overall system.

Equipment and Supplies

Appropriate search equipment readily should be available to staff conducting the inspections. The following items should be available for use during inspections:

- A bar-tapping mallet, made of wood, plastic, leather, or other material of local preference

- Mirrors on extendible handles or poles, to inspect out-of-the-way locations such as the underside of beds, insides of ventilator openings, and other less-accessible portions of the institution

- Metal probes and shims, to detect tampered bars, screens, and other security fixtures and to re-inspect bars that may have sounded irregular when tapped

- In some locations, or for inspections of selected areas, overalls, jumpsuits, or other protective clothing items may be provided to search staff

When not in use, these tools should be secured in an area inaccessible to inmates. When in use, they should be under staff control and in no case should an inmate be issued this equipment to perform any inspections.

Recordkeeping and Follow-up

Every effective security inspection system must have appropriate inspection forms, follow-up forms on necessary repairs, and memo reports on serious breaches that are discovered. The basic security inspection form should contain, at a minimum: the name of the zone, the inspecting staff member's name, the various component areas of the assigned zone, and the results of the inspection of each component. It is insufficient to sign off for the entire zone; the inspecting staff member must certify to the complete inspection of each specific area noted on the form.

Any staff member discovering a critical breach of security during an inspection must notify specified officials at once. Noncritical discrepancies can be handled through routine channels. Critical breaches ordinarily require more complete investigation. In those cases, procedures should state the responsibility of the involved staff member requiring them to supply any additional information or memoranda to complete the investigative effort.

At the end of their shift, all assigned staff members must turn in the forms to a predetermined area such as the control center, the shift supervisor's office, or the chief of security's office. In all cases, these forms must be reviewed promptly for compliance and any noted discrepancies should be followed up immediately.

The chief of security must bring to the appropriate department head's attention any persistent unrepaired breaches.

Staff

In designing the inspection system, the chief of security should consult with other department heads and select the staff to conduct the inspections. Any replacements or relief coverage should come from within the affected department. The chief of security's office should maintain a list of staff assignments for security inspections. Any inspection form not turned in on schedule should be reported to the responsible department head for prompt action.

The support of all department heads is critical to the program's success. The department heads must emphasize to staff during in-house training and other supervisory contacts the importance of compliance with the system. When the chief of security reports a problem to a department head, prompt resolution should be given a high priority.

Ordinarily, employees should conduct inspections in their own areas. A well-designed inspection system will include not only correctional officers, but also the job supervisors and other employees who are responsible for specific areas of the facility. It is reasonable to expect that staff members in a given area, the maintenance shops, for example, will conduct the inspections in that area. They are in those areas daily and should be required to conduct contraband searches. Even though security staff may conduct periodic searches of these areas also, the importance of this principle cannot be overstated; security is everyone's business.

Just as is the case with other searches, staff cannot perform security inspections effectively without training. New employees require training in professional techniques; more experienced staff require a regular program of refresher training. These sessions should cover not only the mechanics of searches, but also new contraband production or escape technologies devised by inmates. Staff who are aware of new, more ingenious means of breaching security are better prepared to detect them.

Special Housing and Management Units

20

Maintaining full control of inmates, and protecting those who cannot or will not function properly in the general population, requires having the resources to separate those offenders from the rest of the population. Special housing units of various types fill that role. This chapter will discuss the general conditions of confinement for disciplinary detention, administrative segregation, protection-type units, and special management units.

Witness protection programs are not discussed in detail in this publication, but are referenced, where appropriate.

A typical institution should have between 10-15 percent of its housing capacity capable of being used for special housing status. This provides staff the flexibility they need to safely and securely manage the institution; few institutions are designed with too many cells in this category.

Types of Special Housing

Although many operational procedures for special housing are similar, these statuses are different in their purpose and implementation.

Disciplinary Detention

Disciplinary detention is a single-cell status of confinement that involves punitive separation from the general population. Placement in disciplinary detention only may be ordered after a finding of a serious rule violation in an impartial hearing, and when there is no adequate alternative means to control the inmate's behavior.

With certain safeguards, an inmate who is seriously disruptive, threatens life or property, or cannot otherwise be controlled in administrative segregation and who cannot be transferred safely to the institution hospital may be moved temporarily to disciplinary detention. Ordinarily placement in this status is for a relatively brief period of time, during which the inmate has very limited access to programs.

To be placed in this status, the inmate must be afforded a due process hearing before an impartial hearing officer or body. The inmate must be given advance notice of the charges, be provided the opportunity to appear in person, be provided with a staff representative if he or she wishes one, have the opportunity to present evidence and call reasonably available witnesses, and be advised of the decision and the reasons for it.

Administrative Segregation

Administrative segregation is a nonpunitive confinement used to house inmates whose continued presence in the general population may pose a serious threat to life, property, self, staff, or other inmates, or to the security or orderly running of the institution. Inmates in this category are pending investigation for a trial on a criminal act or are pending transfer. This placement may be for relatively extensive periods of time and certain programs are provided. To be placed in this status, the inmate must be provided with notice of the reason for placement in special housing, with a sufficient degree of specificity so that a reasonable person would understand those reasons.

Protective Custody

Protective custody is a status of confinement for inmates requesting or requiring protection from the general population, because their safety and well-being may be jeopardized. This is not a punitive status.

Although they must be separated from the general population (sometimes for long periods of time), inmates in this status should be allowed to participate in as many as possible of the programs afforded the general population, providing such participation does not threaten institutional security. Protective custody voluntary placements may be provided with notice, but involuntary placement cases must be provided with the same type of notice as for administrative segregation.

Special Management

Special management is a status of confinement equivalent to long-term administrative detention that is used when short-term controls cannot safely and securely control specific high-risk offenders. Ordinarily, an inmate in this status presents a severe danger to others, a severe escape risk, or other unusual management factors, which require a higher level of control. Most agencies provide a full due process hearing before placement in this type of unit. This hearing in most cases is very much like that for a disciplinary detention placement.

Design Issues

Special housing units have different needs than the rest of the institution needs that should be taken into account during the institution's design stage. Special housing units must be totally secure from both internal escape and external intrusion and allow the efficient movement of personnel and materials, while containing the inmate population and denying unauthorized access to the unit. To the extent possible, new facilities, as well as existing institutions and units that are adapted for special housing use, should incorporate the design elements noted below.

Special Housing Needs

- The nature of the unit and the need for separation dictate that housing within these units should consist of individual cells that are arranged to permit good visual supervision by a minimal number of staff. Ideally, cells should be grouped to allow the clustering of similarly classified inmates and should accommodate, with some flexibility, groups of individuals requiring separation within the unit.

- A secure control center is a desirable feature in such units. It is a must in all new facility designs. Also, many systems include a secure escape route or "safe harbor" area for staff in the event of an inmate takeover of the unit.

- Movement should be controlled by using a sally port and a control center; the control center function for special management units may be a part of the institutional control center function.

- All special housing units must be well ventilated, adequately lit, and appropriately heated. Each unit must meet applicable fire and safety requirements. A battery backup lighting system should be available in the unit for the control center, as well as for all stairwells, corridors, and key office areas. If the unit has a separate unit control center, all of its electronic systems should be fully operational under power outage conditions.

- At the end of a range (row) of cells, appropriately situated range grilles and cutoff doors should prevent inmates from leaving the area immediately in front of the cells, and should be included in the design, to increase compartmentalization and staff safety. Handcuff ports should be cut in all unit gates and doors, so that restraints can be removed without unnecessarily risking staff safety.

- A centrally monitored smoke detection system should be installed in the unit, to meet life safety codes and to provide for staff and inmate safety. A smoke detection system will enable the prompt response to a fire and minimize injury to inmates and staff, as well as damage to the physical plant. This system should be monitored remotely in the control center, and also should have an audible alarm to notify those in the unit of an emergency.

- Cells should be equipped with beds that are securely fastened to the floor or wall. They should employ fortified lights and other fixtures, including seats and desks.

- Agencies have found the use of prefabricated cells, with beds, shelves, and plumbing already cast in place, to be a cost-effective strategy for new construction. With such an approach, it also may be possible to incorporate a design that includes rounding off the

Source: CRSS

Special housing units include cells that are appropriately secure.

corners of beds, desks, and other cell furnishings, so as to reduce the potential for injuries to staff and inmates when tactical action is required in the close confines of a cell.

- To reduce the possibility of damage by high-security inmates, and for long-term cost savings, all special housing unit toilet fixtures should be security-type fixtures.

- In new design, consideration should be given to installing a shower stall in each cell, to increase safety and eliminate staff time involved in moving inmates to a separate shower area.

- Ideally, strip cells should not be a part of a special housing unit; they should be in the medical area, and be operated under the supervision and control of health personnel.

- The total number of inmates within one unit will depend on staffing patterns, population pressures, and resources, but, in general, it should not exceed 150 inmates.

- Space should be provided within the unit for recreation activities, if possible, and whether inside recreation space is available or not, outside recreation should be available to each inmate. To accommodate inmate separation and staff time in managing exercise periods, new designs should provide as many exercise spaces as possible within the limits of the project.

- Outside yards should be located immediately adjacent to the unit, and multiple yards should be constructed with appropriate razor ribbon on all fences. The fence configuration should avoid a long, narrow configuration, which lends itself to unprofessional "dog run" or "pen" nicknames. The yard fences themselves should be anchored, and brackets spot welded to prevent their removal and use as weapons. Overhead fencing or expanded metal covers, or razor wire on the fences around the perimeter of the yards, will prevent inmates in them from moving from yard to yard, or from escaping altogether. In addition, it will deter inmates from the compound from coming over a fence and attacking inmates in special housing status while exercising.

A security vestibule should be installed at the entrance to each recreation yard, to protect inmates in restraints, who can be vulnerable to attack by other inmates in the yard who already have been uncuffed.

A vestibule will allow safe removal of the handcuffs before the inmates actually are admitted into the recreation area.

Weight bars can be used as weapons or battering rams, and no weight equipment should be installed in any exercise area. Other recreational equipment may be provided, such as basketballs or a fixed chin-up or dip bar.

Unit dayrooms, if available, can be used to expand recreation opportunities when single-inmate recreation requirements complicate the task of finding enough time and areas to provide all required recreation. In high-security settings, dayrooms should be designed to serve a discrete group of inmates such as one range or pod with a minimum of travel distance.

It may be beneficial in some units to consider installing laundry equipment in the unit itself, to reduce the flow of contraband into the unit.

Provision should be made to accommodate sick call and routine medical services within the unit, which will minimize inmate movement through, and exposure to, the general population. More extensive medical treatment should be provided in the hospital of the main institution, of course.

Offices should be located in the unit, and designed so that staff have the opportunity to visually monitor inmate movement and activities but still have the privacy necessary for confidential discussions.

Space also should be provided to accommodate the storage of staff equipment, inmate property, and the physical processing activities when inmates enter or leave the unit. This space should be located so as to expedite the flow of inmates to and from the unit, and this function is particularly critical when inmates are moved regularly to and from the courts.

Appropriate breathing equipment should be available to staff in special housing units, to include both standard and voice-enhanced gas masks that enable staff to function if any significant amount of any chemical agent is deployed. These items should be stored in a secure location, but one with easy accessibility. There also should be at least two wall-mounted self-contained breathing packs in the unit in case of fire. Staff should be trained in the use of this equipment at least annually.

Staff in these units (and other posts in the more remote areas of the institution, as well) must have personal body alarms as a means of alerting supervisory personnel in the event of an emergency. Not only is staff safety greatly improved, but quick intervention facilitated by body alarms can prevent a small disturbance or assault from building to unmanageable proportions before responding staff can arrive.

A shadowboard for handcuffs, restraint chains, and leg irons should be installed in the unit, to facilitate easy issue of, and accountability for, these items.

Operational Issues

The following operational features should characterize special housing operations of all types.

Procedural safeguards should be in place to ensure that the keys to range grilles and other critical unit doors never enter the area in front of the cells, and, to the extent possible, never come in contact with inmates. The keys to the unit should be removed from the unit during the later portion of the evening watch and most of the morning watch, as an additional safeguard when staffing levels in the unit are low; they can be maintained on another nearby post, or carried by a compound patrol officer, who can respond quickly if there is a need to obtain the keys for an emergency.

Ideally, only one inmate should be confined in each cell or room; it is inconsistent (in principle) with the mission of such a unit to house inmates in multiple occupant cells. This is, admittedly, a statement of the ideal situation in today's crowded institutions. However, when high-security cases are double-bunked, opportunities can be created for pressure, assault, sexual activity, and other negative behavior. Potential liability problems certainly are increased when known predators are housed with other inmates. Moreover, when inmates are housed two to a cell, and one is handcuffed for removal, the cellmate is given an excellent opportunity to assault the restrained inmate before staff can intervene. Finally, when two inmates are in a cell, and staff have to use force to move one or both of them, they are faced with a dramatically more difficult problem than when only one is involved. Having said all that, many systems successfully manage special housing unit programs with multiple-occupant cells, albeit with careful screening and supervision.

After being thoroughly searched, all inmates admitted should be dressed in institution clothing, without a belt, and furnished a mattress and bedding. Cloth or paper slippers may be substituted for shoes, if desired. Inmates should not be segregated without clothing, mattresses, blankets, or pillows, except when prescribed by the medical officer for medical or psychiatric reasons.

Personal property items must be strictly controlled to prevent their use for high-risk activity. Anything presenting a potential danger for escape or assaults must be kept out of the unit.

Excessive personal property should be impounded while the inmate is in the unit. The more property available, the more places to conceal contraband, and the more difficult it is for staff to properly search a cell. Inmates in long-term special housing units may be permitted some personal property commensurate with that permitted in the general population.

Smoking materials should be limited, if not prohibited. Some facilities have installed electrical cigarette lighters so that matches are not needed, thus reducing the risk of arson or bomb-making.

All unit and inmate records should be maintained in a secure location and access to them restricted to authorized staff.

As undesirable as it may be, in units where there is a mixture of several statuses of inmates–administrative segregation, disciplinary detention, and protective custody, for instance–inmates from one category must never be permitted to have contact with those of other categories. Protected cases, in particular, would likely be subjected to threats, taunts, and other types of intimidation, but such a practice increases the actual physical risk to the inmates, and to the staff who work in the unit.

Inmates who are so seriously disturbed that they are likely to destroy clothing or bedding or to create a disturbance that would be seriously detrimental to others are a special case. The medical department should be notified of them immediately, and a program of treatment and control should be instituted with medical officer's concurrence. In some instances, agency policy calls for the use of "four-point" restraints for specific periods of time for this type of inmate. Each such situation should be managed in accord with procedures that are strictly reviewed by medical and mental health staff, as well as those in the operational chain of command.

Each special housing unit should have an organized, scheduled program for maintaining sanitation and hygiene, including arrangement of items in the cell, proper bed making, general unit sanitation, and so forth. Sanitation should be a high priority. Just because it is a high security area, there is no reason that a special housing unit cannot be kept neat and clean.

Unit inmates should be able to maintain an acceptable level of personal hygiene, and toilet tissue, soap, toothbrushes, and other personal care items should be provided; often, a retrievable kit of toilet articles is issued. Laundry and barbering services should be provided on the same schedule as for the general population. Each inmate should have the opportunity to shave and shower at least three times each week, unless these procedures present an undue safety or security hazard.

Inmates should be secured alone in shower stalls, for their own safety, as well as that of other inmates and staff. Unit procedures should include the use of lockable shower enclosures with handcuff ports in the grilles. Ideally, these doors should be equipped with electric, selective locking devices, but manual locks certainly are adequate. By handcuffing inmates before opening the doors, a great many forced moves can be eliminated, and the safety of staff will be improved during the moves to and from showers.

Except in special cases, no more than two inmates should be out of a cell at a time in a special housing unit; this will reduce the risk to staff if a problem occurs. Again, this is an ideal; the realities of day-to-day operations often require more than two inmates recreating together, after proper screening and with appropriate supervision.

When out of their cells, each inmate should be escorted by a minimum of two officers, and should be in handcuffs. Local practice will dictate whether the cuffs are applied in front or in back, and whether leg irons are needed for some cases.

Ordinarily (and again ideally), recreation in special housing units should be on an individual basis. If specially screened, small groups may be approved to recreate together. The most preferable number would be a maximum of two, although that is a difficult goal to attain. The type of inmate confined in this unit presents a clear risk to staff and other inmates, and in many cases, single recreation still will be necessary, to provide appropriate separation for predatory or extremely violent individuals. In addition to protecting other inmates, and reducing the possibility of conveying contraband, single recreation status generally results in fewer problems for staff, as it is easier to control or subdue one inmate than two or more.

Unless safety or security dictates otherwise, inmates in special housing units should exercise outside their cells a minimum of one hour per day, five days per week.

The fences in the recreation yards should be searched and inspected regularly for tampering, including before and after each recreation period.

In some large units, it may be beneficial to establish a separate recreation staff position, to meet all applicable recreation requirements.

While inmates are recreating, staff should take that opportunity to search their cells.

Inmates moving to and from the yards should be counted and searched thoroughly. This search should include the use of a walk-through metal detector in and out of the yard, and a thorough search of the clothing the inmate is wearing. This is a prime area

for escape, and nothing to aid in escape should go out to the yard, nor should materials from the yard go back into the unit for unauthorized use there.

A satellite law library should be maintained in each special housing unit, containing basic legal materials, and supplemented, as necessary, with items from the main institution law library. Short-term units may have all legal materials delivered from the main institution law library. A properly secured typewriter can be made available in the room and used for legal work; access should be on a sign-up basis, with priority for those with imminent court deadlines. Because a satellite law library of this type is a natural place for inmates to exchange notes and contraband, each such area should be searched before and after each time an inmate uses it.

Legal correspondence and contacts with attorneys should be permitted.

Reading material may be provided on a circulating basis or on request from the institution library.

Each special housing unit inmate should be seen daily by a member of the medical staff, and the individual log sheet of each inmate should be so noted.

Each unit should have a urine testing program for detecting unauthorized drug use. At a minimum, this program should test a random sample of the unit population each month.

Special housing unit inmates should be permitted social correspondence privileges unless there are compelling reasons to the contrary. Inmates in disciplinary status may be subject to some restrictions. Only unit staff should receive, inspect, and deliver incoming and outgoing mail for special housing unit inmates.

Social visitors should be notified of any necessary restriction to ordinary visiting procedures, to spare them disappointment and unnecessary inconvenience. If ample time for correspondence exists, the burden of notification may be placed on the inmate.

Phone calls may be available to inmates in special housing units on a restricted basis. Calls from inmates in disciplinary segregation status should be restricted to those specifically related to legal matters that cannot be handled through correspondence.

While commissary should be restricted (as to quantity and type of items) for disciplinary detention cases, those privileges may be afforded all other special housing unit inmates, consistent with those available to general population inmates. Staff also may limit the type of packaging materials allowed in the unit, and should enforce additional inspection requirements, to prevent the flow of contraband into the unit.

Packages delivered to special housing units should be subject to special handling and inspection procedures, to prevent the entry of contraband. Boxes and other packing materials are prime avenues for introducing contraband and should be disposed of as "hot trash."

A picture file should be maintained on each inmate in the unit, to identify those who may be particularly disruptive to the orderly running of the unit or dangerous to staff or other inmates. Procedures and design features (close supervisory review of recreation groups, appropriate door and gate controls, and other operational details) should ensure that inmates who are known to be hostile toward each other are never allowed to come into contact.

Nonpermanent, part-time, contract, consultant, and volunteer personnel should be permitted access to special housing units only upon the warden's approval. They should be directly supervised at all times.

There should be a written plan for evacuation of the unit in the event of an emergency. Inmates should receive instructions regarding evacuation procedures as a part of the admissions procedure.

Videotaping of incidents in the unit is a valuable management tool. Whenever staff are aware that a forced cell move is going to be necessary or that some other problem is about to occur, a videotape should be made of the event. This provides an excellent means of documentation for disproving future allegations of staff brutality, and often vividly shows the degree of resistance with which staff have to contend from recalcitrant inmates. In many cases, it prevents violent resistance, especially if the inmates know that the tape will be available to use against them in disciplinary or prosecution proceedings. It also provides an extra level of motivation for staff to remain professional in their actions.

A regular psychological review schedule should be in place for all special housing unit inmates; ideally, a permanently assigned staff position would be valuable for intake screening, periodic reviews, crisis intervention, mental health referrals, and other purposes.

While inmates requiring psychotropic medication ordinarily should not be confined in a special housing unit, those drugs and other "hot" prescription or controlled medications, in no instance, should be stored on the unit. That practice presents a tremendous potential for abuse, overdose, theft, extortion, or resale. Instead, individual doses should be brought to the unit for each inmate, and staff should insure by personal observation that the inmate takes each dose. The administration of that medication should be logged, so that a complete medical record is maintained on each inmate being so treated. A psychiatrist carefully should monitor all inmates receiving psychotropic medications, to modify dosages and types of medication, as necessary.

Staff should encourage long-term special housing unit inmates to participate in programs, and a staff member from the education department may be designated to work with the inmates in the unit. However, because of the need to control these inmates more closely, correspondence courses are the most appropriate avenue for these programs, rather than a classroom setting. While not all inmates will use such programs, they should be made available, both as constructive methods of occupying time, as well as for the inherent benefits of education, should they elect to participate. Nonetheless, operational or staffing compromises never should be made for program reasons.

The security roster should include rotation of staff assignments to special housing units, to prevent staff from becoming overly familiar with long-term offenders in the unit, and perhaps letting down their guard, accommodating inmates, or otherwise compromising security. Rotation after six months is recommended for line staff, with one-year tours of duty for others.

In addition to maintaining a complete inventory of all tools kept in the unit and those coming in with work crews, tools should be under direct staff supervision at all times. The loss of any tools in a unit such as this is a grave risk. Every possible precaution should be taken to prevent this from happening.

Inmate workers from the general population should be admitted rarely. Their presence significantly increases the potential for contraband introduction, as well as other management problems. Any general population inmates entering and leaving the unit should be searched carefully and closely maintained under direct staff supervision at all times.

The use of inmate clerks and barbers, particularly, presents a risk in a high-security setting. No inmate clerks should be used. This precludes access to unauthorized information and prevents staff from becoming accustomed to an inmate with high-supervision requirements being in a position that allows freedom of movement. Inmate barbers can be in a prime position to move contraband and information about the unit, and that function should be performed under very close supervision. Porters or orderlies should be limited in their movement in the unit, and the number of inmates permitted out for cleanup work at any given time should be strictly controlled.

Classification

Some form of classification or stratification can assist greatly in the day-to-day operation of a special housing unit, allowing program and security decisions to be made on a rational basis.

- In a *disciplinary detention* setting, it may be very simple, involving very little differentiation of privileges. Most inmates are in this status for a relatively short period of time, and most privileges already have been withdrawn for that time.

- In *administrative segregation*, some stratification may be possible, depending on whether an inmate is in transit, awaiting a disciplinary hearing, or awaiting some initial screening or classification decision.

- *Protective custody* inmates conceivably could be from all different classifications; the degree of separation and program activity provided largely will be linked to the available staff and the physical limitations of the unit itself.

- *Special management* cases most often are subject to very rigid controls, with inmates starting out with a completely individualized program   one that allows no contact with other inmates and contact with staff only when in restraints. Most such units (but not all) have a program of graduated housing and privileges, depending on the inmate's conduct over time. Eventual release is to an institution; it is rare that an inmate is released to the community from this type of setting.

Supervisory Oversight

Special housing unit operations should be monitored on a regular basis. Prior comments about supervisory visibility are particularly important to recount here; top officials personally should observe and evaluate confinement conditions and discuss individual problems with the inmates.

Managerial and professional visits should be logged, and conducted in accordance with the following schedule:

- Shift supervisor–once each shift

- Health care official–daily

- Caseworker or social worker–daily

- Counselor–daily

- Religious representative–weekly (employees only, not volunteers or nonstaff)

- Chief of security–not less than weekly

- Deputy warden (custody)–weekly

- Warden–weekly

- Psychologist or psychiatrist–as requested by staff or inmate. This individual should interview each inmate confined for more than thirty days and prepare an evaluation report with recommendations.

Case Review and Records

Once an inmate is in special housing status, some management group (the classification team, unit team, or disciplinary committee) should review his or her status at least every seven days for the first two months, and every thirty days, thereafter. A psychologist should make a thirty-day evaluation to ensure the inmate's mental health status is acceptable. The inmate should be offered the opportunity to attend these review meetings.

The review committee should provide the inmate with a written decision stating the basis for its decision, as well as a summary of the information presented to and considered by the committee. If the review committee determines the inmate should remain in the unit, the inmate should be able to appeal that decision to the warden.

Each review should include an evaluation of the following information regarding the inmate:

- Reason for placement

- Disciplinary record

- Past criminal record

- Conduct record in other institutions

- Mental health status

- Involvement in criminal activity while in custody

- Attitude toward authority

- Institutional record on work assignments

- Adjustment to institution programs

- Willingness and ability to live with other inmates

- Record of violent reactions to stressful situations

- Habitual conduct or language that may provoke or instigate stressful, perhaps violent, situations

Because of the sensitivity of the types of cases, permanent logs should be maintained by the senior officer on duty in the unit. These records should include the following:

- A record of all admissions and releases including date of action, time of action, reason for admisson or release, and authorizing official or committee

- A record of visitors, including all official visits by staff members, and the time, date, and signature of the visitor

- Notations of unusual behavior by individual inmates or the unit as a whole

- Information from and observations by staff members which should be forwarded for staff action and observation to future shifts

Individual records completed (and initialed by the employee performing the action) on each shift for each inmate should contain a record of all activities required by policy, such as showers, exercise, administration of medication, law library access, education and religious visits, and other activities. The record of medical visits should include the initials of the medical staff member conducting the visit. Comments on unusual occurrences or behavior also should be entered in the record. This type of information provides invaluable documentation when questions arise regarding policy compliance, or if litigation should result from any of the allegations made by inmates regarding unit operations. The individual record sheet should be forwarded to the inmate's central file upon release from the unit. A copy of such a form is included in Appendix D.

All official visitors on the unit should sign a bound ledger maintained at the entrance, to document their presence. Supervisory and management staff, in particular, should be logged. These visits will help insure that high standards are maintained, and provide management support for the staff who are working this difficult assignment.

Releases

Release from most special housing units may be authorized by the following officials or groups:

- The committee or person authorizing the inmate's placement in the unit

- The disciplinary committee

- The classification committee

- The inmate's unit management team

Local policy should specify which level of authority may release inmates in each category. For instance; the classification team ordinarily would not release inmates held at the order of the disciplinary committee. Release from some special management units may require the warden's written approval, or perhaps even that of an official from the agency's headquarters office.

Releases usually are authorized when one or more of the following conditions exist:

- The inmate has completed the assigned time in disciplinary detention

- The inmate is transferred to a more restrictive unit or institution

- The original condition requiring the inmate's placement in the unit no longer exists

- New information or evidence indicates that the inmate is no longer a threat to himself or herself or others

Food Service Issues

Some large-scale special housing operations have a self-contained capability for preparing, serving, and dining within the unit, but this approach may be economically impractical for units with a relatively small number of inmates. Other options for providing meals to inmates in locked housing units include microwave reheating of pre-prepared trays, use of thermal trays, and direct service from steam tables in the unit. Whatever method is used, the following principles should apply:

- Ideally, only staff should transport, prepare, and serve food for the unit. In no case should inmate food servers be used. This prevents pressure and/or extortion activities associated with one inmate delivering food to another in this type of unit.

- There must be strict inventory controls on all potentially dangerous or sensitive items necessary for the food service process that are brought into the unit.

- Special housing units should be served the same institution meals provided to the general population. If meals are moved to the unit in mobile carts, those carts should be locked and ideally should be moved only by staff, although in most systems that is not the case.

- Care should be taken to serve food at proper temperatures. Special diet meals prepared or delivered through separate methods must be maintained at acceptable temperature levels. Time elapsed from arrival to service is critical in nonmicrowave operations, even when using thermal trays or containers.

- Supervisors should assess serving techniques, temperatures, and quality of the food itself. To that end, the food service administrator and other kitchen staff regularly should make rounds in the unit at meal time, to assist security staff in properly serving the meals.

- Meals should be served with lightweight plastic utensils.

Special Management Unit Operations

Special management units fill a unique role in many institutions, so extra comment on their operations is warranted.

General

Assignment to such a unit should be a classification decision that is based on documented information supporting a finding that the individuals involved are so dangerous that they require extraordinary controls. The philosophy of the unit should be nonpunitive. It should be a deterrent measure that is imposed to prevent future misconduct by the relatively few inmates in every system who clearly and consistently demonstrate their inability to function under traditional institutional regulations. These typically include those found to have committed murder, serious assaults, extortion, gang-related activities, or any actions which threatened others or the orderly operation of the institution.

A specific system of written policies and procedures supporting functional security practices must be in place for the unit. Policy for the unit should include the following elements:

- The purpose of the unit

- The chain of command in the unit

- A clear description of the process for assignment to the unit

- Definition of the role of the unit team

- Security procedures in use in the unit

- A description of any status levels within the unit used to motivate inmates, available programs and their criteria, and how inmates may progress through the system and earn release

- Other operational details, such as commissary, food service, religious programs, and so forth

The admission criteria, and the process required to carry it out, must be specific and fully described; all involved in the process must be fully aware of the need to adhere to the criteria precisely. To do otherwise will jeopardize the credibility of the program, and conceivably could result in court intervention. The admission process should incorporate an impartial review, and an opportunity to appeal the decision for placement.

Every transfer to the unit must be fully documented. No inmate ever should arrive in the unit without a documented determination that he or she (there are female special management inmates, as well) clearly needs the controls offered in the unit.

After intake, each inmate should be provided a copy of the rules and regulations of the unit, including the schedule of disciplinary penalties for rule infractions.

Throughout the inmate's stay in the unit, his or her case should receive a meaningful review by unit staff every thirty days. Any higher-level reviewing officials should be provided with a complete summary of the inmate's conduct, and any recommendations for release or other status change.

Staff in the unit should have a role in the decision-making process, particularly the correctional staff assigned there, who know the inmates far better than anyone else. Their input should include information on attitude, relationships with other inmates and with staff, personal appearance, cell cleanliness, and overall response to supervision.

Post orders should emphasize safe inmate movement procedures and effective security inspections. All unit staff should be provided with training that enhances their ability to deal with the inmates housed in this unit, as well as the stresses of duty in a high-security setting.

Staffing

The staffing pattern of units in this category will be determined by the mission and design of the unit. For the most part, only the most senior officers should be assigned to units of this type. While newer officers

Source: Capitol Communication Systems, Inc.

Secure recreation areas for special housing offenders are an important design feature.

certainly can be placed on posts here as well to gain experience, they should be under the careful over-sight of experienced personnel.

The unit management concept may be used in some types of special housing units as well–notably protective custody and special management units. While this may not be applicable to all such units, it does provide many of the same managerial and com-munication benefits as in a general-population setting.

The following staffing pattern is recommended for a long-term special management unit of 150 inmates:

- One senior supervisory correctional officer (of shift commander rank) or a unit manager

- One case worker

- Two counselors

- One secretary or clerk

- Fifteen correctional posts providing twenty-four-hour coverage. This includes ten posts (four on days, two on evenings, and two on morning watch) actually working the inmate-contact areas and five posts (two each on days and evenings, and one on the morning watch) in a unit control center. If no unit con-trol center is in use, these numbers may be adjusted accordingly. Other design factors may require additional posts for recreation or as activities and escort officers. Indeed, the basic officer coverage needs of a special man-agement unit, particularly on the day shift (when recreation and shower activity are high) may require even more posts. These staffing decisions must be made on an individualized assignment basis. Notice that these are posts, not positions; the actual number of positions will be dictated by the agency's relief factor.

Separate Special Management Institutions

Many correctional systems now have separate institutions dedicated to confining large numbers of inmates who present an unusually serious risk to the security, safety, and orderly operation of a typical institution. These institutions–sometimes popularly called "supermax" facilities–consist essentially of multiple special management units.

Administratively, there are both advantages and disadvantages to housing all special management inmates in a separate institution. The concentration of security resources and staffing at one location is costly, but it also frees up the other institutions in the system to operate more openly, and in a less costly manner. The inherent security problems of managing such a concentration of high-risk offenders is offset by the fact that other institutions in the system are at lower risk. The media and legal attention that these institutions seem to draw are balanced against the reduction in serious problems throughout the system. While there is not complete unanimity in the field of corrections on this issue, the prevailing view seems to be that these institutions have a useful role in some correctional systems.

Most institutions of this type operate with some type of stratification system, which is intended to motivate inmates to good conduct, which, in turn, will lead to greater privileges in the institution and eventual transfer to another institution of lesser security. Custody classifications of the inmates involved may encourage the establishment of smaller specialized units.

Several important concepts should be recalled when discussing these facilities.

First, inmates housed in these locations or in individual special management units in most cases are not going to require permanent confinement in a setting such as this. In many, if not most, instances, the inmate is engaged in a pattern of current conduct that is dangerous, but which may not be long-term. This type of highly controlled environment may deter future misconduct when the inmate eventually is released to a regular institution. Age (as is well recognized) may play a factor in diminishing the likelihood of violent acts. Circumstances upon release may be totally different; in many instances, an inmate is situationally involved in an incident that requires a

period of special management housing, but will not again engage in that conduct. Whatever the reason, it is worthwhile bearing in mind that some inmates in these units likely will be able to function successfully in a less-secure setting, having experienced the impact of this highly controlled environment.

However, it also is important to note that not every inmate who requires such a setting will present the typical classification profile of an inmate requiring extreme security measures. Most correctional systems now use a standardized classification system, often reducing inmate background and behavioral characteristics to some type of numerical form. But, these systems, useful as they are, do not capture exactly every potential risk or danger inherent in an inmate. They certainly cannot predict exactly an inmate's reaction to sex pressure, temptation to become involved in drug dealing, propensity to act anew on past gang associations, or other factors. Thus, virtually all such institutions and units will house inmates who technically may not appear to be high-security cases, but whose actual conduct or history clearly demonstrates the need for unusually close supervision and control. The critics of this type of institution often seize on this apparent inconsistency, and it is important in both policy and public information contacts to clarify the complexities involved in assigning inmates to this type of setting.

Also, institutions of this type always are going to be scrutinized, whether by the courts or the media, and often by both. Thus, it is critical that policies are not only functional but legal, and that staff are particularly careful to follow them in every way. As a practical matter, this means that the remarks earlier in this publication about administrative visibility and professionalism are perhaps more important in institutions and units of this type than in any other setting. Inmates in these institutions can present unusually difficult challenges taunting and threatening staff, throwing urine and feces, assaulting employees and other inmates, refusing to come out of cells, refusing to allow staff to apply restraints–challenges that sometimes can generate imprudent or improper staff actions.

Facility administrators must be sure that they are out and about in the institution, talking to staff and inmates, and being alert to potential problems. Appropriate supervisory controls must be in effect at every level and for every activity, to prevent incidents such as these from becoming the basis for employee misconduct or litigation.

Finally, staff in institutions like this many tend to adopt a "macho" attitude, a callous approach to dealing with inmates, or a complacency (born from the view that the controls in place are so strict that nothing could happen). Managerial staff constantly must be alert to the development of these attitudes, any one of which could lead to a serious incident.

Tool Control

21

Tool control is critical in any institution, no matter how small, or what its security level. This general heading also includes such things as controls over hazardous materials throughout the facility, food service implements, and needles and syringes in the medical area.

General

A well-designed tool control program will:

- Provide for secure storage and perpetual accountability of all tools

- Control unauthorized or improper use

- Provide adequate supervision

- Prevent loss or damage

- Provide a positive means of identification

- Specify methods of purchase, issue, receipt, and disposal of tools

- Identify the need for specific items

The chief of security has primary responsibility for developing and supervising the tool control program in all departments. The chief also should be sure necessary checks and inspections (whether they are carried out by security personnel or staff from the various departments) are in place, to assure the effective operation of the program.

Every employee is responsible for following established tool control policies and procedures. But first, and foremost, security staff should set the standard for tool control in their own tool use. There is no excuse for security staff not properly marking, storing, inventorying, and using tools. By setting a proper example, security staff greatly increase the likelihood that tool control in other departments will be in line with policy.

Although responsible for the overall operation of the program, the chief of security should be aided by the department heads, each of whom is responsible for control in his or her own area. Department heads should ensure compliance with established policy by the employees under their supervision, with the chief of security providing any necessary advisory assistance.

Employees using tools should be issued metal or plastic tags bearing their names, to serve as a receipt for all issued tools. When an employee is terminated, resigns, retires, or is separated from service, he or she must turn in all name tags. If a name tag system of this type is not used, each employee should be issued an identifying number that is coded in a log. Temporary or paper receipts should not be used without the chief of security's approval. Loss of a tag must be reported to the chief of security and immediately followed by a written report.

Classification of Tools

Tools should be divided into a minimum of two categories—Class A and Class B.

- Class A tools are those such as files, knives, saw blades, ladders, ropes, extension cords, lift devices, grinders, and others presenting inherent safety or security risks. Class A tools should be used only under the direct supervision of staff, and always placed in a secure tool storage area when not in use. Poisonous chemicals, dangerous drugs, acids, and hypodermic needles also should be controlled with the Class A methods.

- Class B tools, such as light pliers, short power cords, and others, constitute a lower level of risk. They may be stored, issued, and used under less stringent conditions, but the institution or department still must account for them.

The classification of a tool determines the degree of staff control needed over inmate use of that piece of equipment. However, it must not be assumed that a particular tool, by virtue of its classification as nonhazardous, does not represent a risk to institutional security or personal safety. Each and every tool must be considered as potentially hazardous and treated accordingly.

Also, the classification of tools as hazardous or nonhazardous differs significantly between maximum- and minimum-security institutions. For example, ladders would be considered hazardous in a secure institution, but nonhazardous in an open camp setting. In view of this, each institution should develop its own lists of Class A and Class B tools.

Storage

Tools should be kept only in designated secure tool rooms and other approved storage areas. The location and design of these storage areas should be determined by the facility's layout, taking into consideration the needs of various shops and departments. The chief of security should approve storage facility design and placement, ensuring that the areas are secure from inmate access and suitable for secure tool issue.

Shadow boards generally are agreed to be the best storage method for those tools, especially those that can be adapted to suspension from a rack, hook, or peg. Each tool should have its own pegged shadow, or silhouette, on the board, and the shadow should closely mimic the outline of each tool so that quick inspection of the board will reveal any missing tools.

- Tools of the same type should be stored individually and never be stacked.

- All shadow boards accessible to inmates should be secured by an expanded metal locked screen.

- Tools that cannot be adapted to the shadow board should be stored in a locked cabinet or room.

- A careful inventory of these tools should be maintained with the tools.

- If a tool is removed from the inventory, the corresponding shadow immediately should be removed from the shadow board.

- Tools on repair or checked out to a job site should be replaced by a tool chit or durable tag. Temporary or paper tags are not acceptable for this purpose.

- Copies of sample tool accountability forms are included in Appendix D.

- Class A tools, regardless of type or location, always should be stored separately from Class B tools, under double lock and key. Typically, the shadows for Class A and Class B tools are different colors; often Class A shadows are red.

- Tool carts and toolboxes are an effective means of controlling tools that must be moved to remote work sites. They can be rolled out of the central tool room in the morning and returned at the end of the day, with appropriate accountability maintained by the employee checking out the tools. A complete inventory of everything on the cart should travel with it, so that staff quickly can ascertain if all items are there, and a copy also should be filed in a secure cabinet in the tool room. The same principles apply to tool belts, or pouches, checked out of the tool room. However, class A tools should not be issued as part of a standard tool pouch.

- A system should be in place to assure that new tools brought into the institution are placed on an inventory and properly etched before being put into service. The etching system should include a code for the shop to which the tool is issued, as well as an individual tool number.

Several specialized tool use and storage situations require elaboration.

Shop grinders only should be used under direct staff supervision. All grinders should be secured with full guards on the grinding wheels, and locking devices on the main electrical switchboxes feeding them. In the alternative, the wheels themselves can be removed by staff to a secure tool room, when not in use. Broken grinding wheels immediately should be removed from the institution and properly discarded.

Any hacksaw blades, files, other cutting blades, and similarly hazardous tools in use throughout the day should be removed from the shop area and turned in to the control center or some other location outside the secure perimeter at the end of each work day.

Hacksaw blades should be mounted on rings, issued using a durable receipt system, and only in amounts necessary for one day's use. In addition to storing blades in the control center, a running hacksaw blade inventory should be maintained there. Broken or worn blades must be turned in, and all parts accounted for, in order for a new blade to be issued.

Acetylene torches present a very grave hazard. The tips and mixing chambers should be controlled by staff at all times and removed from the institution at the end of each day. The usual inventory and checkout procedures apply to them, also. The tanks themselves can be used to jury-rig a flame-thrower or bomb, and should be safely and securely stored at the end of the work day as well.

In a secure setting, extension and step ladders must be secured and tracked through an inventory system. Storage inside the rear sally port is a common option, so that they can be available easily when it is necessary to move them inside. Alternatively, ladders may be stored outside the perimeter or chained to a fixed object in an area easily supervised, such as from a tower.

Identification and Inventory

All new tools purchased or otherwise acquired by the institution should be approved by the chief of security and received at an outside receiving area. There, they can be properly categorized, marked, and moved to secure storage. A copy of a sample tool receiving form is included in Appendix D.

All tools should be marked with a separate code identifying the department, and individual shop or work detail to which the tool is assigned, as well as having an individual tool number that is etched on it, so that it can be identified easily on inventories and checkout logs.

Tools that cannot be marked without damage, such as surgical instruments, micrometers, and small drill bits, should be inventoried and kept in locked storage when not in use.

Tool inventories should be posted on all corresponding shadow boards, tool boxes, and tool kits. In addition to tool records in the tool room and the department to which the tools are issued, the chief of security should maintain a separate tool file for each area in which tools are stored. Audit sheets, with the signature of the periodic audit official and date of the audit, should be maintained in each folder. All lost or replacement tool reports also should be kept in this folder. A copy of such a form is included in Appendix D.

All tools should be accounted for at the beginning and end of each work day, and a log or other record of that check should be completed and forwarded periodically to the chief of security.

A complete tool inventory should be conducted at least every three months, by a person designated by the chief of security. All tools must be inventoried according to category Class A or Class B. A minimum of three copies of the inventory should be prepared, with copies going to the chief of security, supervisor for the shop or area where the tools are located, and the shop, department, or detail itself. A copy of a sample tool inventory form is included in Appendix D. Any addition to or deletion from an inventory should be followed immediately by a typewritten explanatory inventory supplement and circulated to each of the involved departments.

The institution must establish procedures for ensuring control of all outside tools while they are in the facility. Inventories should be made of all tools and equipment used by civilian contractors working inside the institution, and be maintained by the chief of security, the maintenance supervisor, and the job supervisor.

Institution tools also should be inventoried by gate officers as the tools go in or out of the institution, so that if they are lost or inadvertently left at a job site, there is a way of reconstructing what is missing.

Lost, Excess, or Broken Tools

At a minimum, all areas that maintain tools should verify and account for all tools at the beginning and end of each shift. Missing tools should be reported immediately to the shift supervisor, chief of security, and responsible department head.

Written reports should follow as soon as possible, preferably no later than the end of the shift during which the loss was discovered. The report should identify the missing item and describe the circumstances of the incident. The chief of security, shift supervisor, and the department involved should maintain copies of the report until the tool is found or the incident is closed.

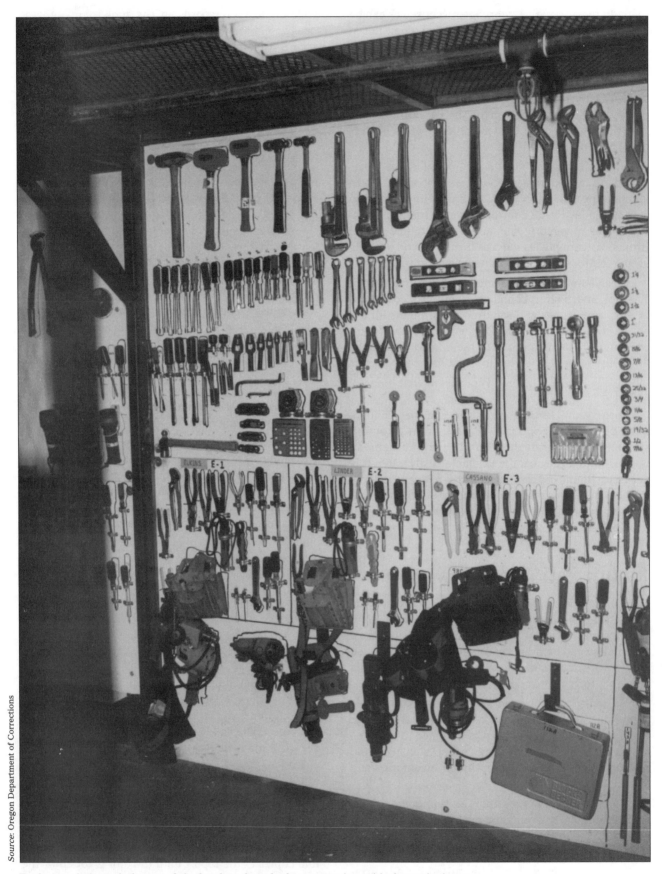

Source: Oregon Department of Corrections

Tool control, through the use of shadow boards and other means, is a critical security issue.

Procedures should be established to ensure that reasonable efforts are made to recover lost tools. Inmates who had access to the missing tool should be detained at the site of the loss until a thorough search is made. When a lost tool is recovered, a report detailing the circumstances of the discovery should be submitted to the chief of security.

A procedure for the disposal of excess or unserviceable tools must be part of any tool control program, to ensure that they remain unavailable to staff and inmates. Each department head should determine what tools are excess or unserviceable. The list of these tools should be submitted to the chief of security, who will arrange for their disposal.

Excess or spare tools never should be kept in the institution. Instead, they should be kept in a secure storage area outside the perimeter, in order to avoid substitutions that undermine tool accountability.

Hazardous Chemicals

The control of hazardous substances is an important adjunct to the control of tools. Chemicals such as bleaches, acids, alcohols, solvents, gasoline, and others must be under complete staff control, with a full inventory program in use. American Correctional Association and National Fire Protection Association (NFPA) storage requirements should be strictly followed.

The amount of hazardous materials maintained in the institution should be kept to an absolute minimum. Properly constructed storage areas, and properly designed containers must be used for all hazardous materials. Controls on these compounds should be monitored carefully by the chief of security.

Special Areas–Kitchen and Hospital

- Kitchen knives and yeast are discussed in detail in Chapter 13 on food service operations. However, as a point of emphasis, these items should be subject to the strictest possible controls, because of their inherently dangerous nature.

- Close inventory and storage controls should be maintained on all medications, sharps, needles, syringes, medical instruments, and all such discarded items until they leave the institution for proper disposal.

- Large quantities of medications should be kept in a vault or safe, with a master inventory. Regular issue quantities should be maintained in a secure, but somewhat more accessible area, with shift-to-shift accountability and a running inventory.

- If a rolling response cart (crash cart) with medications, needles, and syringes is kept in the hospital, then when it is not in use, it must be stored in a secure area, so that no inmates can gain access to it.

- Other than over-the-counter items, all medications should be dispensed by medical staff.

- The combination for the hospital safe should be highly controlled. It should be issued to the warden and deputy warden in a sealed, countersigned envelope, for storage so that in the absence of key hospital staff, access still would be possible.

- Strict procedures should be in place to ensure accountability of needles and syringes in the medical area. Inventory, issue, and disposal methods should emphasize not only security, but in the instance of used items, universal precautions against disease transmission.

- Tools used in the barber or beauty program should be shadowed, kept in a locked metal container, and placed on an inventory.

- The signout sheet for tools issued also should be secured to prevent an inmate from accessing it and changing it.

Special Areas and Concerns

22

A number of other general areas require special mention. This chapter covers the security-related concerns in those programs or activities.

Commissary Operations

Commissaries are the stores of institutions, and like stores on the outside, they sometimes are targets of burglaries, shoplifting, and outright theft. Commissaries also sometimes serve as a clearing point for other money-related projects, such as inmate fund-raising activities; they, too, have a certain risk attached.

The following considerations should be part of the security department's interest in commissary operations:

- The keys to the commissary should be part of the restricted key program.

- The commissary and all associated warehouse areas should be constructed so as to prevent inmate break-in. Walls, ceilings, and floors should be completely secure. Entrances should be equipped with institution-type locks. Windows, if there are any, should be secured with grilles.

- The inmate service areas should be functional, but should also provide sufficient security to prevent over-the-counter theft. Items on display should be situated in such a way as to prevent shoplifting.

- Adequate physical and procedural safeguards should be in place to deter and detect theft by inmate commissary workers.

- Commissary records should be maintained in a secure location. Because these records may be the only proof of inmate fund balances, they should not only be safe from theft, but also should be safe from fire–thus the need for fireproof file cabinets. Commissary records should be stored, and all bookkeeping work done on them, in an area that is secure from inmates. No inmate should have access to the financial records of another inmate.

- Commissary items themselves should be selected to preclude any presenting obvious security risks, such as aerosol cans and bleaches, and a method should be in place to ensure that security staff have input into the selection of all items.

Delivery of commissary items to inmates in special housing circumstances is a separate area of concern. In high-rise jails, special housing units, and medical areas, inmates often physically cannot go to a commissary and order over the counter. They must fill out a commissary order form and wait for the items to be delivered to them. This causes three areas of concern:

(1) Some types of items suitable for general population inmates may not be appropriate for inmates in these units. Security staff carefully should screen the commissary list for items that should be prohibited or repackaged before delivery to the unit.

(2) Similarly, the security needs of the unit may dictate different quantities of commissary purchasing than would be the case for inmates in general population; security staff must work with commissary

Comissary operations must be well organized and secure from unauthorized inmate access.

personnel to include those limitations in the purchasing process.

(3) The delivery process may provide an avenue for the flow of contraband into a secure unit; careful searches of the commissary items and the delivery cart are clearly in order.

As a related note, in some facilities money is collected in connection with inmate programs (such as arts and crafts sales) or is left for inmates by visitors. Those funds should be under continuous and careful staff control once they are received. Often, the money is placed in a locked box or other repository with an accompanying receipt (the original of which is provided to the person making the purchase or leaving money for the inmate). There should be a log of staff access to the box and all transactions, to ensure accountability. When the box is opened, the funds should be counted and reconciled with the receipts inside. This is best done jointly, by the person responsible for keeping the box and the commissary employee picking the funds up for deposit to an official account.

Inmate Discipline

Effective, fair, and consistent inmate discipline is absolutely essential in any correctional system. While discipline and enforcement of rules can help develop inmate self-discipline and self-control–things that ultimately will help them conform to accepted standards for society–security staff are particularly concerned with discipline to prevent misconduct and disturbances.

While discipline usually is thought of as a formal process, the real foundation of institution discipline is in the human factor. Staff must inform inmates of the rules and regulations, make clear their expectation that they be followed, and then enforce them in a firm, fair, and consistent manner. If the regulations change, staff need to tell inmates in advance. If the penalties for an infraction change, staff should tell inmates at the time. If a warning for a minor, first infraction is appropriate, staff need to do that in an effective way. And if inmates persist in misconduct, or engage in serious misconduct, then staff intervention has to be prompt and professional.

Inmates easily will sense and exploit staff inequities in enforcing the rules of the institution. There is no more quick way to disorder in an institution than lowering standards and expectations, unless it is allowing them to slip gradually and then suddenly enforcing them without providing inmates notice of the new approach. All of this points to the need for consistent application of rules throughout the institution. Inmates, if pressed, will say that strict rules are not the real problem in most institutions–it is inconsistency in the application of even the most innocuous rules. Staff need to work hard to avoid that situation.

Once beyond that frame of reference, then the remaining, basic disciplinary functions involving security staff are the preparation of incident reports, the conduct of disciplinary hearings, and the operation of the special housing unit (discussed in Chapter 20).

Incident Reports

Correctional officers (and all other staff, as well) are required to prepare incident reports that accurately and briefly reflect reportable inmate misconduct. In many instances, low-level misconduct can and should be resolved informally. But types of more serious misconduct must be reported, even if an informal disposition later is applied. Agencies should provide clear training to staff on how to make decisions about the threshold for reportable misconduct. In some organizations, the inmate rules, regulations, and misconduct code actually include guidelines to that effect, either for the correctional officers or for staff on disciplinary committees.

Once it has been determined, though, that a misconduct report is required, the staff member should fill out the required form as promptly as possible. The report should be neat, clear, and to the point. All possible witnesses, and the disposition of any evidence, should be referenced. If necessary, supporting memoranda can be provided, and memos from other staff can be attached, if they are available. In most instances, this is the end of the reporting officer's involvement, although staff assigned to investigate the incident may interview the reporting officer at a later time.

Discipline Hearings

In most institutions, (after some preliminary determination of probable guilt has been made by an investigator or unit team hearing) chairing the disciplinary committee is a task delegated to the chief of security. In some systems, a single hearing officer (often a former security official) is responsible for conducting hearings. For those reasons, this publication briefly will discuss the disciplinary process.

Correctional discipline in the United States is broadly governed by case law established by the Supreme Court in *Wolff v. McDonald* (418 U.S. 539, 1974). This case, briefly, requires that:

- An inmate be advised in advance of the charges against him or her

- A written notice of a forthcoming hearing and all rights at that hearing be provided

- The inmate be afforded the right to be present at the hearing unless security would be jeopardized

- The inmate may call for witnesses and present documentary evidence

- Staff assistance must be provided, if the inmate requests it

- The inmate must be advised of the decision and the reasons for it, and must be provided a written copy of that information

The chief of security, and other staff members assigned to be involved in the disciplinary process, must be completely familiar with these general requirements, as well as any others that the agency has in its own policies and procedures. Failure to abide by them is quite likely to result in an overturn on appeal of the decision in that case, and possibly could result in civil liability for those involved.

Each agency will have different rules and regulations on inmate discipline. The important factor for line staff is accurate, complete reporting of all incidents.

Programs

Knowledgeable correctional managers–whether from a security background or not–know or should know the value of programs in the total operation of an institution. Programs productively occupy inmate time. They provide structured activities outside the housing unit, which take a portion of the supervision load off security staff. They give inmates a sense of purpose and a method of orienting their institutional lives around something that is goal-oriented, personally satisfying, and productive for the future. In short, programs are an important–and greatly underacknowledged–component of institutional security. While the intended focus of this guide is on the other elements of security, some mention of the value of programs is warranted.

First, it is important to underline the fact that ideally, security staff have a well-founded interest in telling program staff how they can run their programs, not that they cannot run them. The goal of security staff in relation to programs is enforcing reasonable and necessary security measures, while avoiding the imposition of a repressive atmosphere that suppresses programs.

For example, if a regular search procedure put into place for inmates going to and from the education department is done correctly and obviously is for good cause, inmates will still go to school. If it is done with an unprofessional, perhaps harassing attitude, school attendance may drop off, and the inmates may go to the yard or back to the housing unit instead of being in school.

Who is the loser here? The education staff, who have fewer inmates to teach? The inmates, who may or may not take up the classwork another time (since time is one thing they do have)? Or the housing unit and yard officers, who suddenly have many more inmates to supervise and control? Clearly, security staff have an interest in seeing that programs go on with as little interruption as possible.

To support security, not complicate it, each institution and agency should have a well-balanced program of inmate activities, including work, basic recreation programs, education, and treatment. The following basic programs have been tested in day-to-day institution operation; they enhance, not detract from, security.

Work

Inmate idleness is a continuing problem in many of today's institutions and requires special mention. With high levels of crowding, many institutions have large numbers of inmates who are unassigned, and others who only have a nominal job assignment–less than full time in most cases. With few jobs, accountability problems increase, and opportunities for misconduct grow correspondingly. The more jobs available, the lower the chance of problems. To the greatest extent possible, job assignments should include compensation in the form of money, good time, or other rewards.

Education

A large percentage, if not a majority, of inmates coming into today's institutions have significant literacy deficits. Educational programs can be one of the keys to preparing offenders for their eventual return to society, and also to more functional living in the institution. But they also provide constructive time-structuring, which, in itself, is a valuable effect of any program.

Counseling

These programs also are important in establishing interpersonal skills, improving inmate anger management capabilities, and, of course, in helping inmates develop the ability to deal with substance abuse problems. They also help establish and maintain important lines of communication between staff and inmates.

Vocational Training

Vocational training should be available in the institution to stimulate inmates to improve their job skills and work habits. Participation in these programs basically should be voluntary, but well-designed incentive programs may be used.

Recreation Programs

Recreation is important to the overall functioning of an institution, and well-equipped, but basic, recreation facilities should be available to inmates on a daily basis. Qualified staff should be available to plan, organize, and carry out these programs.

Religious Counseling

These services and programs, directed by a well-trained chaplain are also a necessity. The Religious Freedom Restoration Act makes this a particularly important area for administrators to support.

Mental Health, Dental, and Medical Services

These programs must be provided to the inmate population in keeping with legal requirements, as well as in the interest of operating a humane facility. Also, institutions must be in compliance with the Americans

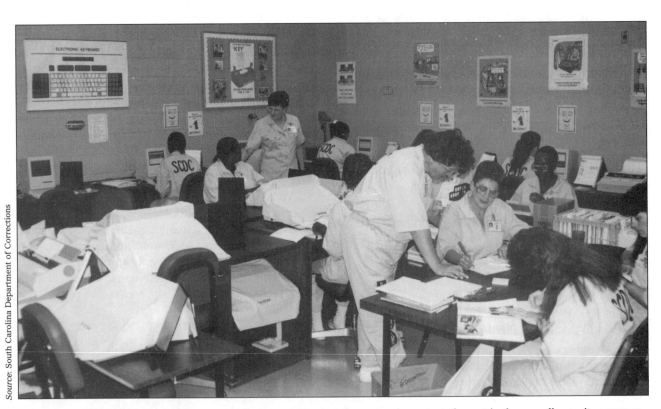

Source: South Carolina Department of Corrections

Programs not only help offenders prepare to return to society, but also are an important element in the overall security program.

with Disabilities Act (ADA), so that disabled inmates can take part in all institution programs.

Institution budgets usually are laden with requests for new security equipment, refurbished offices, or a new cellblock–but few visible dollars are budgeted for inmate programs. Knowledgeable administrators also make sure every year that the budget contains something that inmates can recognize as being for them. Whether it is new bleachers for the ball field, a new floor for the indoor recreation area, or a new paint and plaster job in the visiting room, this added touch can go a long way toward enhancing inmate morale and showing that the administration does care about their living conditions.

Security Procedures

While this publication does not address individual programs in any further detail, this section is intended to discuss briefly the basic points of interaction between program and security staff. That discussion falls into three major areas–security procedures in the program areas, inmate accountability, and volunteers and contract personnel.

Program personnel–regardless of whether they are teachers, recreation specialists, trade instructors, mental health staff, or others–are subject to the same security procedures as any other employee. If the facility is operating under the correctional worker concept, they even are provided the same basic and refresher training as correctional officers. While it is true that in some correctional systems there are significant, very distinct, role divisions between security staff and the nonuniformed workforce, there is a great deal of agreement on the proposition that some security awareness on the part of all staff is a desirable situation, to the degree labor-management agreements and local practice permit.

The skills most often recognized as important for nonsecurity staff include the following:

Proper key handling. Every employee who is issued keys is responsible for controlling those keys and preventing inmate access for use or copying.

Proper tool control. Whether it be scissors, cutting pliers, or solvents, proper security measures for such items are the responsibility of all employees who have them in their work area.

Awareness of security breaches. Each staff member must be alert to tampered bars, broken locks, and other elements of the physical security of the institution. In most systems with a comprehensive security inspection system, program employees are integrated into the portion of the system involving their department.

Alertness to inmate activities. Every employee is another set of eyes and ears for the institution's intelligence-gathering operation, and is responsible for not only alertness to signs of unrest or problems, but for reporting them to the proper institutional officials. Because of this, all institution staff should receive training in the indicators of a potential disturbance.

Knowledge of basic correctional skills. This is needed so that all staff and volunteers will be able to assist during institutional emergencies.

Inmate Accountability

Every staff member in an institution bears some responsibility for making sure that the institution remains secure from escape. This is a matter of public duty and duty to fellow employees. But it also is a matter of self-interest, because if an individual staff members sees or becomes aware of a potential security risk and does nothing about it, there always is the possibility that that person could be involved in an escape, be taken hostage, be injured, or even be killed.

Staff in program areas are responsible for the whereabouts of the inmates in their areas. This includes:

- Keeping records of those assigned to the area

- Using the pass system to control inmates moving in and out of the area

- Making census checks

- Using outcount procedures correctly

- Assisting in emergency counts and other unplanned activities relating to accountability

Security staff need to work closely with program personnel in making sure that these accountability-related activities are carried out properly. This is done as a regular part of the institution's training program. However, on a day-to-day basis, security staff also should be aware of the state of accountability in program areas.

Volunteers and Contract Personnel

Security personnel often interface regularly with program personnel who use volunteers and contract personnel to carry out their programs. Religious, recreation, and education programs are particularly oriented to the use of these nonstaff personnel.

The following areas represent major interface activities between security staff and other departments in this regard:

- Establishing background-screening criteria for volunteers and contractors that meet the security needs of the institution

- Providing an orientation, or orientation materials, that acquaint all such personnel with the security needs and procedures of the institution

- Creating, authenticating, and issuing passes for all such individuals

- Performing searches and identifying volunteers and contract personnel coming into the institution

- Providing escort to certain areas of the institution

While there is a great deal of benefit to having the services of these individuals available to the institution, a few basic cautions are important to remember.

- Ordinarily, such personnel should be limited in their access to special housing units and other sensitive areas; direct staff supervision is required when they are granted such access.

- Nonemployees usually may not carry security keys; some contract personnel may be issued a limited key ring for their specific work area.

- Inmates may target nonemployees for manipulation; employees supervising contract personnel and volunteers must be alert to the signs of an improper relationship or other impermissible activity.

- A higher level of personal search–equivalent to that used for inmate visitors–may be used for personnel in these categories.

Factories and Mechanical Shops

The security department must have a close, cooperative relationship with staff working in the factory and maintenance areas of the institution. Large numbers of inmates are assigned there each day. Inmate accountability is critical. Tools and hazardous materials are in regular use. Proper control of those items is vital. Movement of materials and inmates through the perimeter are a regular feature of these operations. If

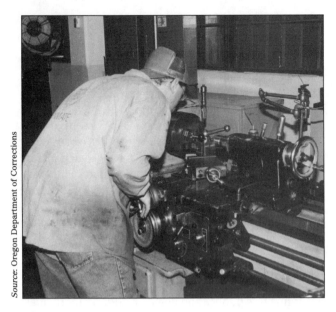

Source: Oregon Department of Corrections

Industrial employment is one of many vital programs that contribute to institution security.

security staff do not have the proper influence and oversight into these departmental activities, inmates certainly will exploit the inevitable breaches.

This chapter discusses several major areas of joint concern: general security procedures, inmate accountability, tool control, movement through the perimeter, and outside contractors.

General Security

Factory and maintenance staff are responsible–as any other employee–for being aware of the institution's general security procedures. They should be provided basic and refresher training that conveys the basics of security. Even though some division of responsibility may exist between uniformed and nonuniformed staff, in day-to-day activities factory and maintenance personnel must be responsible for the following areas:

- Proper key handling and control

- Awareness of security breaches and potential breaches

- Alertness to inmate actions and attitudes that could signal potential problems

Inmate Accountability

Because so many inmates are in factories and shop areas, or are moving throughout the institution on work details, inmate accountability takes on a particular importance. Staff in these departments are responsible for the inmates assigned to them, through careful implementation of procedures described elsewhere in this publication, to include:

- Keeping accurate records of those assigned to the department and individual work areas

- Using the pass system to control inmates moving in and out of factories or shops

- Making census checks on a regular basis to ensure that all assigned inmates are in their proper place

- Using the outcount procedures correctly, when inmates cannot be returned to the unit for a count

- Effectively using the crew kit card system to account for all inmates assigned to work crews

- Assisting in emergency counts and other unplanned activities relating to accountability

Security staff need to work closely with staff in these departments, to be sure that these accountability procedures are implemented properly. This certainly would include regular tours by the shift supervisor through shops and factory areas, to personally ascertain the status of accountability systems.

Tool Control

Tool control is so important that Chapter 21 is devoted to it. Yet, every employee using or responsible for any type of tool must be totally familiar with the institution's tool control policy and procedures, and use them without fail.

Security staff can play an important role in assuring that the tool control program in these areas is working as intended. Training, regular tours of the areas, actual checks of inventories and tool storage areas, and other measures are a major part of the oversight and assistance process that is the responsibility of the security department.

Movement Through the Perimeter

Inmate work crews, raw materials, finished factory goods–all move through the perimeter. On a day-to-day basis, traffic through the gates for these purposes is an essential part of the institution's life. In particular, facilities with major factory operations may have regular truck deliveries and pickups that tie up rear gate operations for a large part of the day.

Security staff have a great deal to do with this traffic. They control the gates. They search the vehicles and payloads. In many instances, they search the

inmates as they come and go. And they are constantly aware of the potential for escape or contraband introduction inherent in all of those activities.

However, to a large degree, the interface between security, factory, and maintenance staff centers around coordinating these gate-related activities. Also, the security department is responsible for maintaining the gate pass and crew kit systems that maintenance staff, in particular, rely on as they move inmates around the institution. Finally, the chief of security must be active in overseeing the methods of search used by nonsecurity personnel at the gates.

Outside Contractors

Security personnel must take an active role in the management of all construction, maintenance, and factory-related activities that involve outside contractors. Many institutions rely on contract resources to carry out major physical plant renovation and building. The supervision of these activities, supervision of the individuals involved, and control of all tools and materials are major elements of concern to security personnel. Security staff should be involved in the process of managing outside contractor activities in the following ways:

- Establishing background screening criteria that meet the security needs of the institution

- Providing an orientation, or orientation materials, that acquaint all contractor personnel with the security needs and procedures of the institution

- Creating, authenticating, and issuing passes for all such individuals

- Performing searches and identification of contract personnel coming into the institution

- Searching and inventorying all tools and materials, both coming into and leaving the institution

- Providing escort to certain areas of the institution

A few basic controls are needed on contractor's personnel to further enhance proper security.

- Contractors' personnel ordinarily should not be permitted to carry keys, other than to their own tool boxes. Searches of contractor personnel should be of the same type as those for inmate visitors (walk-through metal detector and a search of any tool boxes, tool pouches, lunch containers, or other hand-carried items).

- These individuals should be advised in writing of the consequences (including criminal prosecution) of violating any institution regulations. When contractor personnel are in regular contact with inmates, inmates may try to influence them improperly; training/orientation materials and staff supervision should emphasize this possibility.

- Contractor personnel ordinarily should not be permitted in locked housing units; direct staff supervision is mandatory in the rare event that they absolutely must be granted such access.

- To facilitate the use of contractor personnel and avoid misunderstandings about the security procedures that will be in force while working in the institution, security and maintenance staff should hold a preconstruction conference with the contractor's key staff before any major construction project commences. In this session, the search, tool accountability, and security considerations that will be enforced throughout the project should be explained fully to the contractor. This is a prime opportunity to make last minute adjustment of procedures outlined in the contract itself, to avoid security breaches or unnecessary delays in construction due to misunderstandings and faulty procedures.

Finally, just as with other areas, staff working in the maintenance and facilities departments require guidance for their security-related activities. This best can be done by compiling a comprehensive facilities manual that contains information regarding tool control, use of hazardous materials, principles of correctional construction management, and other related topics. A manual of this type also will provide a benchmark for the administration to use to evaluate the efficiency of these departments.

Infectious Diseases

Contagious disease processes are a major concern today, and particularly with the increased incidence of the Human Immunodeficiency Virus (HIV), hepatitis, and tuberculosis (TB) in society, as well as in institutions. The closed correctional environment offers great potential for rapid disease spread to both inmates and staff. The risk to security staff–who may encounter blood or spit during altercations with inmates, needles during shakedowns, and other hazardous situations–is particularly high.

This situation creates the need for a well-developed set of policies and procedures to deal with this potential problem. While this publication will not go into detail about the medical management of these diseases, a number of basic procedures and principles are important for all staff–security and nonsecurity–to know.

- The starting point for any institutional program of this type is education about disease prevention. Staff must be aware of the major disease processes, their methods of transmission, and the means to prevent that transmission.

- Staff must not only know about the principle of universal precautions, but also know how to apply it and have the proper equipment to do so. For instance, staff should be provided with the option of carrying latex gloves and a belt pouch, for quick access to basic protection.

- Proper cleaning and sanitation supplies must be available in all areas.

- Staff should be trained in proper restraint procedures for combative inmates, including the use of protective equipment.

- Staff should be trained in proper search techniques, so as to minimize the risk of needle sticks and other risky contact with potentially contaminated items.

- There must be a procedure available to staff to allow them to receive infectious disease testing; in that process, appropriate informed consent procedures must be in place.

- Staff must be trained in the proper storage and disposal procedures for infectious waste and other materials, and those procedures must be in accord with all state and federal regulations.

- Staff who are in a position to know the infectious disease status of inmates or other staff–such as the chief of security–must know and adhere to all privacy requirements.

- Procedures must be in place to isolate inmates with infectious diseases (those transmitted through casual contact such as tuberculosis) from the general population until evaluated by the medical staff. Management of these housing units may be the joint responsibility of the chief of security and the head of the medical department.

- Procedures must be in place to separate from other inmates, and safeguard staff from, offenders who are carrying an infectious disease and who pose a threat to others by virtue of a history of assaults of any type, or who credibly threaten to assault others. Management of housing units for such cases is the responsibility of the chief of security, in consultation with the medical staff.

Investigative Activities

Institutions are, indeed, small cities–cities with crime problems. Employees are the eyes and ears of the city's government. Security staff, in general, are in some ways analogous to the city police. The institution's special investigative supervisor is the city's detective. Procedures must be in place to report and handle crimes.

Investigative Supervisor

A supervisory correctional officer should be selected and trained to act as the institution's special investigator. This employee should receive training in investigative techniques, perhaps through the local law enforcement community. The investigative supervisor should be responsible for conducting inquiries into internal inmate and staff-related improprieties. The incumbent should be able to develop a comprehensive base of intelligence information about inmate activity within the institution, as well as intelligence summaries and evidence packages suitable for court.

The investigative supervisor should be responsible for developing a method for identifying the most dangerous inmates in the population, and compiling a readily available file of pictures and basic identifying information on them, so that staff can easily learn about inmates who require additional attention or levels of supervision.

The investigative supervisor should work actively and cooperatively with other law enforcement agencies and the agency's internal affairs staff regarding institution-related investigations, such as introduction of contraband and other significant cases.

The tools available to the investigative supervisor may include:

- Staff reports, including confidential shift reports filed by staff on all posts, which reflect unusual occurrences and activities–"tidbits" of information that only may mean something to the investigative supervisor

- Data collected on incident reports and other activities, reflecting trends and significant events

- Confidential inmate sources

- Results from monitoring of selected inmate correspondence

- Confidential sources in the community

- Telephone monitoring data

- Tapes of closed circuit TV monitors in visiting and other areas

- Other information that is based on technical interception

The supervisor should be provided with computer capability, as well as a secure storage area (preferably a safe or vault) to store evidence and contraband.

Crime Notification

Local policy should specify the steps to be taken in notifying local law enforcement agencies of a crime in the institution, particularly identifying what level of management is authorized to make such a referral. The following steps should be included in local policy:

Whenever an criminal offense may have been committed in an institution–whether by inmate, staff member, visitor, or others–it must be reported promptly to a supervisor.

The next step is to isolate the crime scene. All inmates should be removed from the area and it should be secured.

The first employees to arrive at a crime scene must secure the area. Staff who are not involved in protecting the crime scene should not be permitted in the area.

The scene should remain fully isolated until the warden authorizes qualified investigative personnel to enter the area and begin an investigation.

Items at the scene should remain in the exact position where they are found until trained investigators properly process the evidence.

Each institution should outline specific procedures to be followed in the event it becomes necessary to conduct searches that are not routine and that may result in criminal prosecution.

In most cases, criminal referrals will come from either the warden, investigative supervisor, or in an emergency, the shift supervisor.

When a criminal referral is made, all facility staff must cooperate fully with the investigative agency and make available any information or evidence bearing on an offense being investigated.

Requirements Regarding the Investigation of Crimes

The Supreme Court has established certain rights of criminal suspects regarding self-incrimination, including a requirement that a suspect be advised of his or her right to counsel. To assure compliance with this requirement (called the *Miranda* warning, after the lead case on this issue), the following points are important in managing the criminal referral process:

- The two main considerations in the investigation of a crime committed in an institution are the identification and isolation of the suspected offender as a matter of internal security and safety, and the prosecution of the offender. To achieve the second consideration–successful prosecution–staff must comply carefully with applicable constitutional requirements.

- In the usual case where prosecution is a possibility, institutional staff should not question suspects. When the investigation has narrowed to several suspects, they may be isolated from the rest of the population until the arrival of the appropriate law enforcement officials, who assume the responsibility of the investigation for purposes of prosecution.

- A suspect should not be questioned further about the incident without being given the required warning regarding his or her rights. However, because the *Miranda* decision concerns only questioning, a suspect freely may volunteer a statement about the offense without being asked any questions. Also, nothing prevents the questioning of witnesses; it is only when a person is suspected of involvement in the offense that questioning must be suspended and the *Miranda* warning given.

- A suspect must be advised of his or her *Miranda* rights before any questioning begins. In addition to reading the warning to suspects and permitting them to read it themselves, suspects should be asked to sign a form containing the warning, indicating that they do understand their rights and whether or not they waive them. A copy of such a form is included in Appendix D. If circumstances do not permit the use of a written form, the warning and waiver can be made orally.

- At times, the customary method of investigation–completely turning over the interrogation of suspects to the appropriate investigative

agency–may have to be abandoned. For instance, the warden may decide that staff promptly must pursue questioning of suspects to stop an escape, discover plans for a disturbance, or prevent retaliation by associates of an assault victim. On such occasions, questioning the suspect for internal security purposes likely will affect the prospect of successful prosecution of the inmate offender. Failure to properly advise suspects of their rights is advisable only when the benefits gained clearly outweigh the value lost by the inability to properly prosecute the case. In these circumstances, the statement, and only tangible evidence (such as weapons or escape tools) located as a result, probably will be inadmissible at trial. Also, any statement subsequently given to any other investigative agency likely will be so tainted that it will be inadmissible, and the prospect of a successful prosecution is therefore endangered.

- When the investigative agency has completed its investigation, institution disciplinary action may be taken. It is generally not necessary to await the outcome of a criminal trial to do so, especially if there will be a long delay before the trial.

It is impossible in this brief section to spell out the complete legal background and details and to anticipate all the problems that may arise. Troublesome cases and local problems not covered here should be discussed with the appropriate investigative agency and the agency's legal counsel.

Acts of Violence

Acts of violence are a special case. They present an immediate need for handling the incident as a potential criminal referral. The chief of security is responsible for establishing procedures to be followed in the event of serious assaults, homicides, and other acts of violence committed in the institution. All such guidelines should be reviewed and approved by the central office legal staff.

Procedures to handle acts of violence should include, but not be restricted to, the following topics:

- Responsibility of the shift supervisor and the department supervisor involved

- Steps to assure the preservation of evidence

- Notification of appropriate investigative and law enforcement agencies

- Interrogation and segregation of witnesses and handling of suspects

- Notification of next of kin

- Notification of the central office

Since acts of violence can occur anywhere within the institution and can be discovered or witnessed by any member of the staff, all staff members must be thoroughly familiar with these procedures.

Transportation Activity

23

Even though it means foregoing all of the stable security measures associated with the institution itself, for a variety of reasons, every correctional system must transport inmates outside the secure perimeter from time to time. When outside the secure perimeter, inmates are in a somewhat better position to escape from custody than when they are in the institution. That means that staff have to have, and carefully follow, planned security measures whenever they have inmates under escort or in transit.

Trip Arrangements

In general, trip planning and arrangements should include provisions for:

- Conferring with other staff members regarding trip date, departure time, financial arrangements, transportation, and type of accommodations available

- Determining whether special provisions are needed for infirm inmates

- Learning who to contact in the event of unusual incidents or emergencies

- Reviewing of post orders by transporting officers

- Obtaining any necessary records

- Securing other pertinent information regarding the inmate, including his or her adjustment while in confinement

- Reading and signing the escort instructions prior to departing on the trip

The chief of security carefully should select the escorting officers and provide them with instructions governing their responsibilities. They should have completed their probationary period, and the officer-in-charge should have a minimum of three years' experience. When groups of three or more inmates are transported, a shift supervisor-level employee should be in charge. Staff selected for escort duty should remember that they are representatives of their institution and agency, and they should conduct themselves in a professional manner. They should treat inquiring citizens courteously without divulging information about inmate movement.

The record office should furnish the necessary records, including commitment papers or a copy of them, a photograph, and a brief description of the inmate. Central file records should be furnished in the case of a permanent transfer to another institution.

Medical staff should determine the need for any medical services in conjunction with inmate transfers. Medical staff should furnish escorting officers with a report on medical or psychiatric cases, covering any prescribed medication, or suggestions for special handling. In special situations, a member of the medical staff may be detailed to the trip to provide treatment for any medical problems that may arise. In the absence of a medical staff member, a medical kit may be provided to the trip supervisor, along with full training in its use.

Transportation of inmates in restraints should be carried out quietly, with as little public display as possible. Inmates to be transferred or moved under escort must not be allowed to have contact with the public or make any public statements. Specific escort plans and schedules never should be discussed with the inmates involved. Inmates should be notified of the trip just prior to departure. To the extent possible, after notification of a scheduled trip, the inmate should not make or receive any phone calls, visit with anyone, or make any public statements.

Prior to departure on an institutional transfer trip, staff should notify the warden of the receiving institution of the departure time, expected arrival time, number of inmates, and all other pertinent information. If difficulties delay the arrival, the warden at the receiving institution must be notified by telephone, radio, or other method. If the delay is serious or lengthy, both sending and receiving institutions should be notified.

Property and Searches

The officer-in-charge of the trip should be present when the inmate dresses for the trip, and should thoroughly strip search the inmate and all property. All clothing should be removed. No part of the body should be overlooked, especially locations where keys, money, razor blades, or small bits of metal might be concealed. Hair, mouth, the spaces between fingers and toes, soles of the feet, all bandages, dentures, custom built shoes, canes, crutches, and artificial limbs also should be inspected thoroughly. Prior to actually transporting an inmate, a final, thorough inspection by the escort officer is required, including a search with a handheld metal detector. Ideally, a second set of inspected clothing should be furnished. Care should be taken to make certain the inmate does not acquire any unauthorized items after the search.

Inmates should take a minimum of personal property and funds with them, depending on the duration of the trip. For relatively brief escorted trips, items accompanying the inmate ordinarily should be limited to toilet articles, combs, hair brushes, and eyeglasses. The inmate's remaining personal property should be inventoried and stored in a secure area of the institution, although in some circumstances (single cell and relatively short trip) the property may be secured in the inmate's cell.

On bedside visits or funeral trips where the escort officer is responsible for money belonging to the inmate under supervision, the officer should provide a receipt for inmate funds at the time the money is received. At the conclusion of the trip, a complete itemized report of the expenditures should be submitted.

For permanent transfers, items should be limited to the amount that can be packed and sealed in a box measuring approximately 12 x 12 x 15 inches. The balance of the property should be forwarded to the receiving institution. For permanent transfers, the agency's typical business office procedures will be used to transfer inmate funds.

Restraint Equipment and Weapons

Being legally responsible for an inmate's custody, the officer usually is given great discretion in the type of restraint equipment employed on an escorted trip. All institutions should maintain an adequate supply of restraint equipment for use in escort activity. This equipment should be of a standard type and brand, and should be maintained in good operating condition. However, the use of restraint equipment does not eliminate the need for continuous, alert supervision during the trip.

Restraint equipment typically consists of leg irons, handcuffs, handcuff covers, and waist chains. Restraint belts and leather cuffs for mental health cases, and plastic restraint devices (which ordinarily are used only temporarily when enough regular handcuffs are not available) also should be on hand. All restraint equipment should be double locked.

The inmate should not be shackled to a stationary object in a moving vehicle, unless his or her past conduct indicates it is necessary to safeguard the security of persons and property. In such cases–which should be extreme in nature–the factual reasons for doing so should be fully documented.

Agency policy should specify the circumstances under which "black box" restraint covers may be used; often this decision is linked to the inmate's custody level, with maximum-security inmates most often qualifying for such use.

Firearms always must be carried and used in conformance with applicable county, state, and federal law. Except for the regular transfer of large groups of inmates, such as by bus or to court, the use of firearms by an escorting officer should be approved on a case-by-case basis–usually by the warden. While some systems maintain that firearms ordinarily should not be carried by officers traveling in the same car with inmates, others require that high-security inmates be transported by two officers–one armed and one unarmed. In any case, appropriate safeguards must be in place to ensure that the inmate never has the opportunity to seize any weapon.

Individual agency policy may vary on the specific circumstances under which weapons may be fired, and

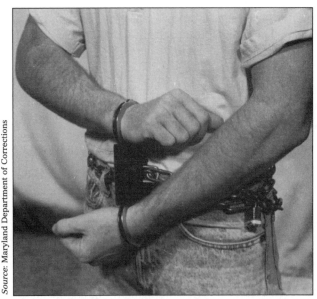

Source: Montgomery County, Maryland, Detention Center

Source: Maryland Department of Corrections

Proper use of restraint equipment, sometimes including a "black box," (above, right) is vital to safe, secure inmate transportation.

whether verbal warnings or warning fire are required before actually firing at an inmate. In many agencies, firearms may be used to disable in the event of an escape attempt, only after the inmate disregards orders to halt, and after a warning shot has been fired. Use of firearms under these circumstances must be undertaken only with full regard for public safety. Firearms should not be used to prevent escape of inmates recognized or known to have been committed as juveniles.

Other Transportation Issues

The mode of transportation best suited to the situation and nature of the trip always is recommended. Normally, bus or automobile is most appropriate. Bus operations are so common and such a significant aspect of inmate transportation that a separate section follows on that topic. Transfer by train is a little-used travel option in this era, but the general principles of other modes of transportation apply broadly to train travel, as well. Automobiles and vans are the major remaining mode of travel.

Once a vehicle is issued, the transporting officer must search it, ensuring that it is free of contraband, weapons, or any article that might aid an escape attempt. The officer also shall perform a safety check of the vehicle and ensure that it is fully fueled and that all communication systems (radio and cell phone) are operating properly. To ensure that contraband is not put in a vehicle after this inspection has been completed, the vehicle should be locked and kept under some form of supervision.

In sedans and vans used to transport inmates, a safety shield should be installed between the front and rear seats. Additional brackets can be installed in other institutional vehicles so, if necessary, the shield may be transferred between vehicles. If shields are not available, one escorting officer should sit in the back seat with the inmate. Inmate trips by sedan or van should be as direct as possible, and accomplished in an inconspicuous manner, avoiding all possible traffic congestion, signal lights, railroad crossings, and other delaying situations. When possible, staff should establish several routes to frequently traveled destinations (such as hospitals and court), so as not to establish a predictable pattern. The chosen route should be finalized with institution staff prior to departing.

When traveling by car or van, rest stops should be made where there is no building or traffic congestion. Isolated gas stations in rural areas involve the fewest hazards. Inmates should not be taken into public dining rooms. If stops for meals are necessary, carryout or drive-through service is recommended.

When traveling to crowded areas, parking problems should be anticipated. All vehicles and civilians should be viewed as possible threats. The escort officer always shall be very cautious and observant of his or her surroundings. A well-formulated plan should be in place to prevent officers from becoming separated from inmates for any reason.

When travel by plane is necessary, the movement must be completed within Federal Aviation Administration (FAA) guidelines. All questions regarding restraints, firearms, and so forth should be referred to the FAA

163

prior to scheduling a trip by plane. To the extent possible, rest stops in airports and other public areas should be arranged with a minimum of public contact.

Inmates sometimes are escorted to the funeral of a relative or to the bedside of a dying relative, using one or more methods of transportation. As in other transportation-related situations, careful supervision is required, commensurate with the inmate's custody level. The following guidelines should govern such trips:

- An officer-in-charge of a funeral or bedside visit carefully should review the inmate's central file prior to departure to determine whether any special or significant factors exist that may compromise security.

- Any guidelines regarding the use of restraint equipment on such a trip should be decided in advance. Depending on the situation, additional restraints may be applied. Ordinarily, it is not necessary to use restraint equipment on minimum-custody inmates.

- The escorting officer should instruct the inmate regarding forbidden practices such as making statements to news media or making unauthorized contact with the public, family, or friends.

- The inmate and the escort should be inseparable throughout the trip.

- Layovers should be planned to ensure that acceptable jail facilities are available.

- The inmate should be returned to the institution immediately following the termination of the visit by the most expeditious route and means.

Transportation of inmates between an institution and court–whether by car, van, or other conveyance–should be accomplished inconspicuously. Sufficient time should be allowed to park the vehicle and safely move to the court area. Constant alertness is necessary to avoid contact with the public, or others who may be interested in the inmate. While transporting inmates for this purpose, some systems assign a chase vehicle with an armed officer.

Officers should be properly stationed in the court-house to cut off every avenue between the inmate and reporters, photographers, lawyers, family, and the general public, and to be able stop an escape attempt. The officer-in-charge should be thoroughly familiar with the general floor plan, stairways, elevators, and hallways of the building in which the courtroom is located.

Illness or death en route is a possibility, particularly during long trips. If an inmate becomes ill or injured en route and no medical staff is available, arrangements should be made for an examination by qualified medical personnel as soon as possible. If necessary, the home institution should be contacted for further instructions.

If an inmate dies while in transit, it will be necessary to arrange for the coroner and local and state police authorities to remove the body while still within the state in which the death occurred. A receipt for the body should be obtained from the coroner. The officer-in-charge immediately should notify the institution of the death, and provide a statement of the time, place, and apparent cause of death. If injury or death occurred by violence or under other unusual circumstances, the nearest law enforcement officer should be notified to meet the escorting officer at the scene.

If an inmate escapes while in transit, the officer-in-charge should use all resources immediately available to apprehend the inmate. The officer-in-charge also should take immediate action to notify the nearest law enforcement agency. The officer should radio or phone the originating institution. Notification should include a summary of the circumstances surrounding the escape and any information that might be useful in conducting the search. The supervision of other inmates never should be relaxed in order to pursue an escaping inmate.

Bus Operations

Transportation of large numbers of inmates by bus can pose special problems, many of which cannot be fully anticipated. Therefore, the following section is not intended to be all-inclusive, but should be used as a guide in developing local operating procedures.

General

Bus officers ordinarily should be assigned to a bus as part of the regular roster rotation. Employees selected for assignment to bus duty should: have a minimum of three years' correctional experience; be required to complete training in bus operations; and, have passed the state commercial drivers' examination. They also should be required to complete training courses in the use of restraint and defensive equipment. A senior correctional supervisor should be in charge of each bus–responsible for complete trip preparation, supervision of all bus personnel and inmates on board, and the secure, safe transportation of inmates.

The bus should be operated safely at all times. The maximum cruising speed should not exceed the speed limit of the road on which the bus is traveling.

Each officer assigned to the bus should be familiar with Interstate Commerce Commission Motor Carriers' Safety Regulations and should be able to operate the bus in accordance with these regulations. Bus drivers should make every effort to familiarize themselves with the mechanical aspects of its operation. A bus never should be taken on a trip unless it is in proper running order and good repair.

The bus supervisor is responsible for inspecting and searching the bus prior to leaving on a trip to ensure that it is in good running order and that there has been no sabotage or concealment of weapons.

On-the-road Issues

It is imperative that personnel responsible for the bus operation have proper rest intervals between trips. When a bus is away from its home institution, the employees responsible for its operation need sufficient time to keep the bus in good sanitary and mechanical condition.

The warden of each institution along the planned route should assist the bus supervisors in the following ways:

- Make available institution garages and mechanics for needed repairs and supply material for repairs

- Furnish gasoline, oil, and lubricants, as needed

- Supply inmate details for cleaning the vehicles

- Furnish meals for inmates en route

- Furnish transportation for bus officers to the nearest suitable motel or place of lodging

- Provide a safe and secure place for bus storage and parking

- Promptly furnish receipts for all inmates, as well as for property and fuel

Appropriate high-quality meals should be provided for use on the bus, ideally prepared by a civilian food service staff member and picked up by a member of the bus crew, who will inspect them for quality of contents, proper wrapping, proper packaging, and correct quantities. Prior to taking the lunches or dinners to the departure point, any discrepancies must be corrected. Any bus thermos containers should be cleaned by a designated staff member and locked in a secure area until they are filled by a staff member.

Before starting a day's travel, the bus supervisor should communicate with each institution to be visited that day. When possible, the bus supervisor should notify institutions on the day's route of the following information:

- Estimated time of arrival

- Total number of inmates to be received or housed overnight, and number of those to continue on the bus the next day

- Proposed departure time and next day's destinations

- Number of seats that will be available on departure

- Types of inmates on the bus, so that the institution will be prepared to handle any problems or special cases

Bus departures should be scheduled so as to arrive at the designated institution during working hours, if possible. When a bus is to arrive at an institution on a Saturday, Sunday, or holiday, the supervisor should notify the institution as far ahead of time as possible. The bus supervisor should report to the warden any delay in departure, indicating the estimated length of the delay and the reason.

In the event of an emergency situation, the bus supervisor should notify the originating and receiving institutions. If there is an unexplained delay in arrival of a bus, institutions on the bus route should take appropriate action to locate the bus and determine its status.

All buses should have two-way radios with two or more frequencies, one of which allows access to state law enforcement officials. Bus officers also should have portable radios for maintaining contact with any officer who has to leave the bus. Many agencies also are equipping bus staff with cellular phones, which provide an alternate means of communication in many locales.

Bus Supervision and Inmate Management

The bus supervisor should handcuff all inmate passengers, even minimum-custody inmates, checking all restraint equipment to determine that it is applied correctly. Handcuffs should be used as a security measure, and not as punishment. They should not be tightened to the point where they cut off circulation.

Leg irons and handcuff covers (black boxes) should be used at the discretion of the bus supervisor. Discretion should be exercised in using handcuff covers. They should be used only as a last resort for added control and security. The problems they create when eating and drinking or using toilet facilities should be kept in mind. Handcuff covers may be used in the following situations:

- For use on special runs, when a bus is required to transport unruly inmates to another institution because of a disturbance

- For use on inmates who are considered extreme escape risks

- For use on inmates with severe assault records

- For use on individual inmates who are disruptive at the beginning of the transfer or become disruptive during the trip

The bus supervisor should be certain a thorough strip search is performed on each inmate during processing and again before boarding the bus. A portable transfrisker should be used to determine if offenders are hiding any metal objects within their body cavities.

No personal property should be given to inmates while on board a bus. This includes items such as trial records, judgment and commitment orders, personal legal papers, correspondence, photographs, pens and pencils, excess smoking materials, toilet articles, and so forth. Individual records, correspondence, or other official records, as well as clothing and other personal effects of officers, fire extinguishers, or any articles that may be used as weapons should not be stored in the inmate compartment of the bus. Such articles should be stored in a secure place accessible only by the bus crew.

Officers assigned to supervise inmates should have a clear view of the entire bus compartment and should be able to prevent inmate contact with civilians or introduction of contraband from the outside. Inmates should not be permitted to make contact with unauthorized persons, make telephone calls, or mail letters in transit or at stopovers (except when an inmate is held over for several days).

Any staff who will be armed during the trip should be in a separate, secure compartment, so that he or she has no direct contact with inmates.

At least two officers should remain aboard the bus while inmates are in transit, including during rest and lunch stops. Vehicle stops should be short and can be kept to a minimum by obtaining takeout lunches for all crew members and having them eat them on the bus.

Staff should have a photo identification card for each inmate on the bus, and that identification and other relevant records should accompany the inmate in transit. Each inmate should be checked against the ID when boarding or disembarking.

Inmates should be assigned seats when placed on the bus, and should not be permitted to leave them without the bus supervisor's authorization.

Firearms and Restraints

Firearms only should be used when absolutely necessary to prevent escapes and serious assaults. Depending on agency policy, the factors justifying the use of deadly force will vary. Many agencies require that, before firing at an individual, officers give verbal warning and then fire a warning shot in a safe direction. When it is necessary to fire at an individual, the shots should be directed to disable, and only when there is no risk to the public.

Employees with firearms should be held strictly accountable for the condition of their weapons and for their proper use. The standard sidearm for security personnel escorting the bus should be a high-capacity 9 mm pistol and a 12-gauge shotgun. Officers carrying firearms should not come in contact with inmates. Sidearms should be carried in shoulder or belt holsters and not be exhibited to inmate passengers.

The bus supervisor should be responsible to see that adequate arms, ammunition, handcuffs, leg irons, flashlights, flares, red flags, and fire suppression equipment are properly issued and stored before the trip begins, as well as during stopovers and at the end of the trip.

The supervisor should be certain that more than one officer has keys to the handcuffs and/or leg irons. Officers holding keys should not come in direct contact with inmates except when directed by the bus supervisor to remove handcuffs or leg irons. Firearms, handcuffs, leg irons, hacksaw blades, and devices for removal of defective restraints should be stored in a secure compartment that is inaccessible to inmates. Some systems use a removable, secure equipment container to hold all such items, such as an armored box on wheels that easily can be moved from the bus to the armory.

Bus Security and Upkeep

Bus windows should be blocked from the outside, limiting window movement to a four-inch opening.

Stopovers at night generally should be at institutions. When making overnight stopovers at a jail, the sheriffs and jailers should be instructed fully on any special procedures for handling the inmates. Law enforcement personnel should be advised that visitors should not be permitted; any letters written by inmates should be held for the bus supervisor. Inmates should not be permitted to receive communications, packages, money, or articles from anyone.

The bus should be maintained in a clean and sanitary condition and should be ready for operation at all times. The toilets must be kept clean, and the supervisor should see that inmates use them in a sanitary manner. Close supervision should be exercised by one of the bus officers over any inmate cleaning detail.

The bus supervisor should make certain that the bus is locked when left unattended. The bus never must be left standing with keys in the ignition or loose on board. Buses should not be parked in areas where they would attract undue attention.

When staff quarters are not provided by institutions where stopovers are made, the bus should be left at the institution and alternate transportation arranged for taking the crew to and from a motel.

An adequate supply of water should be kept in the bus tanks at all times, and a supply of ice, paper cups, and disposable containers for used cups should be furnished for inmate use.

Special Situations

A number of disruptive or potentially dangerous situations can occur while a bus is in transit that can interrupt normal operations. The bus crew always should be alert to the possibility that an unexpected incident is a diversion, intended to allow inmates on the bus an opportunity to escape.

(1) If an escape occurs directly from the bus, the bus supervisor should request assistance from the appropriate law enforcement agencies, notify the originating and receiving institutions, and attempt to apprehend the escapee without risking the security of the remaining inmates.

(2) If the bus is attacked by outside parties, the bus supervisor should radio for assistance from the nearest law enforcement agency. The bus should continue moving unless it is crippled by breakdown or sabotage.

(3) If a hostage situation occurs on a bus, the bus supervisor should secure the bus perimeter, request assistance from the nearest law enforcement agency and the institution, determine the number of staff and inmates involved, determine what weapons the hostage takers have, and identify the resources available to gain release of the hostages.

(4) If a staff member or an inmate becomes ill, the bus supervisor should seek assistance from the nearest

appropriate medical facility and, if necessary, request assistance from a local law enforcement agency.

(5) If a staff member or an inmate dies, the bus supervisor should notify the local coroner or medical examiner, secure a body receipt from him or her, and record the pertinent data, including name of the deceased and time, date, cause, and place of death.

(6) In the event of a fire on board the bus, the bus supervisor should stop the bus and use the available fire-fighting equipment. He or she immediately also should request assistance from local fire and police authorities. If evacuation is necessary, the supervisor should secure the bus perimeter, provide for weapons control, and evacuate the inmates, while maintaining accountability. The bus staff should fight the fire only if it seems possible for them to do so while maintaining security.

(7) If a disturbance that cannot be controlled with available resources occurs on a bus, the bus crew should isolate the bus from civilians and request assistance from the nearest law enforcement agency. When sufficient assistance is available, the bus crew should attempt to regain control of the situation using the equipment available, including chemical agents, restraints, and disturbance batons. Firearms only should be used to protect life and to prevent escapes and only the minimum force necessary to control the situation should be used.

(8) If a bus transporting inmates is involved in a traffic accident, the bus supervisor should secure the bus perimeter, request assistance from a local law enforcement agency, and obtain medical assistance for any injured. If the bus is disabled, the bus supervisor should request advice from the home institution.

(9) If a flood, snow storm, or ice storm occurs, the bus supervisor should contact the highway patrol to determine road conditions along the planned route. If the weather precludes safe operation of the bus, the bus supervisor should request further instructions from the home institution.

(10) In the event of a possible tornado, the bus should not proceed into the area of danger. The bus supervisor should establish and maintain radio contact with law enforcement agencies along the bus route. If a tornado is approaching, the crew should notify local law enforcement agencies by radio of the situation, stop the bus beneath a highway overpass or in as safe an area as is possible, and order the inmates to exit the bus and lie flat on the ground. Officers on board should form a secure perimeter and try to maintain full visibility of all inmates. When the emergency has passed, the supervisor should

return all inmates to the bus and take a careful count of all inmates and staff.

(11) If a bus fails to function properly on startup at the institution, the bus supervisor should notify the chief of security and other appropriate personnel in order to restore the bus to working order. If a bus fails to operate properly on the road, the supervisor should request assistance from the nearest law enforcement agency. If the failure is such that temporary housing is required, the supervisor should request assistance and advice from the home institution.

Use of Force

24

On occasion, in every institution, staff have to use force to control an individual inmate or a group of inmates. While confrontation avoidance techniques–the use of interpersonal skills to defuse a situation–often are successful and should be tried whenever it is safe to do so, sometimes staff must intervene forcefully. Most use-of-force situations fall into one of two categories–nonlethal and lethal. This chapter will address them using that division, after a few general comments. It will not cover the use of precautionary restraints, such as using handcuffs to move inmates in special housing units, or in transit from one institution to another. This chapter should be read with particular attention to its links to the emergency preparedness section of the guidelines.

General

As a foremost principle, force should be used only as a last resort, after all other reasonable efforts to resolve a problem have failed. When force is absolutely necessary, staff must use only the minimum amount necessary to:

- Prevent escapes and protect the public

- Control the inmate

- Ensure the safety of staff, inmates, and others in the institution

- Prevent serious property damage

- Ensure institution security and safety

Training is critical when it comes to the use of force. Whatever the agency policy is–and there is

considerable variation in practice around the country–staff need to know it. They need to know what levels of force are authorized, the conditions under which it may be used, and who may authorize it. Whether it be deadly force reserved only to the warden's authorization or the more common application of restraints to subdue a combative inmate, this is an important area that the agency's training program needs to address clearly.

To achieve these ends, specific initial and annual refresher training must be provided to all staff who may be called upon to employ any level of force in managing an inmate. The training should include a detailed presentation on the department philosophy related to the use of force and its relationship to successful inmate management.

Those sessions should cover confrontation avoidance procedures, the application of all types of restraints, and reporting procedures. Training should emphasize the principle that only the least amount of force necessary should be employed to control a situation, and that force and restraints may not be used as retribution or punishment. The training must be specific for individual control methods, such as direct physical control, chemicals, and electronic controls. The training must characterize the different types of force on a continuous scale from the least aggressive (officer presence, verbal commands) to the most aggressive (lethal). The training should use actual scenarios to demonstrate sound decisionmaking.

There are very clear legal implications to the use of either nonlethal or lethal force. Inmates can–and have–died during or after the application of even relatively low levels of force. Staff inadvertently can cause serious physical injury to an inmate. In some instances, the imprudent use of lethal force could jeopardize members of the public. No one wants these kinds of incidents to occur, and agency staff must be familiar with the limitations of their authority, and the implications of misuse of force.

Nonlethal Force

Staff should be trained in the application of nonlethal force and the application of restraints to gain control of an inmate when:

- The inmate commits an assault upon staff or inmates

- The inmate destroys property

- The inmate attempts suicide or harms himself or herself

- The inmate is violent or displays signs of imminent violence

Staff may be required to use force immediately–with or without the direction of supervisory personnel–when an inmate's actions present an immediate, serious threat to the inmate, staff, others, property, or to institution security and safety.

When immediate use of force is not necessary, staff should rely on a calculated use-of-force strategy–such as when an inmate is in a relatively isolated area (a cell, for instance) and presents no immediate threat. Ordinarily, staff should attempt to resolve the situation verbally, but if that attempt fails, calculated force may be used.

Many calculated use-of-force situations lend themselves to a preliminary effort to persuade the inmate to comply with staff orders. Confrontation avoidance often can defuse a potentially dangerous situation and eliminate the need to use force to control an inmate. Ordinarily, the chief of security or shift supervisor, a member of the mental health staff, unit staff, or others who know the inmate assesses all available information, and one or more of them attempts to persuade the inmate to comply. These attempts to resolve the situation peacefully should be videotaped, when possible.

Use-of-force Teams

If confrontation avoidance attempts are unsuccessful, the coordinated use of a tactical team may be required. In the past, the accepted way to remove a defiant inmate from a cell or otherwise move a recalcitrant inmate was to gather the available staff and send them into the area, relatively unprepared to do

the job. Today, many correctional systems have adopted a trained team approach to this task. The results of this change appear to be fewer injuries to staff and inmates, and a far more professional approach to a very difficult, and sometimes dangerous, task.

(1) This strategy ordinarily involves five or more staff specifically trained in extraction techniques. Each member of the team wears a helmet, face shield, jumpsuit, gloves, boots, and pads. Team members are pre-briefed by the team leader (usually of senior correctional supervisor rank) as to the situation, all relevant facts about the inmate, and the responsibilities of each team member.

(2) The first team member into the area should be responsible for pinning the inmate to the wall or floor (using a shield, when possible), the second member for securing the left upper portion of the body, the third member for securing the right upper portion of the body, the fourth member for securing the left lower portion of the body, and the fifth member for securing the right lower portion of the body. The third member should apply handcuffs to the inmate's wrists (behind the back), and the fifth member should apply leg irons to the inmate's legs. Assignments of the portions of the body are made as the team members see it, to account for the inmate being sideways on a bed or otherwise not in an upright position. Talk should be kept to an absolute minimum while the team is at its task. To the extent possible, staff should try to protect the inmate's head and neck.

(3) If necessary, staff also may use chemical agents, or nonlethal weapons (such as a stun gun that temporarily incapacitates). These methods only may be used with the approval of top command staff (that is, the chief of security, deputy warden, warden, or duty officer).

(4) When these methods are believed necessary, and there is time to do so, command staff should confer with medical personnel to determine if there are any medical reasons why a particular type of control device should not be used. If there are, then an alternate means of control should be selected.

(5) If an inmate refuses to move once restrained, staff may physically move him or her by lifting and carrying the inmate, but the inmate should not be lifted or carried by the restraints.

(6) Medical staff should examine an inmate who has been subject to the use of these methods. This should occur immediately after control has been regained. Treatment may include flushing eyes and other decontamination techniques, as well as a more

While not a day-to-day factor in correctional operations, tactical response capability is critical in emergencies.

complete medical examination if there is an indication of an injury warranting advanced treatment.

Communicable Disease Safeguards

Staff must take appropriate precautions to prevent injury and prevent exposure to communicable diseases during all use-of-force actions.

- Appropriate protective gear should be provided for planned use-of-force actions.

- Training should emphasize the methods of transmission of communicable diseases.

- Staff with a skin disease or skin injury should not participate in use-of-force actions unless it is an emergency.

- When staff enter an area where there is reason to believe body fluids may be present, additional protective devices shall be available and used by those staff entering that area.

- Following such incidents, areas contaminated with blood or other body fluids must be sanitized as soon as any investigation is complete; all required biohazard safeguards should be used in that process.

Prolonged Use of Restraints

Sometimes it is necessary to maintain an inmate in restraints for significant periods of time, to control dangerous or threatening conduct. In such cases, a progressive restraint policy should be used–meaning that staff should use the least-restrictive method to control the inmate, based on an assessment of past and current conduct. This would include, respectively, hard restraints without waist chain or waist belt, hard restraints with waist chain or waist belt, four-point soft restraints with hard restraints to the bed, and finally, four-point hard restraints to the bed.

Because of the severity of the four-point procedures, some additional information is necessary. Highly assaultive and aggressive inmates may be placed immediately in whatever level of restraints their conduct requires, including four-point restraints, employing vinyl, leather, or handcuff-type equipment, to restrain an inmate by hands and feet to a bed or other stationary object. This should be an uncommon procedure, and while with proper safeguards it can be accomplished by security personnel, in some systems, this procedure is used only in medical units, and under medical supervision. Ordinarily, only the warden or qualified medical staff may approve the use of four-point restraints on an inmate.

Soft restraints (such as vinyl or leather) should be the starting point for all four-point restraint situations, unless such restraints previously have proven ineffective for that inmate, or were ineffective when initially applied. Restraint chairs are available commercially, which rely on heavy straps to restrain highly aggressive, dangerous, and violent inmates.

The conditions under which an inmate is held in four-point restraints are critical. Inmates should be placed face-down to prevent complications from vomiting, but should be rotated periodically to prevent undue soreness or stiffness. The surface upon which the inmate is restrained must have a mattress and blanket or sheet; inmates must not remain naked or without bed covering, and must be provided clothing that is appropriate to the temperature in the cell, unless ordered otherwise by medical staff.

When an inmate is placed in four-point restraints, medical personnel must assess the inmate, ensure appropriate breathing and response, and ensure proper circulation, at least twice during each eight-hour shift. In institutions without twenty-four hour medical coverage, the shift supervisor may conduct checks for the first eight hours, but after that time, medical staff should become involved in the process.

Line staff should check the inmate at least every thirty minutes for circulation impairment and other problems. The shift supervisor personally should check the inmate every two hours to determine if the inmate has regained control and may be released from that level of restraint. At this two-hour point, the inmate should be given a chance to use the toilet, unless doing so likely would allow the inmate to become violent again.

Documentation is critical for this type of restraint situation. All staff checks, medical reviews, changes of clothing or position, and other events must be recorded. Any relapse in conduct, refusal by the inmate to take advantage of the opportunity to use the toilet, or other noteworthy actions must be logged as well, using the individual unit log sheet or a separate form that should be placed in the inmate's central file when the episode is over.

Releasing an inmate from restraints or applying lesser restraints ordinarily is the shift supervisor's decision. Inmates should not be retained in four-point restraints for more than eight hours without some additional level of management review and safeguards against abuse of the procedure.

If an inmate has been brought under control with the use of four-point restraints, but still displays a need for restraints, whenever possible, ambulatory restraints should be used. Ambulatory restraints allow the inmate to eat, drink, and take care of other needs without staff intervention. This is an excellent means of transitioning an inmate from a more restrictive restraint status to unrestrained status.

Reporting and Incident Review

All use-of-force incidents, including those involving the nonroutine use of restraints, must be carefully documented and investigated. This will protect staff from unfounded allegations and deter the unwarranted use of force. Of particular importance is the need to be specific in describing what actual steps were taken to control the inmate. It is not enough to say, "The minimum amount of force required was applied." Staff must be very detailed in reporting the measures used in a use-of-force situation. This is critical in defending staff against litigation that may result from such situations.

When possible, all planned use-of-force incidents should be videotaped. Any variation from established procedures should be documented carefully, as they are prime candidates for litigation or adverse public attention. Full documentation, including preservation of any videotape relating to the incident, is especially important in such cases.

All use-of-force incidents should be documented immediately in a standard format, and any videotapes and associated records should be reviewed formally by an administrative team consisting of the chief of security and at least two other department heads. This team should determine whether the type and extent of force used was appropriate under the circumstances, and in addition to critical findings, they also should praise staff when their performance was positive (see box, below).

The warden personally should go over the review team's report, all documentation, and the videotape (if available) on every use-of-force incident–planned

---

Use-of-force Incident Reviews

Administrative team reviews of use-of-force incidents should include an assessment of the following elements:

– Whether there was an opportunity for voluntary compliance, and if so, how effective it was

–Professionalism and conduct of the supervising officer and all involved line staff

–Proper use of protective gear, including proper and improper equipment

–Level of force employed, including any indication that excessive force was used particularly to the inmate's thorax (chest and back), throat, head or extremities during or after the time when the inmate was resisting staff

–Technique for application of restraints, to ensure there was no indication that excessive force or pressure was applied

–Time required for the operation to be completed

–Continued and appropriate use of protective equipment

–Proper and continuous use of the video camera throughout the incident

– Presence and role of a medical staff member

–Proper use of a stun gun, chemical agents, or pepper mace, if employed

–Verbal content of the incident, including whether any employees used inappropriate or unprofessional language

and unplanned. A summary report of the team's findings also should be forwarded for review to the central office security administrator, who should track all use-of-force incidents in the agency.

Use of Chemical Agents and Other Nonlethal Devices

The warden may authorize the use of chemical agents or nonlethal weapons when:

- The inmates involved are armed or barricaded

- They cannot be approached without danger to staff, inmates, or others

- A delay in restoring control would constitute a serious hazard to the inmate or others, or would likely result in a major disturbance or serious property damage

Medical staff should be consulted prior to staff using chemical agents and other nonlethal weapons, unless the circumstances are such that immediate use is necessary. Whenever possible, the inmate's medical file first should be reviewed to determine whether the inmate has any diseases or condition (asthma, emphysema, bronchitis, tuberculosis, or heart or lung diseases) which would be dangerously affected if a chemical agent or nonlethal weapon were to be used.

When using a chemical agent aerosol dispenser, it should not be used at a range closer than four feet. It should not be intentionally dispersed into the eyes, although the inmate must be touched on the face by the chemical in order for the agent to be effective. The recommended method is to dispense the chemical at the inmate's lower facial areas in one short (two-second) burst. If control is not achieved within fifteen seconds after the initial discharge, a second (two-second) burst per individual may be used. Once control is established, the inmate immediately must be examined by medical staff and the eyes flushed with cold water within five minutes after exposure, unless the inmate will not cooperate.

Other nonlethal devices also are available, including beanbag rounds, stun and "stingball" munitions, and electrical stunning devices. Each agency should develop specific procedures for the use of these devices, to include guidance on:

- The circumstances under which they may be used

- Who may authorize such use

- Any limitations on the category of inmate or area of the institution where they may be used

- Reporting requirements following such use

- Input from medical staff prior to such use and medical examination requirements after use

Special Circumstances

Staff occasionally may be required to use force on a pregnant, handicapped, or mentally ill inmate, or an aggressive inmate with open cuts, sores, or lesions. In such instances, consultation with medical staff is essential for all but true emergencies. The condition of the inmate must be assessed carefully to determine whether the situation is serious enough to justify the use of physical force.

- When pregnant inmates must be restrained, necessary precautions (determined by the medical staff) shall be taken to ensure the fetus is not harmed.

- Mentally ill and handicapped inmates may require special handling, as well. It may be necessary to restrain such an inmate at the institutional hospital or at a local medical facility.

- Inmates with open cuts or wounds present a very high risk to staff in a restraint situation. Unless an emergency dictates otherwise, they should be approached carefully, by staff wearing prescribed necessary protective gear.

Use of Lethal Force

Firearms only should be used in cases where there is no other avenue to prevent serious consequences. The decision to use firearms should not be taken lightly and should be governed by considerations such as the location of the incident and the effectiveness of firearms in the situation.

Agency policy should make clear that firearms are to be used as a last resort to:

Prevent Escape: Agency policy will differ on this issue, but in many jurisdictions, in the event of an escape or attempted escape, a verbal order to halt first must be given. If the order is not obeyed, a warning shot may be fired, but only if there is no apparent risk of injury to an innocent person. If the warning shot is ineffective in stopping the escape attempt, firearms may be used to disable the potential escapee or any person assisting in the escape. An outside-assisted escape or escape attempt presents additional concerns to individual safety. Where an inmate attempting escape (or a person actively assisting an inmate in an escape) initiates action to cause physical harm, staff may use necessary force to control the

173

situation. In such cases, no verbal commands to stop or warning shots are necessary. Firearms ordinarily are not used in minimum-security level institutions, and may not be used if the staff member recognizes a potential escapee as an inmate sentenced under juvenile statutes.

Prevent Loss of Life or Grievous Bodily Harm: Firearms may be used by staff when there is a reasonable belief that the actions of another person are likely to result in the loss of life or grievous bodily harm to staff, inmates, or others. Whenever possible, firearms are to be used in the same manner as for escapes; that is, a disabling shot may be fired following an unsuccessful verbal order to stop and a safely directed warning shot. Verbal orders or warning shots, however, are not required when the staff member reasonably believes a danger of death or grievous bodily harm is imminent. Only the warden may order the use of firearms as a means to resolve a hostage situation. Warning shots should not be fired in an attempt to resolve a hostage situation, nor should firearms be used to create a diversion.

Protect Property: Firearms may be used to prevent damage to, or the destruction of, property when the loss of this property could contribute directly to an escape or attempted escape, grievous bodily harm, or death. This would include firing on persons attempting to damage or disable a fire truck during a fire within the institution, or inmates trying to break into a building where weapons or other security items are stored. Firearms should be used as a last resort, with a disabling shot fired following an unsuccessful verbal order to stop, and a warning shot.

No employee should be assigned duties involving firearms prior to the successful completion of the agency's firearms familiarization training course or a suitable equivalent. All staff subject to being placed on a post requiring the use of firearms also must satisfactorily complete an approved firearms refresher training course each year.

The warden may authorize staff to carry firearms when transporting inmates, participating in escape hunts, or being assigned to security posts requiring firearms. Post orders, disturbance plans, and escape plans must include authorization and instructions for the carrying and use of firearms. This would include the deployment of firearms outside the perimeter during fog patrol or low-visibility conditions, as determined by the appropriate emergency plan.

Staff may carry a firearm when transporting an inmate in the community, being especially cautious when members of the public are nearby. The guidelines for the use of a firearm during the course of an escape in the community are the same as for those in force at an institution, with the important condition that such use does not endanger the public.

Staff also may carry a firearm when transporting an inmate by commercial air carrier. Federal aviation regulations allow law enforcement officials, when necessary in the performance of their duties, to travel while armed. A required form must be completed before leaving the institution. When a flight does not involve the actual escort of an inmate, the weapon must be declared, unloaded, and placed in checked baggage.

A written report should be submitted each time a firearm is discharged while on duty, prior to the end of the staff member' shift. If a person is injured during an incident involving the use of firearms, immediate medical attention must be provided.

The agency should authorize, in accord with the needs of the individual institutions in the system, suitable identification that reflects the employee's status as being approved to carry a firearm under applicable laws and regulations. These IDs shall be maintained and closely accounted for by the chief of security. Lost or stolen IDs must be reported in writing. In systems where security staff are not already sworn law enforcement officers, staff assigned to posts involving the use of firearms (with the exception of tower and perimeter patrol) should be issued badges, which are to be displayed only when necessary to establish the staff member's authorization to carry a firearm, such as on an escape hunt. Agency policy should specify the parameters for, and limitations of, staff use of such badges.

Visiting Operations

25

Visiting is an important program for inmates and their families. Regrettably, some offenders exploit personal contact with visitors to introduce contraband or have impermissible kinds of physical contact. To prevent those kinds of activities, security staff must impose close controls on visiting rooms and the activities that go on in them. While each institution should have detailed visiting room regulations, basic controls fall into the general areas of visitor identification, visitor searches, visiting supervision, inmate searches, and visiting area searches.

Since visiting is a particularly sensitive activity, shift supervisors should pay special attention to it, as well as to entrance operations, in general. In cases where visits must be denied, terminated, or otherwise disrupted, supervisory personnel must be available to assist line staff. The shift supervisor should make certain decisions, including the decision to search or detain a visitor, or to notify law enforcement personnel of a possible law violation.

Visitor Identification

Visitors should be on an approved list generated by unit staff; no one should be permitted to arrive at the institution and visit an inmate without advance review and approval. Once determining a visitor is on the approved list, that person should establish his or her identity with a positive picture identification, such as a driver's license. If the individual cannot produce adequate identification, the visit should not be allowed. Some systems require that this picture ID be left at the processing point as part of the release identification process.

When they are approved to visit, and before being permitted into the visiting areas, all visitors should be subject to a "blacklight" procedure. This involves obtaining a portable ultraviolet light source, a supply of reflective ink, and a variety of distinctive stamps to be used on a random basis. Any visitor to the institution should be stamped with the ultraviolet-sensitive ink upon entry and checked with the ultraviolet light source before being allowed to leave. This procedure is effective with large groups as well as individual inmate visitors. This will ensure that the departing person was not an inmate attempting to escape by posing as a visitor.

Visitor Searches

Visitors and their belongings should be searched thoroughly before being allowed in the visiting area. This search process involves several elements. The visitor should deposit all nonessential items in a locker provided by the institution, or should return those items to their vehicle, if they so choose. The visitor retains the key to the locker throughout the visit. Any items going into the visiting room (diaper bags, purses, and so forth), should be carefully searched by security staff before the person is allowed into the visiting room.

The visitor should be required to successfully pass through a walk-through metal detector; a hand-held metal detector should be used to search those who set off the walk-through unit. The walk-through metal detector speeds the search of incoming visitors, and acts as a deterrent against the introduction of contraband in the institution. If a visitor repeatedly

Walk-through metal detection equipment at entrances and internal traffic points contributes greatly to contraband and weapon control.

does not clear this process, or refuses to submit to a search, he or she should be denied the privilege of visiting.

If visitors are permitted to deliver personal property items or money to the institution (practices that are not highly recommended), these items should not be opened or conveyed in the presence of inmates. A separate process should be established for this purpose (such as through the mail room), so as to not unduly complicate the visiting search and identification process. Food items, if permitted (although again, not recommended), also should be thoroughly searched; these items also are an excellent means for the introduction of contraband.

Finally, if visitors are required to travel any significant distance from the initial receiving/search point to the actual visiting area, then a second search may be required at the actual point of entry into the visiting room.

Visiting Supervision

Proper design and direct supervision of the visiting room will prevent many problems and detect others. The visiting area should be close to the main entrance, have appropriate search and storage areas for visitors, an adequate shakedown area for inmates, and other necessary features, including a child care or children's play area.

The staff post, itself, should provide direct visual supervision of the entire area. Chairs and tables should be arranged in a way that allows direct lines of sight. Blind spots created by any columns, pillars, or other design features should be compensated for with mirrors visible from the visiting officer's station.

Staff should be quick to intervene when inappropriate conduct begins. In particular, excessively intimate behavior is not only against institution rules, but is offensive to other inmates and visitors. It should be clear to all involved that any improper conduct will result in the termination of visiting and a possible incident report for the involved inmate.

In many systems, closed-circuit television is used to aid in supervision of the visiting room. If tilt and pan capability is available in the camera mount, then by enclosing the cameras in appropriately tinted enclosures, no one in the visiting room will be able to tell if they are under surveillance or not.

The most experienced staff should be on duty for the heaviest scheduled visiting days. Ordinarily, the days off for the regular visiting room officers should be adjusted so that they are present on both weekend days.

Some institutions permit soft drinks and food to come into the visiting area from the outside. This is a prime avenue for contraband; vending machines should be considered.

Traffic to the rest rooms in the visiting area always is a potential avenue for contraband introduction. Visitors can hide items in the rest room, or transfer items from clothing or a body cavity, for passage to an inmate. Similarly, inmates can use the rest room to hide items received from a visitor in a body cavity. Officers should be aware of any unusual conduct associated with this area.

Closed-circuit television can be used to supplement officer coverage in visiting areas.

Inmate Searches

Inmates should be strip searched before and after all visits. Pat searches are not sufficient. A suitably private area should be available, and staff should post in the area a list of all permissible items that may be taken into the visiting room. In particular, searches after visits must be very thorough. Staff should be alert to any indication of items hidden in body cavities, of course. But clothing, shoes, and all other items also should be given strict scrutiny.

Inmate orderlies working in the visiting room, either during, before, or after visiting hours, should be strip searched as well. All cleaning supplies and equipment they use should be carefully searched.

Visiting Area Searches

The visiting room should be thoroughly searched before and after each visiting period. Handheld metal detectors can be used to inspect cushions. Rest rooms should be given special attention. All trash in the visiting area should be cleared out daily and handled as hot trash, removed by staff. This will prevent the possibility of a visitor hiding contraband in the trash, to be removed later by an inmate orderly.

General Emergency Preparedness

26

Daily operations in a modern correctional institution require extraordinary vigilance. Crowding, idleness, understaffing, budget constraints, and other organizational problems can create an environment of stress and tension in the inmate population. Outside events can trigger adverse inmate reactions. A fire or natural disaster can create a need for immediate staff action. An imprudent staff action or decision can precipitate a crisis. Fog or other weather conditions can have an impact on normal operations. Emergency situations of any type can arise instantly. Staff have to be prepared for any one of those events–and many more.

Central Office Role

The agency's central office plays a key role in ensuring that all institutions are prepared for a crisis situation, and the security administrator is the central figure in that process. Every institution emergency plan must be reviewed and approved by the administrator, who also must pay particular attention to the plans during audits.

Setting up joint training among institutions and with other agency personnel is often the administrator's responsibility, as is identifying the location of key equipment and supplies that might have to be redeployed in a crisis. The administrator is responsible for ensuring that all relevant emergency preparedness information is conveyed in training, and that specialty training for tactical personnel is of a high quality and carried out on a timely basis.

Establishment of a central office emergency preparedness plan, including operation of a command center for prolonged crises, is a critical task for the security administrator. During an actual crisis, the security administrator must be prepared to coordinate resources from other institutions and agencies, as well as to actually go to the location of the incident, if need be.

Institutional Role

Effective emergency response capability at the institution level is vital in assuring security and public safety. The conventional wisdom holds that order usually is most effectively restored through an immediate response, but there also are many instances where a more measured response is required. Contingency plans need to be flexible enough to envision all possible resolution scenarios.

The chief of security is responsible for developing emergency plans in cooperation with all other department heads. But to ensure full readiness, the institution should conduct emergency plan training and drills with other state and local agencies that may be involved in providing emergency support to the facility. An annual administrative review of all plans should be an integral part of the emergency plan system. The warden should sign each plan, officially indicating that it is accurate and current.

There are a number of common procedures that should be followed in most crises, and which should be reflected in all emergency plans. This section will discuss those common elements, with the following chapters containing specific response elements for the most common emergencies.

Response Strategy for Emergencies

Response strategies for every emergency should contain provisions to:

– Ensure the integrity of the perimeter, so that the public is not at risk

–Contain the crisis to the minimum area possible within the institution

–Ensure all staff are accounted for and safe

–Ensure that all inmates are accounted for and safe

–Notify appropriate officials and necessary staff, using an accurate, up-to-date list of all employee addresses and telephone numbers

–Muster any necessary local and agency-wide resources, as well as resources from other cooperating agencies near the site of the crisis

–Ensure due process for all participants who may be charged with criminal acts

–Preserve evidence for future prosecution

–Maintain security during any evacuation activities

–Ensure appropriate information is released to the media

–Take proper postemergency action to care for inmates and restore normal operations

---

Format of the Plan

The specifics of each emergency plan should follow the same general pattern. While this will vary from agency to agency, the balance of the emergency plan information in these guidelines will follow the following basic categorical breakdown:

(1) Prevention

(2) Initial Reaction and Notification

(3) Command Issues and Command Center Operations

(4) Resource Assembly and Post Assignments

(5) Accounting for Staff and Inmates

(6) Firearms and Ordnance

(7) Physical Plant and Utilities

(8) Equipment

(9) Media Relations

(10) Reporting

(11) Postemergency Action

(12) Training

(13) Other specific plan information, including relevant backup materials

The balance of the information in this chapter is intended to serve as a general guide to the content and structure of all institution emergency plans. This material should be common to almost all plans. The subsequent chapters on individual plans will not repeat this general content, unless necessary to highlight a specific point.

Prevention

As a critical element of training, each emergency plan should contain an extensive section on prevention. It is better to identify and correct conditions that may lead to a disturbance, fire, or escape, than to have to deal with the actual event. Each of the plans should be as detailed as possible on this point, so that staff–when they review the plans each year–receive a strong reminder of the type of things that they should be alert to in their daily activities.

Generally, these preventive factors should include:

• The importance to both staff and inmates of managerial visibility and approachability

• Effective security auditing that discovers security deficiencies, so they can be corrected before inmates exploit them

• Consistently enforcing all rules and regulations

• Effective communications between inmates and staff, among staff, and particularly between line and supervisory personnel

• The need to provide appropriate programs and services of all types (food, medical care, and so forth)

- Management systems, such as sanitation, safety and security inspections, contraband deterrence and detection, tool and key control, and inmate accountability

- Sensitivity to changes in inmate actions or the institution atmosphere

- The value of a risk-assessment program in identifying possible trouble spots, and correcting them as soon as possible. Such systems may include the use of objective indicators (tests, review of incident data, sick call data) or more subjective elements (staff and inmate interviews) to assign levels of risk to a situation or institution.

Notification

The first notification of a problem is likely to come into the control center or to the shift supervisor. The person receiving the alarm should know, in no uncertain terms, who they are to notify in the chain of command. The ramifications of that decision are discussed in greater detail in the section that follows. However, in addition to supervisors, line staff also must be advised that there is a problem.

Many institutions have in-house systems to immediately alert staff that there is an emergency, and which provide for an immediate staff response capability to the area of an emergency. These procedures should not only be included in the emergency plans, but contained in post orders and in other procedures, as well.

Perimeter staff should be alerted at once to any actual or impending crisis. Also, staff should remember that any real or contrived crisis can be used to conceal an escape attempt or otherwise accomplish some improper end. If there are specific perimeter-related aspects to the emergency, then the plan should specify how and when perimeter posts should be reinforced.

Housing unit staff should be alerted as soon as practical if there is a potential threat that may cause disruption in housing operations. Staff members who are not staffing critical posts, or who do not have inmates under their supervision at the time of an emergency should report to a predesignated location and await further instructions.

These early warnings allow employees to perform tasks that may be crucial to successful resolution of the emergency such as: performing an inventory and lockdown of all tools and hazardous substances, holding or releasing assigned inmates in the area, or reporting to a predetermined central assembly area for accountability and reassignment at the direction of the warden.

Each institution also should develop an emergency alert system for off-site security personnel who may be needed to report at once. Autodialers and pyramid-style telephone trees are good methods for quickly alerting large numbers of employees of an emergency situation. Institutions employing autodialers should have a backup telephone tree system in the event that the autodialer mechanism is rendered inaccessible or inoperative.

The plans also should specify a priority order for identifying and recalling personnel from nonsecurity departments. In most systems, it is understood that employees from all disciplines likely will become a part of any large-scale response effort. However, recalled personnel never should enter the facility without explicit direction to do so and no one should be permitted to enter or leave the institution without presenting valid identification.

Control center and command staff should know the procedure for notifying other state and local law enforcement agencies during an emergency. Command staff, in particular, should be familiar with the role those groups play in a crisis and in a post-emergency investigation.

The ground rules for other agency involvement should be developed before a crisis. Planning sessions with other agency representatives, formal memos of agreement, and joint training exercises can form a three-part process that ensures that when a crisis occurs, everyone involved knows not only what they should do, but what the other parties in the response team are supposed to do. The importance of joint training with these organizations has been demonstrated repeatedly.

Command Issues and Command Center Operations

In the first moments of an emergency, the control center officer, the shift commander, or both, usually are the ones who receive the information and make the initial response decisions. Clearly, the chief of security, deputy warden, and warden are the ones to be notified as soon as possible. But for a few moments in any crisis–before anyone else really is available to take command, the shift commander is in charge.

Because of that fact, emergency plans, training, and all policy should be extremely clear about what levels of response can be ordered by interim command staff before the official chain of command solidifies. For instance, it would not be unusual for the shift commander to be authorized to deploy chemical agents to repel inmates in a serious crisis. It normally would not be within the shift commander's authority to use firearms inside the institution (that almost always is reserved for the warden alone), but it certainly could be permissible for him or her to order warning or disabling shots from towers. The degree of authority the shift supervisor has to order an immediate lockdown should be clear. In short, the amount of latitude the shift commander has in the early moments of an emergency must be spelled out clearly.

Similarly, as higher-level command staff arrive, they, too, must know what the limits to their authority is. Can the chief of security order the use of firearms against participants in a serious, fast-moving disturbance where the use of weapons inside might save lives, but before the warden or deputy warden arrives or can be contacted? Under those same circumstances, may the deputy give that order before the warden is available? These are difficult, but critical, issues that must be resolved in advance, and clearly spelled out in the emergency plans and post orders.

If the plans are clear on this point, then at each stage of the crisis there should be no question about who can order what. However, once the chain of command has stabilized, the warden eventually will be in charge. The deputy warden supervising the security department may be given responsibility for developing a complete response strategy, based on the situation at hand. The chief of security probably will be tasked with mustering the tactical resources necessary to carry out the overall response strategy. Individual department heads no doubt will be called upon to support this effort, drawing on their expertise and experience.

As soon as there is an indication that an incident is likely to develop into a major or prolonged crisis, a command center should be activated. The command center should be located in an area that is readily accessible to key staff, but not likely to be disrupted during a crisis. It should not be the institution's control center, nor should it be the warden's office. However, proximity to those locations–as long as the area is totally secure–is a key asset. The plan also should identify an alternate command center, should the primary location become unavailable or unsafe.

The primary purpose of the command center is to enable the control center and other sections of the facility to function as normally as possible during the crisis by reducing conflict between everyday procedures and emergency procedures. Careful planning and coordination are required to ensure that conflicting orders are not issued to staff or other persons involved in both everyday and emergency operations.

In some cases, an external command center may be necessary, established by the central office security administrator or a regional counterpart. It should be located reasonably close to the disturbance and may be staffed by key administrators from other portions of the agency. Representatives of other state, county, and municipal agencies should report to the external command center for briefings and instruction. Staff in this area may be responsible for establishing staging areas from which employees belonging to assisting agencies should base their operations.

The following general functions should be organized and carried out in the command center:

- Assigning and placing personnel, including tactical resources

- Maintaining accurate records of all ongoing reports of incidents and staff actions

- Decision making regarding the crisis

- Communicating with the central office and other agencies involved in managing the crisis

Access to the command center should be limited to those who have an official need to be there. Some agencies institute a pass system for this purpose, to include the possibility of admitting representatives from other involved agencies. In no case should media representatives be permitted in the command center.

The command center should have the basic equipment, supplies, and materials to manage a crisis. In addition, contingency plans should be available for obtaining additional supplies and equipment as they become necessary. Basic furnishings should include:

- Computers, desks, chairs, file cabinets, and other necessary office equipment

- Telephones (including cell phone capability), radios, and other communications equipment enabling contact with: the control center, towers, patrol vehicles, the warden's office, key security staff, and local law enforcement personnel. It also should contain open line capability linking the command center to the central office; sufficient phone capability should be in place for adequate communications with other law enforcement agencies involved in managing the crisis (state police, sheriff's office, and the FBI).

- A telephone directory listing all numbers for employees, outside agencies, and sources of emergency equipment and other crisis-related resources

- A taping system that will allow historical and investigative review of all telephone activity

- Written copies of all emergency plans

- Current plot plans of the facility and maps of the local area

The command center should be staffed by experienced personnel, including the warden, the deputy warden(s), key management personnel and other specialists, and selected clerical staff. The prescribed chain of command should be clearly denoted, in the event top staff are taken hostage or become incapacitated.

If the crisis is prolonged, then a relief schedule for command staff must be established. In some cases, this is difficult to enforce, because these officials feel a particular responsibility to keep involved in the management of the situation. However, when it is evident that the problem is going to last beyond eight-to-ten hours, then command personnel immediately need to make schedule adjustments that will ensure sound, well-rested decision makers are in charge at all times.

Other key personnel should be on a standby basis, including maintenance employees familiar with the utility and water system switches and valves, employees qualified to use welding and cutting torches and other specialized tools, medical staff, a public information officer, and representatives of other agencies responding to the emergency.

Resource Assembly and Post Assignments

Once the scope of the problem begins to become apparent, the plan should provide for the assembly of resources in a coordinated manner. Many plans–escape plans being the most prominent example–will have special posts established. The plans should be clear about who may authorize the activation of such posts, and how staff placed on the posts are to be briefed on the situation and their specific responsibilities. The plan should identify posts that are not critical to the facility's continued operation, and which security and nonsecurity personnel who staff these posts may be called on to assist in other areas.

When an alarm sounds, employees from nonessential posts should be prepared to report to a designated location and await further instructions, but these posts should not be vacated without receiving a specific order to do so. The specification "essential" or "nonessential" should be a part of the post orders for each post, and the master list of these posts should be kept in the control center and the shift supervisor's office. Any nonessential post employee who is involved in the supervision of work crews first should ensure that all tools are secured and all inmates are returned to their housing units as quickly as possible before leaving the post.

As staff are called up and arrive on-site, there should be specific areas identified in the plans for them to assemble, be briefed, and, if necessary, receive equipment. If outside personnel (nonagency) are involved, then a separate assembly and briefing area should be identified.

If the crisis is prolonged, then a relief schedule for all staff–and particularly disturbance control or tactical personnel–must be established. Fatigue and stress can cause performance problems and this should be taken into account as soon as it becomes evident that the situation is going to last more than one shift.

Accounting for Staff and Inmates

Command staff must respond to the immediate problems the emergency presents. But one of the most important initial tasks is staff and inmate accountability. If possible, an inmate count should be taken immediately. To the extent possible, command personnel need to know which inmates are involved, which are not, and if there are any injured or missing.

Ordinarily, employees supervising inmates outside the housing areas should be instructed to return the inmates to their units. If there are problems in the units, the employees should keep inmates in other secure areas until further instructions are received. Plans should specify the conditions under which essential inmate workers are to be returned to their quarters or remain at their job sites.

Staff and visitor records should be researched, to begin to account for everyone in the institution. Reviewing rosters is a cumbersome method for accounting for every employee, and many departments do not operate on daily rosters, in any case. To have a ready, but relatively simple, means of accounting for staff, some systems require staff to surrender a picture ID when they enter the institution. Issue of a numbered receipt, the use of a well-organized card file, or even a numbered board-and-keyhook arrangement can speed retrieval of the ID when staff leave the secure portion of the institution. In some systems, all staff and visitors are issued a computer-encoded identification card, which they use when entering and leaving the institution. Most of these automated systems allow for an immediate printout that show who is in the institution. This, then, can be used to arrive at the desired status report on who is in the institution and who is not. Whatever method is used, a tracking process for staff should remain intact and active throughout the entire course of the emergency. After the initial identification is complete, the system can be used as the basis for all emergency timekeeping.

The identity and probable location of all missing staff should be reported immediately to the command center. While a great deal of confusion surrounds the initial moments of a crisis, this is a critical step to initiate. Command staff need to know if there are any missing staff who may be hostages or trapped in a burning building, and they must account for any visitors or volunteers from the community.

A designated timekeeper should track all personnel, including their arrival and departure time, and if possible, the post to which they are assigned. The timekeeping system used also may be used to keep an up-to-date list of personnel within the institution.

Finally, each emergency plan–no matter what the nature of the crisis–should have the agency's hostage statement included in it. This statement clearly should indicate that no one held hostage has any authority, and that no inmate is to be released while holding anyone under duress. This requirement is particularly relevant for plans relating to disturbances and escape, although any emergency conceivably could be used as a diversion for a hostage-type escape, and, thus, all plans should contain this information. Hard as it may be to accept, staff, contract personnel, volunteers, and others in the institution must know that, in the final analysis, they may be expendable in the interest of maintaining the security of the institution and assuring public safety.

Firearms and Ordnance

In the event of an emergency that may involve armory-related activities, the warden should assign at least one employee to the armory at once–usually the regular armory officer. This employee should assume command of the armory and remain there until the "all clear" signal is given. In all likelihood, additional staff will be assigned to assist the armory officer if largescale weapon and equipment issue is necessary. While the armory operation is discussed in much greater detail elsewhere in the guidelines, it is critical that armory security be maintained at all costs, that equipment (and particularly firearms) only be issued to staff who are specifically qualified for its use, and that personnel can account for all equipment and supplies issued.

Approved ordnance items should be identified in relevant emergency plans, along with critical use data. That should include specifications on which

chemical agents may be used indoors, and which may be used only outdoors. Also, saturation calculations for each area of the institution should be included; this data tells staff how many of each type of chemical agent delivery device will be sufficient to safely saturate each part of the facility. For instance, even a one-blast dispersion round would expel too much gas in a single cell, two might be sufficient for a small indoor recreation area, but four might be needed in a full-size gymnasium. This information will allow staff to attain the minimum safe-level saturation, gaining the full effect of the gas without causing permanent physical damage to the occupants.

Physical Plant and Utilities

It may be necessary to shut down utility services quickly, and emergency plans should include a description of the location of all utilities, switches, and mains–both inside and leading to the institution. All such controls should be secure from normal inmate access, and ideally, critical controls and equipment should be outside the secure perimeter.

Plans should anticipate the loss of commercial electric power and specify alternate means for providing electricity. The maintenance department should ensure that all emergency generators are maintained in working order and are readily available for prolonged service during emergency situations. The maintenance supervisor should assign this responsibility to a specific staff member.

Parking areas and marshalling points should be established to handle the increased vehicular traffic common in emergencies. Separate areas should be designated for media and emergency vehicle parking, to reduce confusion and promote safety.

Equipment

Each emergency plan should include a detailed list of all available emergency equipment, including its location and the names of personnel responsible for collection, storage, issuance, and retrieval. If the available equipment is insufficient, alternative resources should be listed with a description of arrangements made for obtaining it.

Media Relations

Correctional systems are often a focal point of public and media interest when there is an incident. Key aspects of the media portion of each emergency plan should include a clear statement that the agency head, warden, or public information officer are the only authorized points of contact with the media. No comments of an official nature should be disseminated by anyone other than one of these authorized persons. All employees contacted by the news media should refer inquiries to the designated public information officer.

When the public information officer makes contact with the media representatives, he or she should make an initial information release and then establish a method and schedule for any subsequent updates. This may be accomplished by hourly briefings in a designated area, by telephone, or by other suitable means. By cooperating with the news media and keeping them informed, the institution enhances its credibility and ensures the accuracy of accounts reaching the public.

Each emergency plan should include a list of contacts at local newspapers and television and radio stations. The public information officer should be responsible for notifying the media of escapes after the central office, local law enforcement, and other government agencies have been informed.

In many emergencies, the agency will be involved in a response that relies on other members of the law enforcement community and other portions of government. In such cases, it is vitally important that there be very close coordination between the public information efforts of all involved. This is particularly the case when hostages or other sensitive internal crisis situations are under way. All those speaking to the media must speak with one voice with regard to crisis-sensitive issues, to avoid increasing the level of tension in the institution and complicating the resolution of the crisis.

The institution should designate an area in which news media personnel can gather. This designated media center should contain telephones, access to toilet facilities, and adequate seating and work areas. It should be located out of the main flow of staff traffic, so that civilians are not in contact, and do not interfere, with tactical response preparations or other support activities.

Regular media briefings should be scheduled, within limits established by the warden, and with due regard to tactical considerations. No information should be released if it would compromise the solution to the crisis.

Reporting

Debriefing of involved personnel should occur as soon after the emergency as is possible. Information resources used to compile reports should include videotapes, logs, and memos from employee and other witnesses on their observations and actions. Written statements should be clear enough to aid in the identification of inmate participants, when possible.

The following individuals should submit reports at the end of an emergency, or if it is protracted, prior to leaving the facility at the end of their shift:

- Shift supervisors

- Employees witnessing the incident

- Civilian or other witnesses to the event, or those who were involved in its aftermath

- Employees who notified other agencies

- Hostages

- Other staff members with pertinent areas of responsibility or having relevant information

An employee should be assigned to keep a written chronological log of events as they occur–ordinarily in the command center. He or she should be relieved if the emergency continues beyond the length of a single shift. A specific employee should be assigned to work with the chief of security to collect video and audiotape, and write written records of the emergency and all subsequent actions.

Employees responsible for maintaining these records should receive any necessary clerical assistance. Computerization of this process is highly recommended.

Postemergency Action

An all-clear signal should be given when it has been determined that the emergency is over. The warden should notify the shift supervisor, who ordinarily would be the official notifying all posts through the control center. All employees should remain on duty to assist in the return to full normal operations. A complete count and picture identification of all inmates should be initiated.

Steps should be taken to assure inmates are served meals, cared for medically, and that other typical services are restored as soon as it is safe to do so. Supervisory personnel should be particularly attentive to preventing retaliatory action in the aftermath of a disturbance, hostage situation, or similar event.

As a particularly important follow-up process, employees directly involved in an incident should be debriefed, or interviewed, by trained mental health personnel, to determine the effect their experience has had on them. In cases where there is an indication of post-event psychological trauma, the agency should have procedures for providing appropriate follow-up care.

Training

Emergency plans are an excellent training tool, and review and coverage of the plans in annual refresher training is a major way to retain staff familiarity with them. The formal process for training staff on the emergency plans should include:

- Instructions on the emergency plan

- Critical concerns under emergency conditions, such as how to react if taken hostage

- Other pertinent staff directions

In addition, every employee should be required to personally review all plans at least once a year, as a further training method. This personal review should be documented by the employee signing out a copy of the plans, and when they are returned, signing a form or sheet attesting that they have been reviewed. There is no way of predicting who will be on duty in a critical post in a time of crisis. A senior officer may be in an acting supervisor's position, a department head may be acting as a deputy warden–each of these individuals and staff at every other level needs to know the overall plan for response.

While emergency plans are highly confidential and never should go inside the institution, staff should be able to check them out for detailed review. Also, the training officer should have easy access to them for reference in the development of training programs.

Simulated exercises can be used to train staff in some aspects of emergency plans. An example would be a "tabletop" exercise of primary decision makers in a mock scenario. Another example would be to announce an emergency, lock down all inmates, and account for inmates and staff. An expanded version would be to add a hostage scenario with emergency response teams callups. Some form of these exercises should be done every one-to-three months.

Full mobilization exercises are real-world drills intended to train staff in the broader aspects of the emergency plan, usually involving at least one outside agency. An example would be to announce an emergency, lock down all inmates, and introduce a scenario of a disturbance with hostages and a fire. The command center would be activated, and emergency teams would report and prepare for deployment. The exercise would bring in fire protection equipment, and staff might conduct medical injury triage of simulated injuries. This level of exercise might occur once or twice a year, preceded by notification to other agencies and the agency's central office. Exercises of this type should be followed by a report to the agency's security administrator.

Inmates also should receive an orientation to the following relevant portions of some emergency plans, as part of the admission and orientation process:

- Rules for inmate conduct during emergencies and emergency plan training

- An explanation of the goals of the emergency in terms of preservation of life and prevention of injury

- An explanation of the intention to use force under escape and emergency management situations

Escape

27

Despite the best of efforts, the escape-proof institution has yet to be built. But good planning and effective security practices can reduce the probability of escape and increase the rate of recapture after an escape has occurred. To that end, each facility should have an up-to-date escape prevention and apprehension plan.

Prevention

Of course, prevention is the key to any escape plan. Indeed, in the aggregate, escape prevention is probably the single most influential activity in a correctional institution. Measures that help reduce the occurrence of escape attempts include:

- Alert detection and prompt reporting of unrest or tension, or abnormal changes in inmate conduct

- An effective system of accountability, tool and key control, security inspections, and other basic security measures

- Appropriate classification and classification review of all inmates, including accurate designation of high-risk cases

- Provision of appropriate work and living assignments

- Prompt correction of construction or damage-related security breaches, including providing adequate interim security coverage until repairs are made

Initial Reaction and Notification

The institution's escape plan should specify that any unauthorized absence be reported immediately to the control center and shift supervisor. When it is determined that an inmate is missing or unaccounted for, or that an actual escape is in progress or has occurred, the plan should specify the order of notification of institution officials.

Ordinarily, the institution's radio system, tower intercoms, phones, and pager systems are used for this purpose. Typically, once the initial determination is made that there is an escape-type situation, the warden, deputy wardens, chief of security, and shift supervisor are the first to be notified. Ordinarily, the chief of security is responsible for implementing the escape plan. In his or her absence, the senior shift supervisor should take charge.

If staff live in the vicinity of the institution, or if it is necessary to warn the community, prearranged signals may be sounded, such as a horn or whistle. The warden should determine the method for sounding a general alarm, because alarms can cause increased tension and apprehension in the facility, and in the surrounding community. As soon as an escape occurs, the senior official in command should decide if off-duty employees are needed to reinforce the on-duty staff. If the decision is made to contact them, autodialer or pyramid-calling systems should be used.

On command issues and command center operations, the relevant provisions of the general emergency plan apply.

Resource Assembly and Post Assignments

The plan should include information on which positions are critical to the immediate operation of the facility and which positions may be vacated, freeing staff members to assist in the search–whether it be inside the institution or in the community. Adequate staff coverage should be maintained to provide normal supervision of inmates not involved in the escape hunt.

Certain posts will be staffed in the event of an escape. Extra staff should be assigned to the armory. The armory officer immediately should prepare for the issue of arms, ammunition, and other controlled equipment. However, authorization to actually issue and receive arms should come from the warden, deputy warden, or chief of security. All perimeter posts should be reinforced.

One employee should be responsible for notifying all law-enforcement agencies in the surrounding area, once the senior commander has determined that an escape actually has occurred. These agencies should be contacted by telephone; their telephone numbers should be listed as a part of the plan.

The plan should describe how to organize inside search parties, what areas are to be searched, and other relevant inside search-related information. The escape plan also should contain a list of outside posts that must be staffed during a search for escapees, with designations such as "primary," "secondary," "mobile," "stationary," or other relevant labels. The priority in which these posts are covered should depend on the particulars of the escape, considering the time, means of departure, and direction of travel.

All employees receiving weapons (for outside posts) should be thoroughly familiar with their appropriate and safe use. Employees may be issued batons or similar devices in lieu of firearms.

Officers on outside search posts should be provided with an instruction kit containing relevant maps, a telephone location list (for use if radios are not issued to officers on such posts), and descriptions of post duties with search assignments. Escape post orders should include the proper method for covering that post, the importance of concealment and necessity of avoiding unnecessary conversation, and specific radio frequencies and usage information.

All employees on escape posts should be instructed in the use of tact and good judgment for their contacts with the public. The plan should clearly state the limits of the authority correctional personnel have when they are not accompanied by police officers. Personnel should be trained to cooperate fully with other agencies.

The plan should specify legal limitations in vehicle and house searches, as well as in other areas where the search for escapees intrudes on community privacy. Plans also should stress the importance of abiding by the law in all respects, including avoiding speeding and other traffic infractions. Employees should be instructed in recognizing, preserving, and turning over to the appropriate officials, any potential evidence, to assure its value for prosecution.

Escape Intelligence

Coordinating information is essential to recapturing an escapee. Accordingly, law enforcement agencies should be promptly supplied the following:

- Name of the escapee

- Escapee's sex, race, nationality, date of birth, age, weight, hair and eye color, social security number, and state of residence

- Photographs of the escapee

- Escapee's crime and length of sentence

- Federal Bureau of Investigation and state police numbers, if available

- Fingerprint classification

- Escapee's last known residence, past associates, or other likely places or groups to which he or she might return

- Escapee's driver's license and vehicle information, if known

- A statement of whether the escapee is considered dangerous

- The name and title of the person who should receive notice of the apprehension, if by another agency

The investigative supervisor should begin to coordinate all escape-related intelligence-gathering, including coordination with law enforcement personnel. One employee should be detailed to obtain current identification information and pictures of the escapees. Copies of these photographs and an accompanying description should be given to the search leader, all local law enforcement agencies, and any nearby residents. Specific information to be given to law enforcement agencies at the time of an escape is listed in the box on page 188.

An employee should be assigned to collect the escapee's property, mail, and visiting lists, which should be taken to the investigative supervisor. A staff member familiar with the composition of inmate central files should review the file of all involved for other information that may help in apprehension.

The plan also should identify who is responsible for prompt notification of all alerted agencies and the central office, when an escapee has been recaptured. If the institution becomes aware that the escapee has been involved in another crime (such as assault, hostage-taking, kidnapping, theft, or the destruction of property), local law enforcement agencies should be informed of that fact.

In accounting for staff and inmates, the relevant provisions of the general emergency plan apply. In this situation, a good picture count, conducted as quickly as possible, is essential in knowing who is missing.

Firearms and Ordnance

The plan should specify who may authorize firearms to be issued and carried during an escape search. Under normal circumstances, firearms should not be issued during escapes from community facilities. An exception to this policy may be made when a substantial crime has been committed during the escape.

Armed employees should be aware of the agency's policy on the use of force, and particularly that firing a weapon in the community may endanger innocent parties. Staff must be clear that firearms should be used only as a last resort. Weapons use is appropriate for the following:

- The prevention of loss of life or grievous bodily harm

- The prevention of escapes

- The protection of property, under some circumstances

Agency policies will differ on this point, but in general, a verbal warning should precede the use of firearms. Again, depending on agency policy, if the warning is ineffective in stopping the inmate, the officer should discharge a warning shot in a safe direction. If that fails to have the intended effect, shots may be fired to disable the escapee. If, in any situation, the employee believes that there is an immediate and overriding threat to life, a shot to disable may be fired without warning.

Physical Plant and Utilities

An expert should be assigned to make any repairs involving the welding of tool-resistant bars. Until all repairs are completed, sufficient staff should be assigned to the damaged area to preclude other escape attempts that would exploit the temporary breach in security. On equipment, the relevant provisions of the general emergency plan apply.

Media Relations

The institution should implement its general media plan provisions. Data to be released to the media on escapees should include: name, age, place of conviction, crime committed, and sentence. Other information that does not violate privacy statutes may be issued, including a picture. When an inmate is recaptured, the public information officer should provide details of the apprehension to the news media.

Reporting

As soon as it is determined that an actual escape has taken place, the warden must notify the designated central office official. Follow-up reports, whenever possible, should contain information on:

- The method of escape, including how the inmate accessed the area from which the escape occurred, whether other inmates were involved, and a complete description of the appearance and clothing of all escapees

- A careful description of any cut bars, window sashes, or fences, or other damage to the security features of the institution, accompanied by photographs

- An evaluation of the factors which may have led to or enabled the escape

189

- Proposed changes to institutional policy or procedures designed to prevent similar escapes in the future

A copy of a sample form for reporting escapes is included in Appendix D. Less serious escape attempts need not be followed up by detailed reports. It should be sufficient to describe them as a part of the warden's and chief of security's regular reports to the central office.

Postemergency Action

The relevant provisions of the general emergency plan apply. It is important that any lockdown or other restrictions applied to the general population be as brief as possible. There is no reason to punish the rest of the inmates for the actions of one or a few. On training, the relevant provisions of the general emergency plan apply.

Specific Plan Information

Hostages

When hostages are taken in the course of an escape, the following guidelines should be followed:

- "OFFICIALS WHO ARE TAKEN HOSTAGE, REGARD-LESS OF RANK OR POSITION, LOSE ALL COMMAND AUTHORITY. NO ORDER FROM ANY HOSTAGE SHOULD BE HONORED." This statement should

be included in a prominent location in all post orders and in all emergency plans.

- No inmate or group of inmates using hostages should be permitted to leave the facility with a hostage; movement of a hostage-taker within the institution should be curtailed to the extent possible.

- Hostages never should be exchanged.

- No weapons should be given to offenders in exchange for hostages.

Additional information on this topic is contained in Chapter 33, on the hostage emergency plan.

Canine Operations

The use of canine units to track escapees is a long-standing practice in corrections. Earlier references (in the section on searches) to canine operations, with regard to selection and training, should be noted.

In the event of an escape, the canine unit supervisor and other canine unit staff also should be immediately notified by phone, radio, or pager. The area will be sealed off and an appropriate scent article obtained and bagged without further contamination. The canine unit, as quickly as possible, will establish a direction of travel and attempt to locate the subject. Additional qualified personnel will be made available as needed, to assist the canine unit. Firearms may be issued to canine-unit personnel upon the authorization of the warden, on the same basis as they are issued to other staff involved in escape-related activities.

Bomb Plan

28

All bomb training should emphasize–above all else–the concept, **"evacuate people not bombs**." This point cannot be driven home too strongly, and this statement should be included in bold-faced type and underlined in each copy of the bomb plan. The plan should be developed in close cooperation with local authorities with particular expertise in this area, that is, the military, the police, and others.

The bomb plan should consider safety in the following priority:

(1) Public safety

(2) Employee safety

(3) Inmate safety

(4) Protection of property, under certain circumstances

(5) Restoration of order and control

Prevention

Preventing the introduction of a bomb hinges on sound perimeter security and equally sound search practices. If the provisions of the sections of this publication dealing with entrances and searches are applied, the risk of a bomb from the outside is minimal. Institutions with a perimeter or building envelope in close proximity to the public (in highly urbanized settings, for instance) must rely on perimeter patrols, closed circuit television surveillance, and clean design to reduce the possibility that a bomb can be concealed successfully at the perimeter itself.

Fabrication of a bomb inside by inmates is a potential problem that cannot be ignored. Indeed, the chemicals in matchheads are the most common substances used in prison-made bombs, although other materials have been used, as well. While many institutions are beginning to restrict smoking, and others have installed special common-access cigarette lighters, this still is a potential problem in many facilities. While it is relatively easy for inmates to camouflage this activity, staff should be alert to large quantities of discarded matchbooks, significant increases in the consumption of matches, or other signs that an inmate may be accumulating this substance. The presence of wires, broken light bulbs, or other items that could be used in a bomb also should be cause for staff action.

Initial Reaction and Notification

If a bomb threat is received over the phone or through other means, it is important to document as much information as possible at that time. Some bombers are unusually willing to give out information over the phone, and that fact should be taken advantage of, to the extent possible. The person receiving a telephoned bomb threat should try to keep the caller on the line and elicit as much of the following information as possible, including the following:

- The caller's sex and voice, the time of the telephone call, any background noises, and whether or not the person placing the call sounds familiar

- The time of detonation. Find out the exact time at which the bomb is set to explode. The current time should be confirmed with the caller to establish the interval remaining.

- The exact location and appearance of the bomb

- The exact nature of the explosive device (pipe bomb, satchel charge, molotov cocktail), the activating mechanism used, the type of combustible or explosive used, and if the bomb is booby-trapped in any way

- What individual or organization claims responsibility for the bomb

A sample form to record this information is included in Appendix D.

When the employee receiving the call tries to elicit this information, he or she should remain as calm as possible. The best way to get as many details as possible is to avoid spending too much time on any one line of questioning. If a caller readily shares the time the device is set to go off, but hesitates to reveal its location, the listener should direct the line of questioning to other details. Later in the call, the listener may be able to return to that subject.

If possible, the person receiving a bomb threat should notify the shift supervisor, while still engaging the caller. This could be done by handing another staff member a note, or cautiously using another phone line. The value of this action is to allow supervisory personnel to begin to react as quickly as possible.

When a bomb, or suspected bomb, is found in the institution, the control center or shift supervisor should be notified immediately. The supervisor receiving that notification should secure the affected area, and contact the warden and other staff identified in the facility's bomb plan. When time permits, the warden should notify the agency head, who, in turn, may notify additional agency personnel, if so indicated.

If a suspicious item is discovered, it should not be touched. Instead, the discoverer should make sure the area is cleared and the person in charge of the search is notified. When qualified bomb squad personnel arrive and determine that a bomb exists, they have the option of deciding whether or not it is appropriate to remove the device from within the institution.

Command Issues and Command Center Operations

When a bomb threat has been received, evaluation is a critical first step. The senior command official must determine whether the crisis is a false alarm, sometimes with no more information than was contained in the call. If evacuation is deemed necessary, he or she should order employees and inmates evacuated by the safest means possible from the area.

If the caller discloses the location of the bomb or clues indicate a probable location, the threatened area should be evacuated and sealed off until bomb squad personnel arrive. In all cases, staff must be aware of the priority need to evacuate people, not to discover or remove a bomb.

The command center should be activated, as provided in the general plan chapter. In the event that there is some reason to believe the bomb is located near the command center, the secondary command center should be activated, instead.

Any announcements made after the threat is received should be broadcast on the public address system. Two-way radio transmissions should be terminated, because the signals broadcast from radio sets can trigger some detonating devices. Because magnetic fields also can set off an explosion, handheld metal detectors should not be used in the bomb search unless they are specifically cleared for use by the bomb squad.

Institution staff should not attempt to move or disarm a bomb of any type. Homemade bombs are extremely unstable because they usually are made poorly. Under no circumstances should anyone other than a qualified bomb squad professional try to move, defuse, cover, disconnect, hose down, or tamper with any object suspected of being a bomb.

All bomb plans should include prearranged agreements with qualified police agencies staffed with trained bomb disposal units. These trained units should conduct or supervise all necessary bomb searches, movement, or disarming activity.

Resource Assembly and Post Assignments

The relevant provisions of the general emergency plan apply. In this instance, if command staff estimate there is any potential risk that a bomb actually is in the institution, then callup of the local bomb squad–as identified in the plan–should be the principal course of action.

Procedures should be in place to clear bomb squad personnel and their equipment through the entrance as quickly as possible. Other than securing the area, institution staff should not be involved in bomb removal or disarming activities, although they may provide supplies and equipment, as needed.

On accounting for staff and inmates, the relevant provisions of the general emergency plan apply. If the bomb is in a housing unit, then the inmates should be evacuated to a secure area (gymnasium, auditorium, yard), counted there, and maintained under heightened security until the unit again is safe for reoccupancy.

On firearms and ordnance, the relevant provisions of the general emergency plan apply. While a heightened perimeter awareness may be called for, no weapons ordinarily are issued in such an instance.

Regarding physical plant and utilities, plot plans of the entire institution should be available to the bomb squad personnel for reference. The head of the maintenance department may be called upon to advise bomb squad personnel regarding details of the building, utilities, or other physical plant features of the area where the bomb is located.

On equipment, the relevant provisions of the general emergency plan apply. It is extremely important that staff do not use radios during a bomb emergency, as radio signals may induce enough current in a bomb's wiring to activate the device. Loudspeakers and public address systems are the recommended means of communicating until the situation has been cleared safely.

On media relations, the relevant provisions of the general emergency plan apply.

As far as reporting goes, the warden should follow up every bomb threat with a complete report listing all actions taken during the initial receipt of the threat, the evacuation, the search, methods of detection and removal, and return to normal operations.

On both postemergency action and for training, the relevant provisions of the general emergency plan apply.

Specific Plan Information

The institution's basic evacuation plan should be followed, to the degree that the situation indicates. Evacuation routes used during a bomb emergency should be the same as those planned for use during a fire. If an entire building is to be cleared, all inmates and employees should be moved to a safe place away from the building but inside the facility perimeter. Elevators should not be used to evacuate a building.

If the complete evacuation of the institution is required, the warden should consult the evacuation plan and the central office to determine where the inmates can be moved and the method to do so in this particular situation. In the event of an evacuation, the only personnel authorized to remain in the cleared area are police, firefighters, officials assisting in the search, and volunteers requested by the warden.

Disaster Plan

29

Natural disasters are brought about by the forces of nature–severe storms, hurricanes, tornadoes, earthquakes, volcanic eruptions, or floods. Human disasters include fires, explosions, hazardous chemical spills, toxic waste, or radioactive contamination. Both of these general categories of emergencies require similar management action.

The disaster plan should be detailed enough to ensure that predetermined, approved procedures can be implemented swiftly. The plan should contain sufficient information to guide staff actions from the initial notification of a potential disaster until the final cleanup has occurred and the institution has returned to normal operation.

Prevention

In most cases, there is little or nothing that staff can do to prevent a natural disaster. However, staff should be alert to the indications that a weather-related problem is imminent. That will allow early preparations, as indicated elsewhere in the plan.

Initial Reaction and Notification

The plan clearly should indicate who has the authority to declare a state of emergency in the event of a natural or human disaster. Typically, this authority belongs jointly to the warden and the agency head, but when time does not permit consultation, the warden may make the declaration.

When the central office has been notified, the agency head may decide that the governor's office should be advised. That office, if the situation so warrants, may alert the National Guard and civil defense authorities, so their assistance can be available. This points out the need for early joint agency cooperation for developing this type of plan. The institution's disaster plan should be a part of the local civil defense emergency response plan and be coordinated accordingly. In a crisis, the National Guard may be asked to provide transportation, perimeter lighting equipment, emergency generators, and additional staff. Local civil defense authorities also may supply needed equipment, feeding facilities, and emergency medical treatment.

Command Issues and Command Center Operations

To avoid overreaction to a crisis situation, it may be useful to develop plans for differing levels of disaster response, using one of three generally recognized emergency levels:

Level I: A situation that requires staff to secure the facility, but which does not require evacuation of the site

Level II: A situation that requires staff to secure the facility and conduct a partial evacuation

Level III: A situation that requires staff to secure the facility and conduct a total evacuation

Detailed information on these **three levels is** included in the final portion of this chapter.

Typical command center operations should be implemented, unless the nature of the disaster renders the area unsafe for use. In that case, the alternate command center should be used. If that area, too, is unsafe, then the warden should choose a location that is as secure as possible, has maximum communication capability under the circumstances, and is capable of supporting the minimum functions of a command center.

In most areas, the relevant provisions of the general emergency plan apply. Also, review the discussion at the end of the chapter on the different levels of response.

Training

While all of the general features of staff emergency-plan training apply, additionally, as part of their initial orientation to the facility, all newly admitted inmates should be made aware of the features of the disaster plan that directly affect them. Unit staff periodically should review those procedures in town hall meetings or through other methods.

Specialized Disaster Response Information

The Level I Crisis

In the Level I crisis, institution operations will be disrupted, but there is no imminent threat, and officials anticipate that most, if not all, of the physical plant will remain intact, or at least functional. The following steps should be taken, as the situation dictates:

(1) An emergency count should be made. Security devices (handcuffs, chains, and so forth) should be readily available.

(2) Depending on the conditions, a roving patrol (or additional patrols) should be activated to maintain perimeter security.

(3) All buildings should be secured to prevent or minimize damage during the emergency. Only buildings with functions supporting a necessary and immediate service should remain occupied by staff and inmates.

(4) Hazardous material, including firearms and ammunition, should be removed from all but essential posts.

(5) All portable equipment not in use should be stored inside buildings or in some other logical, safe place.

(6) Personnel should be assigned to periodically inspect both buildings and equipment to ensure their continued security throughout the emergency.

A determination should be made in advance, of posts and services considered essential for continued operation during an emergency. Personnel whose routine functions will be considered nonessential during an emergency should be reassigned to other areas to provide necessary services. Inmates whose normal assignments have been identified as nonessential should be secured in a housing unit, but may remain available for assignment to areas that provide essential services.

The plan should establish procedures to ensure that the food service department functions as normally as possible. If necessary, additional staff members from nonessential posts may be assigned to food services. Inventories should be maintained on all food items and procedures should be in place for obtaining additional food during the emergency. Menus should be planned to maintain maximum use of existing inventories. If conditions permit, inmates should continue to eat in the dining room and also, provision should be made to feed staff at the facility for the duration of the crisis.

Additionally, procedures should include providing for collection and storage of as much drinking and sanitary water as possible. Plans for waste product removal and disposal should be included in the disaster plan. The maintenance department supervisor should ensure that water, sewage, steam, and electrical systems continue to function during the emergency.

Although the type and severity of the emergency will determine the deviation from normal routine, the disaster plan must specify procedures to accommodate the medical needs of inmates and of any staff injured on the job during the emergency. The medical portion of the plan should include:

- Around-the-clock staff coverage with reassignment of medical personnel, including those from other institutions, or other state and local facilities, if necessary

- Maintaining an inventory of necessary medical supplies, as well as a prearranged means for obtaining additional supplies from other sources

• Procedures for the medical evacuation of sick or injured inmates or staff to appropriate state, local, or private facilities

Inventories should be maintained of all clothing and laundry supplies that may be needed during the emergency. Only essential laundry services should be continued during the crisis.

The disaster plan should include a list of all facility vehicles appropriate for emergency use, listing the seating capacity of each vehicle. Preidentified staff should coordinate all activities involving vehicles, identifying a pool area, dispatching them on an as-needed basis, and ensuring their prompt return to the pool. Fuel tanks should be kept at least half full at all times. Additional sources of transportation should be identified and prior arrangements made for their acquisition, if necessary.

If the type of inmate in the institution lends itself to such action, the warden may choose to make inmate work squads available to the local community to assist civil defense or specified authorities during, and in the aftermath of, civic emergencies. Prior coordination of such work activities should be reflected in the plan.

The Level II Crisis

The Level II disaster plan should anticipate the need for partial evacuation to another site. This would include steps similar to those described for Level I crises in the following areas:

• Buildings and equipment

• Essential and nonessential services

• Command center

• Communications

• Emergency power

• Water and sewage

• Maintenance

• Medical services

• Emergency equipment

• Work squad availability

The following additional functions should be included in the Level II plan:

(1) A written internal-search plan of the institution should be implemented and the inmate count verified.

Source: West Virginia Regional Jail Authority, Central Regional Jail

Most laundry operations are centralized, but some special housing units have separate laundry equipment to reduce contraband trafficking opportunities.

(2) Rosters and post descriptions required at Level I should be supplemented to include positions needed for transporting evacuated inmates to alternate locations.

(3) A partial evacuation requires a detailed staff/inmate transportation schedule to facilitate the movement.

(4) Inmates should be listed on a roster by custody or supervision categories, to facilitate the selection of appropriate vehicles and staff supervision levels.

(5) Each vehicle containing inmates leaving the institution should be counted when loading and unloading to ensure the accuracy of the count.

(6) The plan should provide for the assignment of sufficient personnel to provide the necessary security at the alternate site.

(7) Evacuation priority should be given to inmates with medical problems, followed by inmates whose services are not needed. Remaining staff and inmates should be reassigned to safe and secure areas within the institution.

(8) Because of the high escape risk they represent, inmates under close- and maximum-custody, and those under a death sentence, should be secured in a separate area with extra supervision. They should be the last to be moved in an evacuation of any type.

(9) In addition to following Level I procedures, food service staff should be reassigned to the sites

receiving evacuated inmates. Contingency plans should be activated that allow for the provision of additional food at evacuation locations.

(10) There should be provisions for sufficient clothing and bedding at the alternative locations to meet the needs of the evacuated inmates.

The Level III Crisis

If, in the warden's estimation, the crisis situation warrants total evacuation, most of the procedures required at Levels I and II must be initiated, with additional measures, as well. Total evacuation is a complex undertaking, involving a number of factors.

(1) The plan may permit some volunteers–staff and selected inmates–to remain at the institution to conduct periodic surveillance of buildings and equipment, but it also must provide for their evacuation, if the situation worsens.

(2) A written plan for the orderly shutdown of all utilities should be included in the plan.

(3) Inmates under a death sentence should be transported in full restraints and, upon arrival at a temporary confinement site, must be housed separately from the rest of the population.

(4) Provision should be made at the temporary evacuation site to establish a staff rotation roster to maintain security and provide necessary services during the crisis.

(5) The agency should be prepared to use the Interstate Compact, if at any point it becomes necessary to arrange for additional temporary housing for the inmates.

(6) Lastly, there should be a plan for returning evacuated inmates to their original institution after the emergency is over.

Additional Information on Responses to Specific Natural Disasters

There are several specific types of natural disasters that could affect a correctional facility in a significant way. Because they are likely events in many parts of the country, the following section details additional response information for each of them.

Tornado

A tornado is an erratically moving, funnel-shaped windstorm capable of enormous destruction. Tornados follow a general pattern, but may vary as shown in the chart below.

Tornados form from thunderstorms and are always accompanied by rain and often by severe hail. Depending on their strength, they are capable of lifting objects weighing several tons, tossing them to great heights, and depositing them far from their point of origin. Certain geographic areas seem prone to tornadoes, but no location is exempt. They cause their greatest damage not by wind speed, but by massive and sudden reductions of air pressure. When the air pressure outside a structure or object is reduced drastically, the structure will explode if it is not capable of rapidly equalizing the pressure loss. The severe pressure imbalance combined with very strong circular winds results in great destruction. Several minutes prior to and after a tornado, large clouds of dirt and

Elements of a Tornado

CONDITION	NORM	POSSIBLE RANGE
Ground speed	10-25 miles per hour	2-65 miles per hour
Duration	2-40 minutes	Up to 180 minutes
Width of path	200-500 feet	Up to 2 miles
Length of path	1,200-2,500 yards	250 miles
Wind speed	150+ miles per hour	75-300+ miles per hour
Direction	Northeast	96 percent true

dust may be generated by the storm, reducing the visibility to zero.

Although communications within the institution are not likely to be interrupted, outside telephone lines may be severely damaged. Exterior base station antennas also may be destroyed, limiting radio communication to the use of portable units. An electrical blackout can occur if the emergency generator is disabled and outside power sources, lines, or substations are damaged.

If the institution receives sufficient warning that it is in the path of a tornado, staff immediately should take the following actions:

- Activate the command center.

- Order a total lockdown of the institution.

- Instruct all employees not otherwise assigned to take shelter.

- Discontinue all visiting and volunteer group activities, and offer those persons the option of leaving the institution or taking shelter in the institution, but not remaining with inmates. Visitors and volunteers should be allowed to leave at any time, regardless of the location of the storm.

- Make assignments of on-duty and off-duty personnel on a minute-to-minute basis, as needs arise. The severity of the disaster at the institution and in the surrounding community, the time of occurrence, and the staff and inmate reaction will determine the number of staff available and the level of response required.

- After the storm passes, order that a head-count be taken and perform an immediate radio check between the control center and each unit officer to ascertain if the officer is duty-ready. Immediately check any area that fails to respond.

- Order the senior medical employee on duty to organize a medical triage system in the event of injuries.

- Order at least two officers to make a walking check of the perimeter. If damage to any perimeter fence or other structures has occurred, a lockdown should remain in effect until repairs are completed or until armed staff are assigned to secure the point of damage.

- If all outside communications are disabled and cellular communications also are disrupted, dispatch an officer to the nearest operable telephone to notify appropriate personnel and agencies.

- The facility manager should assess damages and issue clearances to enter obviously damaged areas or to use damaged systems or equipment. If possible, damaged areas should be photographed before work is started, and cleanup should not commence without the warden's permission. The chief of security has the final authority to clear security features of the institution for duty status.

Earthquake

An earthquake is a sudden disturbance in the earth's surface that may result in topographic changes. Depending on the severity and time of the occurrence, the facility may experience total isolation from all forms of relief, support, or communications for an extended period of time. Aftershocks may pose a continuing hazard. Discharges of geothermal steam, natural gas, sulfuric gas, pumice, ash, or dust may occur. Due to the creation of unusual electromagnetic fields, two-way radio communications may be interrupted. Proximity to large bodies of water may result in flooding.

The following is a simple scale of severity for use in determining the damage to expect:

Minor earthquake: Cracked or broken windows; separation of water, sewer, steam, and gas and/or oil pipes; total or partial power failures; total or partial telephone and/or radio disruption; and, minimal structural damage or loss of life

Moderate earthquake: Any or all of the foregoing, plus small fissures in the earth; cracked walls and/or floors; large-scale glass breakage; severe window and door jamming due to foundation support shifts; breaches in security fencing; and some injuries or loss of life

Severe to massive earthquake: Any or all of the foregoing, plus extensive building damage; violent and severe changes in topography; large earth fissures or shears resulting in total disruption of all ground transportation; gas or particulate discharge; moderate to severe flooding; and multiple injuries and moderate to heavy loss of life

If a severe disruption occurs, the command center should be activated. If it is in a damaged location, the backup or a tertiary location may be used. In some cases, the command center actually may be an individual rather than a specific location, and that person may have to be mobile.

Outside communication may be difficult; however, every effort must be made to contact the appropriate local authorities at the earliest opportunity. Every telephone and radio in the institution should be tried, as failure may not be total.

The warden also should try to notify the agency head, who should notify other personnel or outside agencies, as necessary. In many instances, the National Guard will be mobilized in the area regardless of whether it is needed to support the institution, so if evacuation becomes necessary at some time, these initial contacts can be important.

In a moderate to severe quake, multiple injuries may occur, and structural damage may prevent medical personnel from administering aid to the injured. Officers in affected units may be required to provide first aid until assistance arrives and may have to render aid through the bars due to jammed doors and/or nonfunctional locks.

Assignments of both on- and off-duty personnel must be made as developments occur. The severity of the disaster, number of injuries at the institution and in the surrounding community, the time of occurrence, and the type of communication available will determine staff usage and response.

Because of the unpredictable pattern of aftershocks, it may be impossible to declare a distinct "all clear." The warden should direct actions with this in mind, as continuing danger may alter planning and carrying out subsequent actions. However, immediate actions should include but not be limited to:

- Ordering a lockdown of the institution and obtaining a complete unit-by-unit, area-by-area, assessment of injuries. If conditions allow, medical personnel should provide triage for injuries, either at a central location or in the individual units.

- Determining the status of operations and control functions, including damage to fences, buildings, communications, power, lighting, and video security systems

- Ordering a walking perimeter inspection by not less than two officers to ascertain if security has been breached, and posting armed officers at any breaches until repairs are completed

- Determining the amount of structural damage in each cell, to ascertain if occupancy is safe, if an escape could occur, or if further shocks could cause any significant risk

- Maintaining order, until communications with the outside are reestablished and relief personnel arrive

Depending on the type and severity of the earthquake, ordinary services may be disrupted for an extended period of time. Toilet fixtures may back up or not operate, creating unsanitary and possibly dangerous health problems. Disruption of all potable water services may occur. All approved drinking fluids should be conserved and rationed once a survey of supplies on hand is obtained.

It also is important to remember that the sudden, massive nature of earthquake destruction, and the uncertainty of knowing when the earthquake has subsided can create significant emotional stress, and supervisory or professional mental health intervention may be required. Also, staff naturally will be concerned about their families and homes. While the needs of the institution come first, every effort should be made to let staff learn as much information as they can about the status of their interests in the community. Likewise, the agency should make efforts to advise inmate families of the status of their loved ones in the institution.

Flood

A flood is a major high-water event that disrupts normal traffic and other patterns in the vicinity of the institution, or in rare cases, the institution itself. Major floods can have the most impact on three diverse, but critical, areas of a correctional operation–communications, urban services, and normal personnel relief.

Because floods ordinarily can be anticipated, the command center should be activated before conditions become serious. Assignments of both on and off-duty personnel should be made as developments occur. The amount of advance warning, the personnel available for response, and the severity of the disaster will determine staff assignments and the pattern of reliefs used.

As the flood threat develops, the following actions should be taken:

(1) A weather information log should be kept, which includes time of each entry, forecast conditions, anticipated arrival of the flood, and the person to whom the information has been relayed. Information sources that may be monitored frequently include the following:

- Television channels

- AM and FM commercial radio stations

- U.S. Weather Service

- State police district headquarters

- State emergency management agency

(2) Severely ill inmates should be assessed by medical personnel to ascertain if any are borderline hospital transfer cases. If so, they should be transported while vehicular traffic is still a safe option.

(3) If a lockdown is necessary, several cold meals and snacks should be prepared while utilities are still functional. However, if a hot meal is planned, it is important that enough hot food for all inmates is ready before serving begins, as interruption of utility service during serving adversely may affect serving routines.

(4) Telephone lines to the outside may be rendered inoperative because of damage to the lines, switching gear, or power supplies. Inside phone lines likely will function as long as electrical power is supplied. If regular phone service is unavailable, then radio and cellular phones will be the key methods of communication.

(5) Water and electricity may be disrupted after flood conditions begin. However, contamination of water may occur before indications of intrusion are noticed. Evidence of contamination includes the presence of air in lines, rust or debris in water, or excessive hydrostatic pressure. Key staff must be familiar with the location of and procedures for shutting off the water supply to the institution.

(6) If a major flood is forecast, efforts should be taken to stockpile potable water. All available clean containers should be filled with tap water, covered, and sealed for future use. To maximize the stored resource, hot water should be stored. It will cool by the time it is used.

(7) Excessive hydrostatic pressure may occur during flood conditions, causing toilets, sinks, and basins to back up and overflow, particularly on the ground or first-floor levels. The resultant raw sewage contamination is very hazardous to health. Areas where backup occurs should be emptied and isolated until cleanup efforts are undertaken. Inmates assigned to clean up should be supplied with rubber gloves and boots.

(8) The institution should be equipped with an emergency generator capable of continuous operation for 100 hours. When in use, the warden should be advised periodically of the remaining time available for generator operation, based on available fuel supplies.

(9) Major floods may impede or disrupt travel by foot or vehicle. In addition, attempts by personnel to reach the facility may be limited by other state agencies, including the National Guard or state police. As a result, relief may be delayed for hours or even days, and creative patterns of rotating available personnel may be required to maintain proper security.

(10) Should a flood penetrate the compound and an employee or inmate is in danger, rescue attempts should be undertaken only if there is no significant risk to the potential rescuers. Additionally, the presence of debris washed into the area provides an avenue for escape. Logs, brush, or other items washed up against a fence, for instance, could be used as a bridge over the perimeter fence.

(11) Personnel allowed outside the building should be watchful, especially for dogs, cats, horses, livestock, wild animals, rodents, and reptiles that might have been washed onto the property. Animals under these conditions are extremely fearful, possibly injured, and should not be approached.

(12) Personnel inside the institution, particularly those on the ground floor, also should watch for rodents, reptiles, and other vermin seeking shelter and safety.

Other Disasters or Disruptions

Plans to respond to other disasters, such as an accident at a nearby industrial location or transportation line, also should be developed by the agency. The nature and extent of such plans will be determined by proximity to the potential hazard, as well as the specific risk posed. In most cases, these plans will incorporate the basic elements of the Level I-III planning.

Fog and extended inclement weather can disrupt institution operations, even though they do not cause extensive physical damage or risk. Inclement weather plans should include provisions for controlled movement, enhanced perimeter supervision, and in some cases, curtailment of programs (including work) that ordinarily involve inmate movement outside secure building envelopes. If meal service must be provided in a central dining room in a campus-style facility, then extra supervision, sequential meal service, and even greater perimeter security are indicated.

Disturbance Plan

30

Disturbances are complex and varied events that can be caused by a variety of factors. Although historically, crowding, idleness, faulty security, lack of staff and staff training, substandard facilities, and lack of programs all have played roles contributing to major disturbances, they cannot be viewed as the only potential causes. Major disturbances also have been attributed to spontaneous acts and noninstitutional, or outside, causes.

Prevention

Although many disturbances have been triggered by a single incident, in most cases, those incidents were only sparks igniting an already volatile situation. Many of the variables involved in creating such a situation are well known and can be anticipated by correctional administrators. If they can be detected and corrected in advance, the possibility of a disturbance can be reduced substantially. For that reason, this section discusses four major causes of disturbances: the institution environment, inmate characteristics, administrative policies and procedures, and outside events and their impact on the institution.

The Institutional Environment

Inmates respond to their environment. Living conditions often play a part in the cause of disturbances. Design features–some long corridors, repeated doorways, and hard finishes–can be hypnotic and may contribute to depersonalization of the overall institution setting. Plumbing, heating, lighting, and ventilation are sometimes inadequate. Noise control may be poor to nonexistent. The result can be

that thousands of inmates live in environments that are not only uncomfortable, but frequently unhealthy. Much of this is attributable to the age of many institutions; some facilities still in use today were built prior to 1900.

Disturbances are not confined to outmoded facilities; they occur in some of our most modern facilities, also. But the physical aspects of an institution can contribute to the origins of disturbances and certainly can have an impact on how a disturbance is managed. Correcting obvious deficiencies in these living conditions can help eliminate at least some underlying tensions.

Crowding in correctional institutions is a particular problem. As of late 1996, the correctional population (not including jails) in the United States was more than one million–an all-time high. Moreover, there is every reason to believe that figure will continue to grow. In most institutions, two or more inmates live in cells designed for one. In many institutions, dormitories and other areas are housing far more inmates than they were designed to house, if they were intended to be housing units at all. It is not uncommon for inmates who should be confined in cells to be living in dormitories, instead.

As institutions and living quarters increase in population, the ability to effectively control inmates decreases. Support facilities, including gymnasiums, kitchens, dining rooms, industries, and medical facilities, are all severely stressed. Program resources are inadequate for the increased numbers they must serve. Inmate/staff ratios usually increase. Depersonalization of services and inadequate security then become a possibility.

In all fairness, many agencies have received excellent support from their funding authorities to try to avoid these circumstances. But when they are present, the possibility of a disturbance can increase dramatically. Small, well-designed institutions with individual cells are more effective in reducing tension and disturbances within the institution. But unfortunately, large, crowded, poorly designed correctional institutions with open dormitories are the reality with which many correctional administrators must contend. Therefore, administrators constantly should be seeking innovative methods for improving facilities of this type, and neutralizing the inherent drawbacks of the physical plant with regard to housing. Of primary importance, work programs and other activities can provide an alternative to enforced idleness and thus decrease institutional tension.

Characteristics of the Inmate Population

The characteristics of the inmate population cannot be overlooked as a basic factor in the cause of many disturbances. Indeed, when one looks at the correctional population profile today, it is a marvel that there are not more problems, considering the lack of resources available on a day-to-day basis to deal with these individuals.

Most United States correctional facilities are populated primarily by young, unmarried, minority males from the lower social and economic strata of society. A disproportionate share of these individuals are educationally deficient, emotionally unstable, and prone to violence or other socially deviant behavior. They are frequently the products of broken homes, unskilled, and have unstable work records. They are apt to have prior criminal records, low self-esteem, and no major goals in life. Personal failure in a culture firmly oriented toward material success is a prevalent common denominator among these offenders. These are people with significant needs–needs which have not been met by society but with which the correctional system is somehow expected to contend.

Ironically, despite the fact that inmates have committed serious violations of the law, most tend to become responsible members of the institutional community once they are confined. In general, they want the institution to run smoothly, and they want their lives to be as pleasant and as safe as possible given the circumstances. No one stands to lose more in a disturbance than the inmates. They have the greatest risk of being injured or killed, losing personal property, or having to tolerate a long postdisturbance lockdown. In most disturbances the majority of the inmates want order restored and issues resolved as quickly as possible.

But there are also some special groups within the general correctional population who, for a variety of reasons, are especially prone to cause problems that may erupt into violence and disorder.

- Some inmates are sociopaths, angry at society and lacking normal ethical values. They are prone to destroying property and injuring others, and they can be particularly prone to involvement in disturbances.

- Growing numbers of former mental health patients have made their way into the correctional system in recent decades, and other inmates develop mental health problems while in custody. These inmates often can be involved in "trigger incidents" for much larger disturbances, and can cause general unrest in the general population.

- Many inmates confined today have significant histories of substance abuse. While that background may not directly dispose inmates to instigate or participate in disturbances, it may be part of a larger constellation of factors–gang membership, aggressive or impulsive action patterns–that may contribute to a predisposition to disturbance participation.

- In recent years, prison gang membership has increased; polarization of a population and the individual acts of misconduct associated with gang activity can contribute to a disturbance-prone situation.

- While no longer a major factor in institution unrest, revolutionary organizations have found correctional populations fertile fields for recruitment over the years. Individual misconduct, as well as specific acts of rebellion can precipitate an unplanned disturbance, but members of these organizations also deliberately may plan disruptions of institution operations.

Fortunately for institution staff, inmates do not often unite because, in general, they have difficulty sharing goals and objectives. It is common for an inmate leader to command a large following of loyal supporters, but it is unusual for such a leader to control an entire institution for any length of time. When inmates become frustrated, however, leaders have an easier time agitating and convincing others to join them in aggressive acts. When tension builds, a condition of emotional contagion often develops.

Rumors can run rampant, and crowds can become mobs. Emotionally stimulated inmates may experience an unusual sense of psychological unity, while losing a sense of self-discipline. Then, the climate becomes ripe for a disturbance.

Administrative Problems

A correctional institution, like any other business, industry, or government agency, must be guided by competent, professional management. And while many disturbances can be traced to circumstances beyond the control of correctional administrators, a significant number can be directly attributed to internal agency or administrative factors.

Poor managerial practices found in correctional institutions have included:

- Undefined, or poorly defined, lines of authority and responsibility

- Poor communications

- The absence of clearly described and easily understood rules and regulations

- Precipitous changes in policy or procedures, or inconsistent application of them. In most institutions, considerable attention has been paid to establishing security procedures to prevent disturbances. In too many cases, the aftermath of a disturbance disclosed that security procedures were inadequate or, if not adequate, were not being followed. Inmates quickly become aware of breaches of security, and will try to take advantage of them. Sound security procedures need to be established and continuously monitored to ensure breakdowns are not exploited.

- Unjustified revocation of privileges

- Partiality or favoritism in dealings with inmates and staff members

- Indecisive responses to legitimate grievances

- Problems in hiring, training, and retaining qualified personnel

A common and serious problem has been the high rate of turnover in correctional management, which can contribute to instability. Regrettably, appointments as agency heads appear to be no less political than they were decades ago, when (in 1978) an ACA survey disclosed that only three of the fifty state directors of corrections had been in their jobs more than three years. Those in charge of appointing correctional officials should ensure that they put competent individuals at the helm and then protect the chosen administrators from needless political interference. Systemwide improvements may be needed, but constant and sudden change is almost always detrimental to the stability of agencies and institutions.

The high turnover of correctional officers and other line staff can be another serious problem. In most jurisdictions, pay is relatively low, stress is high, and new staff often are given the least desirable jobs and shifts. It hardly is surprising that in many institutions more than 50 percent of all new correctional officers fail to complete their first year on the job. Inexperienced officers cannot be expected to deal with serious crises as wisely and effectively as more seasoned staff members. Taken together, these factors can set the stage for internal management problems that can stir inmate unrest.

Inadequate financing and stringent budget practices (often stemming from political considerations) have been at the root of some personnel, physical plant, and program issues that have led to disturbances. As noted, many agencies have received strong funding support, but others are not so fortunate. Even organizations that have found the dollars for new construction find it difficult to obtain ongoing funding for annual operating budgets.

Noninstitutional Causes

Just as correctional administrators must be aware of conditions and practices within the institution which can precipitate disturbances, they also must be aware of factors outside the facility that may create tension and hostility in the institution. Steps may be taken to remedy institutional causes through proper management, but the administrator may be severely handicapped in managing factors arising in the larger community. A constant awareness and understanding of these conditions must be maintained, and staff should be educated about their importance and possible consequences.

In an era of ever-increasing violent crime, the American public–or at least their elected representatives–has responded by demanding greater punishment and retribution. This growing punitive attitude is a major factor that must be considered in looking at the cause of prison problems. Inmates read the newspapers, watch television, and listen to the radio. They hear politicians and others call for harsher punishment. Inmates also have been subject to major changes in sentencing and enforcement policies, which have the effect in many jurisdictions of abolishing parole and good time, and lengthening prison terms overall. These conditions tend to make inmates resentful and hostile–conditions that predispose them to act out against lawful prison authority.

Finally, there are many apparent inequities and complexities in the criminal justice system. The most frequent target of attack is disparity in sentencing practices. Other inequities are related to the maxim "the rich man (woman, majority member) goes free while the poor man (woman, minority member) goes to prison."

Indicators of Potential Problems

Regardless of the underlying conditions, there are a number of generally recognized advance indicators of potential problems.

- An atmosphere of sullenness or restlessness among the inmates

- Inmate unwillingness to communicate with staff

- Large numbers of requests for cell, dormitory, or job transfers

- An increase in requests for placement in administrative segregation

- Large numbers of requests for institutional transfer

- Inmate avoidance of meals

- An increase in commissary purchases

- An increase in inmate self-segregation by race or ethnic group, or an increase in unusual inmate gatherings

Several of these elements are worthy of some elaboration:

An increase in gang activity can signal coming problems. Despite the best efforts of staff, rival gangs develop in institutions, and employees must be alert to signs of gang activity and report any unusual incidents immediately. Inmate-organized martial arts (which often are a visible sign of gang intimidation) should not be permitted. Institution rules should limit the number of inmates allowed to congregate in corridors, yards, gymnasiums, libraries, and other common areas. Known gang leaders should be under close observation and supervision. Accurate systems should be devised for recording, reporting, and tracking gang activities.

Racial segregation can lead to problems. Management should be alert to the possibility that particular subgroups may come to dominate specific living areas, job assignments, or basic recreational activities. Steps should be taken to prevent disproportionate representation of racial or ethnic groups in these areas. In addition, efforts should be made to hire and promote minority employees, ensuring a racially balanced staff at all levels of authority.

In many disturbances, food has been a factor. Efforts should be made to ensure that food is properly prepared and served. Food, kitchen equipment, and utensils should be handled in a hygienic manner and servers should be clean and neatly dressed. The dining area should be pleasant and sanitary. Portions should be equally divided and precautions should be taken against shortages of popular items. When substitutions are made, equally desirable foods should be selected as replacements. A rotation system should be devised which enables each housing unit occasionally to be served first. Daily menus should be posted, clearly indicating items that certain religious groups avoid. At meals where pork is a featured entree, an equally attractive substitute should be provided. Importantly, complaints about the meal program to supervisors or food service workers should not be ignored.

Unequal or reduced access to certain programs and services can generate unusual tensions; sometimes this is an unintended side effect of crowding. These areas can include medical services, basic recreation programs, correspondence, visiting with family members and close friends, telephone access, and commissary.

Initial Reaction and Notification

Public safety should be an overriding concern in all disturbance plans, followed closely by staff safety, inmate safety, and then protection of property. When a disturbance begins, staff immediately should notify the control center, shift supervisor, or both. With the widespread use of radios throughout institutions, they also can be used to alert other supervisors at the same time. Other command staff, as specified in the plan, should be called at once.

Immediate steps should be taken to secure and reinforce the perimeter. Towers should be staffed by at least two officers, and gate areas should be secured and staffed by experienced, reliable personnel.

Containment in the interior of the institution also is critical. Certain areas, systems, and supplies are particularly vulnerable during emergencies, and emergency plans should specify that the areas noted in the box on page 207 be secured and reinforced by additional staffing and other measures, before an actual threat to their security materializes.

Areas of Containment

A list of priority containment areas and their items of potential value to inmates.

AREA	CONTENTS
Record rooms	Files and areas with computers that may hold official records, data or inmate file information
Mechanical and industrial shops	Tools and weapons
Medical areas	Medicines, supplies, and equipment
Officer uniform rooms	Clothing, uniforms, and personal belongings
Commissary	Food and other commodities
Power plant	Tools and access to institutional power systems
Warehouse	Equipment and food
Kitchen	Equipment, weapons, and food
Barbershop	Weapons

Probable routes of inmate escape should be anticipated and included on the list of vulnerable areas. Initial staff call-up procedures shall include prioritization, to include specification of the order for alerting command personnel, tactical personnel, and other key employees. An area such as a visiting room or other location out of sight of the inmate population should be designated for the assembly of all stand-by forces.

The warden should notify the appropriate central office officials when an emergency arises, and when events permit that phone call. The original notification should contain as much background and basic facts as are known, followed by updates as new information becomes available. In the event that a disturbance occurs during a weekend or after regular business hours, the central office duty officer, or other designated alternate officials, should be notified. The agency head is responsible for informing the governor and other designated officials, if necessary.

Command Issues and Command Center Operations

The disturbance control plan should be very specific as to who is authorized to do what in the early moments of a disturbance. When the warden and other top staff have arrived, things generally are clear. But before all of the proper officials can be contacted, the plan needs to be very concise as to who

can order the use of what chemical agents, in what locations, and under what circumstances. The plan needs to tell the shift commander if he or she has the authority to use deadly force inside the compound if there is no other command staff member present and if lives are at stake. The plan must anticipate at least a general response to every reasonably foreseeable situation during the period when the chain of command may not yet be complete. Some of this information, no doubt, will be contained elsewhere in agency policy. But it should be stated very plainly in the disturbance control plan, so there is no doubt when a crisis arises.

General features of this portion of the plan should include:

- An emphasis on flexibility; the type of initial response will depend on the nature of the disturbance and an initial assessment by the warden, or the senior command official on site at the time.

- Guidance on containing the situation: locking grilles, securing buildings, locking inmates in cells to the extent possible

- Taking advantage of any opportunities to communicate with participants. If the incident has been nonviolent, a short initial discussion with the inmate group may be appropriate. Inmates should be advised that their grievances will be considered if they stop their actions. As a general rule, bargaining with inmates who are resisting authority is not encouraged, but the warden may deem negotiation appropriate.

- Removal, as soon as possible, of all nonparticipating inmates from the involved area. Nonparticipants left with rioters can be intimidated, coerced into joining the insurrection, or harmed. They should be isolated from the disturbance to the extent allowed by the situation, and should be provided with shelter, clothing, food, and medical attention. The last thing that should happen is ignoring their basic needs or making them think they are being punished, which would risk the possibility of them turning against staff–something that would greatly complicate the situation. If rioters jeopardize the life of other inmates, the procedures followed should be the same as those used to aid employees in danger.

- Obtaining assistance from other institutions or agencies if a disturbance cannot be controlled by local personnel. These requests should be coordinated through the head of the agency. If, in the warden's judgment, the severity of the situation justifies the use of force at levels not available from institutional resources, he or she should call in support forces.

- Provisions for the safety of other staff during disturbances. Employees involved in the restoration of order should be properly equipped to do their jobs, and well trained, and should not be sent into a confrontational situation without sufficient resources to ensure that inmates will not overwhelm the responding personnel.

Resource Assembly and Post Assignments

The relevant provisions of the general emergency plan apply. As additional employees become available, they should be deployed to other parts of the institution to meet possible threats, or to secure areas. The shift supervisor should assume initial command of personnel involved in the response to the disturbance area.

In addition to mustering the formal tactical team and assembling any necessary equipment (more information about this topic is contained in a later chapter), additional staff should be formed into disturbance control squads that also have been trained in crowd control techniques, and in subduing and restraining inmates. Extra staff should be placed in the control room, in the armory, on ground posts between towers, in the power plant, and on strategic points on overlooking buildings. All other noninvolved posts inside the institution should be reinforced as staff become available. At least one staff member should be assigned to coordinate the use of fire equipment.

Nonsecurity personnel should be deployed as needed. In systems relying on the correctional worker concept, this may include nonsecurity staff being assigned to armed posts or tactical response and disturbance control teams.

It is particularly important that the perimeter be reinforced as quickly as possible. Vehicle headlights should be used for illumination if the lighting or power system has been disabled.

Utility and water cutoffs should be protected if they are threatened by the location or the type of disorder. Members of the maintenance staff familiar with the utility layout and operation should be available in case they are needed.

If a situation is prolonged, relief schedules must be established for all disturbance control and tactical personnel. The stress and fatigue of being in what is essentially a combat-ready situation for long periods of time must be taken into account.

The warden and other key command personnel should not respond to the location of the disturbance, but rather to the command center. While it may be natural for them to want to be involved in the immediate management of the situation, it is far more important for them to be safe and to have at their disposal all of the resources of the command center.

Accounting for Staff and Inmates

The relevant provisions of the general emergency plan apply. Since a disturbance may serve as a cover for an escape attempt or can include hostage-taking, this is a particularly important area for the plan to cover.

Firearms and Ordnance

The relevant provisions of the general emergency plan apply. The decision to use lethal force is critical, and the plan clearly should spell out who has the authority to use it, and under what circumstances. Gas saturation data for all areas of the institution, and guidelines for permissible types of ordnance, should be spelled out clearly.

Physical Plant and Utilities

The relevant provisions of the general emergency plan apply. Early in the disturbance, any inmates threatening key features of the physical plant should be told in no uncertain terms that institutional property will be protected by weapons. Although all parts of the facility should be safeguarded, special attention should be given to the areas that are frequent targets of rioters: pharmacies, records offices, commissaries, storerooms and warehouses, knife cabinets, control centers, power plants, and vehicle pools. Staff members should be prepared to fight fires occurring in any section of the institution.

The relevant provisions of the general emergency plan apply for equipment, media relations, reporting, and postemergency action.

Training

In the area of training, the relevant provisions of the general emergency plan apply. Preidentified tactical teams should be trained in advanced tactical skills and in the use of both lethal and nonlethal force. However, all staff should be well trained in general disturbance control procedures so that they can be called upon to serve on regular disturbance control teams. As noted earlier, employees should be thoroughly familiar with the plan and review it at least annually.

Specific Plan Information

General

Although every reasonable effort to regain control must be made from the beginning of a disturbance, actions taken should be based on careful analysis and should follow a planned strategy. While restoration of order will proceed differently in every situation, the following principles generally can be applied:

- Tactical forces should be properly equipped and deployed in sufficient numbers to restore order without a risk of being overwhelmed by inmates.

- Birdshot should be used inside buildings instead of double aught buckshot shotgun

rounds, which can be lethal when used at close range.

- Rifles should be used only in specific situations, and must be issued exclusively to staff trained in their use.

- Whenever possible, large groups of inmates should be split into smaller groups for easier control.

- Leaders should be isolated from the rest of the group at the first opportunity.

- Under proper conditions, smoke, flash grenades, and stinging (but nonlethal) rounds should be used to cover moves and to confuse rioters.

- High-pressure fire hoses may be useful in controlling inmate movement.

- Photographs and videotapes should be made whenever possible, to provide information for subsequent prosecution or internal investigations.

- Once the disturbance has ended, inmates who took an active role should be segregated from the rest of the population as soon as possible.

- Inmates or staff who have been injured should be identified and attended to immediately.

- Retaliation by employees against inmates should be forbidden, and active supervision should be a priority to ensure that this does not take place.

During the disturbance, all employees should attempt to identify inmate participants, and pay special attention to leaders, agitators, those displaying aggressive behavior or destroying property, and inmates holding hostages or committing felonious acts. Positive identification is essential and accurate records must be kept. Whenever possible, an employee witnessing an incident should ask another staff member to corroborate it. Photographs, videotapes, and films are admissible as evidence when proper procedures have been followed and the chain of evidence has not been broken. The main participants in the disturbance should be referred for possible prosecution; others should be handled through the institution's disciplinary policy.

While a disturbance control plan will necessarily contain a great deal of generic information, there are at least two contingencies for which staff should be prepared within the general scope of the plan–violent and nonviolent disruptions of institution operations.

Nonviolent Actions

When a nonviolent disturbance (such as a food strike, for instance) begins, tactical and other staff should be placed on stand-by alert. Efforts should be made to isolate the protesters from the nonparticipating population. Security personnel should be deployed to prevent the spread of the problem and to observe and react if violence should occur. Other inmates should be returned to their housing units; command staff should consider whether to lock down the rest of the institution to minimize the possibility of other disorderly or disruptive action.

Generally, it is preferable to establish a dialog and negotiate with the participants. Negotiation may end the immediate problem, but care must be exercised to avoid reinforcing disruptive behavior. Administrators should maintain the image of being in command of the situation. Inmates are aware that the administrators cannot permit rebellion and need not negotiate with them. No bargaining or concessions should be made with inmates who continue in a state of resistance, but this posture should not preclude administrators from talking to the leaders of a disturbance in an effort to regain control by peaceful means.

Inmate demands to negotiate with outside parties, such as the governor or the news media, should be refused. Care should be exercised in making any promises to inmate groups. Promises made should be kept in good faith; indiscreet promises can lead to awkward or dangerous situations in the future.

When sufficient tactical personnel and equipment have been assembled and related preparations made, inmates should be issued an order to surrender. If they refuse to do so, they should be removed from the area of the disturbance and placed in secure housing. If the use of force becomes necessary, the minimum amount required should be employed.

Violent Actions

In the event of a disturbance that initially is, or becomes, violent, staff must take prompt action. Generally, the response strategy in such situations is characterized as being in one of six levels.

(1) *First Level Response*–After a violent outburst, the situation subsides, but there still are some inmates who are not under complete staff control, although they appear to be interested in talking toward a solution. The warden may choose to authorize staff to attempt to reason, but not negotiate, with the disorderly group. All inmate grievances should be heard and consideration should be given to those that are legitimate, contingent on the participants' immediate, peaceful surrender.

(2) *Second Level Response*–The situation is violent, or a First Level approach is unsuccessful, but there are signs that a nonforceful solution still is possible. A formal order should be issued to disperse and return to quarters or an alternate location; inmates should be instructed to release any hostages. The order should specify a time limit for compliance and offer no alternatives, but may be repeated at reasonable intervals to ensure that all inmates are aware of what is required of them. However, care should be taken to avoid repeating the order so many times that it loses its impact.

(3) *Third Level Response*–A show of force is going to be needed. Sufficient quantities of well-equipped staff (who clearly are capable of handling the situation) should be assembled in locations that are visible to the inmates, and at key access points to the area where the inmates are located. The show of force should be organized to achieve the greatest psychological effect.

(4) *Fourth Level Response*–Some actual tactical action is going to be necessary, probably gas, smoke, and water. These tactical agents should be used only to gain inmate compliance with issued orders, never for punitive or retaliatory purposes. The exact type of ordnance authorized for use should be stated in the authorization. At this stage, disturbance control and tactical personnel will have to move in and restrain, search, and remove the insurgents.

(5) *Fifth Level Response*–More forceful tactical force is needed to control the situation. Large-scale tactical resources should be assembled, depending on the area in which the disturbance occurs and the number of inmates involved. Chemical agents, distraction devices, and other methods should be used to minimize the risk to staff and ensure a prompt resolution to the situation. There must be sufficient numbers of tactical and disturbance control teams to control the situation with total certainty.

(6) *Sixth Level Response*–Severe threats to life and/or property are evident, and firearms must be used as a method of last resort, followed up by tactical force in overwhelming numbers. Weapons should be issued only under the specific authorization and direct command of the warden. Depending on agency policy, the use of weapons ordinarily is appropriate when there is an assault taking place (with danger of bodily harm to inmates or institutional employees), to stop an escape, and to prevent arson.

Employee Job Action

31

While most employees would not engage in such activity (and indeed in most jurisdictions it would be illegal to do so), an employee job action is a possibility under some circumstances. Such a situation may involve a group of employees walking off assigned posts or failing to report for duty at the scheduled time.

Prevention

Prevention in this case hinges on sound communications and reasonably applied personnel practices. If staff believe they can communicate constructively with supervisors, they will be less likely to engage in mass action. If they believe that the agency is applying its personnel regulations fairly, it is less likely they will want to protest as a group. In short, treating employees fairly is the single most effective preventive factor regarding an employee job action.

Some labor organizations have been known to press institution administrators rather vigorously, and to use the threat of "blue flu" or other devices to gain concessions. Managerial personnel carefully should weigh any action taken in response to such pressure, ensuring that the actions they take are fair to employees and are fully within the scope of any formal labor-management agreement. Care should be taken not to overreact to minor incidents, thus provoking a more serious problem.

Initial Reaction and Notification

Often, the first person to know about a problem of this type will be the shift supervisor. But in some instances, the employees may make their intentions known in advance. Whatever the means, the warden should be advised at once, followed by the deputy wardens, chief of security, and other department heads. The degree of immediate notification and staff callup required will be determined by the nature and extent of the initial situation. However, the central office should be notified at once, and in some instances, the state police may be placed on standby, as well.

Command Issues

The relevant provisions of the general emergency plan apply. To the extent possible, inmate activities should continue in a routine manner, depending on the number and abilities of available employees. It may be necessary to postpone or eliminate some activities until enough personnel are available to cover necessary posts and supervise all programs. The support and goodwill of the inmate population is of utmost importance during this time of crisis. Therefore, based on staff availability and the level of compliance of the inmate population, program schedules may be adapted in the following order:

(1) Maintenance of a normal program schedule

(2) Adoption of a "holiday" schedule

(3) Selective lockdown, with routine meal service in the dining room and limited programs

(4) Total lockdown, serving all inmate meals in cells, with limited program access

If the command center is activated, procedures should ensure that it is secure from unauthorized personnel, particularly striking employees.

Resource Assembly and Post Assignments

The lack of personnel may lead inmates to believe there is diminished security, thus increasing the possibility of an escape attempt. Particularly vulnerable areas should be identified in each institution's plan, along with response strategies for dealing with each potential vulnerability.

In the event of a work stoppage by line correctional officers, all other available staff members and supervisory correctional officers should be used to staff necessary areas. Minimum staffing requirements and essential posts that must be filled should be listed as part of the plan. All off-duty personnel should be notified of the work stoppage and advised to report to work as required. Unit management staff should be assigned to work in their respective units, when possible. Only weapons-qualified personnel should be assigned to towers, outside hospital details, and transportation duties. Upon arrival at assigned posts, all newly assigned personnel should read the post orders.

Compulsory overtime may be necessary during such a situation. It also may be necessary to institute work shifts of twelve-on, twelve-off. In extreme situations, the institution may wish to set up sleeping areas for staff who live long distances from the facility and do not have the time to go home between shifts.

If, in the warden's judgment, there still are not enough personnel to staff all essential posts, it may be necessary to request assistance from other resources. If the work stoppage has spread to other institutions, support from forces outside the agency may be called in to assist. If possible, the decision to call support forces should be coordinated through the agency head. If that person is not immediately available and the warden believes that the situation has caused a serious breach in security, the warden should call in outside agencies and notify superiors of the actions taken at the earliest opportunity.

The food service manager should plan on preparing and serving three meals per day to inmates and employees. Serving schedules should be coordinated through the deputy warden. Inmate food service workers should report to their regular work areas under the food service manager's supervision and should be used in their normal capacities if, in the warden's opinion, their presence does not create a security risk.

Accounting for Staff and Inmates

The relevant provisions of the general emergency plan apply, but in addition, it may be necessary to institute special personnel tracking systems. For instance, supervisory personnel may have to personally call every employee and order them to work, making a record of their response and whether they ultimately reported for duty or not. This information could be used later in any adverse action proceedings against the employee, since automated callup procedures or even "pyramid" calling by nonsupervisory staff could be challenged on several grounds.

Firearms and Ordnance

Ordinarily, no issues involving this area should arise. However, only staff fully trained and qualified for weapons should be issued firearms.

Physical Plant and Utilities

The relevant provisions of the general emergency plan apply. The security and continued operation of key posts, such as the powerhouse, water treatment plant, or other areas should be addressed.

Equipment

Necessary equipment should be provided to replacement employees, including, but not limited to, firearms, flashlights, keys, radios, batons, and gas.

Media Relations

The news media often give coverage to any employee work stoppage at an institution. The warden or designated public information officer (who may be from the central office if there are systemwide implications) should keep the news media informed of developments. The emphasis should be on the stability of current operations and the fact that there will be no risk to the public. Staff should be ready to implement any other necessary aspects of the institution's general media plan.

Reporting

The relevant provisions of the general emergency plan apply. This type of situation is certain to require a great deal of additional reporting. The personnel regulations of the agency and state largely will determine, for instance, whether the incident will become the subject of litigation. Consequently, local administrators should confer early and often with central office staff to determine what ongoing documentation should be maintained, and in what form it should be submitted when the crisis has passed.

For postemergency action and training, the relevant provisions of the general emergency plan apply.

Specific Plan Information

Should a disturbance by the inmate population arise in conjunction with an employee work stoppage, the institution's disturbance plan should be implemented without delay.

During an employee work stoppage, vehicular traffic in the vicinity of the institution may be an issue. In addition, employees directly taking part in the work stoppage may be near the institution's entrance, interrupting vehicular traffic. Delivery truck drivers may refuse to cross what they perceive to be a picket line, although a formal strike may not have been declared. If this occurs, on-duty personnel may be required to make pickups of food, medicines, and supplies.

Local police should direct traffic and see that the employees involved in the work stoppage do not cause property damage or harm to individuals entering the institution.

Any discussion with employees involved in a work stoppage should be for informational purposes only. All grievances should be identified and reported to the agency head or other designated labor-management official. Any agreement reached at one facility ultimately may affect all institutions, and so only the agency head should make formal commitments to employees in the process of resolving any disputes of this type.

Fire Plan

32

Fires in a high-security correctional institution pose one of the most grave threats imaginable for both staff and inmates. The fire-control plan should outline institutional fire policy and procedures, and identify equipment and training necessary to provide a safe environment for employees, inmates, and visitors.

Prevention

The most important aspect of any fire protection program is prevention. The first ingredient of a good fire prevention program is the use of safe building materials and furnishings that meet National Fire Protection Association (NFPA) and other applicable standards.

In particular, the use of certain types of foam rubber mattresses presents an extreme hazard, as the toxic fumes from their combustion quickly can incapacitate or kill staff and inmates in a confined area. No such mattresses should be in use.

Some institutions are beginning to severely limit smoking, and in a few instances, systems are prohibiting smoking entirely. While this is largely for health reasons, it also has very clear fire-prevention benefits. Noncombustible receptacles should be available for smoking materials, and other noncombustible containers should be readily accessible throughout the institution for flammable liquids, rags, and other burnables. These latter containers should be capped by tightly fitted lids, except when in use. A plan for daily disposal of contents and cleaning of the containers should be formulated.

Paints and other flammable materials should be stored in an approved, properly constructed building which meets NFPA codes. The enclosure must be adequately ventilated, have an approved drain system, and the lights and switches must be explosion-proof. Unapproved auxiliary heaters should not be used in paint storage areas, and no smoking signs should be posted prominently.

Regular inspection of fire and emergency equipment and regular review of procedures should be required by agency policy and institutional procedures, in compliance with applicable fire codes. The basics of the fire plan should include these other preventive elements:

- Documentation by an independent, qualified source that the institution complies with all applicable fire safety codes

- Regular inspection by the fire or safety officer

- Annual review of the entire fire-control plan

- Weekly fire and safety inspections by a member of the administrative staff

- Quarterly testing of fire equipment, including the fire alarm and smoke detection systems

- Certification by a qualified inspector that travel distances to exits are in compliance with the National Fire Safety Code

- Testing power generators at least every two weeks, and the repair or replacement of any inoperable equipment

Weekly, quarterly, and annual inspections for the entire institution should evaluate the following conditions:

- Compliance with safety codes

- Results of fire drills

- Visual observation of all emergency equipment and facilities

- Degree of readiness of all fire-extinguishing equipment

- Placement and operational readiness of alarm and detection systems

- Compliance with requirements for fire-resistant furnishings and facilities

- Trash collection procedures

- Condition of exit signs

- Travel distance to exits

- Emergency lighting

- Evacuation plans

Fires often occur in unoccupied areas such as shops, warehouses, and industries buildings. Inspection procedures should ensure that these areas are free of fire hazards at the end of the regular workday. Inspections of these nonhousing areas should be made on each shift when they are not in use. These inspections should be documented in the shift log, and the fire or safety supervisor immediately should be advised–in writing–of any deficiencies noted. Some institutions use an inmate fire watch program, in which specifically selected inmates are assigned to such areas during selected nonworking hours.

All staff should be aware of the following fire-related concerns:

- All flammable liquids must be stored and dispensed in accordance with applicable codes and standards.

- Oily rags and other waste subject to spontaneous combustion must be disposed of in self-closing containers.

- Paper or cardboard containers never should be used for trash storage; only noncombustible containers should be used.

- Flammable waste should not be stored in shops at night.

- Exposed wiring should be reported and repaired promptly.

Initial Reaction and Notification

The relevant provisions of the general emergency plan apply. If the institution has a staff or inmate fire brigade, they should be alerted at once.

The plan should be very specific on the procedure for calling local fire authorities, and the numbers to be called should be on an automatic dialer and prominently posted in the control center. In facilities with automatic tie-ins between the institution's fire detection system and a local fire department, there must be clear instructions for the control center officer on how to handle false and questionable alarms.

Post orders should contain specific information on how employees are to respond to fires. This should include instructions for reporting, how to decide whether to take immediate suppression action, how to decide to evacuate the area, and other key elements.

The confusion caused by a fire, and the vehicular traffic that can result if fire trucks are brought into the institution, can be used by inmates to conceal an escape attempt. The perimeter should be on full alert during a fire-related problem.

Command Issues and Command Center Operations

The relevant provisions of the general emergency plan apply. If the fire is in an area that implicates, and hampers the effective operation of, the command center, then the command center should be relocated to the alternate site.

Resource Assembly and Post Assignments

The relevant provisions of the general emergency plan apply. Any staff or inmate fire brigade personnel should be cleared to the area where their equipment is stored, and permitted to access the site of the fire.

Accounting for Staff and Inmates

The relevant provisions of the general emergency plan apply.

Firearms and Ordnance

The relevant provisions of the general emergency plan apply.

Physical Plant and Utilities

The relevant provisions of the general emergency plan apply. Responding fire personnel from the community should be familiarized already (through ongoing joint training and tours) with the location of all standpipes and hydrants, but institution staff should be available to assist in locating them, should there be any problems. A standpipe is a vertical hydrant into which water is forced by mechanical means to obtain pressure sufficient to reach the top of the institution's tallest building.

Equipment

Adequate fire control equipment is an absolute necessity. It is usually more economical to arrange for a local fire department to provide for the facility's major fire protection. When this is not practical, the facility should secure the services of experts in the fire safety field to advise on the fire prevention measures and equipment necessary to provide adequate protection. Fire protection equipment to be considered should include:

- A fire truck equipped with lined hose, nozzles, ladders, hydrant wrenches, small tools, and other needed items

- Fire extinguishers of all types

- Fire hydrants and standpipes, properly located, and with sufficient water pressure and volume

- Automatic smoke detectors, fire alarms, and sprinkler systems, which ordinarily are required in all new construction

- Emergency lighting that provides sufficient illumination for exit areas and stairwells during emergencies

Media Relations

The relevant provisions of the general emergency plan apply.

Reporting

The relevant provisions of the general emergency plan apply. Regardless of magnitude, all fires should be investigated by a qualified fire or safety inspector. Staff must be aware of the need to preserve a fire site and any associated evidence, when there is reason to believe that an arson investigation may result from an incident. Reports of all in-house investigations should be forwarded to the warden.

Agency policy and state statute will provide criteria for notifying the fire marshal or other authorities when a fire occurs. In cases where the cause of the fire is not easily determined, the fire marshal's office should assist in the investigation. In those cases, institution staff should cooperate fully and provide all information and evidence necessary for the completion of the inquiry.

Postemergency Action

The relevant provisions of the general emergency plan apply.

Training

Training should acquaint staff with fire safety, fire prevention, and fire-fighting techniques. Specific fire control training should be provided to personnel who have been selected to operate fire control equipment, such as members of an institution's fire brigade. The importance of good housekeeping standards must be a part of any staff or inmate fire prevention training. Because an escape attempt is a real possibility during an emergency such as a fire, that contingency should be addressed in the fire training program.

The designated fire or safety supervisor, in cooperation with all department heads, should schedule and supervise monthly fire drills. Prior notification of the drills should be limited, to increase the training effect of an unanticipated situation.

Specific Plan Information

Definitions

Class A Fires: Fires consuming ordinary combustible material such as wood, paper, or clothing. A pressurized, water-based fire extinguisher is appropriate for this type of fire.

Class B Fires: Fires consuming flammable and combustible liquids, grease, and gases. A foam, dry chemical, or carbon dioxide (CO_2) extinguisher is appropriate for this type fire.

Class C Fires: Fires burning in energized electrical equipment. A dry chemical or CO_2 extinguisher is appropriate for this type fire. A water-based extinguisher must never be used on a Class C fire.

Class D Fires: Fires consuming combustible metals such as magnesium, titanium, zirconium, and sodium. A dry powder extinguisher is necessary to extinguish such a fire.

Hydrostatic Test: A type of fire extinguisher examination intended to determine the balance of its chemical contents.

Procedures

The cooperation and assistance of local fire authorities should be solicited in the development of the plan.

Evacuation routes should be posted on unit bulletin boards and in other prominent areas. In particular, staff should be intimately familiar with the means for the orderly release of inmates from locked areas in case of an emergency.

Weekly inspections of the evacuation routes should be made by various staff, with a report filed with the shift supervisor after each inspection.

To provide an early warning of fires from any source, whether of inmate or mechanical-failure origin, a product-of-combustion smoke detection system can identify smoke particles and should be installed in each housing unit, with separate detection heads in each pod, at a minimum. This equipment should be linked to a central annunciator panel, in an area that is monitored twenty-four hours a day by staff who can call local fire departments quickly if the need arises. This system also should be tied in with a sprinkler network that will act to quickly suppress any serious fires.

Self-contained breathing units, or air packs, should be in key areas, such as the control center, shift supervisor's office, special housing units, and other critical areas, such as the industrial building and shops, where a fire hazard might be high. They should be mounted on the wall in such a way that a staff member only has to back up to the pack, slip his or her shoulders into the harness and lift it off the wall mount. This is a quick, easy method for donning this gear, and by mounting them in staff-controlled areas, where they can be observed easily, tampering is less likely and inspection is easier.

Hostage Plan

33

Definitions

A hostage is any person (an employee, visitor, or inmate) who is held against his or her will by another person for purposes of escape or monetary gain, or in any other manner that places the hostage in danger of bodily injury or death. No person–regardless of rank or other attribute–has any authority while being held hostage.

Hostage situations are perhaps the most serious emergencies with which an institution administrator may have to deal. Hostage-taking can be a desperate spur-of-the-moment action or a premeditated act. The hostage-taker may have been caught in a wrongdoing or in an escape attempt, or may be attempting to intensify pressure on institution management. Whether it is one hostage in a room or dozens in several areas of the institution, lives are at risk–lives of people the administrator very well may know and work with every day. The pressures and the stakes in such a situation are immense.

Prevention

The relevant provisions of the general emergency plan apply. As a general matter, supervisors should be alert to staff assignments that might lend themselves to a potential hostage-taking situation: employees alone in isolated areas, or staff in offices without proper windows. Personal body alarms, while not a complete preventive measure, somewhat can deter hostage-taking situations from developing.

Initial Reaction and Notification

In addition to the notification steps in the general plan, some immediate, concrete actions are necessary in the event a hostage is taken. The shift supervisor should isolate the crisis area to restrict the hostage-taker's movement, to prevent the spread of the situation, and to preclude additional staff or inmates from being taken hostage.

- The perimeter should be alerted and reinforced.

- A general lockdown should be considered.

- Any available trained hostage negotiators should be summoned.

- Tactical personnel should obtain equipment and prepare for action.

- The central office should be advised, when the situation allows the time to do so.

Command Issues and Command Center Operations

Decisionmakers in the command center must make key decisions quickly in the initial stages of a hostage situation. As it develops, the warden must consider the following possible approaches to the situation:

- Contain the situation and demand surrender.

- Negotiate surrender and release of all hostages.

- Use chemical agents to force surrender.

- Use snipers or sharpshooters to disable the hostage taker.

- Deploy tactical staff for an actual assault; ensure that they understand that the amount of force used should not exceed that necessary to prevent a hostage taker from escaping, or causing bodily harm or death to a hostage.

If circumstances permit, the decisionmaker should progress from one of the lower-level responses to the higher-level response. It is virtually impossible to return to negotiation after an assault has taken place. Therefore, it is important to remember that the initial response chosen may preclude the use of other actions later.

Authorization for the use of deadly force requires that an informed judgment be made by the warden regarding the situation at hand. Any use of firearms may involve the full spectrum of deadly force, ranging from firing-to-wound-or-disable to a full assault. Consequently, the assessment of the advisability of using firearms to resolve a hostage situation should be based on agency policy and established procedures for the use of force. If armed personnel must be deployed, then it is absolutely critical that they are fully qualified in the use of those weapons, that only approved weapons and ammunition be issued, and that they know the rules of engagement–under what circumstances they may fire, and what the effect of that fire is to be.

However, in many cases, time is a factor that works in favor of the authorities. Good judgment and sound security practices often are the principal means of bringing about the safe release of hostages. As long as the hostages are not being harmed or an escape is not actually under way, the most common strategy is to delay the use of force and to keep talking.

Hostage scenarios will be complicated considerably if there are multiple hostages, and even more so if they are held in multiple locations. This not only makes negotiations more complex, but also makes any necessary tactical action far more difficult.

Resource Assembly and Post Assignments

The relevant provisions of the general emergency plan apply.

Accounting for Staff and Inmates

The relevant provisions of the general emergency plan apply.

Firearms and Ordnance

The relevant provisions of the general emergency plan apply.

Physical Plant and Utilities

The relevant provisions of the general emergency plan apply. In some situations, water, electricity, and heat may be cut off to increase pressure on the hostagetakers. Mechanical services personnel should be ready to take such action, if needed.

Equipment

The relevant provisions of the general emergency plan apply.

Media Relations

The relevant provisions of the general emergency plan apply. Ordinarily, the identity of hostages is not released until the incident is resolved.

Reporting

The relevant provisions of the general emergency plan apply. In virtually all cases, a criminal investigation will result, so all reports should be prepared with that in mind.

Postemergency Action

Debriefing–the formal, systematic questioning of a witness, released hostage, or hostage taker–is an important part of the management of the crisis. This is a means for staff to obtain useful information that may assist in the successful outcome of a current or future hostage situation. Debriefing sessions should be conducted as soon as possible after the incident, to obtain information while it still is fresh in the hostage's mind. The information obtained in a quick debrief is available for any continuing negotiations, but also later for use if criminal charges are filed. Thoroughness in questioning at this stage eliminates having to recall the subject after he or she has been reunited with family and has turned attention to different concerns.

Training

Specific training for hostage negotiators is important. While the information that follows in the "Specific Plan Information" section is important, agencies should make every attempt to secure specialized hostage-negotiation training for key staff. Also, agency negotiators should train jointly with tactical personnel on a regular basis. These two functions inextricably are linked, and joint training will ensure the decisions and acts of both parties support a successful outcome. In addition, if the plan relies on negotiators from another agency, those individuals should be included in this training.

Hostage Survival

- Be cautious of heroics. Do not act foolishly.

- Be cooperative and obey the hostage taker's demands without appearing either servile or antagonistic.

- Look for a protected place to take shelter in case either authorities or inmates assault your location.

- Keep calm. Think about pleasant scenes or memories; try to recollect books or movies. A calm mind will help you remain functional.

- Keep a low profile. Avoid the appearance of observing any crimes that rioters commit. Look down or away. Avoid interfering with their discussions or activities.

- Do not threaten the hostage takers or indicate that you intend to testify against them. If they are attempting to conceal their identities, make no indication that you recognize them.

- Be reluctant to give up your identification or clothes; loss of these things is demoralizing and inmates will use these items in bargaining. Be especially resistant to exchanging clothing with an inmate; being indistinguishable from the inmates could put you in danger during an assault.

- Because of the stress of the situation, you may have difficulty retaining fluids. Drink water and eat, even if you are not hungry; it is important to maintain strength.

- Be conscious of your body language as well as your speech. Do not say or do anything to arouse the hostage-taker's hostility or suspicions. Act neutral and be a good listener if your captors want to talk.

- Be cautious about making suggestions; you may be held responsible if something you suggest goes wrong.

- Think of persuasive reasons the hostage-takers should keep you and any other hostages alive and unharmed. Encourage captors to let the authorities know your whereabouts and condition.

- Suggest possible ways in which you or other hostages may help in negotiations. If you, as a hostage, serve as a communicator between the hostage taker and the authorities, convey all messages accurately.

- If there is a tactical assault and shots are fired, drop quickly to the floor and seek cover. Keep your hands on your head. When appropriate, identify yourself, but do not resist being apprehended.

- There is a feeling of tremendous psychological and physiological relief when you are released. Debriefing gives you the opportunity to discuss what happened to you and your reactions. Express your feelings freely and deal openly with your reactions and any problems you may have subsequently.

- Although you must appear disinterested while being held hostage, observe all you can. To aid in the debriefing process, make notes as soon after your release as you can. These actions will help in the subsequent prosecution of the hostage takers.

Staff training for every employee–directed at what to do if taken hostage–is a vital survival skill in the correctional setting. It is important for persons being held hostage to remember that, whatever their position in the agency, they have no authority while under duress, and their orders will not be obeyed. Hostages must also remember the important points noted in the box on page 221.

Specific Plan Information

Hostage incidents can involve a single hostage taker and one hostage in one location, or multiple hostage takers holding numerous captives in multiple areas throughout the institution. The specifics of the situation will determine the response. However, a number of basic principles apply to all such situations.

(1) The first objective is to convince a hostage taker to safely release the hostage and to surrender.

(2) Many agencies have trained hostage negotiators in each institution; others have one or more such personnel who quickly may be sent to an institution where a hostage situation is underway.

(3) Negotiations should be conducted authoritatively, but at the same time, the negotiator immediately must let the hostage taker know that negotiators have no final authority; everything discussed in negotiations must be approved by someone higher in the organization.

(4) All records on the hostage taker should be retrieved and a mental health professional should be standing by for consultation, if an extended situation develops.

(5) The hostage taker's family or friends should not be brought to the scene; their presence may adversely affect the inmate's mental state and provoke a violent act directed at the hostage. Involving family or friends should be approved only as a last resort.

(6) The area where the incident is contained never should be unsecured; the hostage taker and captives should not be permitted to move without authorization from the situation commander.

(7) No action should be taken against the hostage taker without the approval of the warden unless there is an imminent threat to the life of the hostage.

(8) A bullhorn or public address system should not be used for negotiations unless there is no other alternative, because the impersonal nature of these methods may interfere with the development of trust and rapport in the negotiation process.

(9) If negotiations cannot be conducted safely face-to-face, which often is the case, then the phone system should be used. Negotiation over the telephone allows a personal, private conversation and provides the negotiator with a maximum amount of protection and safety. It also enables the isolation and simplification of the negotiation process.

(10) Face-to-face negotiations allow more accurate assessment of the mental state of the hostage taker, but should be undertaken only after rapport has been established through some other mode of communication. They should be carried out only from a safe position; often some form of barricade is needed to assure that the negotiator is not harmed or taken captive.

A key principle of hostage negotiations is the likelihood that hostages will be released unharmed as time passes. This is because:

- Basic needs for normal intake patterns of food and water, and regular sleep, increase as time passes.

- The anxiety and tension of the initial situation tend to abate over time; most persons begin to think more rationally and less emotionally after the early stage of a crisis passes.

- The Stockholm Syndrome (explained later) begins to develop.

- Hostages have an increased opportunity to escape.

- Intelligence gathering permits better decision making.

- Increased rapport and trust develop between the negotiator and hostage taker.

- The hostage taker's expectations may be reduced.

- The incident may simply fade, with the hostage taker allowing the hostages to walk out with no expectation of anything in return.

Staff conducting face-to-face negotiations also should consider the following issues:

- Obtain a verbal agreement guaranteeing that negotiators will not be harmed.

- Do not talk to a hostage taker who is menacing negotiation staff with a weapon.

- Ordinarily, meet face-to-face with no more than one hostage taker at a time.

- Always maintain direct eye contact and never turn your back on a hostage taker.

- Always have an escape route and be aware of body space; estimate what the hostage taker's body space needs are and how much pressure will be put on him or her by encroaching on that space.

- Do not push the hostage taker into taking desperate measures; as long as he or she believes there is a hope of achieving something in the negotiation process, talks will be likely to continue.

- Be conscious of both verbal and nonverbal communication; listen actively, but discreetly.

- Avoid deadlines; remember, time is on the side of the negotiator.

- Give hostages only minimal attention and do not give away advantages you can use as bargaining chips.

- Do not negotiate on demands for additional weapons.

- Be honest and authoritative, but make sure the hostage taker understands that the negotiator does not have the final authority on any issues.

- Be wary of nonagency negotiators; conventional wisdom holds that, in most instances, they should not be used.

The hostages themselves play an important part in the management of a hostage crisis. Although each hostage will react uniquely, a common set of behaviors, labeled the Stockholm Syndrome, is a likely occurrence in lengthy hostage situations. The Stockholm Syndrome is characterized by one or more of the following behaviors:

- The hostages develop positive feelings toward their captors.

- The hostages develop negative feelings toward authorities.

- The hostage takers begin to develop positive feelings toward their hostages.

All three of these behaviors do not have to be present. Although it may not occur to the same extent with all hostages, it should be assumed that at least some features of this syndrome will be displayed unless the hostage has been abused or isolated. From the standpoint of the negotiators, this behavior set has both positive and negative aspects. The positive aspect is that the stronger the manifestation of the Stockholm Syndrome, the less likely it is that the hostage taker will kill the hostages. Negative aspects include:

- Information coming from the hostages during and after the crisis may be unreliable.

- The hostages may deliberately or unconsciously misrepresent the hostage taker's argument; they may become de facto advocates of their captors.

- The hostages may act in a manner counter to the commands of the person in charge of their rescue, causing interference with rescue plans.

- The syndrome also may affect the performance of the negotiator. If, after hours of attempting to build rapport and establish trust, it becomes evident that an assault is necessary, it may be emotionally difficult for a negotiator to distract the hostage taker during the initiation of an assault. This points out the need for alternate, or relief hostage negotiators in prolonged hostage situations.

If negotiations fail, or there is reason to believe the hostage is about to be harmed, a tactical assault may be the only course of action. While negotiations proceed, tactical planning, preparing, and positioning should be taking place. Planning and implementation should be directed by the warden or designee, in coordination with the chief of security.

Decisions about weaponry, types of ammunition, positioning and rules of engagement for snipers, and many other details must be pre-identified in the hostage plan and quickly put into effect. Pictures of the hostages, and other identifying information must be provided to the tactical teams. All staff should be thoroughly familiar with the mission and their specific role. Every attempt should be made to safeguard the hostages in a tactical operation.

Inmate Work/Food Strike Plan

34

Generally, nonviolent disturbances, such as food and work strikes, can be anticipated somewhat. They often occur during business hours, when the employee workforce is greatest in number. While they can spread into a more serious, violent disturbance, they usually do not present those complications.

Prevention

Since nonviolent disturbances usually involve planning, leadership, and organization within the inmate population, institution intelligence measures and informants can alert personnel to organized inmate actions. This gives the administration an opportunity to take action to abort the pending disturbance before it occurs, or to be better prepared to handle it.

Initial Reaction and Notification

The relevant provisions of the general emergency plan apply.

Command Issues and Command Center Operations

The following management strategies can help assess the nature of the problem:

- When word of a potential strike is received, heighten all forms of communications.

- Be alert to inmates putting up handbills or notes regarding a mass action.

- Watch for inmates circulating in groups, agitating, taking names, or perhaps pressuring other inmates to participate.

- Watch for inmates posted at the housing unit, the dining room, or at work area doors, as if to intimidate others from entering.

- Identify additional known or emerging inmate leaders, and isolate them from the general population.

While taking these steps, the following parallel actions should be taking place:

- Inmates should be told that staff will not tolerate disruptive activities or individuals; it should be clear that inmates who do become involved in rebellious behavior will be disciplined, accordingly.

- Supervisory staff should convey to the inmates their readiness to deal with valid grievances in a reasonable manner, but not while under duress.

- Tactical staff should be placed on alert, if deemed appropriate, and assembled in an area that allows for a prompt reaction.

- The perimeter should be reinforced.

- Consideration should be given to whether the institution should be locked down until there is a reasonable belief that the tension has abated.

- If a clear inmate leadership structure exists, consideration may be given to discussing issues with them; this approach, however, has the drawback of essentially validating the prestige and authority of those inmates with the rest of the population.

- A full-institution interview strategy can be used, with staff conducting private interviews with all inmates. This allows inmates to speak freely without peer pressure, and permits staff to obtain a more complete picture of the true sentiments of the population. It also allows informants to safely provide information about leaders and any other planned action that may be forthcoming.

Resource Assembly and Post Assignments

The relevant provisions of the general emergency plan apply. Housing unit posts may be reinforced, and unit management staff used to interview and interact with inmates, to gather information about the causes of the strike.

Accounting for Staff and Inmates

The relevant provisions of the general emergency plan apply.

Firearms and Ordnance

In most cases, this type of incident will not involve the use or weapons and ordnance; however, a standby issue of chemical agents may be in order as a precautionary measure.

Physical Plant and Utilities

The relevant provisions of the general emergency plan apply.

Equipment

The relevant provisions of the general emergency plan apply.

Media Relations

The relevant provisions of the general emergency plan apply.

Reporting

The relevant provisions of the general emergency plan apply.

Postemergency Action

The relevant provisions of the general emergency plan apply.

Training

The relevant provisions of the general emergency plan apply.

Tactical Operations

35

The tactical option to resolving institution disturbances–whether it is presented to inmates as a threat or actually used–is important enough to have its own chapter. The use of calculated force raises life and death issues, as well as important public safet concerns.

The formation and use of tactical response teams and disturbance control squads are inherent and important parts of most institutions' emergency response capabilities. While every employee (within agency regulations) should be trained in basic crowd control tactics, most facilities also have specially trained tactical teams that provide the main response force in a crisis. This chapter deals primarily with the more specialized tactical response teams (variously called SORT, CERT, SWAT); disturbance control teams of more general use should receive a subset of the training recommended.

Team Guidelines

All team members should be experienced and volunteer for this teams; no probationary employees should be involved, unless a newly activated institution does not have enough career staff to form a full team. Each team member should meet the following criteria. Note: all members do not need to be correctional officers:

- Have completed all required agency inservice training

- Be thoroughly familiar with all emergency plans of the institution, as well as the layout of the facility, including all buildings, key utility features, and the working properties of all locking systems

- Be fully qualified in the use of weapons, chemical agents, and other emergency equipment, including complete familiarity with all agency rules and regulations pertaining to the use of force, firearms, and chemical agents

- Be able to withstand physical and mental stress, including being able to remain on duty for extended periods of time

- Have a home telephone and reside within a reasonable distance (ordinarily not more than forty-five minutes travel time) away from the institution

Team members should participate as a group in annual refresher training, but also must attend at least one monthly training session, or exercise, as a group, to ensure that they retain the minimal degree of proficiency. The warden, deputy warden, chief of security, and certified trainers in relevant specialties should evaluate the members of the tactical squad on specific performance criteria developed by the agency. Quarterly evaluation sheets completed by team leaders should remain on file in the chief of security's office, with copies forwarded to the personnel office and placed in the individual's official personnel file. In addition, team leaders should ensure that appropriate comments are included on annual employee service rating forms. Failure to meet performance standards should result in removal from the team.

Outside Tactical Resources

Staff from other agencies sometimes are necessary to supplement the institutional security force.

Tactical Team Equipment

Tactical teams should be equipped suitably for personal protection, as well as to perform the assigned task. Typical issue items include:

- Gas masks (mask with speaker for team leader)

- Protective helmet and face guard

- Jump suits (coverall type) or other suitably durable and comfortable clothing

- Disturbance control batons

- Protective shields

- Ballistic-resistant vests

- Electronic stun equipment and handheld restraint devices (optional)

- Handcuffs, standard, nickel-plated steel; ten ounce

- Plastic handcuffs (for temporary use only)

- Firearms, if authorized by the warden

- Chemical agents appropriate for the intended use

- Other ordnance, including smoke grenades, stun rounds, stingballs, and flash-rounds

---

Tactical and other support forces may be requested by the command center from the following sources:

(1) Central office security administrator

(2) Other institutions

(3) State highway patrol

(4) Municipal police departments

(5) County sheriff's department

(6) Local fire department

(7) Local ambulance service

(8) Civil defense

Ordinarily, only agency employees should be used within the secure confines of the institution. Assisting personnel from other agencies should be used outside the perimeter unless the situation warrants otherwise. Should the crisis escalate to the point where the on-site commander finds it necessary to request additional support from the National Guard, a request should be submitted to the agency head, with complete details of the present situation and an outline of the additional support needed. The agency head then should initiate a formal request to the governor's office for that support.

Upon arrival at the institution, the officer-in-charge of other agency or forces outside the detail should report to the command center, where he or she should receive a thorough briefing on:

- The current situation

- Housing and food arrangements for long-term deployment

- Current policy on the use of force and media contacts.

- Other supporting materials needed to ensure outside forces are thoroughly and completely familiar with all portions of the institution

All support and reserve forces from other institutions should be mustered at a central point outside the disturbance area, and be placed under the operational control of the warden.

Intelligence-gathering Activities

Specific staff should be assigned to gather information about the areas involved in the disturbance, to be used in operational planning. Speed of collection, evaluation, and transmission of information is vital to the success of the emergency operation. Strict security should be maintained at all levels, with particular attention paid to the handling of documents, maps, phone and radio traffic, or any other form of communication that might convey tactical information to unauthorized personnel. No release of information should be made concerning any aspect of tactical operations except by the duly appointed public information officer.

The following information is of particular interest in evaluating the situation and making decisions regarding tactical and negotiation responses:

- Location and nature of the disturbance

- Type of weapons and equipment being used by inmates

- Extent of damage, as well as the location of any barricades, blocked grilles or doors, or other hindrances to tactical operations

- Hostages held

- Number of persons needing aid

- Availability of communications to the area

- Approximate number of inmates involved

For both intelligence-gathering and general documentation, staff trained in proper use and maintenance of video cameras should be available during an emergency. A current list of these employees should be part of the emergency plans and be maintained in the command center. Videotape recorders should be used to document all possible aspects of the situation, including those where physical confrontation is probable, as well as (if possible) what specific areas look like before entry by response teams. Photographing these events provides evidence and documentation and may provide an element of control by acting as a deterrent to violence. Care should be taken to protect the operator of the camera or videotape recorder. As a related sidelight, video equipment for this purpose, as well as for any legitimate educational uses, should be secured from unauthorized inmate access and use.

Tactical Strategies

The actual tactics of disturbance response are impossible to specify. Each institution is different. Each situation is different. Each set of available staff resources is different. Each set of available facts is different. However, there are a number of guidelines that are applicable to most situations:

(1) If force is necessary, it must be overwhelming, but only in the amount necessary to restore order.

(2) Never commit to a tactical action that does not assure total control of the inmates as the final outcome, because if inmates prevail, then in the next encounter, staff will be fighting combatants wearing staff riot gear, perhaps using staff weapons.

(3) Always retain a backup tactical capability, which can be quickly deployed, if necessary.

(4) If nonagency resources are called upon, use them to replace agency staff; nonagency personnel should not be used inside the institution, except in extreme cases.

(5) Gas, distraction devices, and other strategies are excellent methods of confusing and disabling inmates; their use is recommended. However, only pre-approved weapons and munitions must be used.

(6) If lethal weapons are sent inside an institution, they must be protected at all costs from inmates seizing them. In many cases, this means having covering weapons, as well.

(7) Multiple points of access should be used whenever possible; tactical forces should come at the inmates from as many routes as possible, at the same time.

(8) Let the physical plant work for the tactical force. If inmates can be driven and contained into an area defined by the design features of the institution, take advantage of that fact.

(9) If there are hostages involved, tactical personnel need to be briefed on their location, appearance, and possible types of threats to them by their inmate captors.

Canine Operations

The use of canine units in institutions for tactical purposes is not widespread, but with appropriate controls, it can be a useful supplemental method for obtaining control over inmates. Canine dogs may be used as support for tactical staff, guarding strategic areas and patroling for duty during emergency situations. Canines may be used to "backup" officers in emergency situations. Canines may be used in other emergencies where such use is properly cleared through the warden.

Canines never should be used as a means of punishment, and no greater amount of force should be used by a canine unit than is necessary to control the emergency involved. The earlier references (in the section on searches) to canine operations, with regard to selection and training, should be noted. All incidents involving the use of force by a canine unit shall be reported and investigated in the same manner as other use-of-force incidents. Weapons may be issued to canine unit personnel upon the authorization of the warden, on the same basis as they are issued to other staff involved in disturbance control activities.

Postincident Action

Proper supervision must be on-site in the aftermath of a disturbance. Command staff must ensure that line employees are properly supervised as inmates are subdued, restrained, searched, and moved to secure housing. Retaliatory action–particularly on a systematic basis–must be prevented.

229

As soon as a disturbance is under control, appropriate follow-up steps should be taken, including the following:

- Segregate all leaders and agitators.

- Take appropriate care of all nonparticipants.

- Account for all inmates and staff members.

- Provide appropriate medical screening and care; document all injuries.

- Assess status of all work and recreation activities.

- Provide secure, and progressively less restrictive, meal service.

- Conduct a thorough investigation into the cause and course of the disturbance; interview ringleaders and active participants.

- Interview all those involved in the disturbance and obtain their statements for subsequent prosecutions.

- Immediately repair damage done to institutional physical security features, making sure to photograph all damage before making the repairs.

- Secure and label participants' personal belongings.

Any disturbance-related investigation not specifically referred to an outside investigative agency should be conducted by the institution's investigative supervisor. This investigator should furnish the warden, deputy warden, chief of security, and state attorney's office (when applicable) with formal reports of all investigative findings.

ACA Policies

(Current as of January, 1997)

Appendix A

Public Correctional Policy on Conditions of Confinement

Introduction:

Correctional systems must provide services and programs and administer the detention, sanctions, and punishments ordered by the courts in an environment that protects public safety and provides for the safety, rights and dignity of staff, accused or adjudicated offenders, and citizens involved in programs.

Policy Statement:

Maintaining acceptable conditions of confinement requires adequate resources and effective management of the physical plant, operational procedures, programs and staff. To provide acceptable conditions, agencies should:

A. Establish and maintain a safe and humane population limit for each institution based upon recognized professional standards;

B. Provide an environment that will support the health and safety of staff, confined persons and citizens participating in programs. Such an environment results from appropriate design, construction and maintenance of the physical plant as well as the effective operation of the facility and programming of offenders;

C. Maintain a professional and accountable work environment for staff that includes necessary training and supervision as well as sufficient staffing to carry out the mission of the facility;

D. Maintain a fair and disciplined environment that provides a range of programs and services appropriate to the needs and requirements of offenders, in a climate that encourages responsible behavior.

Public Correctional Policy on Crowding and Excessive Workloads in Corrections

Introduction:

Overpopulation of correctional programs and facilities can negate the effectiveness of management, program, security, and physical plant operations and can endanger offenders, staff, and the public at large. High population density within correctional facilities may be associated with increased physical and mental problems, more frequent disciplinary incidents, higher rates of assault and suicide, and decreased effectiveness in programs and services. When the population of a correctional program or facility exceeds capacity, maintaining safe and reasonable conditions of confinement and supervision becomes increasingly difficult, and may become impossible. Excessive workloads in institutional and community corrections dilute effectiveness of supervision and support services and threaten public safety.

Policy Statement:

The number of offenders assigned to correctional facilities and community services should be limited to

231

levels consistent with recognized professional standards. Correctional agencies should:

A. Establish and maintain safe and humane population and workload limits for each institution and service program based on recognized professional standards;

B. Develop, advocate, and implement, in coordination with the executive, legislative, and judicial branches of government, emergency and long-term processes by which offender populations can be managed within reasonable limits;

C. Anticipate the need for expanded program and facility capacity by using professional population projection methodologies that reflect both demographic and policy-related factors influencing correctional population growth;

D. Advocate for the full development and appropriate use of pretrial/adjudication release, probation, parole, community residential facilities, and other community services that are appropriate for offenders that, as a consequence, reduce the number of offenders in crowded facilities; and

E. Develop, advocate, and implement plans for necessary additional facilities, staff, programs and services.

Public Correctional Policy on Design of Correctional Facilities

Introduction:

The effectiveness and efficiency of correctional staff in maintaining security and delivering services can be either enhanced or limited by the physical plants in which they operate. Quality design combines long-term cost efficiency with maximum programming flexibility thus assisting a correctional system in accomplishing its mission.

Policy Statement:

Correctional architecture is unique, involving the design of facilities that are functionally and environmentally supportive of the needs and activities of a confined society. The design of such facilities is a multidisciplinary process. To improve the design quality and operational adequacy of new and renovated correctional facilities, correctional agencies should:

A. Define operations of all facilities prior to design, including written specifications of the facility's mission and functional elements, basic operating procedures, and staffing patterns so the design can fully support intended correctional operations;

B. Ensure that the design of correctional facilities provides appropriate space for offender activities, including industrial operations, education and training, recreation, and other program and treatment services;

C. Select architects and engineers on merit, as demonstrated by either successful completion of prior correctional projects, or by successful completion of other projects combined with access to recognized correctional expertise;

D. Design correctional facilities through a multidisciplinary process that directly involves correctional professionals, criminal justice planners, architects and engineers, and that also seeks the contribution of other groups and disciplines who have an interest in the facility's design, including those involved in the facility's day-to-day operations;

E. Ensure that facility designs conform to applicable laws, rules, regulations, and codes governing the jurisdiction. The design should conform to nationally recognized professional standards and should encourage direct interaction in the supervision of offenders, consistent with staff safety;

F. Maintain project oversight to ensure design objectives are met;

G. Recognize the need for early selection of key staff, so they can participate in the design and construction process, and/or so they can coordinate initial activation of the facility. Initial activation activities include recruiting staff, transitional training, preparing equipment and supply orders, and documenting operational procedures;

H. Engage in an ongoing process of research and evaluation to develop, improve, and recognize the most operationally effective and cost-efficient design features, equipment technologies, and procedures.

Public Correctional Policy on Female Offender Services

Introduction:

Correctional systems must develop service delivery systems for accused and adjudicated female offenders that are comparable to those provided to males. Additional services must also be provided to meet the unique needs of the female offender population.

Policy Statement:

Correctional systems must be guided by the principle of parity. Female offenders must receive the equivalent range of services available to other offenders, including opportunities for individualized programming and services that recognize the unique needs of this population. The services should:

A. Ensure access to a range of alternatives to incarceration, including pretrial and post trial diversion, probation, restitution, treatment for substance abuse, halfway houses, and parole services;

B. Provide acceptable conditions of confinement, including appropriately trained staff and sound operating procedures that address this population's needs in such areas as clothing, personal property, hygiene, exercise, recreation, and visitations with children and family;

C. Provide access to a full range of work and programs designed to expand economic and social roles of women, with emphasis on education; career counseling and exploration of nontraditional vocational training; relevant life skills, including parenting and social and economic assertiveness; and prerelease and work/education release programs;

D. Facilitate the maintenance and strengthening of family ties, particularly those between parent and child;

E. Deliver appropriate programs and services, including medical, dental, and mental health programs, services to pregnant women, substance abuse programs, child and family services, and provide access to legal services; and

F. Provide access to release programs that include aid in achieving economic stability and the development of supportive family relationships.

Public Correctional Policy on Offenders with Special Needs

Introduction:

The provision of humane programs and services for the accused and adjudicated requires addressing the special needs of these offenders. To meet this goal, correctional agencies should develop and adopt procedures for the early identification of offenders with special needs. Agencies should provide the services that respond to those needs and monitor and evaluate the delivery of services in both confined and community settings.

Policy Statement:

Correctional systems should assure provision of specialized services, programs and conditions of confinement to meet the special needs of offenders. To achieve this, they should:

A. Identify the categories of offenders who will require special care or programs. These categories include:

1. Offenders with severe psychological needs, mental retardation, significant psychiatric disorders, behavior disorders, multiple handicaps, neurological impairments, and substance abuse;

2. Offenders who are physically handicapped or chronically or terminally ill;

3. Offenders who are elderly;

4. Offenders with severe social and/or educational deficiencies, learning disabilities, or language barriers;

5. Offenders with special security or supervision needs, such as protective custody cases, death row inmates, and those who chronically exhibit potential for violent or aggressive behavior; and

6. Sex offenders for whom appropriate treatment may reduce the risk of reoffending conduct.

B. Identify offenders needing such special services and provide such services in a manner consistent with professional standards. Such services and programs may be provided within the correctional agency itself, or by referral to another agency that has the necessary

233

specialized program resources, or by contracting with private or voluntary agencies or individuals that meet professional standards;

C. Maintain appropriately trained staff and/or contractors for the delivery of care, programs, and services;

D. Maintain professionally appropriate record keeping of services and programs provided;

E. Evaluate the quality and effectiveness of services provided; and

F. Provide leadership and advocacy for legislative and public support to obtain the resources needed to meet these special needs.

Public Correctional Policy on Purpose of Corrections

Introduction:

In order to establish the goals and objectives of any correctional system, there must be a universal statement of purpose which all members of the correctional community can use in goal setting and daily operations.

Policy Statement:

The overall mission of criminal and juvenile justice, which consists of law enforcement, courts, and corrections, is to enhance social order and public safety. As a component of the justice system, the role of corrections is:

A. To implement court-ordered supervision and, when necessary, detention of those accused of unlawful behavior prior to adjudication;

B. To assist in maintaining the integrity of law by administering sanctions and punishments imposed by courts for unlawful behavior;

C. To offer the widest range of correctional options, including community corrections, probation, institutions, and parole services, necessary to meet the needs of both society and the individual; and

D. To provide humane program and service and opportunities for accused and adjudicated offenders which will enhance their community integration and economic self-sufficiency, and which are administered in a just and equitable manner within the least restrictive environment consistent with public safety.

Public Correctional Policy on Correctional Staff Recruitment and Development

Introduction:

Knowledgeable, highly skilled, motivated, and professional correctional personnel are essential to fulfill the purpose of corrections effectively. Professionalism is achieved through structured programs of recruitment and enhancement of the employee's skills, knowledge, insight, and understanding of the corrections process.

Policy Statement:

Correctional staff are the primary agents for promoting health, welfare, security, and safety within correctional institutions and community supervision programs. They directly interact with accused and adjudicated offenders and are the essential catalysts of change in the correctional process. The education, recruitment orientation, supervision. compensation, training, retention, and advancement of correctional staff must receive full support from the executive, judicial, and legislative branches of government. To achieve this, correctional agencies should:

A. Recruit personnel, including ex-offenders, in an open and accountable manner to ensure equal employment opportunity for all qualified applicants regardless of sex, age, race, physical disability, religion, ethnic background, or political affiliation, and actively promote the employment of women and minorities;

B. Screen applicants for job-related aspects of physical suitability, personal adjustment, emotional stability, dependability, appropriate educational level, and experience. An additional requisite is the ability to relate to accused or adjudicated offenders in a manner that is fair, objective, and neither punitive nor vindictive.

C. Select, promote, and retain staff in accordance with valid job-related procedures that emphasize merit and technical competence. Voluntary transfers and promotions within and between correctional systems should be encouraged;

D. Comply with professional standards in staff development and offer a balance between operational requirements and the development of personal, social, and cultural understanding. Staff development programs should involve use of public and private resources, including colleges, universities, and professional associations;

E. Achieve parity between correctional staff and comparable criminal justice system staff in salaries and benefits, training, continuing education, performance evaluations, disciplinary procedures, career development opportunities, transfers, promotions, grievance procedures, and retirement; and

F. Encourage the participation of trained volunteers and students to enrich the correctional program and to provide a potential source of recruitment.

Public Correctional Policy on Use of Appropriate Sanctions and Controls

Introduction:

In developing, selecting and administering sanctions and punishments, decision-makers must balance concern for individual dignity, public safety and maintenance of social order. Correctional programs and facilities are a costly and limited resource; the most restrictive are generally the most expensive. Therefore, it is good public policy to use these resources wisely and economically.

Policy Statement:

The sanctions and controls imposed by courts and administered by corrections should be the least restrictive consistent with public and individual safety and maintenance of social order. Selection of the least-restrictive sanctions and punishments in specific cases inherently require balancing several important objectives–individual dignity, fiscal responsibility and effective correctional operations. To meet these objectives, correctional agencies should:

A. Advocate to all branches of government–executive, legislative and judicial–and to the public at large, the development and appropriate use of the least-restrictive sanctions, punishments, programs and facilities;

B. Recommend the use of the least-restrictive appropriate dispositions in judicial decisions;

C. Classify persons under correctional jurisdiction to the least-restrictive appropriate programs and facilities; and

D. Employ only the level of regulation and control necessary for the safe and efficient operation of programs, services, and facilities.

Public Correctional Policy on Use of Force

Introduction:

Correctional agencies administer sanctions and punishments imposed by courts for unlawful behavior. Assigned to correctional agencies involuntarily, offenders sometimes resist authority imposed on them, and may demonstrate violent and destructive behaviors. Use of legally authorized force by correctional authorities may become necessary to maintain custody, safety, and control.

Policy Statement:

Use of force consists of physical contact with an offender in a confrontational situation to control behavior and enforce order. Use of force includes use of restraints (other than for routine transportation and movement), chemical agents, and weapons. Force is justified only when required to maintain or regain control, or when there is imminent danger of personal injury or serious damage to property. To ensure the use of force is appropriate and justifiable, correctional agencies should:

A. Establish and maintain policies that require reasonable steps be taken to reduce or prevent the necessity for the use of force, that authorize force only when no reasonable alternative is possible, that permit only the minimum force necessary, and that prohibit the use of force as a retaliatory or disciplinary measure;

B. Establish and enforce procedures that define the range of methods for and alternatives to the use of force, and that specify the conditions under which each is permitted. The procedures must assign responsibility for authorizing such force, ensure appropriate documentation and supervision of the action;

C. Establish and maintain procedures that limit the use of deadly force to those instances where it is legally authorized and where there is an imminent threat to human life or a threat to public safety that cannot reasonably be prevented by other means;

D. Maintain operating procedures and regular staff training designed to anticipate, stabilize and diffuse situations that might give rise to conflict, confrontation, and violence;

E. Provide specialized training to ensure competency in all methods of use of force, especially in methods and equipment requiring special knowledge and skills such as defensive tactics, weapons, restraints, and chemical agents; and

F. Establish and maintain procedures that require all incidents involving the use of force be fully documented and independently reviewed by a higher correctional authority. A report of the use of force, including appropriate investigation and any recommendations for preventive and remedial action, shall be submitted for administrative review and implementation of recommendations, when appropriate.

Sample Outline–
General Audit Format

Appendix B

Institution audits, both internal and external, should be based on policy. Basically, there are three elements to auditing. Auditors should determine (1) what is required by policy, (2) what procedures are in place to implement that policy, and (3) whether (or to what degree) the procedures actually are being implemented. Because every agency's policy and procedures are going to be different–and the resultant audits individually tailored to them–the following general audit guideline only covers the major areas of policy and procedure that should be reviewed in a security audit.

I. Introduction

A. Opening paragraph with auditor's name, dates, places visited

B. Circumstances leading to audit

C. Initial impressions of overall problem

D. Description of assistance

E. Methodology
   1) Staff met
   2) Places visited
   3) Documents reviewed

F. Closeouts held

II. General Impressions

A. Population density

B. Staffing pattern

C. Sanitation

D. Staff visibility

E. Inmate activity level

F. Condition of physical plant

G. Overall morale/atmosphere

H. Staff/inmate relationships

III. Administrative Structure (if applicable)

A. Parent agency

B. Central/regional office organization

C. Institution executive staff

D. Departmental structure

E. Centralized versus decentralized inmate management

F. Policy development

G. Enabling legislative factors

H. Litigation impacting on system

I. Political influences on system

IV. Classification/Inmate Population

A. Salient population characteristics
   1) Demographics
   2) Racial/ethnic
   3) Offense characteristics
   4) Turnover

B. Population capacities

C. Population balance within institution

D. Housing unit assignment procedures

E. Special categories
   1) Protective custody

2) Witnesses

3) Detention/segregation

4) Medical/psychiatric

V. Education/Vocational Training Programs

A. Type

B. Quality

C. Participation level

D. Impact on idleness

E. Tool and hazardous material controls

F. Inmate accountability

VI. Financial Management

A. Major project funding

B. Commissary operations

C. Warehousing safeguards

D. Inmate funds controls

E. Laundry/clothing exchange

VII. Food Service

A. Sanitation

B. Staff supervision of inmates

C. Inmate accountability

D. Tool control

E. Satellite feeding to special housing and medical units

F. Special diets

1) Kosher/Muslim

2) Medical

G. Warehousing procedures

VIII. Health Services

A. Physical plant

B. Outside medical care, escort procedures

C. Dispensing of medications

D. Storage of medications

E. Syringe/medication control

F. Medical services to special housing units

IX. Industrial Operations

A. Extent

B. Number of inmates employed

C. Tool control

D. Inmate accountability

E. Control of contraband

F. Other inherent security problems

X. Inmate Discipline

A. Policy in effect

B. Hearing procedures

1) Composition of committee

2) Structure of hearing

3) Procedures

C. Sanctions available

D. Sanctions applied

E. Conditions of detention

F. Conditions of segregation

G. Time frames for disciplinary action

H. Staff perceptions of effectiveness

I. Inmate perception of system

J. Review of hearing outcomes (appeals)

K. Periodic review of inmates in special housing status

L. Witness protection/protective custody cases

M. Mental health cases

N. Use of restraints/strip cells

XI. Legal

A. Court orders in effect constraining operations

B. Agency legal resources available to staff

XII. Facility Issues

A. Overall physical plant impressions–site, size, and construction

B. Age

1) Design

2) Adaptations

3) Present methods of dealing with crowding

C. Perimeter structures

D. Housing units and other structures

E. Specific concerns or problems

F. Inmate accountability on work details

G. Tool control

H. Flammables/corrosives controls

I. Inmate gate traffic

J. Timeliness of maintenance response to security problems

XIII. Security Practices

A. Overall impression

B. Reliance on physical security versus interpersonal controls

C. Staffing
1) Supervisory visibility
2) Roster management
3) Rotation patterns
4) Assignment records

D. Perimeter security features
1) Construction
2) Towers
3) Complexity
4) Lighting
5) Detection systems
6) Mobile patrols

E. Control center
1) Security
2) Equipment
3) Key control/emergency keys
4) Staffing
5) Post orders

F. Towers
1) Number/arrangement
2) Type weapons/number
3) Other equipment
4) Staffing pattern
5) Inventory of equipment
6) Post orders

G. Rear gate procedures
1) Staffing
2) Tower coverage
3) Vehicle procedures
4) Inmate accountability/gate passes
5) Contraband control
6) Post orders

H. Front entrance
1) Physical plant
2) Inmate processing
3) Visitor processing
4) Metal detectors
5) Ultraviolet stamping
6) ID card usage
7) Post orders

8) Methods for tracking persons in institution

I. Inmate accountability
1) Count procedures
2) Pass system
3) Census checks
4) Picture card ID procedures
5) Crew kit systems

J. Armory/Lockshop
1) Location/access
2) Adequacy of site
3) Inventories
   a) Weapons
   b) Ammunition
   c) Gas
   d) Other equipment
   e) Keys
4) Procedures
5) Key stock
6) Custom key storage system
7) Emergency keys
8) Rotation program
9) Personal weapon use/storage
10) Personal keys

K. Communications
1) Radios
2) Body alarms
3) Intercom
4) Phone systems
5) Roll Calls
6) Logs

L. Housing unit
1) Staffing patterns
2) Construction
   a) Cell design
   b) Access to outside
   c) Multiple occupants
   d) Locking devices
3) Sanitation
4) Ventilation/heating
5) Fire detection/control
6) Evacuation routes
7) Plumbing/showers
8) Electrical service

9) Emergency lighting

10) Post orders

M. Inmate telephone/mail access

1) Phone/mail policy/procedures

2) Phone monitoring capability/usage

3) Mail inspection/censorship practices

4) Inspection of incoming packages

   a) Shakedown

   b) X-ray/other technologies

5) Outgoing packages

6) Publication controls

7) Legal mail/phone policy

N. Visiting procedures

1) Advisement of visiting regulations

2) Searches of inmates

3) Searches of visitors

4) Conditions of visits

5) Staff supervision

6) Attorney visiting area

7) Controlled visiting capability

O. Receiving and Discharge

1) Intake processing

2) Release processing

3) Property permitted

4) Property storage/shipped

5) Admission/orientation program

P. Special housing units

1) Staff coverage

2) Physical security features

3) Control of inmate movement

4) Control of property/contraband

5) Shower procedures

6) Recreation procedures

7) Law library procedures

8) Visiting

9) Food service procedures

10) Personal keys

11) Sanitation

12) Logs

13) Staff mobility in unit

14) Supervisory visibility in unit

15) Procedures for use of force/restraints/chemical agents

Q. Emergency preparedness

1) Types of emergency plans maintained

2) Quality of plan/date

3) Storage of plans

4) Staff training/review of plan

5) Update procedures

6) Content of plans

XIV. Sanitation/Safety

A. Overall impression

B. Specific areas of concern

C. Control of hazardous materials

D. Shop safety/sanitation

E. Industrial safety/sanitation

F. Food service/safety/sanitation

G. Housing unit safety/sanitation

H. Special housing unit safety/sanitation

I. Fire safety program

XV. Staffing/Personnel Management/EEO

A. Overall impressions/morale

B. Internal organization

C. Problematic union contract provisions

D. Preemployment processes

1) Recruitment

2) Qualifications

3) Testing/rating of candidates

4) Interviews

E. EEO issues

F. Turnover

1) Top staff

2) Line staff

G. Exit interview program

H. Promotional practices

I. Time and attendance system

J. Staff development/upward mobility program

XVI. Staff Training

A. Adequate information in preemployment interviews

B. Initial training

1) Academy

2) Local

C. Specialty training

D. In-house/refresher training

E. Firearms/use of force/self defense

F. Interpersonal skills/cultural diversity

XVII. Other Security Issues

A. Inmate organizations

B. Inmate publications

XVIII. Conclusion/Summary of Findings

Sample Roster Materials

Appendix C

Sample Daily Roster

DAY: DATE:

POST	MORNING WATCH	DAY WATCH	EVENING WATCH
Chief of Security		Imhof, K.	
Captain	Jones, B.	Dunigan, C.	Claus, P.
Lieutenant	Huff, J.	Priestly, R.	Hickey, J.
A & B Sergeant	Nunley, G.	Beal, L.	Monyour, N.
C & D Sergeant	Wasco, T.	White, J.	Hunt, Y.
Roster Mgt. Clerk		Scaife, V.	
Building Control #1	Rogers, C.	Harris, J.K.	Mikitus, A.
Building Control #2		Kimmons, J.	
Security Office	Morah, L.	Carpenter, J.	Truvillion, B.
Intake/Discharge		Morrow, J.	
Front Gate #1	Turner, P.	Scaife, F.	Walton, P.
Front Gate #2		Harris, J.A.	Czarnecki, K.
Lobby #1		Foote, S.	Shader, T.
Lobby #2		Rehman, C.	Herandez, E.
Area A & B #1	Cavanaugh, R.	Robles, L.	Anderson, T.
Area A & B #2	Wells, V.	Delitz, D.	Harling, W.
Area C & D #1	Canada, L.	Dunbar, H.	Jones, D.
Area C & D #2	Lathon, F.	Davis, T.	Nichols, T.
Activities Officer	Peppers, W.		Demcak, M.
Maintenance		Glinsey, V.	Rajewski, C.
1-A Wing	Chapa, H.	Robinson, M.	Hannah, O.
1-B Wing	Jusczak, J.	Harper, L.	Wolfe, M.
1-C Wing	Rudd, D.	Lee, S.	Nowaczyk, F.
1-D Wing	Sprovieri, J.	King, R.	Powell, W.
2-A Wing	Galvin, W.	Cerezo, A.	Woody, K.
2-B Wing	Senerchia, S.	Harper, L.	Shaw, J.
2-C Wing	Walker, K.	Carvajal, J.	Healy, R.
2-D Wing	Levon, E.	Larkins, B.	Echevarria, M.
3-A Wing	Jackson, G.	Sawyer, R.	Mickiel, C.
3-B Wing	Solofra, G.	Shermanski, R.	Garmon, N.
3-C Wing	Webb, T.	Carroll, D.	Nenadic, A.
3-D Wing	Lee, D.	Steele, T.	Cozzolino, V.
4-A Wing	Jones, M.	Dominguez, J.	Walker, R.
4-B Wing	Szumacher, W.	Lera, E.	Lippincott, G.
4-C Wing	James, L.	Sharmpine, T.	Williams, D.
4-D Wing	Daniels, L.	Koch, J.	Sullivan, R.
Post #2		Davis, K.	
Recreation Officer		Perry, A.	Hayes, M.
Storeroom Officer		CLOSED	Keith, K.
Barber Shop		Shimanski, S.	
Medical/Dental Ofc.		Bady, C.	
Medical Escort Ofc.		Glasper, D.	

_____   _____   _____
Shift Supervisor   Shift Supervisor   Shift Supervisor

Scheduled and Unscheduled Absenses

DAY: DATE:

MEDICAL	VACATION	HOLIDAY	PERSONAL DAY	REGULAR DAY OFF
				Kelly, W.
				Sarafin, P.
				Baines, D.
				Banovic, R.
				Schelhammer, W.
				Chow, R.
				Dipasquale, P.
				Barone, J.
				Zyrkowski, C.
				Koranda, E.
	TIME DUE	TRAINING	SUSPENSION	Miller, M
				Scaife, F.
				Berggren, K.
				Williams, L.
				Harris, C.
				Seay, A.
ABSENT	EXCUSED ABSENT	SPECIAL ASSIGN	MILITARY	Rodriquez, F.
				Wesley, P.
				Corey, S.
				Seay, E.
				Austin, C.
				Romero, R.
	MATERNITY	DUTY INJURY	OTHER	Mathis, D.
				Windmon, Y.
				Lones, D.
				Czarnecki, K.
				Wendel, W.
				Fegan, M.
				Vallego, M.
				Zriny, T.
				Coleman, G.
				Burg, J.
				Watkins, H.
				Tate, S.
				McNeal, F.
				Bassett, T.

Record of Assignment Changes

DAY: DATE:

SHIFT	POST	OFFICER	STATUS	RELIEVED BY	FROM	SHIFT COM.

Recapitulation Form

DAY: DATE:

AUTHORIZED COMPLIMENT	163
VACANCIES	10
ON DUTY	102
REGULAR DAY OFF	36
ADMINISTRATIVE RELIEF	15
MEDICAL	0
VACATION	0
ABSENT	0
EXCUSED ABSENCE	0
MILITARY	0
TIME DUE	0
HOLIDAY	0
MATERNITY	0
SUSPENSION	0
DUTY INJURY	0
SPECIAL ASSIGNMENT	0
TRAINING	0
PERSONAL BUSINESS DAY	0
OTHER	0
TOTAL	163

Administrative Relief

Name
Wallace, F.
Varela, R.
Ballentine, S.
Pamon, J.
Ross, M.
Feazell, J.
Leak, R.
Varnagis, F.
White, B.
Parker, J.
Lehmann, W.
Glover, J.
Fernendez, J.
Goytia, O.
Walsh, T.

Sample Forms

Appendix D

The following forms are provided for your use. You may adapt and reproduce them according to your needs.

- Signature Sheet
- Your Rights & Waiver of Rights (*Miranda*)
- Request for Storage of Personal Weapon
- Checking Armory Equipment In and Out
- Individual Segregation Record Sheet (two pages)
- Sanitation Checklist (six pages)
- Restricted Key Form
- Tool Inventory
- Tool Receiving Report
- Weekly Tool Report
- Report of Hazardous Tools
- Tool Turn-in Receipt

- Lost Tool Report
- Sample Official Count Form
- Special Census (three pages)
- Weekly Master Security Checksheet
- Daily Inspection Report
- Weekly Inspection Report
- Monthly Security/Sanitation Inspection Schedule
- Inspection of Quarters Sheet
- Daily Security, Sanitation, and Fire Slip
- Standard Escape Report
- Daily Fire, Security, and Energy Checks
- Bomb Threat Information Sheet

Signature Sheet

POST: _____

    I certify that I have read and fully understand the post orders both general and specific for this post. I have also read and fully understand all operations statements and memorandums, which are attached to these post orders, affecting the operation of this post. **TO BE MADE A PART OF ALL POST ORDERS.**

Employee Name	Date	Supervisor's Initials	Employee Name	Date	Supervisor's Initials

Your Rights

Before we ask you any questions, you must understand your rights.

- You have the right to remain silent.

- Anything you say can be used against you in court.

- You have the right to talk to a lawyer for advice before we ask you any questions and to have him with you during questioning.

- If you cannot afford a lawyer, one will be appointed for you before any questioning if you wish.

- If you decide to answer questions now without a lawyer present, you will still have the right to stop answering at any time. You also have the right to stop answering at any time until you talk to a lawyer.

Waiver of Rights

I have read this statement of my rights and I understand what my rights are. I am willing to make a statement and answer questions. I do not want a lawyer at this time. I understand and know what I am doing. No promises or threats have been made to me and no pressure or coercion of any kind has been used against me.

Signed _____

Witness _____

Witness _____

Date & Time _____

Request for Storage of Personal Weapon

I request that I be permitted to store the following weapon(s) in the institution's armory:

Manufacturer   Model & Caliber   Serial #

_____   _____   _____

_____   _____   _____

_____   _____   _____

_____   _____   _____

_____   _____

(Date)   (Requesting Employee)

Approved _____ Date _____

(Chief Security Officer)

Checking Armory Equipment In and Out

Type of Equipment Issued	Signature of Person Receiving Equipment	Time Out	Time In	Initials of Person Issuing Equipment	Date

Individual Segregation Record Sheet

_____
(Institution)

Team/Caseworker _____ Regular Quarters _____

Inmate Name _____ Reg. No. _____ Cell _____
Violation   Date   Time
or Reason _____ Received _____ Received _____
Admittance   Date   Time
Authorized _____ Released _____ Released _____

Date	Shift	Meals B	D	S	SH	EX	Medical PA Signature	Comments (Use reverse if needed)	OIC Signature
	MORN								
	DAY								
	EVE								
	MORN								
	DAY								
	EVE								
	MORN								
	DAY								
	EVE								
	MORN								
	DAY								
	EVE								
	MORN								
	DAY								
	EVE								
	MORN								
	DAY								
	EVE								
	MORN								
	DAY								
	EVE								

Pertinent Information = Epileptic, Diabetic, Suicidal, Homosexual, Assaultive, etc.
Meals: B = Breakfast, D = Dinner, S = Supper
SH = Shower — Yes (Y), No (N), Refused (R)
EX = Exercise (enter actual time period, and inside or outside — i.e., 9:30/10:00 IN; 2:00/2:30 OUT)
Medical PA = Medical Physician's Assistant (nurse) will sign the seg log each shift and the record sheet each time the inmate is seen by him or her.
Comments = Conduct, Attitude, etc. Additional comments documented on reverse side must include date, signature, and title.
Officer in Charge Signature = OIC (Unit Officer) must sign all record sheets each shift.

Individual Segregation Record Sheet

1. Inmate discipline requires that an individual record sheet be maintained on each inmate in segregation. The individual record sheet will reflect all activities affecting each inmate and will be sent regularly to the institution's central file. A standard form has been devised as a result of recommendations received.

2. The Individual Segregation Record Sheet will be completed and maintained in accordance with the following:

   a. The key at the bottom of the sheet is self-explanatory.

   b. The basic information at the top of the sheet, with the exception of the date and time of release, will be completed by the officer in charge/unit officer at time of admittance.

   c. The sheet provides space for a period of up to seven (7) days. The date column will be recorded daily; the shift line will be completed to coincide with the date and time received, recorded at the top of the sheet.

   d. The officer-in-charge/unit officer will sign the sheet in the space provided on line with the shift as indicated. Initials are not acceptable.

   e. The physician's assistant (nurse) will indicate by his/her signature in the proper space when an inmate receives medication, is examined by a medical officer or physician's assistant, or requests to see a member of the medical staff. If no medication is received or request made during a shift, the officer indicates by recording No (N) in the column.

   f. The record sheet is designed for a 7-day period. If confinement to segregation continues beyond a 7-day period, a new sheet will be prepared and the completed form forwarded to central file. Date and time of release will be recorded on the final form.

   g. Additional comments may be noted on the reverse of the form and in each case must be dated and include signature and title of person making the comment.

Sanitation Checklist

SERVING LINE	YES	NO	COMMENTS
1. Are the serving lines clean, including sneeze guards?			
2. Are staff members wearing hair nets or caps and clean dress?			
3. Are inmate servers wearing hair nets or caps and clean dress?			
4. Are the *hot foods* served at 140°? Food Items _____ °F _____ _____ _____ _____ _____ _____ _____ _____ _____ _____ _____			
5. Are *cold foods* served at 45°F? Food Items _____ °F _____ _____ _____ _____ _____ _____ _____ _____ _____ _____ _____			

Sanitation Checklist

DINING ROOM	YES	NO	COMMENTS
1. Are the floors clean and repaired? 2. Are the tables clean? 3. Are the seats clean? 4. Are the walls clean? 5. Are the beverage areas clean?			
KITCHEN PRODUCTION AREAS	YES	NO	COMMENTS
1. Does the general appearance of the department indicate frequent cleaning? 2. Are the floors clean and repaired? 3. Are the walls and ceiling clean and repaired? 4. Are there any overhead pipes that might leak into food or equipment? 5. Are potentially hazardous foods meeting temperature requirements during storage, preparation, display, service, and transportation? 6. Are there adequate facilities for maintaining the food at hot or cold temperatures?			

Sanitation Checklist

KITCHEN PRODUCTION AREAS	YES	NO	COMMENTS
7. Are hands washed and good hygienic practices observed?			
8. Is equipment used in the production area properly cleaned (steam kettle, ovens, grills, can opener, deep fat fryers, mixers, slicing machine)?			
9. Are rolling carts and hot food carts clean?			
10. Are all utensils and equipment in good repair; that is, free of breaks, open seams, cracks, and chips?			
11. Are food contact surfaces of equipment clean to sight and touch?			
12. Are wiping cloths available and clean?			
13. Are wiping cloths properly stored?			
14. Is the importance of frequent handwashing stressed?			
15. Is chewing of tobacco or smoking observed in food production area?			
16. Are the ice and ice handling utensils properly stored?			
17. Is the supply of hot water and cold water adequate?			

Sanitation Checklist

FOOD STORAGE	YES	NO	COMMENTS
1. Are all food products protected from contamination?			
2. Are the containers of food stored off the floor and on a clean surface?			
3. Is all perishable food kept at proper temperature?			
4. Are the potentially hazardous foods stored at 45° or below (for cold food) or 140° or above (for hot food) as required?			
5. Are the frozen foods kept at 0° to 20°?			
6. Are the potentially hazardous frozen foods thawed at refrigerated temperature of 45° or below?			
7. Are cereals, sugars, and so forth kept in tightly covered and labeled containers?			
8. Are the refrigerators equipped with thermometers?			

Sanitation Checklist

DISH WASHING/POT WASHING	YES	NO	COMMENTS
1. Are all dishes properly scraped and, if necessary, soaked before washing?			
2. Are adequate and suitable detergents used?			
3. If the dishes are machine washed: a. Are they washed at 140° or higher for 20 seconds? b. Are they rinsed at 180° or higher for 10 seconds?			
4. If the chemical sanitizer is used for the final rinse, was it properly dispensed and approved?			
5. If the dishes are washed manually, are they washed in water at 110° or higher?			
Are dishes sanitized by immersion in:			
a. water maintained at 170° for 30 seconds; or			
b. chlorine rinse at a temperature of not less than 75°; or			
c. solution containing at least 12.5 ppm of available iodine with ph of not higher than 5.0 and a temperature of not less than 75°?			

Sanitation Checklist

GARBAGE DISPOSAL	YES	NO	COMMENTS
1. Is garbage removed in a timely manner?			
2. Are receptacles and liners non-absorbent?			
3. Are the receptacles covered by tight fitting lids?			
4. Are the receptacles washed and emptied?			
5. Are the receptacles disinfected frequently?			

Restricted Key Form

Key Ring Number and Title _____

Institution _____

Date _____

Time Out _____

Time In _____
                            (Signature)   (Print Name)

Authorized By _____
                            (Signature)   (Print Name)

Employee _____
                            (Signature)   (Print Name)

Control Center Officer _____

Reason Key Was Issued _____

_____

_____

Copies to: Chief Security Officer
                 Department Head Concerned
                 Security Officer

Tool Inventory

_____
(Institution)

Shop or Area _____ Marking _____ Calendar Year _____ Date Prepared _____

Page __ of __ Pages

Qty.	Tool Description	Size	1st Quarter	2nd Quarter	3rd Quarter	4th Quarter
____	_____	____	____	____	____	____
____	_____	____	____	____	____	____
____	_____	____	____	____	____	____
____	_____	____	____	____	____	____
____	_____	____	____	____	____	____
____	_____	____	____	____	____	____
____	_____	____	____	____	____	____
____	_____	____	____	____	____	____
____	_____	____	____	____	____	____
____	_____	____	____	____	____	____
____	_____	____	____	____	____	____
____	_____	____	____	____	____	____
____	_____	____	____	____	____	____
____	_____	____	____	____	____	____
____	_____	____	____	____	____	____

Certified correct _____
          (Shop Area Foreman)

          _____
          (Tool Control Officer)

Approved _____
          (Chief Security Officer)

Quarterly Audits

January _____ C.S.

April _____ C.S.

July _____ C.S.

October _____ C.S.

Tool Receiving Report

To: Assistant Warden (Custody)

From: Tool Control Officer

On _____ , a _____
              (date)   (name and number of tools)

for _____ , was received at the institution.
                         (department)

The classification for this tool is _____ .

This tool was etched and/or coded to conform to policy statement, _____ .

Signature _____
                        (Tool Control Officer)

Copies to: Tool Control Officer
            Work Area Supervisor for whom the tool was purchased

Weekly Tool Report

To: Chief of Security

From: _____
        (Name)   (Title)

I have verified the presence of all tools charged to _____ by _____ and the fact that such tools are stored in the approved and/or prescribed manner as of the end of my workday on _____ .

Tool storage areas identified for warehousing of tool stocks are excluded from the daily accountability, except when there is evidence of forcible entry.

Note: Lost Tool Report

When ANY TOOL is lost, stolen, or misplaced, the chief of security, tool control officer, and shift supervisor shall be notified immediately, by telephone.

A written report covering the details of the loss of tools will be submitted as quickly as time permits. Forward the report to the chief of security with copies to the tool control officer and the shift supervisor. (See Lost Tool Report Form)

Copies to: Tool Control Officer
            Shift Supervisor

Report of Hazardous Tools

Front Entrances ☐
Rear Gate ☐

Security Supervisor

Subject _____ representing _____
(Company)

AM
The following tools were brought into the institution at _____ PM
AM
and were taken out of the institution at _____ PM.

_____

_____

_____

_____

_____

The tools were under the supervision of _____ during their use.

The visitor/mechanic was instructed in the basic supervisory requirements.

_____
(Gate Officer)

Any discrepancies and/or comments _____

_____

_____

Notice: It is a crime to bring any unauthorized weapons, narcotics, ammunition, knives, or other contraband on these premises.

_____   _____
Date   (Signature of Visitor/Mechanic)

                                  _____
                                   (Company Represented)

                                  _____
                                   (Phone)

Tool Turn-In Receipt

To: Tool Control Officer _____ Date _____

The tool(s) described below have been turned in to the tool control officer.

Signature _____
(Employee turning in tool(s))

Description of Tool(s)	**Number Missing**
_____	_____
_____	_____
_____	_____
_____	_____
_____	_____
_____	_____
_____	_____
_____	_____
_____	_____
_____	_____
_____	_____
_____	_____

Turned in by _____
(Work Area Supervisor)

Received in _____
(Tool Control Officer)

Copies to Work Area Supervisor
Chief of Security

Lost Tool Report

To: Chief Security Officer

From _____
(Name)   (Title)

_____
(Department)

The tool(s) listed below have been lost/stolen from this worksite on _____
(Date)

Description of Tool(s)	Number Missing
_____	_____
_____	_____
_____	_____
_____	_____

Circumstances surrounding this loss are as described below:

_____

_____

_____

_____

_____

_____

_____

_____

_____

_____

_____

Copies to: Tool Control Officer
               Shift Supervisor
               Work Area Supervisor

Official Count Form

_____
(Institution)

Date _____

Time _____ PM / AM

Unit	Unit Census	Outcount Section											Out-Count	Count Verification	Unit Count	Unit
		Food Service	Hospital	Clothing Room	Industries	Commissary	Power Plant	Barber Shop								
TOTAL																
Count Verification																

Official preparing count _____
Official taking count _____
Count cleared – time _____

Special Census

A special census is an inmate count taken at an unscheduled time on any day chosen at random. The specific reason for such a census is to let us know if our policy on inmate accountability is being adhered to and to deter inmates from being in unauthorized areas.

When a staff member takes a special census four things have to be noted:

1. Names and numbers of all inmates in your area at the time of census (including inmates assigned to that area on a detail).

2. The determination must be made if the inmates listed are authorized in the area or unauthorized.

3. If an inmate is in the area on vacation, medically unassigned, A & O, etc., this must be noted.

4. Census is to be turned into the Security Supervisor as soon as completed.

Area _____ Date _____ Time _____

Name	Number	Job Assignment	Authorized	Unauthorized	Explain

Note: If more space is needed, attach extra sheet.

Total in area   = _____
Total authorized   = _____
Total unauthorized   = _____

Special Census

Day _____ Date _____ Time Started _____ Time Cleared _____

Detail	Count Called In	Count on Special Census Form	Remarks
* Auto body (383)			
* Auto V.T. (383)			
* AW clerk (216)			
* Business office (214)			
* Commissary (219)			
* C.C.S. office (217)			
* Chapel (230)			
* Dental (238)			
* Education (380)			
Food service			
* Hospital (235)			
* Industry (277)			
Labor 1			
* Laundry (270)			
* CMS office (260)			
* Carpenter shop			
* Construction 2			
* Electric shop			
* Electronics shop			
* Garage (264)			
Landscape			
* Machine shop (263)			
* Paint shop			
* Plumbing shop			
* Power plant (392)			
* Steamfitting (390)			
* Front entrance (348)			
* Visiting room (352)			
Corridor			
* B-Cellhouse (316)			
C-Cellhouse			
D-Cellhouse			
E-Cellhouse			
F-Cellhouse			
G-Dormitory			
J-Dormitory			
K-Dormitory			
L-Dormitory			
M-Dormitory			
* Psychology dept. (242)			
* Record office (365)			
Safety office			
* Storeroom (245)			
* Welding V.T. (385)			
Recreation dept. (gym)			
Recreation dept. (yard)			
* Clothing issue (272)			

(continued)

Special Census (continued)

+			

* Must be notified by telephone.

Total _____

Total _____

Institution count _____

Control room officer _____

(Signature)

Security Supervisor _____

(Signature)

Weekly Master Security Checksheet

_____   _____
(Month)   (Year)

Area	1st week	2nd week	3rd week	4th week	5th week
Business office					
Warehouse					
Laundry					
Commissary					
Chapel					
Food service (except cook/dining room foreman)					
Dental clinic					
Industries (except tool room)					
Safety office					
Education (except VT shops/ classrooms)					
CMS (except shop foreman)					
Administrative systems (except R&D/mail room)					

Daily Inspection Report

Area/Post _____ Shift _____ Date _____

    I certify that I personally checked the items listed below and that all discrepancies are noted below. The shift supervisor was notified immediately of any serious security hazards and work orders were submitted where needed.

_____ Locks	_____ Floor	_____ Tools and Equipment
_____ Bars	_____ Vents	_____ Needles
_____ Doors	_____ Security Screens	_____ Syringes
_____ Grilles	_____ Fire Extinguishers	_____ Narcotics
_____ Windows	_____ Fire Hoses	_____ Other
_____ Walls	_____ Fire Hazards	_____

Discrepancies _____

_____

_____

_____

_____

_____

Officers responsible for the weekly security inspection of the tunnel areas will complete this section on the last workday of the week.

Powerhouse officer's signature _____ Date _____

Security officer's signature _____ Date _____

    The key rings listed below were issued to me during my tour of duty. I personally checked and counted each key and found all to be in good condition with the correct number of keys on each ring, as indicated on the key count tag. Any discrepancies found in the condition or count of keys is noted in the space provided.

Key Ring # _____ Count _____ Discrepancies _____
Key Ring # _____ Count _____ Discrepancies _____
Key Ring # _____ Count _____ Discrepancies _____
Key Ring # _____ Count _____ Discrepancies _____
Key Ring # _____ Count _____ Discrepancies _____

    The officer's signature indicates that he/she made the above security check and key check, and to the best of his/her knowledge, found them secure and in proper condition. Any discrepancies are noted in the appropriate space and action taken to correct these discrepancies.

Morning shift officer's signature _____

Day shift officer's signature _____

Evening shift officer's signature _____

Weekly Inspection Report

Area/Post _____ Shift _____ Date _____

I certify that I personally checked the items listed below and that all discrepancies are noted below. The shift supervisor was notified immediately of any serious security hazards and work orders were submitted where needed.

_____ Locks	_____ Floor	_____ Tools and Equipment
_____ Bars	_____ Vents	_____ Other
_____ Doors	_____ Security Screens	_____
_____ Grilles	_____ Fire Extinguishers	_____
_____ Windows	_____ Fire Hoses	_____
_____ Walls	_____ Fire Hazards	

Discrepancies _____

_____

_____

_____

_____

_____

The key rings listed below were issued to me during my tour of duty. I personally checked and counted each key and found all to be in good condition with the correct number of keys on each ring, as indicated on the key count tag. Any discrepancies found in the condition or count of keys is noted in the space provided.

Key Ring # _____ Count _____ Discrepancies _____
Key Ring # _____ Count _____ Discrepancies _____
Key Ring # _____ Count _____ Discrepancies _____
Key Ring # _____ Count _____ Discrepancies _____
Key Ring # _____ Count _____ Discrepancies _____

The officer's signature below certifies that he/she made the above security check and key check and, to the best of his/her knowledge, found them secure and in proper condition. Any discrepancies are noted in the appropriate space and action has been taken to correct these discrepancies.

Monday _____

Tuesday _____

Wednesday _____

Thursday _____

Friday _____

This form will be turned in to the operations lieutenant on the last workday of the week.

Monthly Security/Sanitation Inspection Schedule

Area Inspected	Day of Week	Inspection Team
Business office and personnel department	Mondays 10:00 A.M.	Assistant warden (operations), chairman, business manager, fire and safety officer
Inmate housing units	Mondays 10:00 A.M.	Assistant warden (programs), chairman, unit manager (of each unit), assistant fire and safety officer
Food service department	Mondays 10:00 A.M.	Health care director, chairman, food service manager, chief security officer
Health care program	Mondays 10:00 A.M.	Industrial director, chairman, hospital administrator, personnel officer
Academic and vocational areas	Mondays 10:00 A.M.	Classification manager, chairman, supervisor of education, chaplain
Industrial operations	Tuesdays 10:00 A.M.	Assistant warden (programs), chairman, industrial director, fire and safety officer
Mechanical services and shop areas	Tuesdays 10:00 A.M.	Assistant warden (operations), chairman, physical plant manager, assistant fire and safety officer
Special service areas: laundry, clothing room, admissions unit, mail and visiting rooms.	Tuesdays 10:00 A.M.	Chief security officer, chairman, chief psychologist, general foreman

———————————————

Warden

Inspection of Quarters Sheet

Date _____

Note: This form will be submitted daily to the shift supervisor by day and evening shift officers.

The following item will be inspected in each cell:

Item	S	U	Discrepancies noted
Walls and ledges			
Shelves			
Floors			
Toilet and sink			
Bars (if applicable)			
Window glass			

In addition to the above, the officer in each housing area will also inspect the following:

Item	S	U	Discrepancies noted
Dayroom floor			
Pillars and walls			
Ceiling and grillework			
Counseling room			
Showers (all areas)			
Ledge above doors			
All other window glass			
Other (as needed)			

INSTRUCTIONS   This check sheet is to be used as a guide by officers making daily security and sanitation inspections. A check mark will be placed in the appropriate column as to the general condition of all areas. Discrepancies should be noted in the proper column. Where more space is needed, the reverse side may be used. When making a comment on the reverse side, please indicate on the front that you have done so.

Shift _____ Area _____ Signature _____

Abbreviations   S = Satisfactory   U = Unsatisfactory

Note: Shift supervisor will note discrepancies and alleviate them if possible, then forward to chief of security for
further action.

Daily Security, Sanitation, and Fire Slip

Post _____

Shift _____ Date _____

Areas checked _____

_____

_____

_____

_____

Discrepancies _____

_____

_____

_____

_____

Use reverse side if additional space required.

_____
(Signature)

Remarks _____

_____

_____

_____

Standard Escape Report

_____
(Institution)

Inmate's name _____ Age _____ Number _____ Date of escape _____

Sentence _____ Offense _____ Custody classification _____

Approximate time remaining to serve _____

Escaped from: Inside perimeter (   ); Outside perimeter (   ); Work release (   ); Other (   )

Number of inmates involved _____ Time of escape _____

Supervising employee (if none, state none) _____

Person first reporting escape _____ Time reported _____

Fired on   Yes (   );   No (   )

Central Office/Regional Office notified _____ Date _____ Time _____

Apprehended _____ Date _____ Time _____

Circumstances surrounding escape _____

_____

_____

_____

Evaluation (staff analysis) _____

_____

_____

_____

Changes in facilities or procedures to prevent similar occurrences: _____

_____

_____

_____

Date report submitted _____ Signature _____

A SEPARATE ESCAPE REPORT SHOULD BE SUBMITTED FOR EACH INMATE INVOLVED

Daily Fire, Security, and Energy Checks

(Policy Statement # _____)

To Safety Manager   Date _____

From _____   Time _____
        (Department)

    I have checked my area of responsibility. All trash receptacles are emptied or covered. Flammable liquids are properly stored or removed. Fire extinguishers are unobstructed. No aisleways are blocked. No known hazards are present. All windows and doors are secure. All windows are closed in heating season. All lighting is off in unoccupied areas. All air-conditioning systems are off when area is unoccupied. Exhaust systems are off when not needed.

Remarks _____

_____

_____

_____

_____

               (Use reverse side for additional remarks)

Officer's name _____
          (Print)   (Signature)

Bomb Threat Information Sheet

Name of recipient _____

Address _____

Telephone number _____

Obtain the following information as quickly as possible when you receive a bomb threat.

1. Exact location of the device _____

   _____

2. Time set for denotation _____

   _____

3. Description of device or packaging _____

   _____

4. Reason for call or threat _____

   _____

In Addition, the following details should be noted:

5. Time and date of call _____

   _____

6. Exact language used by caller _____

   _____

7. Sex of caller _____

   _____

8. Estimated age of caller _____

   _____

9. Peculiar or identifiable accent of caller _____

   _____

10. Describe any identifiable background noises or "off-phone" voices _____

   _____

   _____

   _____

   _____

   _____

   _____

Bomb Threat Information Sheet

Index

Index

emergency generator for, 49
entrance to, 71
equipment standardization in, 55
equipment storage in, 71-74
in escape, 188
firearms, 73; *See also* Firearms; Weapons
gas equipment, 72; *See also* Chemical agents
inspection of equipment in, 73
inventory of, 73
key for, 72, 98
and patrol vehicles, 73
policy on, 72
procedures for, 72-74
security manual topic, 32
security of, 184
subarmories, 72
telephone in, 71
tower vehicles, 73
traffic into, 71-72
weapons, *See* Weapons
Assignments, *See* Post assignments
Audits, 237-41
accreditation, 27
auditors, selection of, 23
conducting, 25-27
of emergency plan, 179
external, 25
format for, 237
internal, 25, 26, 32
outline, sample, 237-41
philosophy of, 23
policy on, 30-31
purposes of, 23
sample outline of, 237-41
security, 23, 25-27, 30, 180, 239-40
structure of, 23
tool control, 145
types of, 25
Authors of this book, 305
Automation
of classification, *See* Classification
computers, *See* Computers
of rosters, 41
of security management, 41-43
Automobile transport, *See* Transportation

B

Barber
services of, 133, 135-36
tools of, 147, 206-07
Bars, 127, 189
Bed
search of, 118
in special housing, 130, 132
Bedding
for evacuated inmates, 198
mattress, *See* Mattresses
Binoculars, 56
Biometrics defined, 41f
Black box restraints cover, *See* Restraints, black box
Blacklight, 117, 175
Blades, 145
Blind spots, 61, 176
Body alarms, 52, 55-56, 107
to deter hostage taking, 219
in special housing units, 132

Body armor, *See* Protective gear
Bomb plan, 191-93
policies and procedures on, 8
Bomb Threat Information Sheet (form), 281
Books, searches of, 118
Boxes, 120
Breathing equipment, *See* Gas masks
Brooms, 118
Buildings
architectural issues, 45-46
clustering, 46
design elements, 45; *See also* Facility design
in disaster, 196, 197
after earthquake, 199, 200
and housing unit design, 46
layout of, 45
and perimeter security, 46, 59
securing of, 207
Bus transportation, 164-68
cellular phone in , 53
death during, *See* Death
disturbance on, 167
emergency on, 165
escape from, 164, 167
fire on, 167
firearms on, 166
food, *See* Food service, food in transit
for funerals, 164
hostage situation on, 167
identification of inmates on, 166
illness of inmate on, *See* Medical, illness of inmate transported
inmate management, 165
maintenance of vehicle, 166
on-the-road, 165
operations, 164
restraints for use on, 164, 165-66
searches of, 162, 166
staff duty on, 164-65
and stopover, 166-67
supervision of, 165
and traffic accident, 167
trip arrangements, 161
vehicle for, 163
vehicle security, 166
water on, 167
weapons on, 162
windows on bus, 166

C

Callouts, *See* Accountability, callouts
Cameras, 47; *See also* Videotaping
Canine operations, 123-24
budget, 123
duties of, 123-24
escape and, 190
firearms with, 190
reports on use of, 123
searches with, 123
staff for, 123
tactical response teams and, 229
training for, 123
Cardiopulmonary resuscitation (CPR), 6, 57
Case review, 136
Cashier's office, 46, 98
Ceilings, security inspection of, 126
Cells

Index

Index

Index

Index

Index

About the Authors

James D. Henderson is one of the most highly experienced and regarded criminal justice professionals in the world. A retired Regional Director for the Federal Bureau of Prisons, he has served as a consultant for numerous federal courts, the American Correctional Association, and the National Institute of Corrections (NIC). He also has served as an independent correctional consultant for numerous states, foreign nations, and private firms.

W. H. "Hardy" Rauch is perhaps the most well-known expert on standards and accreditations in American corrections. A highly experienced administrator when he retired from the Federal Bureau of Prisons, Mr. Rauch was appointed Director of the American Correctional Association's Standards and Accreditation Division where he served until 1996. Under his leadership, the accreditation program became a cornerstone of not only ACA's operation, but of correctional management throughout the United States. In 1996, Mr. Rauch was awarded the E. R. Cass Award, ACA's highest honor.

Richard Phillips is an experienced correctional manager and private correctional consultant who has worked in a variety of juvenile and adult correctional settings at both the state and federal level. He has chaired or been a member of several ACA committees, served as an ACA accreditation auditor, and is the author or contributing editor of various publications for ACA and other correctional organizations.